HTML 4.0 Specification

W3C Recommendation, revised on 24-Apr-1998

REC-html-19980424

HTML 4.0 Specification

W3C Recommendation, revised on 24-Apr-1998

REC-html-19980424

toExcel

San Jose   New York   Lincoln   Shanghai

HTML 4.0 Specification

REC-html-19980424
W3C Recommendation, revised on 24-Apr-1998

Compiled from the W3C Standards by Gordon McComb

Open Documents Standards Library
Published by toExcel

All Rights Reserved. Copyright © 1999 World Wide Web Consortium
Massachusetts Institute of Technology, Institut National de Recherché en Informatique et en Automatique, Keio University
http://www.w3.org/Consortium/Legal/

For information address:
toExcel
165 West 95th Street, Suite B-N
New York, NY 10025
www.toExcel.com

ISBN: 1-58348-259-8

LCCN: 99-63249

Printed in the United States of America

0 9 8 7 6 5 4 3 2 1

toExcel donates a portion of the profits
from every **Open Documents** book
to support the mission of the Open Documents and Open Source communities.

Table of Contents

Abstract 1
Status of this document 1
Available formats 2
Available languages 3
Errata 3
Chapter 1   About the HTML 4.0 Specification 5
   1.1   How the specification is organized 5
   1.2   Document conventions 7
   1.3   Acknowledgments 8
   1.4   Copyright Notice 9
Chapter 2   Introduction to HTML 4.0 11
   2.1   What is the World Wide Web? 11
   2.2   What is HTML? 14
   2.3   HTML 4.0 15
   2.4   Authoring documents with HTML 4.0 18
Chapter 3   On SGML and HTML 21
   3.1   Introduction to SGML 21
   3.2   SGML constructs used in HTML 22
   3.3   How to read the HTML DTD 26
Chapter 4   Conformance: Requirements and Recommendations 33
   4.1   Definitions 33
   4.2   SGML 35
   4.3   The text/html content type 36

Chapter 5 HTML Document Representation 37
- 5.1 The Document Character Set 38
- 5.2 Character encodings 38
- 5.3 Character references 41
- 5.4 Undisplayable characters 44

Chapter 6 Basic HTML Data Types 45
- 6.1 Case information 46
- 6.2 SGML basic types 46
- 6.3 Text strings 47
- 6.4 URIs 47
- 6.5 Colors 48
- 6.6 Lengths 49
- 6.7 Content types (MIME types) 50
- 6.8 Language codes 50
- 6.9 Character encodings 50
- 6.10 Single characters 51
- 6.11 Dates and times 51
- 6.12 Link types 52
- 6.13 Media descriptors 54
- 6.14 Script data 56
- 6.15 Style sheet data 56
- 6.16 Frame target names 56

Chapter 7 The Global Structure of an HTML Document 59
- 7.1 Introduction to the structure of an HTML document 59
- 7.2 HTML version information 60
- 7.3 The HTML element 61
- 7.4 The document head 62
- 7.5 The document body 71

Chapter 8 Language Information and Text Direction 83
    8.1   Specifying the language of content: the lang attribute 83
    8.2   Specifying the direction of text and tables: the dir attribute 86

Chapter 9 Text 95
    9.1   White space 95
    9.2   Structured text 97
    9.3   Lines and Paragraphs 102
    9.4   Marking document changes: The INS and DEL elements 108

Chapter 10 Lists 111
    10.1   Introduction to lists 111
    10.2   Unordered lists (UL), ordered lists (OL), and list items (LI) 113
    10.3   Definition lists: the DL, DT, and DD elements 116
    10.4   The DIR and MENU elements 119

Chapter 11 Tables 121
    11.1   Introduction to tables 122
    11.2   Elements for constructing tables 124
    11.3   Table formatting by visual user agents 144
    11.4   Table rendering by non-visual user agents 152
    11.5   Sample table 161

Chapter 12 Links 165
    12.1   Introduction to links and anchors 165
    12.2   The A element 169
    12.3   Document relationships: the LINK element 176
    12.4   Path information: the BASE element 179

Chapter 13 Objects, Images, and Applets 183
    13.1   Introduction to objects, images, and applets 183
    13.2   Including an image: the IMG element 185
    13.3   Generic inclusion: the OBJECT element 187

13.4 Including an applet: the `APPLET` element 197
13.5 Notes on embedded documents 199
13.6 Image maps 200
13.7 Visual presentation of images, objects, and applets 207
13.8 How to specify alternate text 209

Chapter 14 Style Sheets 211
14.1 Introduction to style sheets 211
14.2 Adding style to HTML 214
14.3 External style sheets 220
14.4 Cascading style sheets 222
14.5 Hiding style data from user agents 224
14.6 Linking to style sheets with HTTP headers 224

Chapter 15 Alignment, Font Styles, and Horizontal Rules 227
15.1 Formatting 227
15.2 Fonts 233
15.3 Rules: the `HR` element 236

Chapter 16 Frames 239
16.1 Introduction to frames 239
16.2 Layout of frames 241
16.3 Specifying target frame information 249
16.4 Alternate content 252
16.5 Inline frames: the `IFRAME` element 254

Chapter 17 Forms 257
17.1 Introduction to forms 258
17.2 Controls 258
17.3 The `FORM` element 261
17.4 The `INPUT` element 263
17.5 The `BUTTON` element 268

17.6   The SELECT, OPTGROUP, and OPTION elements 270
17.7   The TEXTAREA element 276
17.8   The ISINDEX element 278
17.9   Labels 279
17.10 Adding structure to forms: the FIELDSET and LEGEND elements 281
17.11 Giving focus to an element 284
17.12 Disabled and read-only controls 287
17.13 Form submission 289

Chapter 18 Scripts 295
18.1   Introduction to scripts 295
18.2   Designing documents for user agents that support scripting 296
18.3   Designing documents for user agents that don't support scripting 304

Chapter 19 SGML Reference Information for HTML 309
19.1   Document Validation 310
19.2   Sample SGML catalog 311

Chapter 20 SGML Declaration of HTML 4.0 313
20.1   SGML Declaration 313

Chapter 21 Document Type Definition 317

Chapter 22 Transitional Document Type Definition 337

Chapter 23 Frameset Document Type Definition 363

Chapter 24 Character entity references in HTML 4.0 365
24.1   Introduction to character entity references 365
24.2   Character entity references for ISO 8859-1 characters 366
24.3   Character entity references for symbols, mathematical symbols, and Greek letters 371
24.4   Character entity references for markup-significant and internationalization characters ..379

Appendix A: Changes 383
A.1   Changes between HTML 3.2 and HTML 4.0 384
A.2   Changes from the 18 December 1997 specification 388

Appendix B: Performance, Implementation, and Design Notes 395
    B.1   Notes on invalid documents 396
    B.2   Special characters in URI attribute values 397
    B.3   SGML implementation notes 398
    B.4   Notes on helping search engines index your Web site 402
    B.5   Notes on tables 405
    B.6   Notes on forms 411
    B.7   Notes on scripting 412
    B.8   Notes on frames 414
    B.9   Notes on accessibility 414
    B.10 Notes on security 415

Reference 417
    Index of Elements 417
    Index of Attributes 421

Abstract

This specification defines the HyperText Markup Language (HTML), version 4.0, the publishing language of the World Wide Web. In addition to the text, multimedia, and hyperlink features of the previous versions of HTML, HTML 4.0 supports more multimedia options, scripting languages, style sheets, better printing facilities, and documents that are more accessible to users with disabilities. HTML 4.0 also takes great strides towards the internationalization of documents, with the goal of making the Web truly World Wide.

HTML 4.0 is an SGML application conforming to International Standard ISO 8879—Standard Generalized Markup Language [ISO8879].

This version:

  http://www.w3.org/TR/1998/REC-html40-19980424

Latest version:

  http://www.w3.org/TR/REC-html40

Previous version:

  http://www.w3.org/TR/REC-html40-971218

Editors:

  Dave Raggett <dsr@w3.org>
  Arnaud Le Hors <lehors@w3.org>
  Ian Jacobs <ij@w3.org>

Status of this document

This document has been reviewed by W3C Members and other interested parties and has been endorsed by the Director as a W3C Recommendation. It is a stable document and may be used as reference material or cited as a normative reference from another document. W3C's role in making the Recommendation is to draw attention to the specification and to promote its widespread deployment. This enhances the functionality and interoperability of the Web.

W3C recommends that user agents and authors (and in particular, authoring tools) produce HTML 4.0 documents rather than HTML 3.2 documents. For reasons of backwards compatibility, W3C also recommends that tools interpreting HTML 4.0 continue to support HTML 3.2 and HTML 2.0 as well.

A list of current W3C Recommendations and other technical documents can be found at http://www.w3.org/TR.

Public discussion on HTML features takes place on www-html@w3.org.

This document is a revised version of the document first released on 18 December 1997. Changes from the original version *are only editorial in nature.*

Available formats

The HTML 4.0 W3C Recommendation is also available in the following formats:

A plain text file:

 http://www.w3.org/TR/1998/REC-html40-19980424/html40.txt,

A gzip'ed tar file containing HTML documents:

 http://www.w3.org/TR/1998/REC-html40-19980424/html40.tgz,

A zip file containing HTML documents (this is a '.zip' file not an '.exe'):

 http://www.w3.org/TR/1998/REC-html40-19980424/html40.zip,

A gzip'ed Postscript file:

 http://www.w3.org/TR/1998/REC-html40-19980424/html40.ps.gz,

A PDF file:

 http://www.w3.org/TR/1998/REC-html40-19980424/html40.pdf.

In case of a discrepancy between electronic and printed forms of the specification, the electronic version is the definitive version.

Available languages

The English version of this specification is the only normative version. However, for translations of this document, see http://www.w3.org/MarkUp/html40-updates/translations.html.

Errata

The list of known errors in this specification is available at:

`http://www.w3.org/MarkUp/html40-updates/REC-html40-19980424-errata.html`

Please report errors in this document to www-html-editor@w3.org.

Copyright © 1997 W3C (MIT, INRIA, Keio), All Rights Reserved.

Chapter 1

About the HTML 4.0 Specification

Contents

1. How the specification is organized
2. Document conventions
    1. Elements and attributes
    2. Notes and examples
3. Acknowledgments
4. Copyright Notice

1.1 How the specification is organized

This specification is divided into the following sections:

Sections 2 and 3: Introduction to HTML 4.0

The introduction describes HTML's place in the scheme of the World Wide Web, provides a brief history of the development of HTML, highlights what can be done with HTML 4.0, and provides some HTML authoring tips.

The brief SGML tutorial gives readers some understanding of HTML's relationship to SGML and gives summary information on how to read the HTML Document Type Definition (DTD).

Sections 4–24: HTML 4.0 reference manual

The bulk of the reference manual consists of the HTML language reference, which defines all elements and attributes of the language.

This document has been organized by topic rather than by the grammar of HTML. Topics are grouped into three categories: structure, presentation, and interactivity. Although it is not easy to divide HTML constructs perfectly into these three categories, the model reflects the HTML Working Group's experience that separating a document's structure from its presentation produces more effective and maintainable documents.

The language reference consists of the following information:

- What characters may appear in an HTML document.
- Basic data types of an HTML document.
- Elements that govern the structure of an HTML document, including text, lists, tables, links, and included objects, images, and applets.
- Elements that govern the presentation of an HTML document, including style sheets, fonts, colors, rules, and other visual presentation, and frames for multi-windowed presentations.
- Elements that govern interactivity with an HTML document, including forms for user input and scripts for active documents.
- The SGML formal definition of HTML:
  - The SGML declaration of HTML.
  - Three DTDs: strict, transitional, and frameset.
  - The list of character references.

Appendixes

The first appendix contains information about changes from HTML 3.2 to help authors and implementors with the transition to HTML 4.0, and changes from the 18 December 1997 specification. The second appendix contains performance and implementation notes, and is primarily intended to help implementors create user agents for HTML 4.0.

References

A list of normative and informative references.

1.2 Document conventions

This document has been written with two types of readers in mind: authors and implementors. We hope the specification will provide authors with the tools they need to write efficient, attractive, and accessible documents, without over-exposing them to HTML's implementation details. Implementors, however, should find all they need to build conforming user agents.

The specification may be approached in several ways:

- **Read from beginning to end.** The specification begins with a general presentation of HTML and becomes more and more technical and specific towards the end.
- **Quick access to information.** In order to get information about syntax and semantics as quickly as possible, the online version of the specification includes the following features:
  1. Every reference to an element or attribute is linked to its definition in the specification. Each element or attribute is defined in only one location.
  2. Every page includes links to the indexes, so you never are more than two links away from finding the definition of an element or attribute.
  3. The front pages of the three sections of the language reference manual extend the initial table of contents with more detail about each section.

1.2.1 Elements and attributes

Element names are written in uppercase letters (e.g., BODY). Attribute names are written in lowercase letters (e.g., lang, onsubmit). Recall that in HTML, element and attribute names are case-insensitive; the convention is meant to encourage readability.

Element and attribute names in this document have been marked up and may be rendered specially by some user agents.

Each attribute definition specifies the type of its value. If the type allows a small set of possible values, the definition lists the set of values, separated by a bar (|).

After the type information, each attribute definition indicates the case-sensitivity of its values, between square brackets ("[]"). See the section on case information for details.

1.2.2 Notes and examples

Informative notes are emphasized to stand out from surrounding text and may be rendered specially by some user agents.

All examples illustrating deprecated usage are marked as "DEPRECATED EXAMPLE". Deprecated examples also include recommended alternate solutions. All examples that illustrates illegal usage are clearly marked "ILLEGAL EXAMPLE".

Examples and notes have been marked up and may be rendered specially by some user agents.

1.3 Acknowledgments

Thanks to everyone who has helped to author the working drafts that went into the HTML 4.0 specification, and to all those who have sent suggestions and corrections.

Many thanks to the Web Accessibility Initiative task force (WAI HC group) for their work on improving the accessibility of HTML and to T.V. Raman (Adobe) for his early work on developing accessible forms.

The authors of this specification, the members of the W3C HTML Working Group, deserve much applause for their diligent review of this document, their constructive comments, and their hard work: John D. Burger (MITRE), Steve Byrne (JavaSoft), Martin J. Dürst (University of Zurich), Daniel Glazman (Electricité de France), Scott Isaacs (Microsoft), Murray Maloney (GRIF), Steven Pemberton (CWI), Robert Pernett (Lotus), Jared Sorensen (Novell), Powell Smith (IBM), Robert Stevahn (HP), Ed Tecot (Microsoft), Jeffrey Veen (HotWired), Mike Wexler (Adobe), Misha Wolf (Reuters), and Lauren Wood (SoftQuad).

Thank you Dan Connolly (W3C) for rigorous and bountiful input as part-time editor and thoughtful guidance as chairman of the HTML Working Group. Thank you Sally Khudairi (W3C) for your indispensable work on press releases.

Thanks to David M. Abrahamson and Roger Price for their careful reading of the specification and constructive comments.

Thanks to Jan Kärrman, author of html2ps for helping so much in creating the Postscript version of the specification.

Of particular help from the W3C at Sophia-Antipolis were Janet Bertot, Bert Bos, Stephane Boyera, Daniel Dardailler, Yves Lafon, Håkon Lie, Chris Lilley, and Colas Nahaboo (Bull).

Lastly, thanks to Tim Berners-Lee without whom none of this would have been possible.

1.4 Copyright Notice

Copyright © 1997 World Wide Web Consortium, (Massachusetts Institute of Technology, Institut National de Recherche en Informatique et en Automatique, Keio University). **All Rights Reserved**.

Documents on the W3C site are provided by the copyright holders under the following license. By obtaining, using and/or copying this document, or the W3C document from which this statement is linked, you agree that you have read, understood, and will comply with the following terms and conditions:

Permission to use, copy, and distribute the contents of this document, or the W3C document from which this statement is linked, in any medium for any purpose and without fee or royalty is hereby granted, provided that you include the following on *ALL* copies of the document, or portions thereof, that you use:

1. A link or URI to the original W3C document.
2. The pre-existing copyright notice of the original author, if it doesn't exist, a notice of the form: "Copyright © World Wide Web Consortium, (Massachusetts Institute of Technology, Institut National de Recherche en Informatique et en Automatique, Keio University). All Rights Reserved."
3. *If it exists*, the STATUS of the W3C document.

When space permits, inclusion of the full text of this **NOTICE** should be provided. In addition, credit shall be attributed to the copyright holders for any software, documents, or other items or products that you create pursuant to the implementation of the contents of this document, or any portion thereof.

No right to create modifications or derivatives is granted pursuant to this license.

THIS DOCUMENT IS PROVIDED "AS IS," AND COPYRIGHT HOLDERS MAKE NO REPRESENTATIONS OR WARRANTIES, EXPRESS OR IMPLIED, INCLUDING, BUT NOT LIMITED TO, WARRANTIES OF MERCHANTABILITY, FITNESS FOR A PARTICULAR PURPOSE, NON-INFRINGEMENT, OR TITLE; THAT THE CONTENTS OF THE DOCUMENT ARE SUITABLE FOR ANY PURPOSE; NOR

THAT THE IMPLEMENTATION OF SUCH CONTENTS WILL NOT INFRINGE ANY THIRD PARTY PATENTS, COPYRIGHTS, TRADEMARKS OR OTHER RIGHTS.

COPYRIGHT HOLDERS WILL NOT BE LIABLE FOR ANY DIRECT, INDIRECT, SPECIAL OR CONSEQUENTIAL DAMAGES ARISING OUT OF ANY USE OF THE DOCUMENT OR THE PERFORMANCE OR IMPLEMENTATION OF THE CONTENTS THEREOF.

The name and trademarks of copyright holders may NOT be used in advertising or publicity pertaining to this document or its contents without specific, written prior permission. Title to copyright in this document will at all times remain with copyright holders.

Chapter 2

Introduction to HTML 4.0

Contents

1. What is the World Wide Web?
   1. Introduction to URIs
   2. Fragment identifiers
   3. Relative URIs
2. What is HTML?
   1. A brief history of HTML
3. HTML 4.0
   1. Internationalization
   2. Accessibility
   3. Tables
   4. Compound documents
   5. Style sheets
   6. Scripting
   7. Printing
4. Authoring documents with HTML 4.0
   1. Separate structure and presentation
   2. Consider universal accessibility to the Web
   3. Help user agents with incremental rendering

2.1 What is the World Wide Web?

The *World Wide Web (Web)* is a network of information resources. The Web relies on three mechanisms to make these resources readily available to the widest possible audience:

1. A uniform naming scheme for locating resources on the Web (e.g., URIs).

2. Protocols, for access to named resources over the Web (e.g., HTTP).

3. Hypertext, for easy navigation among resources (e.g., HTML).

The ties between the three mechanisms are apparent throughout this specification.

2.1.1 Introduction to URIs

Every resource available on the Web—HTML document, image, video clip, program, etc.—has an address that may be encoded by a *Universal Resource Identifier*, or "URI".

URIs typically consist of three pieces:

1. The naming scheme of the mechanism used to access the resource.
2. The name of the machine hosting the resource.
3. The name of the resource itself, given as a path.

Consider the URI that designates the current HTML specification:

```
http://www.w3.org/TR/REC-html40/
```

This URI may be read as follows: There is a document available via the HTTP protocol (see RFC2068), residing on the machine www.w3.org, accessible via the path "/TR/REC-html4/". Other schemes you may see in HTML documents include "mailto" for email and "ftp" for FTP.

Here is another example of a URI. This one refers to a user's mailbox:

```
...this is text...
For all comments, please send email to
<A href="mailto:joe@someplace.com">Joe Cool</A>.
```

Note. *Most readers may be familiar with the term "URL" and not the term "URI". URLs form a subset of the more general URI naming scheme.*

2.1.2 Fragment identifiers

Some URIs refer to a location within a resource. This kind of URI ends with "#" followed by an anchor identifier (called the *fragment identifier*). For instance, here is a URI pointing to an anchor named **section_2**:

```
http://somesite.com/html/top.html#section_2
```

2.1.3 Relative URIs

A *relative URI* doesn't contain any naming scheme information. Its path generally refers to a resource on the same machine as the current document. Relative URIs may contain relative path components (e.g., ".." means one level up in the hierarchy defined by the path), and may contain fragment identifiers.

Relative URIs are resolved to full URIs using a base URI. As an example of relative URI resolution, assume we have the base URI "http://www.acme.com/support/intro.html". The relative URI in the following markup for a hypertext link:

```
<A href="suppliers.html">Suppliers</A>
```

would expand to the full URI "http://www.acme.com/support/suppliers.html", while the relative URI in the following markup for an image

```
<IMG src="../icons/logo.gif" alt="logo">
```

would expand to the full URI "http://www.acme.com/icons/logo.gif".

In HTML, URIs are used to:

- Link to another document or resource, (see the A and LINK elements).
- Link to an external style sheet or script (see the LINK and SCRIPT elements).
- Include an image, object, or applets in a page, (see the IMG, OBJECT, APPLET and INPUT elements).
- Create an image map (see the MAP and AREA elements).
- Submit a form (see FORM).
- Create a frame document (see the FRAME and IFRAME elements).
- Cite an external reference (see the Q, BLOCKQUOTE, INS and DEL elements).
- Refer to metadata conventions describing a document (see the HEAD element).

Please consult the section on the URI type for more information about URIs.

2.2 What is HTML?

To publish information for global distribution, one needs a universally understood language, a kind of publishing mother tongue that all computers may potentially understand. The publishing language used by the World Wide Web is HTML (from HyperText Markup Language).

HTML gives authors the means to:

- Publish online documents with headings, text, tables, lists, photos, etc.
- Retrieve online information via hypertext links, at the click of a button.
- Design forms for conducting transactions with remote services, for use in searching for information, making reservations, ordering products, etc.
- Include spread-sheets, video clips, sound clips, and other applications directly in their documents.

2.2.1 A brief history of HTML

HTML was originally developed by Tim Berners-Lee while at CERN, and popularized by the Mosaic browser developed at NCSA. During the course of the 1990s it has blossomed with the explosive growth of the Web. During this time, HTML has been extended in a number of ways. The Web depends on Web page authors and vendors sharing the same conventions for HTML. This has motivated joint work on specifications for HTML.

HTML 2.0 (November 1995, see RFC1866) was developed under the aegis of the Internet Engineering Task Force (IETF) to codify common practice in late 1994. HTML+ (1993) and HTML 3.0 (1995, see HTML30) proposed much richer versions of HTML. Despite never receiving consensus in standards discussions, these drafts led to the adoption of a range of new features. The efforts of the World Wide Web Consortium's HTML Working Group to codify common practice in 1996 resulted in HTML 3.2 (January 1997, see HTML32). Changes from HTML 3.2 are summarized in Appendix A

Most people agree that HTML documents should work well across different browsers and platforms. Achieving interoperability lowers costs to content providers since they must develop only one version of a document. If the effort is not made, there is much greater risk that the Web will devolve into a proprietary world of incompatible formats, ultimately reducing the Web's commercial potential for all participants.

Each version of HTML has attempted to reflect greater consensus among industry players so that the investment made by content providers will not be wasted and that their documents will not become unreadable in a short period of time.

HTML has been developed with the vision that all manner of devices should be able to use information on the Web: PCs with graphics displays of varying resolution and color depths, cellular telephones, hand held devices, devices for speech for output and input, computers with high or low bandwidth, and so on.

2.3 HTML 4.0

HTML 4.0 extends HTML with mechanisms for style sheets, scripting, frames, embedding objects, improved support for right to left and mixed direction text, richer tables, and enhancements to forms, offering improved accessibility for people with disabilities.

2.3.1 Internationalization

This version of HTML has been designed with the help of experts in the field of internationalization, so that documents may be written in every language and be transported easily around the world. This has been accomplished by incorporating [RFC2070], which deals with the internationalization of HTML.

One important step has been the adoption of the ISO/IEC:10646 standard (see ISO10646) as the document character set for HTML. This is the world's most inclusive standard dealing with issues of the representation of international characters, text direction, punctuation, and other world language issues.

HTML now offers greater support for diverse human languages within a document. This allows for more effective indexing of documents for search engines, higher-quality typography, better text-to-speech conversion, better hyphenation, etc.

2.3.2 Accessibility

As the Web community grows and its members diversify in their abilities and skills, it is crucial that the underlying technologies be appropriate to their specific needs. HTML has been designed to make Web pages more accessible to those with physical limitations. HTML 4.0 developments inspired by concerns for accessibility include:

- Better distinction between document structure and presentation, thus encouraging the use of style sheets instead of HTML presentation elements and attributes.
- Better forms, including the addition of access keys, the ability to group form controls semantically, the ability to group SELECT options semantically, and active labels.
- The ability to markup a text description of an included object (with the OBJECT element).
- A new client-side image map mechanism (the MAP element) that allows authors to integrate image and text links.
- The requirement that alternate text accompany images included with the IMG element and image maps included with the AREA element.
- Support for the title and lang attributes on all elements.
- Support for the ABBR and ACRONYM elements.
- A wider range of target media (tty, braille, etc.) for use with style sheets.
- Better tables, including captions, column groups, and mechanisms to facilitate non-visual rendering.
- Long descriptions of tables, images, frames, etc.

Authors who design pages with accessibility issues in mind will not only receive the blessings of the accessibility community, but will benefit in other ways as well: well-designed HTML documents that distinguish structure and presentation will adapt more easily to new technologies.

Note. For more information about designing accessible HTML documents, please consult [WAIGUIDE].

2.3.3 Tables

The new table model in HTML is based on [RFC1942]. Authors now have greater control over structure and layout (e.g., column groups). The ability of designers to recommend column widths allows user agents to display table data incrementally (as it arrives) rather than waiting for the entire table before rendering.

Note. At the time of writing, some HTML authoring tools rely extensively on tables for formatting, which may easily cause accessibility problems.

2.3.4 Compound documents

HTML now offers a standard mechanism for embedding generic media objects and applications in HTML documents. The `OBJECT` element (together with its more specific ancestor elements `IMG` and `APPLET`) provides a mechanism for including images, video, sound, mathematics, specialized applications, and other objects in a document. It also allows authors to specify a hierarchy of alternate renderings for user agents that don't support a specific rendering.

2.3.5 Style sheets

Style sheets simplify HTML markup and largely relieve HTML of the responsibilities of presentation. They give both authors and users control over the presentation of documents—font information, alignment, colors, etc.

Style information can be specified for individual elements or groups of elements. Style information may be specified in an HTML document or in external style sheets.

The mechanisms for associating a style sheet with a document is independent of the style sheet language.

Before the advent of style sheets, authors had limited control over rendering. HTML 3.2 included a number of attributes and elements offering control over alignment, font size, and text color. Authors also exploited tables and images as a means for laying out pages. The relatively long time it takes for users to upgrade their browsers means that these features will continue to be used for some time. However, since style sheets offer more powerful presentation mechanisms, the World Wide Web Consortium will eventually phase out many of HTML's presentation elements and attributes. Throughout the specification elements and attributes at risk are marked as "deprecated". They are accompanied by examples of how to achieve the same effects with other elements or style sheets.

2.3.6 Scripting

Through scripts, authors may create dynamic Web pages (e.g., "smart forms" that react as users fill them out) and use HTML as a means to build networked applications.

The mechanisms provided to include scripts in an HTML document are independent of the scripting language.

2.3.7 Printing

Sometimes, authors will want to make it easy for users to print more than just the current document. When documents form part of a larger work, the relationships between them can be described using the HTML LINK element or using W3C's Resource Description Language (RDF).

2.4 Authoring documents with HTML 4.0

We recommend that authors and implementors observe the following general principles when working with HTML 4.0.

2.4.1 Separate structure and presentation

HTML has its roots in SGML which has always been a language for the specification of structural markup. As HTML matures, more and more of its presentational elements and attributes are being replaced by other mechanisms, in particular style sheets. Experience has shown that separating the structure of a document from its presentational aspects reduces the cost of serving a wide range of platforms, media, etc., and facilitates document revisions.

2.4.2 Consider universal accessibility to the Web

To make the Web more accessible to everyone, notably those with disabilities, authors should consider how their documents may be rendered on a variety of platforms: speech-based browsers, braille-readers, etc. We do not recommend that authors limit their creativity, only that they consider alternate renderings in their design. HTML offers a number of mechanisms to this end (e.g., the alt attribute, the accesskey attribute, etc.)

Furthermore, authors should keep in mind that their documents may be reaching a far-off audience with different computer configurations. In order for documents to be interpreted correctly, authors should include in their documents information about the natural language and direction of the text, how the document is encoded, and other issues related to internationalization.

2.4.3 Help user agents with incremental rendering

By carefully designing their tables and making use of new table features in HTML 4.0, authors can help user agents render documents more quickly. Authors can learn how to design tables for incremental rendering (see the TABLE element). Implementors should consult the notes on tables in the appendix for information on incremental algorithms.

Chapter 3

On SGML and HTML

Contents

1. Introduction to SGML
2. SGML constructs used in HTML
   1. Elements
   2. Attributes
   3. Character references
   4. Comments
3. How to read the HTML DTD
   1. DTD Comments
   2. Parameter entity definitions
   3. Element declarations
      - Content model definitions
   4. Attribute declarations
      - DTD entities in attribute definitions
      - *Boolean attributes*

This section of the document introduces SGML and discusses its relationship to HTML. A complete discussion of SGML is left to the standard (see [ISO8879]).

3.1 Introduction to SGML

SGML is a system for defining markup languages. Authors mark up their documents by representing structural, presentational, and semantic information alongside content. HTML is one example of a markup language. Here is an example of an HTML document:

```
<!DOCTYPE HTML PUBLIC "-//W3C//DTD HTML 4.0//EN"
    "http://www.w3.org/TR/REC-html40/strict.dtd">
```

```
<HTML>
   <HEAD>
      <TITLE>My first HTML document</TITLE>
   </HEAD>
   <BODY>
      <P>Hello world!
   </BODY>
</HTML>
```

An HTML document is divided into a head section (here, between <HEAD> and </HEAD>) and a body (here, between <BODY> and </BODY>). The title of the document appears in the head (along with other information about the document), and the content of the document appears in the body. The body in this example contains just one paragraph, marked up with <P>.

Each markup language defined in SGML is called an *SGML application*. An SGML application is generally characterized by:

1. An SGML declaration. The SGML declaration specifies which characters and delimiters may appear in the application.

2. A document type definition (DTD). The DTD defines the syntax of markup constructs. The DTD may include additional definitions such as character entity references.

3. A specification that describes the semantics to be ascribed to the markup. This specification also imposes syntax restrictions that cannot be expressed within the DTD.

4. Document instances containing data (content) and markup. Each instance contains a reference to the DTD to be used to interpret it.

The HTML 4.0 specification includes an SGML declaration, three document type definitions (see the section on HTML version information for a description of the three), and a list of character references.

3.2 SGML constructs used in HTML

The following sections introduce SGML constructs that are used in HTML.

The appendix lists some SGML features that are not widely supported by HTML tools and user agents and should be avoided.

3.2.1 Elements

An SGML document type definition declares *element types* that represent structures or desired behavior. HTML includes element types that represent paragraphs, hypertext links, lists, tables, images, etc.

Each *element type declaration* generally describes three parts: a start tag, content, and an end tag.

The element's name appears in the *start tag* (written `<element-name>`) and the *end tag* (written `</element-name>`); note the slash before the element name in the end tag. For example, the start and end tags of the UL element type delimit the items in a list:

```
<UL>
<LI><P>...list item 1...
<LI><P>...list item 2...
</UL>
```

Some HTML element types allow authors to omit end tags (e.g., the P and LI element types). A few element types also allow the start tags to be omitted; for example, `HEAD` and `BODY`. The HTML DTD indicates for each element type whether the start tag and end tag are required.

Some HTML element types have no content. For example, the line break element BR has no content; its only role is to terminate a line of text. Such *empty* elements never have end tags. The document type definition and the text of the specification indicate whether an element type is empty (has no content) or, if it can have content, what is considered legal content.

Element names are always case-insensitive.

Please consult the SGML standard for information about rules governing elements (e.g., they must be properly nested, an end tag closes all omitted start tags up to the matching start tag (section 7.5.1), etc.).

For example, the following paragraph:

```
<P>This is the first paragraph.</P>
...a block element...
```

may be rewritten without its end tag:

```
<P>This is the first paragraph.
...a block element...
```

since the <P> start tag is closed by the following block element. Similarly, if a paragraph is enclosed by a block element, as in:

```
<DIV>
<P>This is the paragraph.
</DIV>
```

the end tag of the enclosing block element (here, </DIV>) implies the end tag of the open <P> start tag.

Elements are not tags. *Some people refer to elements as tags (e.g., "the P tag"). Remember that the element is one thing, and the tag (be it start or end tag) is another. For instance, the HEAD element is always present, even though both start and end HEAD tags may be missing in the markup.*

All the element types declared in this specification are listed in the element index.

3.2.2 Attributes

Elements may have associated properties, called *attributes*, which may have values (by default, or set by authors or scripts). Attribute/value pairs appear before the final ">" of an element's start tag. Any number of (legal) attribute value pairs, separated by spaces, may appear in an element's start tag. They may appear in any order.

In this example, the id attribute is set for an H1 element:

```
<H1 id="section1">
This is an identified heading thanks to the id attribute
</H1>
```

By default, SGML requires that all attribute values be delimited using either double quotation marks (ASCII decimal 34) or single quotation marks (ASCII decimal 39). Single quote marks can be included within the attribute value when the value is delimited by double quote marks, and vice versa. Authors may also use numeric character references to represent double quotes (") and single quotes ('). For double quotes authors can also use the character entity reference ".

In certain cases, authors may specify the value of an attribute without any quotation marks. The attribute value may only contain letters (a-z and A-Z), digits (0-9), hyphens (ASCII decimal 45), and periods (ASCII decimal 46). We recommend using quotation marks even when it is possible to eliminate them.

Attribute names are always case-insensitive

Attribute values are generally case-insensitive. The definition of each attribute in the reference manual indicates whether its value is case-insensitive.

All the attributes defined by this specification are listed in the attribute index.

3.2.3 Character references

Character references are numeric or symbolic names for characters that may be included in an HTML document. They are useful for referring to rarely used characters, or those that authoring tools make it difficult or impossible to enter. You will see character references throughout this document; they begin with a "&" sign and end with a semi-colon (;). Some common examples include:

- "<" represents the < sign.
- ">" represents the > sign.
- """ represents the " mark.
- "å" (in decimal) represents the letter "a" with a small circle above it.
- "И" (in decimal) represents the Cyrillic capital letter "I".
- "水" (in hexadecimal) represents the Chinese character for water.

We discuss HTML character references in detail later in the section on the HTML document character set. The specification also contains a list of character references that may appear in HTML 4.0 documents.

3.2.4 Comments

HTML comments have the following syntax:

```
<!-- this is a comment -->
<!-- and so is this one,
     which occupies more than one line -->
```

White space is not permitted between the markup declaration open delimiter("<!") and the comment open delimiter ("—"), but is permitted between the comment close delimiter ("—") and the markup declaration close delimiter (">"). A common error is to include a string of hyphens ("——") within a comment. Authors should avoid putting two or more adjacent hyphens inside comments.

Information that appears between comments has no special meaning (e.g., character references are not interpreted as such).

3.3 How to read the HTML DTD

Each element and attribute declaration in this specification is accompanied by its document type definition fragment. We have chosen to include the DTD fragments in the specification rather than seek a more approachable, but longer and less precise means of describing an element's properties. The following tutorial should allow readers unfamiliar with SGML to read the DTD and understand the technical details of the HTML specification.

3.3.1 DTD Comments

In DTDs, comments may spread over one or more lines. In the DTD, comments are delimited by a pair of "—" marks, e.g.

```
<!ELEMENT PARAM - O EMPTY    —named property value —>
```

Here, the comment "named property value" explains the use of the PARAM element type. Comments in the DTD are informative only.

3.3.2 Parameter entity definitions

The HTML DTD begins with a series of parameter entity definitions. A *parameter entity definition* defines a kind of macro that may be referenced and expanded elsewhere in the DTD. These macros may not appear in HTML documents, only in the DTD. Other types of macros, called character references, may be used in the text of an HTML document or within attribute values.

When the parameter entity is referred to by name in the DTD, it is expanded into a string.

A parameter entity definition begins with the keyword <*!ENTITY* % followed by the entity name, the quoted string the entity expands to, and finally a closing >. Instances of parameter entities in a DTD begin with "%", then the parameter entity name, and terminated by an optional ";".

The following example defines the string that the "%fontstyle;" entity will expand to.

```
<!ENTITY % fontstyle "TT | I | B | BIG | SMALL">
```

The string the parameter entity expands to may contain other parameter entity names. These names are expanded recursively. In the following example, the "%inline;" parameter entity is defined to include the "%fontstyle;", "%phrase;", "%special;" and "%formctrl;" parameter entities.

```
<!ENTITY % inline "#PCDATA | %fontstyle; | %phrase; | %special; | %formctrl;">
```

You will encounter two DTD entities frequently in the HTML DTD: "%block;" "%inline;". They are used when the content model includes block-level and inline elements, respectively (defined in the section on the global structure of an HTML document).

3.3.3 Element declarations

The bulk of the HTML DTD consists of the declarations of *element types* and their attributes. The <!ELEMENT keyword begins a declaration and the > character ends it. Between these are specified:

1. The element's name.

2. Whether the element's end tag is optional. Two hyphens that appear after the element name mean that the start and end tags are mandatory. One hyphen followed by the letter "O" indicates that the end tag can be omitted. A pair of letter "O"s indicate that both the start and end tags can be omitted.

3. The element's content, if any. The allowed content for an element is called its *content model*. Element types that are designed to have no content are called *empty elements*. The content model for such element types is declared using the keyword "EMPTY".

In this example:

```
<!ELEMENT UL - - (LI)+>
```

- The element type being declared is **UL**.

- The two hyphens indicate that both the start tag <UL> and the end tag </UL> for this element type are required.

- The content model for this element type is declared to be "at least one LI element". Below, we explain how to specify content models.

This example illustrates the declaration of an empty element type:

```
<!ELEMENT IMG - O EMPTY>
```

- The element type being declared is **IMG**.
- The hyphen and the following "O" indicate that the end tag can be omitted, but together with the content model "EMPTY", this is strengthened to the rule that the end tag **must** be omitted.
- The "EMPTY" keyword means that instances of this type must not have content.

Content model definitions

The content model describes what may be contained by an instance of an element type. Content model definitions may include:

- The names of allowed or forbidden element types (e.g., the UL element contains instances of the LI element type, and the P element type may not contain other P elements).
- DTD entities (e.g., the `LABEL` element contains instances of the "%inline;" parameter entity).
- Document text (indicated by the SGML construct "#PCDATA"). Text may contain character references. Recall that these begin with & and end with a semicolon (e.g., "Hergé's adventures of Tintin" contains the character entity reference for the "e acute" character).

The content model of an element is specified with the following syntax:

(...)

Delimits a group.

A | B

Either A or B occurs, but not both.

A , B

Both A and B occur, in that order.

A & B

Both A and B occur, in any order.

A?

A occurs zero or one time.

A*

>A occurs zero or more times.

A+

>A occurs one or more times.

Here are some examples from the HTML DTD:

```
<!ELEMENT UL - - (LI)+>
```
The UL element must contain one or more LI elements.

```
<!ELEMENT DL     - - (DT|DD)+>
```
The DL element must contain one or more DT or DD elements in any order.

```
<!ELEMENT OPTION - O (#PCDATA)>
```
The OPTION element may only contain text and entities, such as &—this is indicated by the SGML data type #PCDATA.

A few HTML element types use an additional SGML feature to exclude elements from their content model. Excluded elements are preceded by a hyphen. Explicit exclusions override permitted elements.

In this example, the -(A) signifies that the element A cannot appear in another A element (i.e., anchors may not be nested).

```
<!ELEMENT A - - (%inline;)* -(A)>
```

Note that the A element type is part of the DTD parameter entity "%inline;", but is excluded explicitly because of *-(A)*.

Similarly, the following element type declaration for FORM prohibits nested forms:

```
<!ELEMENT FORM - - (%block;|SCRIPT)+ -(FORM)>
```

3.3.4 Attribute declarations

The <!ATTLIST keyword begins the declaration of attributes that an element may take. It is followed by the name of the element in question, a list of attribute definitions, and a closing >. Each attribute definition is a triplet that defines:

- The name of an attribute.
- The type of the attribute's value or an explicit set of possible values. Values defined explicitly by the DTD are case-insensitive. Please consult the section on basic HTML data types for more information about attribute value types.
- Whether the default value of the attribute is implicit (keyword "#IMPLIED"), in which case the default value must be supplied by the user agent (in some cases via inheritance from parent elements); always required (keyword "#REQUIRED"); or fixed to the given value (keyword "#FIXED"). Some attribute definitions explicitly specify a default value for the attribute.

In this example, the name attribute is defined for the MAP element. The attribute is optional for this element.

```
<!ATTLIST MAP
  name         CDATA      #IMPLIED
  >
```

The type of values permitted for the attribute is given as CDATA, an SGML data type. CDATA is text that may contain character references.

For more information about "CDATA", "NAME", "ID", and other data types, please consult the section on HTML data types.

The following examples illustrate several attribute definitions:

```
rowspan      NUMBER     1              -- number of rows spanned by cell --
http-equiv   NAME       #IMPLIED       -- HTTP response header name    --
id           ID         #IMPLIED       -- document-wide unique id--
valign       (top|middle|bottom|baseline) #IMPLIE.D
```

The rowspan attribute requires values of type NUMBER. The default value is given explicitly as "1". The optional http-equiv attribute requires values of type NAME. The optional id attribute requires values of type ID. The optional valign attribute is constrained to take values from the set {top, middle, bottom, baseline}.

DTD entities in attribute definitions

Attribute definitions may also contain parameter entity references.

In this example, we see that the attribute definition list for the LINK element begins with the "%attrs;" parameter entity.

```
<!ELEMENT LINK - O EMPTY                    -- a media-independent link -->
<!ATTLIST LINK
  %attrs;                                   -- %coreattrs, %i18n, %events --
  charset     %Charset;       #IMPLIED      -- char encoding of linked resource --
  href        %URI;           #IMPLIED      -- URI for linked resource --
  hreflang    %LanguageCode;  #IMPLIED      -- language code --
  type        %ContentType;   #IMPLIED      -- advisory content type --
  rel         %LinkTypes;     #IMPLIED      -- forward link types --
  rev         %LinkTypes;     #IMPLIED      -- reverse link types --
  media       %MediaDesc;     #IMPLIED      -- for rendering on these media --
  >
```

Start tag: **required**, *End tag:* **forbidden**

The "%attrs;" parameter entity is defined as follows:

```
<!ENTITY % attrs "%coreattrs; %i18n; %events;">
```

The "%coreattrs;" parameter entity in the "%attrs;" definition expands as follows:

```
<!ENTITY % coreattrs
 "id         ID              #IMPLIED      -- document-wide unique id --
  class      CDATA           #IMPLIED      -- space separated list of classes --
  style      %StyleSheet;    #IMPLIED      -- associated style info --
  title      %Text;          #IMPLIED      -- advisory title/amplification --"
  >
```

The "%attrs;" parameter entity has been defined for convenience since these attributes are defined for most HTML element types.

Similarly, the DTD defines the "%URI;" parameter entity as expanding into the string "CDATA".

```
<!ENTITY % URI "CDATA"
   --a Uniform Resource Identifier,
       see [URI]
   -->
```

As this example illustrates, the parameter entity "%URI;" provides readers of the DTD with more information as to the type of data expected for an attribute. Similar entities have been defined for "%Color;", "%Charset;", "%Length;", "%Pixels;", etc.

Boolean attributes

Some attributes play the role of boolean variables (e.g., the selected attribute for the OPTION element). Their appearance in the start tag of an element implies that the value of the attribute is "true". Their absence implies a value of "false".

Boolean attributes may legally take a single value: the name of the attribute itself (e.g., selected="selected").

This example defines the selected attribute to be a boolean attribute.

```
selected     (selected)   #IMPLIED  —reduced inter-item spacing —
```

The attribute is set to "true" by appearing in the element's start tag:

```
<OPTION selected="selected">
...contents...
<OPTION>
```

In HTML, boolean attributes may appear in *minimized form*—the attribute's **value** appears alone in the element's start tag. Thus, selected may be set by writing:

```
<OPTION selected>
```

instead of:

```
<OPTION selected="selected">
```

Authors should be aware than many user agents **only** recognize the minimized form of boolean attributes and not the full form.

Chapter 4

Conformance: Requirements and Recommendations

Contents

1. Definitions
2. SGML
3. The text/html content type

In this section, we begin the specification of HTML 4.0, starting with the contract between authors, documents, users, and user agents.

The key words "MUST", "MUST NOT", "REQUIRED", "SHALL", "SHALL NOT", "SHOULD", "SHOULD NOT", "RECOMMENDED", "MAY", and "OPTIONAL" in this document are to be interpreted as described in [RFC2119]. However, for readability, these words do not appear in all uppercase letters in this specification.

At times, the authors of this specification recommend good practice for authors and user agents. These recommendations are not normative and conformance with this specification does not depend on their realization. These recommendations contain the expression "We recommend ...", "This specification recommends ...", or some similar wording.

4.1 Definitions

HTML document

An HTML document is an SGML document that meets the constraints of this specification.

Author

An author is a person or program that writes or generates HTML documents. An *authoring tool* is a special case of an author, namely, it's a program that generates HTML.

We recommend that authors write documents that conform to the strict DTD rather than the other DTDs defined by this specification. Please see the section on version information for details about the DTDs defined in HTML 4.0.

User

A user is a person who interacts with a user agent to view, hear, or otherwise use a rendered HTML document.

HTML user agent

An HTML user agent is any device that interprets HTML documents. User agents include visual browsers (text-only and graphical), non-visual browsers (audio, Braille), search robots, proxies, etc.

A *conforming user agent* for HTML 4.0 is one that observes the mandatory conditions ("must") set forth in this specification, including the following points:

- A user agent should avoid imposing arbitrary length limits on attribute value literals (see the section on capacities in the SGML Declaration). For introductory information on SGML attributes, please consult the section on attribute definitions.

- A user agent must ensure that rendering is unchanged by the presence or absence of start tags and end tags when the HTML DTD indicates that these are optional. See the section on element definitions for introductory information on SGML elements.

- For reasons of backwards compatibility, we recommend that tools interpreting HTML 4.0 continue to support HTML 3.2 (see [HTML32]) and HTML 2.0 (see [RFC1866]).

Error conditions

This specification does not define how conforming user agents handle general error conditions, including how user agents behave when they encounter elements, attributes, attribute values, or entities not specified in this document.

However, for recommended error handling behavior, please consult the notes on invalid documents.

Deprecated

A deprecated element or attribute is one that has been outdated by newer constructs. Deprecated elements are defined in the reference manual in appropriate locations, but are clearly marked as deprecated. Deprecated elements may become obsolete in future versions of HTML.

User agents should continue to support deprecated elements for reasons of backward compatibility.

Definitions of elements and attributes clearly indicate which are deprecated.

This specification includes examples that illustrate how to avoid using deprecated elements. In most cases these depend on user agent support for style sheets. In general, authors should use style sheets to achieve stylistic and formatting effects rather than HTML presentational attributes. HTML presentational attributes have been deprecated when style sheet alternatives exist (see, for example, [CSS1]).

Obsolete

An obsolete element or attribute is one for which there is no guarantee of support by a user agent. Obsolete elements are no longer defined in the specification, but are listed for historical purposes in the changes section of the reference manual.

4.2 SGML

HTML 4.0 is an SGML application conforming to International Standard ISO 8879—*Standard Generalized Markup Language* SGML (defined in [ISO8879]).

Examples in the text conform to the strict document type definition unless the example in question refers to elements or attributes only defined by the transitional document type definition or frameset document type definition. For the sake of brevity, most of the examples in this specification do not begin with the document type declaration that is mandatory at the beginning of each HTML document.

DTD fragments in element definitions come from the strict document type definition except for the elements related to frames.

Please consult the section on HTML version information for details about when to use the strict, transitional, or frameset DTD.

Comments appearing in the HTML 4.0 DTD have no normative value; they are informative only.

User agents must not render SGML processing instructions (e.g., <?full volume>) or comments. For more information about this and other SGML features that may be legal in HTML but aren't widely supported by HTML user agents, please consult the section on SGML features with limited support.

4.3 The text/html content type

HTML documents are sent over the Internet as a sequence of bytes accompanied by encoding information (described in the section on character encodings). The structure of the transmission, termed a *message entity*, is defined by [RFC2045] and [RFC2068]. A message entity with a content type of "text/html" represents an HTML document.

The content type for HTML documents is defined as follows:

Content type name:

   text

Content subtype name:

   html

Required parameters:

   none

Optional parameters:

   charset

Encoding considerations:

   any encoding is allowed

Security considerations:

   See the notes on security

The optional parameter "charset" refers to the character encoding used to represent the HTML document as a sequence of bytes. Legal values for this parameter are defined in the section on character encodings. Although this parameter is optional, we recommend that it always be present.

Chapter 5

HTML Document Representation

Contents

1. The Document Character Set
2. Character encodings
   1. Choosing an encoding
      - Notes on specific encodings
   2. Specifying the character encoding
3. Character references
   1. Numeric character references
   2. Character entity references
4. Undisplayable characters

In this chapter, we discuss how HTML documents are represented on a computer and over the Internet.

The section on the document character set addresses the issue of what abstract *characters* may be part of an HTML document. Characters include the Latin letter "A", the Cyrillic letter "I", the Chinese character meaning "water", etc.

The section on character encodings addresses the issue of how those characters may be *represented* in a file or when transferred over the Internet. As some character encodings cannot directly represent all characters an author may want to include in a document, HTML offers other mechanisms, called character references, for referring to any character.

Since there are a great number of characters throughout human languages, and a great variety of ways to represent those characters, proper care must be taken so that documents may be understood by user agents around the world.

5.1 The Document Character Set

To promote interoperability, SGML requires that each application (including HTML) specify its *document character set*. A document character set consists of:

- *A Repertoire*: A set of abstract characters, , such as the Latin letter "A", the Cyrillic letter "I", the Chinese character meaning "water", etc.
- *Code positions*: A set of integer references to characters in the repertoire.

Each SGML document (including each HTML document) is a sequence of characters from the repertoire. Computer systems identify each character by its code position; for example, in the ASCII character set, code positions 65, 66, and 67 refer to the characters 'A', 'B', and 'C', respectively.

The ASCII character set is not sufficient for a global information system such as the Web, so HTML uses the much more complete character set called the *Universal Character Set (UCS)*, defined in [ISO10646]. This standard defines a repertoire of thousands of characters used by communities all over the world.

The character set defined in [ISO10646] is character-by-character equivalent to Unicode 2.0 ([UNICODE]). Both of these standards are updated from time to time with new characters, and the amendments should be consulted at the respective Web sites. In the current specification, references to ISO/IEC-10646 or Unicode imply the same document character set. However, the HTML specification also refers to the Unicode specification for other issues such as the bidirectional text algorithm.

The document character set, however, does not suffice to allow user agents to correctly interpret HTML documents as they are typically exchanged—encoded as a sequence of bytes in a file or during a network transmission. User agents must also know the specific character encoding that was used to transform the document character stream into a byte stream.

5.2 Character encodings

What this specification calls a *character encoding* is known by different names in other specifications (which may cause some confusion). However, the concept is largely the same across the Internet. Also, protocol headers, attributes, and parameters referring to character encodings share the same name—"charset"—and use the same values from the [IANA] registry (see [CHARSETS] for a complete list).

The "charset" parameter identifies a character encoding, which is a method of converting a sequence of bytes into a sequence of characters. This conversion fits naturally with the scheme of Web activity: servers send HTML documents to user agents as a stream of bytes; user agents interpret them as a sequence of characters. The conversion method can range from simple one-to-one correspondence to complex switching schemes or algorithms.

A simple one-byte-per-character encoding technique is not sufficient for text strings over a character repertoire as large as [ISO10646]. There are several different encodings of parts of [ISO10646] in addition to encodings of the entire character set (such as UCS-4).

5.2.1 Choosing an encoding

Authoring tools (e.g., text editors) may encode HTML documents in the character encoding of their choice, and the choice largely depends on the conventions used by the system software. These tools may employ any convenient encoding that covers most of the characters contained in the document, provided the encoding is correctly labeled. Occasional characters that fall outside this encoding may still be represented by character references. These always refer to the document character set, not the character encoding.

Servers and proxies may change a character encoding (called *transcoding*) on the fly to meet the requests of user agents (see section 14.2 of [RFC2068], the "Accept-Charset" HTTP request header). Servers and proxies do not have to serve a document in a character encoding that covers the entire document character set.

Commonly used character encodings on the Web include ISO-8859-1 (also referred to as "Latin-1"; usable for most Western European languages), ISO-8859-5 (which supports Cyrillic), SHIFT_JIS (a Japanese encoding), EUC-JP (another Japanese encoding), and UTF-8 (an encoding of ISO 10646 using a different number of bytes for different characters). Names for character encodings are case-insensitive, so that for example "SHIFT_JIS", "Shift_JIS", and "shift_jis" are equivalent.

This specification does not mandate which character encodings a user agent must support.

Conforming user agents must correctly map to Unicode all characters in any character encodings that they recognize (or they must behave as if they did).

Notes on specific encodings

When HTML text is transmitted in UTF-16 (charset=UTF-16), text data should be transmitted in network byte order ("big-endian", high-order byte first) in accordance with [ISO10646], Section 6.3 and [UNICODE], clause C3, page 3-1.

Furthermore, to maximize chances of proper interpretation, it is recommended that documents transmitted as UTF-16 always begin with a ZERO-WIDTH NON-BREAKING SPACE character (hexadecimal FEFF, also called Byte Order Mark (BOM)) which, when byte-reversed, becomes hexadecimal FFFE, a character guaranteed never to be assigned. Thus, a user-agent receiving a hexadecimal FFFE as the first bytes of a text would know that bytes have to be reversed for the remainder of the text.

The UTF-1 transformation format of [ISO10646] (registered by IANA as ISO-10646-UTF-1), should not be used. For information about ISO 8859-8 and the bidirectional algorithm, please consult the section on bidirectionality and character encoding.

5.2.2 Specifying the character encoding

How does a server determine which character encoding applies for a document it serves? Some servers examine the first few bytes of the document, or check against a database of known files and encodings. Many modern servers give Web masters more control over charset configuration than old servers do. Web masters should use these mechanisms to send out a "charset" parameter whenever possible, but should take care not to identify a document with the wrong "charset" parameter value.

How does a user agent know which character encoding has been used? The server should provide this information. The most straightforward way for a server to inform the user agent about the character encoding of the document is to use the "charset" parameter of the "Content-Type" header field of the HTTP protocol ([RFC2068], sections 3.4 and 14.18) For example, the following HTTP header announces that the character encoding is EUC-JP:

```
Content-Type: text/html; charset=EUC-JP
```

Please consult the section on conformance for the definition of text/html.

The HTTP protocol ([RFC2068], section 3.7.1) mentions ISO-8859-1 as a default character encoding when the "charset" parameter is absent from the "Content-Type" header field. In practice, this recommendation has proved useless because some servers don't allow a "charset" parameter to be sent, and others may not be configured to send the parameter. Therefore, user agents must not assume any default value for the "charset" parameter.

To address server or configuration limitations, HTML documents may include explicit information about the document's character encoding; the META element can be used to provide user agents with this information.

For example, to specify that the character encoding of the current document is "EUC-JP", a document should include the following META declaration:

```
<META http-equiv="Content-Type" content="text/html; charset=EUC-JP">
```

The META declaration must only be used when the character encoding is organized such that ASCII characters stand for themselves (at least until the META element is parsed). META declarations should appear as early as possible in the HEAD element.

For cases where neither the HTTP protocol nor the META element provides information about the character encoding of a document, HTML also provides the charset attribute on several elements. By combining these mechanisms, an author can greatly improve the chances that, when the user retrieves a resource, the user agent will recognize the character encoding.

To sum up, conforming user agents must observe the following priorities when determining a document's character encoding (from highest priority to lowest):

1. An HTTP "charset" parameter in a "Content-Type" field.
2. A META declaration with "http-equiv" set to "Content-Type" and a value set for "charset".
3. The charset attribute set on an element that designates an external resource.

In addition to this list of priorities, the user agent may use heuristics and user settings. For example, many user agents use a heuristic to distinguish the various encodings used for Japanese text. Also, user agents typically have a user-definable, local default character encoding which they apply in the absence of other indicators.

User agents may provide a mechanism that allows users to override incorrect "charset" information. However, if a user agent offers such a mechanism, it should only offer it for browsing and not for editing, to avoid the creation of Web pages marked with an incorrect "charset" parameter.

Note. *If, for a specific application, it becomes necessary to refer to characters outside* [ISO10646], *characters should be assigned to a private zone to avoid conflicts with present or future versions of the standard. This is highly discouraged, however, for reasons of portability.*

5.3 Character references

A given character encoding may not be able to express all characters of the document character set. For such encodings, or when hardware or software configurations do not allow users to input some document characters directly, authors may use SGML character references. Character references are a character encoding-independent mechanism for entering any character from the document character set.

Character references in HTML may appear in two forms:

- Numeric character references (either decimal or hexadecimal).
- Character entity references.

Character references within comments have no special meaning; they are comment data only.

Note. HTML *provides other ways to present character data, in particular* inline images.

Note. In *SGML, it is possible to eliminate the final ";" after a character reference in some cases (e.g., at a line break or immediately before a tag). In other circumstances it may not be eliminated (e.g., in the middle of a word). We strongly suggest using the ";" in all cases to avoid problems with user agents that require this character to be present.*

5.3.1 Numeric character references

Numeric character references specify the code position of a character in the document character set. Numeric character references may take two forms:

- The syntax "&#D;", where D is a decimal number, refers to the Unicode decimal character number D.
- The syntax "&#xH;" or "&#XH;", where H is an hexadecimal number, refers to the Unicode hexadecimal character number H. Hexadecimal numbers in numeric character references are case-insensitive.

Here are some examples of numeric character references:

- å (in decimal) represents the letter "a" with a small circle above it (used, for example, in Norwegian).
- å (in hexadecimal) represents the same character.
- å (in hexadecimal) represents the same character as well.
- И (in decimal) represents the Cyrillic capital letter "I".
- 水 (in hexadecimal) represents the Chinese character for water.

Note. *Although the hexadecimal representation is not defined in* [ISO8879], *it is expected to be in the revision, as described in* [WEBSGML]. *This convention is particularly useful since character standards generally use hexadecimal representations.*

5.3.2 Character entity references

In order to give authors a more intuitive way of referring to characters in the document character set, HTML offers a set of *character entity references*. Character entity references use symbolic names so that authors need not remember code positions. For example, the character entity reference å refers to the lowercase "a" character topped with a ring; "å" is easier to remember than å.

HTML 4.0 does not define a character entity reference for every character in the document character set. For instance, there is no character entity reference for the Cyrillic capital letter "I". Please consult the full list of character references defined in HTML 4.0.

Character entity references are case-sensitive. Thus, Å refers to a different character (uppercase A, ring) than å (lowercase a, ring).

Four character entity references deserve special mention since they are frequently used to escape special characters:

- "<" represents the < sign.
- ">" represents the > sign.
- "&" represents the & sign.
- "" represents the " mark.

Authors wishing to put the "<" character in text should use "<" (ASCII decimal 60) to avoid possible confusion with the beginning of a tag (start tag open delimiter). Similarly, authors should use ">" (ASCII decimal 62) in text instead of ">" to avoid problems with older user agents that incorrectly perceive this as the end of a tag (tag close delimiter) when it appears in quoted attribute values.

Authors should use "&" (ASCII decimal 38) instead of "&" to avoid confusion with the beginning of a character reference (entity reference open delimiter). Authors should also use "&" in attribute values since character references are allowed within CDATA attribute values.

Some authors use the character entity reference """ to encode instances of the double quote mark (") since that character may be used to delimit attribute values.

5.4 Undisplayable characters

A user agent may not be able to render all characters in a document meaningfully, for instance, because the user agent lacks a suitable font, a character has a value that may not be expressed in the user agent's internal character encoding, etc.

Because there are many different things that may be done in such cases, this document does not prescribe any specific behavior. Depending on the implementation, undisplayable characters may also be handled by the underlying display system and not the application itself. In the absence of more sophisticated behavior, for example tailored to the needs of a particular script or language, we recommend the following behavior for user agents:

1. Adopt a clearly visible, but unobtrusive mechanism to alert the user of missing resources.

2. If missing characters are presented using their numeric representation, use the hexadecimal (not decimal) form since this is the form used in character set standards.

Chapter 6

Basic HTML Data Types

Contents

1. Case information
2. SGML basic types
3. Text strings
4. URIs
5. Colors
    1. Notes on using colors
6. Lengths
7. Content types (MIME types)
8. Language codes
9. Character encodings
10. Single characters
11. Dates and times
12. Link types
13. Media descriptors
14. Script data
15. Style sheet data
16. Frame target names

This section of the specification describes the basic data types that may appear as an element's content or an attribute's value.

For introductory information about reading the HTML DTD, please consult the SGML tutorial.

6.1 Case information

Each attribute definition includes information about the case-sensitivity of its values. The case information is presented with the following keys:

CS

The value is case-sensitive (i.e., user agents interpret "a" and "A" differently).

CI

The value is case-insensitive (i.e., user agents interpret "a" and "A" as the same).

CN

The value is not subject to case changes, e.g., because it is a number or a character from the document character set.

CA

The element or attribute definition itself gives case information.

CT

Consult the type definition for details about case-sensitivity.

If an attribute value is a list, the keys apply to every value in the list, unless otherwise indicated.

6.2 SGML basic types

The document type definition specifies the syntax of HTML element content and attribute values using SGML tokens (e.g., PCDATA, CDATA, NAME, ID, etc.). See [ISO8879] for their full definitions. The following is a summary of key information:

- **CDATA** is a sequence of characters from the document character set and may include character entities. User agents should interpret attribute values as follows:
  - Replace character entities with characters,
  - Ignore line feeds,
  - Replace each carriage return or tab with a single space.

User agents may ignore leading and trailing white space in CDATA attribute values (e.g., " myval " may be interpreted as "myval"). Authors should not declare attribute values with leading or trailing white space.

For some HTML 4.0 attributes with CDATA attribute values, the specification imposes further constraints on the set of legal values for the attribute that may not be expressed by the DTD.

Although the STYLE and SCRIPT elements use CDATA for their data model, for these elements, CDATA must be handled differently by user agents. Markup and entities must be treated as raw text and passed to the application as is. The first occurrence of the character sequence "</" (end-tag open delimiter) is treated as terminating the end of the element's content. In valid documents, this would be the end tag for the element.

- **ID** and **NAME** tokens must begin with a letter ([A-Za-z]) and may be followed by any number of letters, digits ([0-9]), hyphens ("-"), underscores ("_"), colons (":"), and periods (".").
- **IDREF** and **IDREFS** are references to ID tokens defined by other attributes. IDREF is a single token and IDREFS is a space-separated list of tokens.
- **NUMBER** tokens must contain at least one digit ([0-9]).

6.3 Text strings

A number of attributes (%Text; in the DTD) take text that is meant to be "human readable". For introductory information about attributes, please consult the tutorial discussion of attributes.

6.4 URIs

This specification uses the term URI as defined in [URI] (see also [RFC1630]).

Note that URIs include URLs (as defined in [RFC1738] and [RFC1808]).

Relative URIs are resolved to full URIs using a base URI. [RFC1808], section 3, defines the normative algorithm for this process. For more information about base URIs, please consult the section on base URIs in the chapter on links.

URIs are represented in the DTD by the parameter entity %URI;.

URIs in general are case-sensitive. There may be URIs, or parts of URIs, where case doesn't matter (e.g., machine names), but identifying these may not be easy. Users should always consider that URIs are case-sensitive (to be on the safe side).

Please consult the appendix for information about non-ASCII characters in URI attribute values.

6.5 Colors

The attribute value type "color" (%Color;) refers to color definitions as specified in [SRGB]. A color value may either be a hexadecimal number (prefixed by a hash mark) or one of the following sixteen color names. The color names are case-insensitive.

Color names and sRGB values

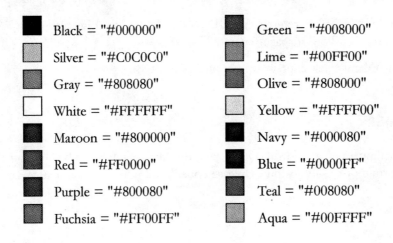

- Black = "#000000"
- Silver = "#C0C0C0"
- Gray = "#808080"
- White = "#FFFFFF"
- Maroon = "#800000"
- Red = "#FF0000"
- Purple = "#800080"
- Fuchsia = "#FF00FF"
- Green = "#008000"
- Lime = "#00FF00"
- Olive = "#808000"
- Yellow = "#FFFF00"
- Navy = "#000080"
- Blue = "#0000FF"
- Teal = "#008080"
- Aqua = "#00FFFF"

Thus, the color values "#800080" and "Purple" both refer to the color purple.

6.5.1 Notes on using colors

Although colors can add significant amounts of information to document and make them more readable, please consider the following guidelines when including color in your documents:

- The use of HTML elements and attributes for specifying color is deprecated. You are encouraged to use style sheets instead.

- Don't use color combinations that cause problems for people with color blindness in its various forms.

- If you use a background image or set the background color, then be sure to set the various text colors as well.

- Colors specified with the BODY and FONT elements and bgcolor on tables look different on different platforms (e.g., workstations, Macs, Windows, and LCD panels vs. CRTs), so you shouldn't rely entirely on a specific effect. In the future, support for the [SRGB] color model together with ICC color profiles should mitigate this problem.

- When practical, adopt common conventions to minimize user confusion.

6.6 Lengths

HTML specifies three types of length values for attributes:

1. **Pixels**: The value (%Pixels; in the DTD) is an integer that represents the number of pixels of the canvas (screen, paper). Thus, the value "50" means fifty pixels. For normative information about the definition of a pixel, please consult [CSS1].

2. **Length**: The value (%Length; in the DTD) may be either a %Pixel; or a percentage of the available horizontal or vertical space. Thus, the value "50%" means half of the available space.

3. **MultiLength**: The value (%MultiLength; in the DTD) may be a %Length; or a relative length. A relative length has the form "i*", where "i" is an integer. When allotting space among elements competing for that space, user agents allot pixel and percentage lengths first, then divide up remaining available space among relative lengths. Each relative length receives a portion of the available space that is proportional to the integer preceding the "*". The value "*" is equivalent to "1*". Thus, if 60 pixels of space are available after the user agent allots pixel and percentage space, and the competing relative lengths are 1*, 2*, and 3*, the 1* will be alloted 10 pixels, the 2* will be alloted 20 pixels, and the 3* will be alloted 30 pixels.

Length values are case-neutral.

6.7 Content types (MIME types)

Note. A *"media type"* *(defined in* [RFC2045] *and* [RFC2046]*) specifies the nature of a linked resource. This specification employs the term "content type" rather than "media type" in accordance with current usage. Furthermore, in this specification, "media type" may refer to the media where a user agent renders a document.*

This type is represented in the DTD by %ContentType;.

Content types are case-insensitive.

Examples of content types include "text/html", "image/png", "image/gif", "video/mpeg", "audio/basic", "text/tcl", "text/javascript", and "text/vbscript". For the current list of registered MIME types, please consult [MIMETYPES].

Note. The content type "text/css", while not currently registered with IANA, should be used when the linked resource is a [CSS1] *style sheet.*

6.8 Language codes

The value of attributes whose type is a language code (%LanguageCode in the DTD) refers to a language code as specified by [RFC1766], section 2. For information on specifying language codes in HTML, please consult the section on language codes. Whitespace is not allowed within the language-code.

Language codes are case-insensitive.

6.9 Character encodings

The "charset" attributes (%Charset in the DTD) refer to a character encoding as described in the section on character encodings. Values must be strings (e.g., "euc-jp") from the IANA registry (see [CHARSETS] for a complete list).

Names of character encodings are case-insensitive.

User agents must follow the steps set out in the section on specifying character encodings in order to determine the character encoding of an external resource.

6.10 Single characters

Certain attributes call for single character from the document character set. These attributes take the %Character type in the DTD.

Single characters may be specified with character references (e.g., "&").

6.11 Dates and times

[ISO8601] allows many options and variations in the representation of dates and times. The current specification uses one of the formats described in the profile [DATETIME] for its definition of legal date/time strings (%Datetime in the DTD).

The format is:

```
YYYY-MM-DDThh:mm:ssTZD
```

where:

```
        YYYY = four-digit year
        MM   = two-digit month (01=January, etc.)
        DD   = two-digit day of month (01 through 31)
        hh   = two digits of hour (00 through 23) (am/pm NOT allowed)
        mm   = two digits of minute (00 through 59)
        ss   = two digits of second (00 through 59)
        TZD  = time zone designator
```

The time zone designator is one of:

Z

indicates UTC (Coordinated Universal Time). The "Z" must be uppercase.

+hh:mm

indicates that the time is a local time which is hh hours and mm minutes ahead of UTC.

-hh:mm

indicates that the time is a local time which is hh hours and mm minutes behind UTC.

Exactly the components shown here must be present, with exactly this punctuation. Note that the "T" appears literally in the string (it must be uppercase), to indicate the beginning of the time element, as specified in [ISO8601].

If a generating application does not know the time to the second, it may use the value "00" for the seconds (and minutes and hours if necessary).

Note. [DATETIME] *does not address the issue of leap seconds.*

6.12 Link types

Authors may use the following recognized link types, listed here with their conventional interpretations. In the DTD, %LinkTypes refers to a space-separated list of link types. White space characters are not permitted within link types.

These link types are case-insensitive, i.e., "Alternate" has the same meaning as "alternate".

User agents, search engines, etc. may interpret these link types in a variety of ways. For example, user agents may provide access to linked documents through a navigation bar.

Alternate

Designates substitute versions for the document in which the link occurs. When used together with the lang attribute, it implies a translated version of the document. When used together with the media attribute, it implies a version designed for a different medium (or media).

Stylesheet

Refers to an external style sheet. See the section on external style sheets for details. This is used together with the link type "Alternate" for user-selectable alternate style sheets.

Start

Refers to the first document in a collection of documents. This link type tells search engines which document is considered by the author to be the starting point of the collection.

Next

Refers to the next document in an linear sequence of documents. User agents may choose to preload the "next" document, to reduce the perceived load time.

Prev

Refers to the previous document in an ordered series of documents. Some user agents also support the synonym "Previous".

Contents

Refers to a document serving as a table of contents. Some user agents also support the synonym *ToC* (from "Table of Contents").

Index

Refers to a document providing an index for the current document.

Glossary

Refers to a document providing a glossary of terms that pertain to the current document.

Copyright

Refers to a copyright statement for the current document.

Chapter

Refers to a document serving as a chapter in a collection of documents.

Section

Refers to a document serving as a section in a collection of documents.

Subsection

Refers to a document serving as a subsection in a collection of documents.

Appendix

Refers to a document serving as an appendix in a collection of documents.

Help

Refers to a document offering help (more information, links to other sources information, etc.)

Bookmark

> Refers to a bookmark. A bookmark is a link to a key entry point within an extended document. The title attribute may be used, for example, to label the bookmark. Note that several bookmarks may be defined in each document.

Authors may wish to define additional link types not described in this specification. If they do so, they should use a profile to cite the conventions used to define the link types. Please see the profile attribute of the HEAD element for more details.

For further discussions about link types, please consult the section on links in HTML documents.

6.13 Media descriptors

The following is a list of recognized media descriptors (%MediaDesc in the DTD).

screen

> Intended for non-paged computer screens.

tty

> Intended for media using a fixed-pitch character grid, such as teletypes, terminals, or portable devices with limited display capabilities.

tv

> Intended for television-type devices (low resolution, color, limited scrollability).

projection

> Intended for projectors.

handheld

> Intended for handheld devices (small screen, monochrome, bitmapped graphics, limited bandwidth).

print

> Intended for paged, opaque material and for documents viewed on screen in print preview mode.

braille

Intended for braille tactile feedback devices.

aural

Intended for speech synthesizers.

all

Suitable for all devices.

Future versions of HTML may introduce new values and may allow parameterized values. To facilitate the introduction of these extensions, conforming user agents must be able to parse the media attribute value as follows:

1. The value is a comma-separated list of entries. For example,

    ```
    media="screen, 3d-glasses, print and resolution  90dpi"
    ```
    is mapped to:

    ```
    "screen"
    "3d-glasses"
    "print and resolution  90dpi"
    ```

2. Each entry is truncated just before the first character that isn't a US ASCII letter [a-zA-Z] (Unicode decimal 65-90, 97-122), digit [0-9] (Unicode hex 30-39), or hyphen (45). In the example, this gives:

    ```
    "screen"
    "3d-glasses"
    "print"
    ```
3. A case-sensitive match is then made with the set of media types defined above. User agents may ignore entries that don't match. In the example we are left with `screen` and `print`.

Note. *Style sheets may include media-dependent variations within them (e.g., the CSS @media construct). In such cases it may be appropriate to use "media=all".*

6.14 Script data

Script data (%Script; in the DTD) can be the content of the SCRIPT element and the value of intrinsic event attributes. User agents must not evaluate script data as HTML markup but instead must pass it on as data to a script engine.

The case-sensitivity of script data depends on the scripting language.

Please note that script data that is element content may not contain character references, but script data that is the value of an attribute may contain them. The appendix provides further information about specifying non-HTML data.

6.15 Style sheet data

Style sheet data (%StyleSheet; in the DTD) can be the content of the STYLE element and the value of the style attribute. User agents must not evaluate style data as HTML markup.

The case-sensitivity of style data depends on the style sheet language.

Please note that style sheet data that is element content may not contain character references, but style sheet data that is the value of an attribute may contain them. The appendix provides further information about specifying non-HTML data.

6.16 Frame target names

Except for the reserved names listed below, frame target names (%FrameTarget; in the DTD) must begin with an alphabetic character (a-zA-Z). User agents should ignore all other target names.

The following target names are reserved and have special meanings.

_blank
　　The user agent should load the designated document in a new, unnamed window.

_self
　　The user agent should load the document in the same frame as the element that refers to this target.

_parent

The user agent should load the document into the immediate FRAMESET parent of the current frame. This value is equivalent to _self if the current frame has no parent.

_top

The user agent should load the document into the full, original window (thus cancelling all other frames). This value is equivalent to _self if the current frame has no parent.

Chapter 7

The Global Structure of an HTML Document

Contents

1. Introduction to the structure of an HTML document
2. HTML version information
3. The HTML element
4. The document head
    1. The HEAD element
    2. The TITLE element
    3. The title attribute
    4. Meta data
        - Specifying meta data
        - The META element
        - Meta data profiles
5. The document body
    1. The BODY element
    2. Element identifiers: the id and class attributes
    3. Block-level and inline elements
    4. Grouping elements: the DIV and SPAN elements
    5. Headings: The H1, H2, H3, H4, H5, H6 elements
    6. The ADDRESS element

7.1 Introduction to the structure of an HTML document

An HTML 4.0 document is composed of three parts:

1. a line containing HTML version information,

60 HTML 4.0 Specification

2. a declarative header section (delimited by the `HEAD` element),
3. a body, which contains the document's actual content. The body may be implemented by the `BODY` element or the `FRAMESET` element.

White space (spaces, newlines, tabs, and comments) may appear before or after each section. Sections 2 and 3 should be delimited by the HTML element.

Here's an example of a simple HTML document:

```
<!DOCTYPE HTML PUBLIC "-//W3C//DTD HTML 4.0//EN"
    "http://www.w3.org/TR/REC-html40/strict.dtd">
<HTML>
   <HEAD>
      <TITLE>My first HTML document</TITLE>
   </HEAD>
   <BODY>
      <P>Hello world!
   </BODY>
</HTML>
```

7.2 HTML version information

A valid HTML document declares what version of HTML is used in the document. The *document type declaration* names the document type definition (DTD) in use for the document (see [ISO8879]).

HTML 4.0 specifies three DTDs, so authors must include one of the following document type declarations in their documents. The DTDs vary in the elements they support.

- The HTML 4.0 Strict DTD includes all elements and attributes that have not been deprecated or do not appear in frameset documents. For documents that use this DTD, use this document type declaration:

  ```
  <!DOCTYPE HTML PUBLIC "-//W3C//DTD HTML 4.0//EN"
          "http://www.w3.org/TR/REC-html40/strict.dtd">
  ```

- The HTML 4.0 Transitional DTD includes everything in the strict DTD plus deprecated elements and attributes (most of which concern visual presentation). For documents that use this DTD, use this document type declaration:

```
<!DOCTYPE HTML PUBLIC "-//W3C//DTD HTML 4.0 Transitional//EN"
        "http://www.w3.org/TR/REC-html40/loose.dtd">
```

- The HTML 4.0 Frameset DTD includes everything in the transitional DTD plus frames as well. For documents that use this DTD, use this document type declaration:

```
<!DOCTYPE HTML PUBLIC "-//W3C//DTD HTML 4.0 Frameset//EN"
        "http://www.w3.org/TR/REC-html40/frameset.dtd">
```

The URI in each document type declaration allows user agents to download the DTD and any entity sets that are needed. The following URIs refer to DTDs and entity sets for HTML 4.0 that W3C supports:

- "http://www.w3.org/TR/REC-html40/strict.dtd"—default strict DTD
- "http://www.w3.org/TR/REC-html40/loose.dtd"—loose DTD
- "http://www.w3.org/TR/REC-html40/frameset.dtd"—DTD for frameset documents
- "http://www.w3.org/TR/REC-html40/HTMLlat1.ent"—Latin-1 entities
- "http://www.w3.org/TR/REC-html40/HTMLsymbol.ent"—Symbol entities
- "http://www.w3.org/TR/REC-html40/HTMLspecial.ent"—Special entities

The binding between public identifiers and files can be specified using a catalog file following the format recommended by the SGML Open Consortium (see [SGMLOPEN]). A sample catalog file for HTML 4.0 is included at the beginning of the section on SGML reference information for HTML. The last two letters of the declaration indicate the language of the DTD. For HTML, this is always English ("EN").

7.3 The HTML element

```
<!ENTITY % html.content "HEAD, BODY">
<!ELEMENT HTML O O (%html.content;)    -- document root element -->
<!ATTLIST HTML
  %i18n;                               -- lang, dir --
  >
```

Start tag: *optional*, End tag: *optional*

Attribute definitions

version = *cdata* [CN]

> **Deprecated.** The value of this attribute specifies which HTML DTD version governs the current document. This attribute has been deprecated because it is redundant with version information provided by the document type declaration.

Attributes defined elsewhere

- lang (language information), dir (text direction)

After document type declaration, the remainder of an HTML document is contained by the HTML element. Thus, a typical HTML document has this structure:

```
<!DOCTYPE HTML PUBLIC "-//W3C//DTD HTML 4.0//EN"
"http://www.w3.org/TR/REC-html40/strict.dtd">
<HTML>
...The head, body, etc. goes here...
</HTML>
```

7.4 The document head

7.4.1 The HEAD element

```
<!-- %head.misc; defined earlier on as "SCRIPT|STYLE|META|LINK|OBJECT" -->
<!ENTITY % head.content "TITLE & BASE?">

<!ELEMENT HEAD O O (%head.content;) +(%head.misc;)-document head -->
<!ATTLIST HEAD
  %i18n;                              -- lang, dir --
  profile     %URI;      #IMPLIED     -- named dictionary of meta info --
  >
```

Start tag: **optional**, *End tag:* **optional**

Attribute definitions

profile = *uri* [CT]

    This attribute specifies the location of one or more meta data profiles, separated by white space. For future extensions, user agents should consider the value to be a list even though this specification only considers the first URI to be significant. Profiles are discussed below in the section on meta data.

Attributes defined elsewhere

- lang (language information), dir (text direction)

The HEAD element contains information about the current document, such as its title, keywords that may be useful to search engines, and other data that is not considered document content. User agents do not generally render elements that appear in the HEAD as content. They may, however, make information in the HEAD available to users through other mechanisms.

7.4.2 The TITLE element

```
<!— The TITLE element is not considered part of the flow of text.
     It should be displayed, for example as the page header or
     window title. Exactly one title is required per document.
  —>
<!ELEMENT TITLE - - (#PCDATA) -(%head.misc;)—document title —>
<!ATTLIST TITLE %i18n>
```

Start tag: **required**, *End tag:* **required**

Attributes defined elsewhere

- lang (language information), dir (text direction)

Every HTML document **must** have a TITLE element in the HEAD section.

Authors should use the TITLE element to identify the contents of a document. Since users often consult documents out of context, authors should provide context-rich titles. Thus, instead of a title such as "Introduction", which doesn't provide much contextual background, authors should supply a title such as "Introduction to Medieval Bee-Keeping" instead.

For reasons of accessibility, user agents must always make the content of the TITLE element available to users (including TITLE elements that occur in frames). The mechanism for doing so depends on the user agent (e.g., as a caption, spoken).

Titles may contain character entities (for accented characters, special characters, etc.), but may not contain other markup. Here is a sample document title:

```
<!DOCTYPE HTML PUBLIC "-//W3C//DTD HTML 4.0//EN"
    "http://www.w3.org/TR/REC-html40/strict.dtd">
<HTML>
<HEAD>
<TITLE>A study of population dynamics</TITLE>
... other head elements...
</HEAD>
<BODY>
... document body...
</BODY>
</HTML>
```

7.4.3 The title attribute

Attribute definitions

title = *text* [CS]

This attribute offers advisory information about the element for which it is set.

Unlike the TITLE element, which provides information about an entire document and may only appear once, the title attribute may annotate any number of elements. Please consult an element's definition to verify that it supports this attribute.

Values of the title attribute may be rendered by user agents in a variety of ways. For instance, visual browsers frequently display the title as a "tool tip" (a short message that appears when the pointing device pauses over an object). Audio user agents may speak the title information in a similar context. For example, setting the attribute on a link allows user agents (visual and non-visual) to tell users about the nature of the linked resource:

```
...some text...
Here's a photo of
<A href="http://someplace.com/neatstuff.gif" title="Me scuba diving">
```

```
    me scuba diving last summer
</A>
...some more text...
```

The title attribute has an additional role when used with the `LINK` element to designate an external style sheet. Please consult the section on links and style sheets for details.

Note. To improve the quality of speech synthesis for cases handled poorly by standard techniques, future versions of HTML may include an attribute for encoding phonemic and prosodic information.

7.4.4 Meta data

As this specification is being written, work is underway that will allow authors to assign richer machine-readable information about HTML documents and other network-accessible resources. The W3C Resource Description Language (see [RDF]) is being developed as a common framework for meta data.

HTML lets authors specify meta data—information about a document rather than document content—in a variety of ways.

For example, to specify the author of a document, one may use the META element as follows:

```
<META name="Author" content="Dave Raggett">
```

The `META` element specifies a property (here "Author") and assigns a value to it (here "Dave Raggett").

This specification does not define a set of legal meta data properties. The meaning of a property and the set of legal values for that property should be defined in a reference lexicon called a profile. For example, a profile designed to help search engines index documents might define properties such as "author", "copyright", "keywords", etc.

Specifying meta data

In general, specifying meta data involves two steps:

1. Declaring a property and a value for that property. This may be done in two ways:
    1. From within a document, via the `META` element.
    2. From outside a document, by linking to meta data via the `LINK` element (see the section on link types).

2. Referring to a profile where the property and its legal values are defined. To designate a profile, use the profile attribute of the HEAD element.

Note that since a profile is defined for the HEAD element, the same profile applies to all META and LINK elements in the document head.

User agents are not required to support meta data mechanisms. For those that choose to support meta data, this specification does not define how meta data should be interpreted.

The META element

```
<!ELEMENT META - O EMPTY              -- generic metainformation -->
<!ATTLIST META
  %i18n;                              -- lang, dir, for use with content --
  http-equiv    NAME    #IMPLIED      -- HTTP response header name   --
  name          NAME    #IMPLIED      -- metainformation name --
  content       CDATA   #REQUIRED     -- associated information --
  scheme        CDATA   #IMPLIED      -- select form of content --
  >
```

Start tag: **required**, End tag: *forbidden*

Attribute definitions

For the following attributes, the permitted values and their interpretation are profile dependent:

name = *name* [CS]

This attribute identifies a property name. This specification does not list legal values for this attribute.

content = *cdata* [CS]

This attribute specifies a property's value. This specification does not list legal values for this attribute.

scheme = *cdata* [CS]

This attribute names a scheme to be used to interpret the property's value (see the section on profiles for details).

http-equiv = *name* [CI]

This attribute may be used in place of the name attribute. HTTP servers use this attribute to gather information for HTTP response message headers.

Attributes defined elsewhere

- lang (language information), dir (text direction)

The META element can be used to identify properties of a document (e.g., author, expiration date, a list of key words, etc.) and assign values to those properties. This specification does not define a normative set of properties.

Each META element specifies a property/value pair. The name attribute identifies the property and the content attribute specifies the property's value.

For example, the following declaration sets a value for the Author property:

```
<META name="Author" content="Dave Raggett">
```

The lang attribute can be used with META to specify the language for the value of the content attribute. This enables speech synthesizers to apply language dependent pronunciation rules.

In this example, the author's name is declared to be French:

```
<META name="Author" lang="fr" content="Arnaud Le Hors">
```

Note. *The META element is a generic mechanism for specifying meta data. However, some HTML elements and attributes already handle certain pieces of meta data and may be used by authors instead of META to specify those pieces: the TITLE element, the ADDRESS element, the INS and DEL elements, the title attribute, and the cite attribute.*

Note. *When a property specified by a META element takes a value that is a URI, some authors prefer to specify the meta data via the LINK element. Thus, the following meta data declaration:*

```
<META name="DC.identifier"
      content="ftp://ds.internic.net/rfc/rfc1866.txt">
```

might also be written:

```
<LINK rel="DC.identifier"
      type="text/plain"
      href="ftp://ds.internic.net/rfc/rfc1866.txt">
```

META and HTTP headers

The http-equiv attribute can be used in place of the name attribute and has a special significance when documents are retrieved via the Hypertext Transfer Protocol (HTTP). HTTP servers may use the property name specified by the http-equiv attribute to create an [RFC822]-style header in the HTTP response. Please see the HTTP specification ([RFC2068]) for details on valid HTTP headers.

The following sample META declaration:

```
<META http-equiv="Expires" content="Tue, 20 Aug 1996 14:25:27 GMT">
```

will result in the HTTP header:

```
Expires: Tue, 20 Aug 1996 14:25:27 GMT
```

This can be used by caches to determine when to fetch a fresh copy of the associated document.

Some user agents support the use of META to refresh the current page after a specified number of seconds, with the option of replacing it by a different URI.

```
<META http-equiv="refresh" content="3,http://www.acme.com/intro.html">
```

The content is a number specifying the delay in seconds, followed by the URI to load when the time is up. This mechanism is generally used to show users a fleeting introductory page. However, since some user agents do not support this mechanism, authors should include content on the introductory page to allow users to navigate away from it (so they don't remain "stranded" on the introductory page).

META and search engines

A common use for META is to specify keywords that a search engine may use to improve the quality of search results. When several META elements provide language-dependent information about a document, search engines may filter on the lang attribute to display search results using the language preferences of the user. For example,

```
<-- For speakers of US English -->
<META name="keywords" lang="en-us"
        content="vacation, Greece, sunshine">
<-- For speakers of British English -->
<META name="keywords" lang="en"
        content="holiday, Greece, sunshine">
<-- For speakers of French -->
<META name="keywords" lang="fr"
        content="vacances, Gr&egrave;ce, soleil">
```

The effectiveness of search engines can also be increased by using the LINK element to specify links to translations of the document in other languages, links to versions of the document in other media (e.g., PDF), and, when the document is part of a collection, links to an appropriate starting point for browsing the collection.

Further help is provided in the section on helping search engines index your Web site.

META and PICS

The Platform for Internet Content Selection (PICS, specified in [PICS]) is an infrastructure for associating labels (meta data) with Internet content. Originally designed to help parents and teachers control what children can access on the Internet, it also facilitates other uses for labels, including code signing, privacy, and intellectual property rights management.

This example illustrates how one can use a META declaration to include a PICS 1.1 label:

```
<HEAD>
  <META http-equiv="PICS-Label" content='
  (PICS-1.1 "http://www.gcf.org/v2.5"
      labels on "1994.11.05T08:15-0500"
         until "1995.12.31T23:59-0000"
         for "http://w3.org/PICS/Overview.html"
      ratings (suds 0.5 density 0 color/hue 1))
'>
  <TITLE>... document title ...</TITLE>
</HEAD>
```

META and default information

The META element may be used to specify the default information for a document in the following instances:

- The default scripting language.
- The default style sheet language.
- The document character encoding.

The following example specifies the character encoding for a document as being ISO-8859-5

```
<META http-equiv="Content-Type" content="text/html; charset=ISO-8859-5">
```

Meta data profiles

The profile attribute of the HEAD specifies the location of a meta data profile. The value of the profile attribute is a URI. User agents may use this URI in two ways:

- As a globally unique name. User agents may be able to recognize the name (without actually retrieving the profile) and perform some activity based on known conventions for that profile. For instance, search engines could provide an interface for searching through catalogs of HTML documents, where these documents all use the same profile for representing catalog entries.

- As a link. User agents may dereference the URI and, perform some activity based on the actual definitions within the profile (e.g., authorize the usage of the profile within the current HTML document). This specification does not define formats for profiles.

This example refers to a hypothetical profile that defines useful properties for document indexing. The properties defined by this profile—including "author", "copyright", "keywords", and "date"—have their values set by subsequent META declarations.

```
<HEAD profile="http://www.acme.com/profiles/core">
 <TITLE>How to complete Memorandum cover sheets</TITLE>
 <META name="author" content="John Doe">
 <META name="copyright" content="&copy; 1997 Acme Corp.">
 <META name="keywords" content="corporate,guidelines,cataloging">
 <META name="date" content="1994-11-06T08:49:37+00:00">
</HEAD>
```

As this specification is being written, it is common practice to use the date formats described in [RFC2068], *section 3.3. As these formats are relatively hard to process, we recommend that authors use the* [ISO8601] *date format. For more information, see the sections on the INS and DEL elements.*

The scheme attribute allows authors to provide user agents more context for the correct interpretation of meta data. At times, such additional information may be critical, as when meta data may be specified in different formats. For example, an author might specify a date in the (ambiguous) format "10-9-97"; does this mean 9 October 1997 or 10 September 1997? The scheme attribute value "Month-Date-Year" would disambiguate this date value.

At other times, the scheme attribute may provide helpful but non-critical information to user agents.

For example, the following scheme declaration may help a user agent determine that the value of the "identifier" property is an ISBN code number:

```
<META scheme="ISBN" name="identifier" content="0-8230-2355-9">
```

Values for the scheme attribute depend on the property name and the associated profile.

Note. *One sample profile is the Dublin Core (see* [DCORE]*). This profile defines a set of recommended properties for electronic bibliographic descriptions, and is intended to promote interoperability among disparate description models.*

7.5 The document body

7.5.1 The BODY element

```
<!ELEMENT BODY O O (%block;|SCRIPT)+ +(INS|DEL)—document body —>
<!ATTLIST BODY
  %attrs;                            —%coreattrs, %i18n, %events —
  onload      %Script;  #IMPLIED     —the document has been loaded —
  onunload    %Script;  #IMPLIED     —the document has been removed —
  >
```

Start tag: **optional**, *End tag:* **optional**

Attribute definitions

background = *uri* [CT]

> **Deprecated.** The value of this attribute is a URI that designates an image resource. The image generally tiles the background (for visual browsers).

text = *color* [CI]

> **Deprecated.** This attribute sets the foreground color for text (for visual browsers).

link = *color* [CI]

> **Deprecated.** This attribute sets the color of text marking unvisited hypertext links (for visual browsers).

vlink = *color* [CI]

> **Deprecated.** This attribute sets the color of text marking visited hypertext links (for visual browsers).

alink = *color* [CI]

> **Deprecated.** This attribute sets the color of text marking hypertext links when selected by the user (for visual browsers).

Attributes defined elsewhere

- id, class (document-wide identifiers)
- lang (language information), dir (text direction)
- title (element title)
- style (inline style information)
- bgcolor (background color)
- onload, onunload (intrinsic events)
- onclick, ondblclick, onmousedown, onmouseup, onmouseover, onmousemove, onmouseout, onkeypress, onkeydown, onkeyup (intrinsic events)

The body of a document contains the document's content. The content may be presented by a user agent in a variety of ways. For example, for visual browsers, you can think of the body as a canvas where the content appears: text, images, colors, graphics, etc. For audio user agents, the same content may be spoken. Since style sheets are now the preferred way to specify a document's presentation, the presentational attributes of BODY have been deprecated.

DEPRECATED EXAMPLE:
The following HTML fragment illustrates the use of the deprecated attributes. It sets the background color of the canvas to white, the text foreground color to black, and the color of hyperlinks to red initially, fuchsia when activated, and maroon once visited.

```
<!DOCTYPE HTML PUBLIC "-//W3C//DTD HTML 4.0 Transitional//EN"
    "http://www.w3.org/TR/REC-html40/loose.dtd">
<HTML>
<HEAD>
  <TITLE>A study of population dynamics</TITLE>
```

```
</HEAD>
<BODY bgcolor="white" text="black"
  link="red" alink="fuchsia" vlink="maroon">
  ... document body...
</BODY>
</HTML>
```

Using style sheets, the same effect could be accomplished as follows:

```
<!DOCTYPE HTML PUBLIC "-//W3C//DTD HTML 4.0//EN"
    "http://www.w3.org/TR/REC-html40/strict.dtd">
<HTML>
<HEAD>
 <TITLE>A study of population dynamics</TITLE>
 <STYLE type="text/css">
  BODY { background: white; color: black}
  A:link { color: red }
  A:visited { color: maroon }
  A:active { color: fuchsia }
 </STYLE>
</HEAD>
<BODY>
  ... document body...
</BODY>
</HTML>
```

Using external (linked) style sheets gives you the flexibility to change the presentation without revising the source HTML document:

```
<!DOCTYPE HTML PUBLIC "-//W3C//DTD HTML 4.0//EN"
    "http://www.w3.org/TR/REC-html40/strict.dtd">
<HTML>
<HEAD>
 <TITLE>A study of population dynamics</TITLE>
 <LINK rel="stylesheet" type="text/css" href="smartstyle.css">
</HEAD>
<BODY>
  ... document body...
</BODY>
</HTML>
```

Framesets and HTML bodies. *Documents that contain framesets replace the* BODY *element by the* FRAMESET *element. Please consult the section on frames for more information.*

7.5.2 Element identifiers: the `id` and `class` attributes

Attribute definitions

id = *name* [CS]

   This attribute assigns a name to an element. This name must be unique in a document.

class = *cdata-list* [CS]

   This attribute assigns a class name or set of class names to an element. Any number of elements may be assigned the same class name or names. Multiple class names must be separated by white space characters.

The id attribute assigns a unique identifier to an element (which may be verified by an SGML parser). For example, the following paragraphs are distinguished by their id values:

```
<P id="myparagraph"> This is a uniquely named paragraph.</P>
<P id="yourparagraph"> This is also a uniquely named paragraph.</P>
```

The id attribute has several roles in HTML:

- As a style sheet selector.
- As a target anchor for hypertext links.
- As a means to reference a particular element from a script.
- As the name of a declared OBJECT element.
- For general purpose processing by user agents (e.g. for identifying fields when extracting data from HTML pages into a database, translating HTML documents into other formats, etc.).

The class attribute, on the other hand, assigns one or more class names to an element; the element may be said to belong to these classes. A class name may be shared by several element instances. The class attribute has several roles in HTML:

- As a style sheet selector (when an author wishes to assign style information to a set of elements).
- For general purpose processing by user agents.

In the following example, the SPAN element is used in conjunction with the id and class attributes to markup document messages. Messages appear in both English and French versions.

```
<!— English messages —>
<P><SPAN id="msg1" class="info" lang="en">Variable declared twice</SPAN>
<P><SPAN id="msg2" class="warning" lang="en">Undeclared variable</SPAN>
<P><SPAN id="msg3" class="error" lang="en">Bad syntax for variable name</SPAN>

<!— French messages —>
<P><SPAN id="msg1" class="info" lang="fr">Variable déclarée deux fois</SPAN>
<P><SPAN id="msg2" class="warning" lang="fr">Variable indéfinie</SPAN>
<P><SPAN id="msg3" class="error" lang="fr">Erreur de syntaxe pour variable</SPAN>
```

The following CSS style rules would tell visual user agents to display informational messages in green, warning messages in yellow, and error messages in red:

```
SPAN.info    { color: green }
SPAN.warning { color: yellow }
SPAN.error   { color: red }
```

Note that the French "msg1" and the English "msg1" may not appear in the same document since they share the same id value. Authors may make further use of the id attribute to refine the presentation of individual messages, make them target anchors, etc.

Almost every HTML element may be assigned identifier and class information.

Suppose, for example, that we are writing a document about a programming language. The document is to include a number of preformatted examples. We use the PRE element to format the examples. We also assign a background color (green) to all instances of the PRE element belonging to the class "example".

```
<HEAD>
<TITLE>... document title ...</TITLE>
<STYLE type="text/css">
PRE.example { background : green }
</STYLE>
</HEAD>
<BODY>
```

```
<PRE class="example" id="example-1">
...example code here...
</PRE>
</BODY>
```

By setting the id attribute for this example, we can (1) create a hyperlink to it and (2) override class style information with instance style information.

Note. *The id attribute shares the same name space as the name attribute when used for anchor names. Please consult the section on anchors with* `id` *for more information.*

7.5.3 Block-level and inline elements

Certain HTML elements that may appear in BODY are said to be "block-level" while others are "inline" (also known as "text level"). The distinction is founded on several notions:

Content model

Generally, block-level elements may contain inline elements and other block-level elements. Generally, inline elements may contain only data and other inline elements. Inherent in this structural distinction is the idea that block elements create "larger" structures than inline elements.

Formatting

By default, block-level elements are formatted differently than inline elements. Generally, block-level elements begin on new lines, inline elements do not. For information about white space, line breaks, and block formatting, please consult the section on text.

Directionality

For technical reasons involving the [UNICODE] bidirectional text algorithm, block-level and inline elements differ in how they inherit directionality information. For details, see the section on inheritance of text direction.

Style sheets provide the means to specify the rendering of arbitrary elements, including whether an element is rendered as block or inline. In some cases, such as an inline style for list elements, this may be appropriate, but generally speaking, authors are discouraged from overriding the conventional interpretation of HTML elements in this way.

The alteration of the traditional presentation idioms for block level and inline elements also has an impact on the bidirectional text algorithm. See the section on the effect of style sheets on bidirectionality for more information.

7.5.4 Grouping elements: the DIV and SPAN elements

```
<!ELEMENT DIV - - (%flow;)*           — generic language/style container —>
<!ATTLIST DIV
  %attrs;                             — %coreattrs, %i18n, %events —
  >
<!ELEMENT SPAN - - (%inline;)*        — generic language/style container —>
<!ATTLIST SPAN
  %attrs;                             — %coreattrs, %i18n, %events —
  >
```

*Start tag: **required**, End tag: **required***

Attributes defined elsewhere

- id, class (document-wide identifiers)
- lang (language information), dir (text direction)
- title (element title)
- style (inline style information)
- align (alignment)
- onclick, ondblclick, onmousedown, onmouseup, onmouseover, onmousemove, onmouseout, onkeypress, onkeydown, onkeyup (intrinsic events)

The DIV and SPAN elements, in conjunction with the id and class attributes, offer a generic mechanism for adding structure to documents. These elements define content to be inline (SPAN) or block-level (DIV) but impose no other presentational idioms on the content. Thus, authors may use these elements in conjunction with style sheets, the lang attribute, etc., to tailor HTML to their own needs and tastes.

Suppose, for example, that we wanted to generate an HTML document based on a database of client information. Since HTML does not include elements that identify objects such as "client", "telephone number", "email address", etc., we use DIV and SPAN to achieve the desired structural and presentational effects. We might use the TABLE element as follows to structure the information:

```
<!-- Example of data from the client database: -->
<!-- Name: Stephane Boyera, Tel: (212) 555-1212, Email: sb@foo.org -->

<DIV id="client-boyera" class="client">
<P><SPAN class="client-title">Client information:</SPAN>
<TABLE class="client-data">
<TR><TH>Last name:<TD>Boyera</TR>
<TR><TH>First name:<TD>Stephane</TR>
<TR><TH>Tel:<TD>(212) 555-1212</TR>
<TR><TH>Email:<TD>sb@foo.org</TR>
</TABLE>
</DIV>

<DIV id="client-lafon" class="client">
<P><SPAN class="client-title">Client information:</SPAN>
<TABLE class="client-data">
<TR><TH>Last name:<TD>Lafon</TR>
<TR><TH>First name:<TD>Yves</TR>
<TR><TH>Tel:<TD>(617) 555-1212</TR>
<TR><TH>Email:<TD>yves@coucou.com</TR>
</TABLE>
</DIV>
```

Later, we may easily add style sheet declaration to fine tune the presentation of these database entries.

For another example of usage, please consult the example in the section on the class and id attributes.

Visual user agents generally place a line break before and after DIV elements, for instance:

```
<P>aaaaaaaaa<DIV>bbbbbbbbb</DIV><DIV>ccccc<P>ccccc</DIV>
```

which is typically rendered as:

```
aaaaaaaaa
bbbbbbbbb
ccccc

ccccc
```

7.5.5 Headings: The H1, H2, H3, H4, H5, H6 elements

```
<!ENTITY % heading "H1|H2|H3|H4|H5|H6">
<!--
   There are six levels of headings from H1 (the most important)
   to H6 (the least important).
-->
<!ELEMENT (%heading;)  - - (%inline;)*   -- heading -->
<!ATTLIST (%heading;)
   %attrs;                               -- %coreattrs, %i18n, %events --
   >
```

Start tag: **required**, End tag: **required**

Attributes defined elsewhere

- id, class (document-wide identifiers)
- lang (language information), dir (text direction)
- title (element title)
- style (inline style information)
- align (alignment)
- onclick, ondblclick, onmousedown, onmouseup, onmouseover, onmousemove, onmouseout, onkeypress, onkeydown, onkeyup (intrinsic events)

A heading element briefly describes the topic of the section it introduces. Heading information may be used by user agents, for example, to construct a table of contents for a document automatically.

There are six levels of headings in HTML with H1 as the most important and H6 as the least. Visual browsers usually render more important headings in larger fonts than less important ones.

The following example shows how to use the DIV element to associate a heading with the document section that follows it. Doing so allows you to define a style for the section (color the background, set the font, etc.) with style sheets.

```
<DIV class="section" id="forest-elephants" >
<H1>Forest elephants</H1>
```

```
<P>In this section, we discuss the lesser known forest elephants.
...this section continues...
<DIV class="subsection" id="forest-habitat" >
<H2>Habitat</H2>
<P>Forest elephants do not live in trees but among them.
...this subsection continues...
</DIV>
</DIV>
```

This structure may be decorated with style information such as:

```
<HEAD>
<TITLE>... document title ...</TITLE>
<STYLE type="text/css" >
DIV.section { text-align: justify; font-size: 12pt}
DIV.subsection { text-indent: 2em }
H1 { font-style: italic; color: green }
H2 { color: green }
</STYLE>
</HEAD>
```

Numbered sections and references
HTML *does not itself cause section numbers to be generated from headings. This facility may be offered by user agents, however. Soon, style sheet languages such as CSS will allow authors to control the generation of section numbers (handy for forward references in printed documents, as in "See section 7.2").*

Some people consider skipping heading levels to be bad practice. They accept H1 H2 H1 while they do not accept H1 H3 H1 since the heading level H2 is skipped.

7.5.6 The ADDRESS element

```
<!ELEMENT ADDRESS - - (%inline;)*—information on author —>
<!ATTLIST ADDRESS
  %attrs;                                —%coreattrs, %i18n, %events —
  >
```

Start tag: **required**, End tag: **required**

Attributes defined elsewhere

- id, class (document-wide identifiers)
- lang (language information), dir (text direction)
- onclick, ondblclick, onmousedown, onmouseup, onmouseover, onmousemove, onmouseout, onkeypress, onkeydown, onkeyup (intrinsic events)

The ADDRESS element may be used by authors to supply contact information for document or a major part of a document such as a form. This element often appears at the beginning or end of a document.

For example, a page at the W3C Web site related to HTML might include the following contact information:

```
<ADDRESS>
<A href="../People/Raggett/">Dave Raggett</A>,
<A href="../People/Arnaud/">Arnaud Le Hors</A>,
contact persons for the <A href="Activity">W3C HTML Activity</A><BR>
$Date: 1998/04/02 00:20:03 $
</ADDRESS>
```

Chapter 8

Language Information and Text Direction

Contents

1. Specifying the language of content: the lang attribute
   1. Language codes
   2. Inheritance of language codes
   3. Interpretation of language codes
2. Specifying the direction of text and tables: the dir attribute
   1. Introduction to the bidirectional algorithm
   2. Inheritance of text direction information
   3. Setting the direction of embedded text
   4. Overriding the bidirectional algorithm: the BDO element
   5. Character references for directionality and joining control
   6. The effect of style sheets on bidirectionality

This section of the document discusses two important issues that affect the internationalization of HTML: specifying the language (the lang attribute) and direction (the dir attribute) of text in a document.

8.1 Specifying the language of content: the `lang` attribute

Attribute definitions

lang = *language-code* [CI]

> This attribute specifies the base language of an element's attribute values and text content. The default value of this attribute is unknown.

Language information specified via the lang attribute may be used by a user agent to control rendering in a variety of ways. Some situations where author-supplied language information may be helpful include:

- Assisting search engines
- Assisting speech synthesizers
- Helping a user agent select glyph variants for high quality typography
- Helping a user agent choose a set of quotation marks
- Helping a user agent make decisions about hyphenation, ligatures, and spacing
- Assisting spell checkers and grammar checkers

The lang attribute specifies the language of element content and attribute values; whether it is relevant for a given attribute depends on the syntax and semantics of the attribute and the operation involved.

The intent of the lang attribute is to allow user agents to render content more meaningfully based on accepted cultural practice for a given language. This does not imply that user agents should render characters that are atypical for a particular language in less meaningful ways; user agents must make a best attempt to render all characters, regardless of the value specified by lang.

For instance, if characters from the Greek alphabet appear in the midst of English text:

```
<P><Q lang="en">Her super-powers were the result of
&gamma;-radiation,</Q> he explained.</P>
```

a user agent (1) should try to render the English content in an appropriate manner (e.g., in its handling the quotation marks) and (2) must make a best attempt to render γ even though it is not an English character.

Please consult the section on undisplayable characters for related information.

8.1.1 Language codes

The lang attribute's value is a language code that identifies a natural language spoken, written, or otherwise used for the communication of information among people. Computer languages are explicitly excluded from language codes.

[RFC1766] defines and explains the language codes that must be used in HTML documents.

Briefly, language codes consist of a primary code and a possibly empty series of subcodes:

```
language-code = primary-code ( "-" subcode )*
```

Here are some sample language codes:

- "en": English
- "en-US": the U.S. version of English.
- "en-cockney": the Cockney version of English.
- "i-navajo": the Navajo language spoken by some Native Americans.
- "x-klingon": The primary tag "x" indicates an experimental language tag

Two-letter primary codes are reserved for [ISO639] language abbreviations. Two-letter codes include fr (French), de (German), it (Italian), nl (Dutch), el (Greek), es (Spanish), pt (Portuguese), ar (Arabic), he (Hebrew), ru (Russian), zh (Chinese), ja (Japanese), hi (Hindi), ur (Urdu), and sa (Sanskrit).

Any two-letter subcode is understood to be a [ISO3166] country code.

8.1.2 Inheritance of language codes

An element inherits language code information according to the following order of precedence (highest to lowest):

- The lang attribute set for the element itself.
- The closest parent element that has the lang attribute set (i.e., the lang attribute is inherited).
- The HTTP "Content-Language" header (which may be configured in a server). For example:

  ```
  Content-Language: en-cockney
  ```
- User agent default values and user preferences.

In this example, the primary language of the document is French ("fr"). One paragraph is declared to be in Spanish ("es"), after which the primary language returns to French. The following paragraph includes an embedded Japanese ("ja") phrase, after which the primary language returns to French.

```
<!DOCTYPE HTML PUBLIC "-//W3C//DTD HTML 4.0//EN"
    "http://www.w3.org/TR/REC-html40/strict.dtd">
```

```
<HTML lang="fr">
<HEAD>
<TITLE>Un document multilingue</TITLE>
</HEAD>
<BODY>
...Interpreted as French...
<P lang="es">...Interpreted as Spanish...
<P>...Interpreted as French again...
<P>...French text interrupted by<EM lang="ja">some
        Japanese</EM>French begins here again...
</BODY>
</HTML>
```

Note. *Table cells may inherit lang values not from its parent but from the first cell in a span. Please consult the section on alignment inheritance for details.*

8.1.3 Interpretation of language codes

In the context of HTML, a language code should be interpreted by user agents as a hierarchy of tokens rather than a single token. When a user agent adjusts rendering according to language information (say, by comparing style sheet language codes and lang values), it should always favor an exact match, but should also consider matching primary codes to be sufficient. Thus, if the lang attribute value of "en-US" is set for the HTML element, a user agent should prefer style information that matches "en-US" first, then the more general value "en".

Note. *Language code hierarchies do not guarantee that all languages with a common prefix will be understood by those fluent in one or more of those languages. They do allow a user to request this commonality when it is true for that user.*

8.2 Specifying the direction of text and tables: the dir attribute

Attribute definitions

dir = LTR | RTL [CI]

This attribute specifies the base direction of directionally neutral text (i.e., text that doesn't have inherent directionality as defined in [UNICODE]) and the directionality of tables. Possible values:

- LTR: Left-to-right text or table.
- RTL: Right-to-left text or table.

In addition to specifying the language of a document with the lang attribute, authors may need to specify the base directionality (left-to-right or right-to-left) of portions of a document's text, of table structure, etc. This is done with the dir attribute.

The [UNICODE] specification assigns directionality to characters and defines a (complex) algorithm for determining the proper directionality of text. If a document does not contain a displayable right-to-left character, a conforming user agent is not required to apply the [UNICODE] bidirectional algorithm. If a document contains right-to-left characters, and if the user agent displays these characters, the user agent must use the bidirectional algorithm.

Although Unicode specifies special characters that deal with text direction, HTML offers higher-level markup constructs that do the same thing: the dir attribute (do not confuse with the DIR element) and the BDO element. Thus, to express a Hebrew quotation, it is more intuitive to write

```
<Q lang="he" dir="rtl">...a Hebrew quotation...</Q>
```

than the equivalent with Unicode references:

```
&#x202B;&#x05F4;...a Hebrew quotation...&#x05F4;&#x202C;
```

User agents must **not** use the lang attribute to determine text directionality.

The dir attribute is inherited and may be overridden. Please consult the section on the inheritance of text direction information for details.

8.2.1 Introduction to the bidirectional algorithm

The following example illustrates the expected behavior of the bidirectional algorithm. It involves English, a left-to-right script, and Hebrew, a right-to-left script.

Consider the following example text:

```
english1 HEBREW2 english3 HEBREW4 english5 HEBREW6
```

The characters in this example (and in all related examples) are stored in the computer the way they are displayed here: the first character in the file is "e", the second is "n", and the last is "6".

Suppose the predominant language of the document containing this paragraph is English. This means that the base direction is left-to-right. The correct presentation of this line would be:

```
english1 2WERBEH english3 4WERBEH english5 6WERBEH
         <----           <----           <----
           H               H               H
------------------------------------------------>
                         E
```

The dotted lines indicate the structure of the sentence: English predominates and some Hebrew text is embedded. Achieving the correct presentation requires no additional markup since the Hebrew fragments are reversed correctly by user agents applying the bidirectional algorithm.

If, on the other hand, the predominant language of the document is Hebrew, the base direction is right-to-left. The correct presentation is therefore:

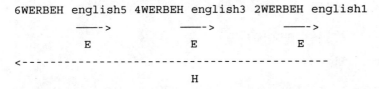

In this case, the whole sentence has been presented as right-to-left and the embedded English sequences have been properly reversed by the bidirectional algorithm.

8.2.2 Inheritance of text direction information

The Unicode bidirectional algorithm requires a base text direction for text blocks. To specify the base direction of a block-level element, set the element's dir attribute. The default value of the dir attribute is "ltr" (left-to-right text).

When the dir attribute is set for a block-level element, it remains in effect for the duration of the element and any nested block-level elements. Setting the dir attribute on a nested element overrides the inherited value.

To set the base text direction for an entire document, set the dir attribute on the HTML element.

For example:

```
<!DOCTYPE HTML PUBLIC "-//W3C//DTD HTML 4.0//EN"
    "http://www.w3.org/TR/REC-html40/strict.dtd">
```

```
<HTML dir="RTL">
<HEAD>
<TITLE>...a right-to-left title...</TITLE>
</HEAD>
    ...right-to-left text...
<P dir="ltr">...left-to-right text...</P>
<P>...right-to-left text again...</P>
</HTML>
```

Inline elements, on the other hand, do not inherit the dir attribute. This means that an inline element without a dir attribute does **not** open an additional level of embedding with respect to the bidirectional algorithm. (Here, an element is considered to be block-level or inline based on its default presentation. Note that the INS and DEL elements can be block-level or inline depending on their context.)

8.2.3 Setting the direction of embedded text

The [UNICODE] bidirectional algorithm automatically reverses embedded character sequences according to their inherent directionality (as illustrated by the previous examples). However, in general only one level of embedding can be accounted for. To achieve additional levels of embedded direction changes, you must make use of the dir attribute on an inline element.

Consider the same example text as before:

```
english1 HEBREW2 english3 HEBREW4 english5 HEBREW6
```

Suppose the predominant language of the document containing this paragraph is English. Furthermore, the above English sentence contains a Hebrew section extending from HEBREW2 through HEBREW4 and the Hebrew section contains an English quotation (english3). The desired presentation of the text is thus:

```
english1 4WERBEH english3 2WERBEH english5 6WERBEH
```

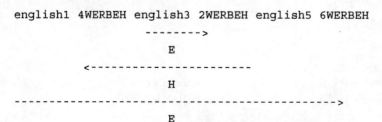

To achieve two embedded direction changes, we must supply additional information, which we do by delimiting the second embedding explicitly. In this example, we use the SPAN element and the dir attribute to mark up the text:

```
english1 <SPAN dir="RTL">HEBREW2 english3 HEBREW4</SPAN> english5 HEBREW6
```

Authors may also use special Unicode characters to achieve multiply embedded direction changes. To achieve left-to-right embedding, surround embedded text with the characters LEFT-TO-RIGHT EMBEDDING ("LRE", hexadecimal 202A) and POP DIRECTIONAL FORMATTING ("PDF", hexadecimal 202C). To achieve right-to-left embedding, surround embedded text with the characters RIGHT-TO-LEFT EMBEDDING ("RTE", hexadecimal 202B) and PDF.

Using HTML directionality markup with Unicode characters. *Authors and designers of authoring software should be aware that conflicts can arise if the dir attribute is used on inline elements (including BDO) concurrently with the corresponding [UNICODE] formatting characters. Preferably one or the other should be used exclusively. The markup method offers a better guarantee of document structural integrity and alleviates some problems when editing bidirectional HTML text with a simple text editor, but some software may be more apt at using the [UNICODE] characters. If both methods are used, great care should be exercised to insure proper nesting of markup and directional embedding or override, otherwise, rendering results are undefined.*

8.2.4 Overriding the bidirectional algorithm: the BDO element

```
<!ELEMENT BDO - - (%inline;)*          -- I18N BiDi over-ride -->
<!ATTLIST BDO
  %coreattrs;                          -- id, class, style, title --
  lang        %LanguageCode; #IMPLIED  -- language code --
  dir         (ltr|rtl)      #REQUIRED -- directionality --
  >
```

Start tag: **required**, *End tag:* **required**

Attribute definitions

dir = LTR | RTL [CI]

> This mandatory attribute specifies the base direction of the element's text content. This direction overrides the inherent directionality of characters as defined in [UNICODE]. Possible values:
>
> - LTR: Left-to-right text.
> - RTL: Right-to-left text.

Attributes defined elsewhere

- lang (language information)

The bidirectional algorithm and the dir attribute generally suffice to manage embedded direction changes. However, some situations may arise when the bidirectional algorithm results in incorrect presentation. The BDO element allows authors to turn off the bidirectional algorithm for selected fragments of text.

Consider a document containing the same text as before:

```
english1 HEBREW2 english3 HEBREW4 english5 HEBREW6
```

but assume that this text has already been put in visual order. One reason for this may be that the MIME standard ([RFC2045], [RFC1556]) favors visual order, i.e., that right-to-left character sequences are inserted right-to-left in the byte stream. In an email, the above might be formatted, including line breaks, as:

```
english1 2WERBEH english3
4WERBEH english5 6WERBEH
```

This conflicts with the [UNICODE] bidirectional algorithm, because that algorithm would invert 2WERBEH, 4WERBEH, and 6WERBEH a second time, displaying the Hebrew words left-to-right instead of right-to-left.

The solution in this case is to override the bidirectional algorithm by putting the Email excerpt in a PRE element (to conserve line breaks) and each line in a BDO element, whose dir attribute is set to LTR:

```
<PRE>
<BDO dir="LTR">english1 2WERBEH english3</BDO>
<BDO dir="LTR">4WERBEH english5 6WERBEH</BDO>
</PRE>
```

This tells the bidirectional algorithm "Leave me left-to-right!" and would produce the desired presentation:

```
english1 2WERBEH english3
4WERBEH english5 6WERBEH
```

The BDO element should be used in scenarios where absolute control over sequence order is required (e.g., multi-language part numbers). The dir attribute is mandatory for this element.

Authors may also use special Unicode characters to override the bidirectional algorithm—LEFT-TO-RIGHT OVERRIDE (202D) or RIGHT-TO-LEFT OVERRIDE (hexadecimal 202E). The POP DIRECTIONAL FORMATTING (hexadecimal 202C) character ends either bidirectional override.

Note. *Recall that conflicts can arise if the* dir *attribute is used on inline elements (including* BDO*) concurrently with the corresponding* [UNICODE] *formatting characters.*

Bidirectionality and character encoding *According to* [RFC1555] *and* [RFC1556]*, there are special conventions for the use of "charset" parameter values to indicate bidirectional treatment in MIME mail, in particular to distinguish between visual, implicit, and explicit directionality. The parameter value "ISO-8859-8" (for Hebrew) denotes visual encoding, "ISO-8859-8-i" denotes implicit bidirectionality, and "ISO-8859-8-e" denotes explicit directionality.*

Because HTML uses the Unicode bidirectionality algorithm, conforming documents encoded using ISO 8859-8 must be labeled as "ISO-8859-8-i". Explicit directional control is also possible with HTML, but cannot be expressed with ISO 8859-8, so "ISO-8859-8-e" should not be used.

The value "ISO-8859-8" implies that the document is formatted visually, misusing some markup (such as TABLE *with right alignment and no line wrapping) to ensure reasonable display on older user agents that do not handle bidirectionality. Such documents do not conform to the present specification. If necessary, they can be made to conform to the current specification (and at the same time will be displayed correctly on older user agents) by adding* BDO *markup where necessary. Contrary to what is said in* [RFC1555] *and* [RFC1556]*, ISO-8859-6 (Arabic) is not visual ordering.*

8.2.5 Character references for directionality and joining control

Since ambiguities sometimes arise as to the directionality of certain characters (e.g., punctuation), the [UNICODE] specification includes characters to enable their proper resolution. Also, Unicode includes some characters to control joining behavior where this is necessary (e.g., some situations with Arabic letters). HTML 4.0 includes character references for these characters.

The following DTD excerpt presents some of the directional entities:

```
<!ENTITY zwnj  CDATA  "&#8204;"—=zero width non-joiner—>
<!ENTITY zwj   CDATA  "&#8205;"—=zero width joiner—>
<!ENTITY lrm   CDATA  "&#8206;"—=left-to-right mark—>
<!ENTITY rlm   CDATA  "&#8207;"—=right-to-left mark—>
```

The zwnj entity is used to block joining behavior in contexts where joining will occur but shouldn't. The zwj entity does the opposite; it forces joining when it wouldn't occur but should. For example, the Arabic letter "HEH" is used to abbreviate "Hijri", the name of the Islamic calendar system. Since the isolated form of "HEH" looks like the digit five as employed in Arabic script (based on Indic digits), in order to prevent confusing "HEH" as a final digit five in a year, the initial form of "HEH" is used. However, there is no following context (i.e., a joining letter) to which the "HEH" can join. The `zwj` character provides that context.

Similarly, in Persian texts, there are cases where a letter that normally would join a subsequent letter in a cursive connection should not. The character zwnj is used to block joining in such cases.

The other characters, `lrm` and `rlm`, are used to force directionality of directionally neutral characters. For example, if a double quotation mark comes between an Arabic (right-to-left) and a Latin (left-to-right) letter, the direction of the quotation mark is not clear (is it quoting the Arabic text or the Latin text?). The `lrm` and `rlm` characters have a directional property but no width and no word/line break property. Please consult [UNICODE] for more details.

Mirrored character glyphs. *In general, the bidirectional algorithm does not mirror character glyphs but leaves them unaffected. An exception are characters such as parentheses (see* [UNICODE], *table 4-7). In cases where mirroring is desired, for example for Egyptian Hieroglyphs, Greek Bustrophedon, or special design effects, this should be controlled with styles.*

8.2.6 The effect of style sheets on bidirectionality

In general, using style sheets to change an element's visual rendering from block-level to inline or vice-versa is straightforward. However, because the bidirectional algorithm relies on the inline/block-level distinction, special care must be taken during the transformation.

When an inline element that does not have a dir attribute is transformed to the style of a block-level element by a style sheet, it inherits the dir attribute from its closest parent block element to define the base direction of the block.

When a block element that does not have a dir attribute is transformed to the style of an inline element by a style sheet, the resulting presentation should be equivalent, in terms of bidirectional formatting, to the formatting obtained by explicitly adding a dir attribute (assigned the inherited value) to the transformed element.

Chapter 9

Text

Contents

1. White space
2. Structured text
   1. Phrase elements: EM, STRONG, DFN, CODE, SAMP, KBD, VAR, CITE, ABBR, and ACRONYM
   2. Quotations: The BLOCKQUOTE and Q elements
      - Rendering quotations
   3. Subscripts and superscripts: the SUB and SUP elements
3. Lines and Paragraphs
   1. Paragraphs: the P element
   2. Controlling line breaks
      - Forcing a line break: the BR element
      - Prohibiting a line break
   3. Hyphenation
   4. Preformatted text: The PRE element
   5. Visual rendering of paragraphs
4. Marking document changes: The INS and DEL elements

The following sections discuss issues surrounding the structuring of text. Elements that present text (alignment elements, font elements, style sheets, etc.) are discussed elsewhere in the specification. For information about characters, please consult the section on the document character set.

9.1 White space

The document character set includes a wide variety of white space characters. Many of these are typographic elements used in some applications to produce particular visual spacing effects. In HTML, only the following characters are defined as *white space characters*:

- ASCII space ( )
- ASCII tab (	)
- ASCII form feed ()
- Zero-width space ()

Line breaks are also white space characters. Note that although   and   are defined in [ISO10646] to unambiguously separate lines and paragraphs, respectively, these do not constitute line breaks in HTML, nor does this specification include them in the more general category of white space characters.

This specification does not indicate the behavior, rendering or otherwise, of space characters other than those explicitly identified here as white space characters. For this reason, authors should use appropriate elements and styles to achieve visual formatting effects that involve white space, rather than space characters.

For all HTML elements except PRE, sequences of white space separate "words" (we use the term "word" here to mean "sequences of non-white space characters"). When formatting text, user agents should identify these words and lay them out according to the conventions of the particular written language (script) and target medium.

This layout may involve putting space between words (called *inter-word* space), but conventions for inter-word space vary from script to script. For example, in Latin scripts, inter-word space is typically rendered as an ASCII space ( ), while in Thai it is a zero-width word separator (). In Japanese and Chinese, inter-word space is not typically rendered at all.

Note that a sequence of white spaces between words in the source document may result in an entirely different rendered inter-word spacing (except in the case of the PRE element). In particular, user agents should collapse input white space sequences when producing output inter-word space. This can and should be done even in the absence of language information (from the lang attribute, the HTTP "Content-Language" header field (see [RFC2068], section 14.13), user agent settings, etc.).

The PRE element is used for preformatted text, where white space is significant.

In order to avoid problems with SGML line break rules and inconsistencies among extant implementations, authors should not rely on user agents to render white space immediately after a start tag or immediately before an end tag. Thus, authors, and in particular authoring tools, should write:

    <P>We offer free <A>technical support</A> for subscribers.</P>

and not:

```
<P>We offer free<A> technical support </A>for subscribers.</P>
```

9.2 Structured text

9.2.1 Phrase elements: EM, STRONG, DFN, CODE, SAMP, KBD, VAR, CITE, ABBR, and ACRONYM

```
<!ENTITY % phrase "EM | STRONG | DFN | CODE |
                   SAMP | KBD | VAR | CITE | ABBR | ACRONYM" >
<!ELEMENT (%fontstyle;|%phrase;) - - (%inline;)*>
<!ATTLIST (%fontstyle;|%phrase;)
   %attrs;                             —%coreattrs, %i18n, %events —
   >
```

Start tag: **required**, *End tag:* **required**

Attributes defined elsewhere

- id, class (document-wide identifiers)
- lang (language information), dir (text direction)
- title (element title)
- style (inline style information)
- onclick, ondblclick, onmousedown, onmouseup, onmouseover, onmousemove, onmouseout, onkeypress, onkeydown, onkeyup (intrinsic events)

Phrase elements add structural information to text fragments. The usual meanings of phrase elements are following:

EM:

Indicates emphasis.

STRONG:

Indicates stronger emphasis.

CITE:

Contains a citation or a reference to other sources.

DFN:

Indicates that this is the defining instance of the enclosed term.

CODE:

Designates a fragment of computer code.

SAMP:

Designates sample output from programs, scripts, etc.

KBD:

Indicates text to be entered by the user.

VAR:

Indicates an instance of a variable or program argument.

ABBR:

Indicates an abbreviated form (e.g., WWW, HTTP, URI, Mass., etc.).

ACRONYM:

Indicates an acronym (e.g., WAC, radar, etc.).

EM and STRONG are used to indicate emphasis. The other phrase elements have particular significance in technical documents. These examples illustrate some of the phrase elements:

```
As <CITE>Harry S. Truman</CITE> said,
<Q lang="en-us">The buck stops here.</Q>

More information can be found in <CITE>[ISO-0000]</CITE>.

Please refer to the following reference number in future
correspondence: <STRONG>1-234-55</STRONG>
```

The presentation of phrase elements depends on the user agent. Generally, visual user agents present EM text in italics and STRONG text in bold font. Speech synthesizer user agents may change the synthesis parameters, such as volume, pitch and rate accordingly.

The ABBR and ACRONYM elements allow authors to clearly indicate occurrences of abbreviations and acronyms. Western languages make extensive use of acronyms such as "GmbH", "NATO", and "F.B.I.", as well as abbreviations like "M.", "Inc.", "et al.", "etc.". Both Chinese and Japanese use analogous abbreviation mechanisms, wherein a long name is referred to subsequently with a subset of the Han characters from the original occurrence. Marking up these constructs provides useful information to user agents and tools such as spell checkers, speech synthesizers, translation systems and search-engine indexers.

The content of the ABBR and ACRONYM elements specifies the abbreviated expression itself, as it would normally appear in running text. The title attribute of these elements may be used to provide the full or expanded form of the expression.

Here are some sample uses of ABBR:

```
<P>
<ABBR title="World Wide Web">WWW</ABBR>
<ABBR lang="fr"
      title="Soci&eacute;t&eacute; Nationale des Chemins de Fer">
   SNCF
</ABBR>
<ABBR lang="es" title="Do&ntilde;a">Do&ntilde;a</ABBR>
<ABBR title="Abbreviation">abbr.</ABBR>
```

Note that abbreviations and acronyms often have idiosyncratic pronunciations. For example, while "IRS" and "BBC" are typically pronounced letter by letter, "NATO" and "UNESCO" are pronounced phonetically. Still other abbreviated forms (e.g., "URI" and "SQL") are spelled out by some people and pronounced as words by other people. When necessary, authors should use style sheets to specify the pronunciation of an abbreviated form.

9.2.2 Quotations: The BLOCKQUOTE and Q elements

```
<!ELEMENT BLOCKQUOTE - - (%block;|SCRIPT)+—long quotation —>
<!ATTLIST BLOCKQUOTE
  %attrs;                            — %coreattrs, %i18n, %events —
  cite        %URI;        #IMPLIED  — URI for source document or msg —
  >
<!ELEMENT Q - - (%inline;)*          — short inline quotation —>
<!ATTLIST Q
```

```
    %attrs;                             -- %coreattrs, %i18n, %events --
    cite        %URI;       #IMPLIED    -- URI for source document or msg --
    >
```

Start tag: **required**, *End tag:* **required**

Attribute definitions

cite = *uri* [CT]

> The value of this attribute is a URI that designates a source document or message. This attribute is intended to give information about the source from which the quotation was borrowed.

Attributes defined elsewhere

- id, class (document-wide identifiers)
- lang (language information), dir (text direction)
- title (element title)
- style (inline style information)
- onclick, ondblclick, onmousedown, onmouseup, onmouseover, onmousemove, onmouseout, onkeypress, onkeydown, onkeyup (intrinsic events)

These two elements designate quoted text. BLOCKQUOTE is for long quotations (block-level content) and Q is intended for short quotations (inline content) that don't require paragraph breaks.

This example formats an excerpt from "The Two Towers", by J.R.R. Tolkien, as a blockquote.

```
<BLOCKQUOTE cite="http://www.mycom.com/tolkien/twotowers.html">
<P>They went in single file, running like hounds on a strong scent,
and an eager light was in their eyes. Nearly due west the broad
swath of the marching Orcs tramped its ugly slot; the sweet grass
of Rohan had been bruised and blackened as they passed.</P>
</BLOCKQUOTE>
```

Rendering quotations

Visual user agents generally render BLOCKQUOTE as an indented block.

Visual user agents must ensure that the content of the Q element is rendered with delimiting quotation marks. Authors should not put quotation marks at the beginning and end of the content of a Q element.

User agents should render quotation marks in a language-sensitive manner (see the lang attribute). Many languages adopt different quotation styles for outer and inner (nested) quotations, which should be respected by user-agents.

The following example illustrates nested quotations with the Q element.

```
John said, <Q lang="en-us">I saw Lucy at lunch, she says
<Q lang="en-us">Mary wants you
to get some ice cream on your way home.</Q> I think I will get
some at Ben and Jerry's, on Gloucester Road.</Q>
```

Since the language of both quotations is American English, user agents should render them appropriately, for example with single quote marks around the inner quotation and double quote marks around the outer quotation:

```
John said, "I saw Lucy at lunch, she told me 'Mary wants you
to get some ice cream on your way home.' I think I will get some
at Ben and Jerry's, on Gloucester Road."
```

Note. *We recommend that style sheet implementations provide a mechanism for inserting quotation marks before and after a quotation delimited by* BLOCKQUOTE *in a manner appropriate to the current language context and the degree of nesting of quotations.*

However, as some authors have used BLOCKQUOTE *merely as a mechanism to indent text, in order to preserve the intention of the authors, user agents should **not** insert quotation marks in the default style.*

The usage of BLOCKQUOTE *to indent text is* deprecated *in favor of style sheets.*

9.2.3 Subscripts and superscripts: the SUB and SUP elements

```
<!ELEMENT (SUB|SUP) - - (%inline;)*    — subscript, superscript —>
<!ATTLIST (SUB|SUP)
   %attrs;                             — %coreattrs, %i18n, %events —
   >
```

Start tag: *required*, End tag: *required*

Attributes defined elsewhere

- id, class (document-wide identifiers)
- lang (language information), dir (text direction)
- title (element title)
- style (inline style information)
- onclick, ondblclick, onmousedown, onmouseup, onmouseover, onmousemove, onmouseout, onkeypress, onkeydown, onkeyup (intrinsic events)

Many scripts (e.g., French) require superscripts or subscripts for proper rendering. The SUB and SUP elements should be used to markup text in these cases.

```
H<sub>2</sub>O
E = mc<sup>2</sup>
<SPAN lang="fr">M<sup>lle</sup> Dupont</SPAN>
```

9.3 Lines and Paragraphs

Authors traditionally divide their thoughts and arguments into sequences of paragraphs. The organization of information into paragraphs is not affected by how the paragraphs are presented: paragraphs that are double-justified contain the same thoughts as those that are left-justified.

The HTML markup for *defining* a paragraph is straightforward: the P element defines a paragraph.

The visual presentation of paragraphs is not so simple. A number of issues, both stylistic and technical, must be addressed:

- Treatment of white space
- Line breaking and word wrapping
- Justification
- Hyphenation
- Written language conventions and text directionality
- Formatting of paragraphs with respect to surrounding content

We address these questions below. Paragraph alignment and floating objects are discussed later in this document.

9.3.1 Paragraphs: the P element

```
<!ELEMENT P - O (%inline;)*         -- paragraph -->
<!ATTLIST P
   %attrs;                          -- %coreattrs, %i18n, %events --
   >
```

Start tag: **required**, End tag: *optional*

Attributes defined elsewhere

- id, class (document-wide identifiers)
- lang (language information), dir (text direction)
- title (element title)
- style (inline style information)
- align (alignment)
- onclick, ondblclick, onmousedown, onmouseup, onmouseover, onmousemove, onmouseout, onkeypress, onkeydown, onkeyup (intrinsic events)

The P element represents a paragraph. It cannot contain block-level elements (including P itself).

We discourage authors from using empty P elements. User agents should ignore empty P elements.

9.3.2 Controlling line breaks

A *line break* is defined to be a carriage return (), a line feed (
), or a carriage return/line feed pair. All line breaks constitute white space.

For more information about SGML's specification of line breaks, please consult the notes on line breaks in the appendix.

Forcing a line break: the BR element

```
<!ELEMENT BR - O EMPTY              -forced line break -->
<!ATTLIST BR
  %coreattrs;                       -id, class, style, title -
  >
```

*Start tag: **required**, End tag: **forbidden***

Attributes defined elsewhere

- id, class (document-wide identifiers)
- title (element title)
- style (inline style information)
- clear (alignment and floating objects)

The BR element forcibly breaks (ends) the current line of text.

For visual user agents, the clear attribute can be used to determine whether markup following the BR element flows around images and other objects floated to the left or right margin, or whether it starts after the bottom of such objects. Further details are given in the section on alignment and floating objects. Authors are advised to use style sheets to control text flow around floating images and other objects.

With respect to bidirectional formatting, the BR element should behave the same way the [ISO10646] LINE SEPARATOR character behaves in the bidirectional algorithm.

Prohibiting a line break

Sometimes authors may want to prevent a line break from occurring between two words. The   entity (or) acts as a space where user agents should not cause a line break.

9.3.3 Hyphenation

In HTML, there are two types of hyphens: the plain hyphen and the soft hyphen. The plain hyphen should be interpreted by a user agent as just another character. The soft hyphen tells the user agent where a line break can occur.

Those browsers that interpret soft hyphens must observe the following semantics: If a line is broken at a soft hyphen, a hyphen character must be displayed at the end of the first line. If a line is not broken at a soft hyphen, the user agent must not display a hyphen character. For operations such as searching and sorting, the soft hyphen should always be ignored.

In HTML, the plain hyphen is represented by the "-" character (- or -). The soft hyphen is represented by the character entity reference ­ (­ or ­)

9.3.4 Preformatted text: The PRE element

```
<!ENTITY % pre.exclusion "IMG|OBJECT|BIG|SMALL|SUB|SUP">

<!ELEMENT PRE - - (%inline;)* -(%pre.exclusion;)—preformatted text —>
<!ATTLIST PRE
   %attrs;                                    —%coreattrs, %i18n, %events —
   >
```

Start tag: **required**, End tag: **required**

Attribute definitions

width = *number* [CN]

> **Deprecated.** This attribute provides a hint to visual user agents about the desired width of the formatted block. The user agent can use this information to select an appropriate font size or to indent the content appropriately. The desired width is expressed in number of characters. This attribute is not widely supported currently.

Attributes defined elsewhere

- id, class (document-wide identifiers)
- lang (language information), dir (text direction)
- title (element title)
- style (inline style information)
- onclick, ondblclick, onmousedown, onmouseup, onmouseover, onmousemove, onmouseout, onkeypress, onkeydown, onkeyup (intrinsic events)

The PRE element tells visual user agents that the enclosed text is "preformatted". When handling preformatted text, visual user agents:

- May leave white space intact.
- May render text with a fixed-pitch font.
- May disable automatic word wrap.
- Must not disable bidirectional processing.

Non-visual user agents are not required to respect extra white space in the content of a PRE element.

For more information about SGML's specification of line breaks, please consult the notes on line breaks in the appendix.

The DTD fragment above indicates which elements may not appear within a PRE declaration. This is the same as in HTML 3.2, and is intended to preserve constant line spacing and column alignment for text rendered in a fixed pitch font. Authors are discouraged from altering this behavior through style sheets.

The following example shows a preformatted verse from Shelly's poem *To a Skylark*:

```
<PRE>
        Higher still and higher
          From the earth thou springest
        Like a cloud of fire;
          The blue deep thou wingest,
And singing still dost soar, and soaring ever singest.
</PRE>
```

Here is how this is typically rendered:

```
        Higher still and higher
          From the earth thou springest
        Like a cloud of fire;
          The blue deep thou wingest,
And singing still dost soar, and soaring ever singest.
```

The horizontal tab character

The horizontal tab character (decimal 9 in [ISO10646] *and* [ISO88591] *) is usually interpreted by visual user agents as the smallest non-zero number of spaces necessary to line characters up along tab stops that are every 8 characters.*

We strongly discourage using horizontal tabs in preformatted text since it is common practice, when editing, to set the tab-spacing to other values, leading to misaligned documents.

9.3.5 Visual rendering of paragraphs

Note. *The following section is an informative description of the behavior of some current visual user agents when formatting paragraphs. Style sheets allow better control of paragraph formatting.*

How paragraphs are rendered visually depends on the user agent. Paragraphs are usually rendered flush left with a ragged right margin. Other defaults are appropriate for right-to-left scripts.

HTML user agents have traditionally rendered paragraphs with white space before and after, e.g.,

```
At the same time, there began to take form a system of numbering,
the calendar, hieroglyphic writing, and a technically advanced
art, all of which later influenced other peoples.

Within the framework of this gradual evolution or cultural
progress the Preclassic horizon has been divided into Lower,
Middle and Upper periods, to which can be added a transitional
or Protoclassic period with several features that would later
distinguish the emerging civilizations of Mesoamerica.
```

This contrasts with the style used in novels which indents the first line of the paragraph and uses the regular line spacing between the final line of the current paragraph and the first line of the next, e.g.,

```
    At the same time, there began to take form a system of
numbering, the calendar, hieroglyphic writing, and a technically
advanced art, all of which later influenced other peoples.
    Within the framework of this gradual evolution or cultural
progress the Preclassic horizon has been divided into Lower,
Middle and Upper periods, to which can be added a transitional
or Protoclassic period with several features that would later
distinguish the emerging civilizations of Mesoamerica.
```

Following the precedent set by the NCSA Mosaic browser in 1993, user agents generally don't justify both margins, in part because it's hard to do this effectively without sophisticated hyphenation routines. The advent of style sheets, and anti-aliased fonts with subpixel positioning promises to offer richer choices to HTML authors than previously possible.

Style sheets provide rich control over the size and style of a font, the margins, space before and after a paragraph, the first line indent, justification and many other details. The user agent's default style sheet renders P elements in a familiar form, as illustrated above. One could, in principle, override this to render paragraphs without the breaks that conventionally distinguish successive paragraphs. In general, since this may confuse readers, we discourage this practice.

By convention, visual HTML user agents wrap text lines to fit within the available margins. Wrapping algorithms depend on the script being formatted.

In Western scripts, for example, text should only be wrapped at white space. Early user agents incorrectly wrapped lines just after the start tag or just before the end tag of an element, which resulted in dangling punctuation. For example, consider this sentence:

```
A statue of the <A href="cih78">Cihuateteus</A>, who are patron ...
```

Wrapping the line just before the end tag of the A element causes the comma to be stranded at the beginning of the next line:

```
A statue of the Cihuateteus
, who are patron ...
```

This is an error since there was no white space at that point in the markup.

9.4 Marking document changes: The INS and DEL elements

```
<!-- INS/DEL are handled by inclusion on BODY -->
<!ELEMENT (INS|DEL) - - (%flow;)*        --inserted text, deleted text -->
<!ATTLIST (INS|DEL)
    %attrs;                              --%coreattrs, %i18n, %events --
    cite        %URI;        #IMPLIED    --info on reason for change --
    datetime    %Datetime;   #IMPLIED    --date and time of change --
    >
```

Start tag: **required**, End tag: **required**

Attribute definitions

cite = *uri* [CT]

> The value of this attribute is a URI that designates a source document or message. This attribute is intended to point to information explaining why a document was changed.

datetime = *datetime* [CS]

> The value of this attribute specifies the date and time when the change was made.

Attributes defined elsewhere

- id, class (document-wide identifiers)
- lang (language information), dir (text direction)
- title (element title)
- style (inline style information)
- onclick, ondblclick, onmousedown, onmouseup, onmouseover, onmousemove, onmouseout, onkeypress, onkeydown, onkeyup (intrinsic events)

INS and DEL are used to markup sections of the document that have been inserted or deleted with respect to a different version of a document (e.g., in draft legislation where lawmakers need to view the changes).

These two elements are unusual for HTML in that they may serve as either block-level or inline elements (but not both). They may contain one or more words within a paragraph or contain one or more block-level elements such as paragraphs, lists and tables.

This example could be from a bill to change the legislation for how many deputies a County Sheriff can employ from 3 to 5.

```
<P>
   A Sheriff can employ <DEL>3</DEL><INS>5</INS> deputies.
</P>
```

The INS and DEL elements must not contain block-level content when these elements behave as inline elements.

ILLEGAL EXAMPLE:
The following is not legal HTML.

```
<P>
<INS><DIV>...block-level content...</DIV></INS>
</P>
```

User agents should render inserted and deleted text in ways that make the change obvious. For instance, inserted text may appear in a special font, deleted text may not be shown at all or be shown as struck-through or with special markings, etc.

Both of the following examples correspond to November 5, 1994, 8:15:30 am, US Eastern Standard Time.

```
1994-11-05T13:15:30Z
1994-11-05T08:15:30-05:00
```

Used with INS, this gives:

```
<INS datetime="1994-11-05T08:15:30-05:00"
     cite="http://www.foo.org/mydoc/comments.html">
Furthermore, the latest figures from the marketing department
suggest that such practice is on the rise.
</INS>
```

The document "http://www.foo.org/mydoc/comments.html" would contain comments about why information was inserted into the document.

Authors may also make comments about inserted or deleted text by means of the title attribute for the INS and DEL elements. User agents may present this information to the user (e.g., as a popup note). For example:

```
<INS datetime="1994-11-05T08:15:30-05:00"
     title="Changed as a result of Steve B's comments in meeting.">
Furthermore, the latest figures from the marketing department
suggest that such practice is on the rise.
</INS>
```

Chapter 10

Lists

Contents

1. Introduction to lists
2. Unordered lists (`UL`), ordered lists (`OL`), and list items (`LI`)
3. Definition lists: the `DL`, `DT`, and `DD` elements
    1. Visual rendering of lists
4. The `DIR` and `MENU` elements

10.1 Introduction to lists

HTML offers authors several mechanisms for specifying lists of information. All lists must contain one or more list elements. Lists may contain:

- Unordered information.
- Ordered information.
- Definitions.

The previous list, for example, is an unordered list, created with the UL element:

```
<UL>
<LI>Unordered information.
<LI>Ordered information.
<LI>Definitions.
</UL>
```

An ordered list, created using the `OL` element, should contain information where order should be emphasized, as in a recipe:

111

1. Mix dry ingredients thoroughly.
2. Pour in wet ingredients.
3. Mix for 10 minutes.
4. Bake for one hour at 300 degrees.

Definition lists, created using the DL element, generally consist of a series of term/definition pairs (although definition lists may have other applications). Thus, when advertising a product, one might use a definition list:

Lower cost

The new version of this product costs significantly less than the previous one!

Easier to use

We've changed the product so that it's much easier to use!

Safe for kids

You can leave your kids alone in a room with this product and they won't get hurt (not a guarantee).

defined in HTML as:

```
<DL>
<DT><STRONG>Lower cost</STRONG>
<DD>The new version of this product costs significantly less than the
previous one!
<DT><STRONG>Easier to use</STRONG>
<DD>We've changed the product so that it's much easier to use!
<DT><STRONG>Safe for kids</STRONG>
<DD>You can leave your kids alone in a room with this product and
they won't get hurt (not a guarantee).
</DL>
```

Lists may also be nested and different list types may be used together, as in the following example, which is a definition list that contains an unordered list (the ingredients) and an ordered list (the procedure):

The ingredients:

- 100 g. flour
- 10 g. sugar
- 1 cup water
- 2 eggs
- salt, pepper

The procedure:

1. Mix dry ingredients thoroughly.
2. Pour in wet ingredients.
3. Mix for 10 minutes.
4. Bake for one hour at 300 degrees.

Notes:

The recipe may be improved by adding raisins.

The exact presentation of the three list types depends on the user agent. We discourage authors from using lists purely as a means of indenting text. This is a stylistic issue and is properly handled by style sheets.

10.2 Unordered lists (UL), ordered lists (OL), and list items (LI)

```
<!ELEMENT UL - - (LI)+              — unordered list —>
<!ATTLIST UL
  %attrs;                           — %coreattrs, %i18n, %events —
  >
<!ELEMENT OL - - (LI)+              — ordered list —>
<!ATTLIST OL
  %attrs;                           — %coreattrs, %i18n, %events —
  >
```

*Start tag: **required**, End tag: **required***

```
<!ELEMENT LI - O (%flow;)*              —list item —>
<!ATTLIST LI
  %attrs;                               —%coreattrs, %i18n, %events —
  >
```

*Start tag: **required**, End tag: **optional***

Attribute definitions

type = *style-information* [CI]

> **Deprecated.** This attribute sets the style of a list item. Currently available values are intended for visual user agents. Possible values are described below (along with case information).

start = *number* [CN]

> **Deprecated.** For OL only. This attribute specifies the starting number of the first item in an ordered list. The default starting number is "1". Note that while the value of this attribute is an integer, the corresponding label may be non-numeric. Thus, when the list item style is uppercase latin letters (A, B, C, ...), `start=3` means "C". When the style is lowercase roman numerals, `start=3` means "iii", etc.

value = *number* [CN]

> **Deprecated.** For LI only. This attribute sets the number of the current list item. Note that while the value of this attribute is an integer, the corresponding label may be non-numeric (see the start attribute).

compact [CI]

> **Deprecated.** When set, this boolean attribute gives a hint to visual user agents to render the list in a more compact way. The interpretation of this attribute depends on the user agent.

Attributes defined elsewhere

- id, class (document-wide identifiers)
- lang (language information), dir (text direction)
- title (element title)
- style (inline style information)

- onclick, ondblclick, onmousedown, onmouseup, onmouseover, onmousemove, onmouseout, onkeypress, onkeydown, onkeyup (intrinsic events)

Ordered and unordered lists are rendered in an identical manner except that visual user agents number ordered list items. User agents may present those numbers in a variety of ways. Unordered list items are not numbered.

Both types of lists are made up of sequences of list items defined by the `LI` element (whose end tag may be omitted).

This example illustrates the basic structure of a list.

```
<UL>
    <LI> ... first list item...
    <LI> ... second list item...
    ...
</UL>
```

Lists may also be nested:

DEPRECATED EXAMPLE:

```
<UL>
    <LI> ... Level one, number one...
    <OL>
        <LI> ... Level two, number one...
        <LI> ... Level two, number two...
        <OL start="10">
            <LI> ... Level three, number one...
        </OL>
        <LI> ... Level two, number three...
    </OL>
    <LI> ... Level one, number two...
</UL>
```

Details about number order. *In ordered lists, it is not possible to continue list numbering automatically from a previous list or to hide numbering of some list items. However, authors can reset the number of a list item by setting its value attribute. Numbering continues from the new value for subsequent list items. For example:*

```
<ol>
<li value="30"> makes this list item number 30.
```

```
<li value="40"> makes this list item number 40.
<li> makes this list item number 41.
</ol>
```

10.3 Definition lists: the DL, DT, and DD elements

```
<!-- definition lists - DT for term, DD for its definition -->
<!ELEMENT DL - - (DT|DD)+              -- definition list -->
<!ATTLIST DL
  %attrs;                              -- %coreattrs, %i18n, %events --
  >
```

Start tag: **required**, End tag: **required**

```
<!ELEMENT DT - O (%inline;)*           -- definition term -->
<!ELEMENT DD - O (%flow;)*             -- definition description -->
<!ATTLIST (DT|DD)
  %attrs;                              -- %coreattrs, %i18n, %events --
  >
```

Start tag: **required**, End tag: **optional**

Attributes defined elsewhere

- id, class (document-wide identifiers)
- lang (language information), dir (text direction)
- title (element title)
- style (inline style information)
- onclick, ondblclick, onmousedown, onmouseup, onmouseover, onmousemove, onmouseout, onkeypress, onkeydown, onkeyup (intrinsic events)

Definition lists vary only slightly from other types of lists in that list items consist of two parts: a term and a description. The term is given by the DT element and is restricted to inline content. The description is given with a DD element that contains block-level content.

Here is an example:

```
<DL>
  <DT>Dweeb
  <DD>young excitable person who may mature
     into a <EM>Nerd</EM> or <EM>Geek</EM>

  <DT>Cracker
  <DD>hacker on the Internet

  <DT>Nerd
  <DD>male so into the Net that he forgets
     his wife's birthday
</DL>
```

Here is an example with multiple terms and descriptions:

```
<DL>
   <DT>Center
   <DT>Centre
   <DD> A point equidistant from all points
             on the surface of a sphere.
   <DD> In some field sports, the player who
             holds the middle position on the field, court,
             or forward line.
</DL>
```

Another application of DL, for example, is for marking up dialogues, with each DT naming a speaker, and each DD containing his or her words.

10.3.1 Visual rendering of lists

Note. *The following is an informative description of the behavior of some current visual user agents when formatting lists. Style sheets allow better control of list formatting (e.g., for numbering, language-dependent conventions, indenting, etc.).*

Visual user agents generally indent nested lists with respect to the current level of nesting.

For both OL and UL, the type attribute specifies rendering options for visual user agents.

For the UL element, possible values for the type attribute are disc, square, and circle. The default value depends on the level of nesting of the current list. These values are case-insensitive.

How each value is presented depends on the user agent. User agents should attempt to present a "disc" as a small filled-in circle, a "circle" as a small circle outline, and a "square" as a small square outline.

A graphical user agent might render this as:

- for the value "disc"
o for the value "circle"
▫ for the value "square"

For the OL element, possible values for the type attribute are summarized in the table below (they are case-sensitive):

Type	Numbering style	
1	arabic numbers	1, 2, 3, ...
a	lower alpha	a, b, c, ...
A	upper alpha	A, B, C, ...
i	lower roman	i, ii, iii, ...
I	upper roman	I, II, III, ...

For example, using CSS, one may specify that the style of numbers for list elements in a numbered list should be lowercase roman numerals. In the excerpt below, every OL element belonging to the class "withroman" will have roman numerals in front of its list items.

```
<STYLE type="text/css">
OL.withroman { list-style-type: lower-roman }
</STYLE>
<BODY>
<OL class="withroman">
<LI> Step one ...
<LI> Step two ...
</OL>
</BODY>
```

The rendering of a definition list also depends on the user agent. The example:

```
<DL>
  <DT>Dweeb
  <DD>young excitable person who may mature
     into a <EM>Nerd</EM> or <EM>Geek</EM>

  <DT>Cracker
  <DD>hacker on the Internet

  <DT>Nerd
  <DD>male so into the Net that he forgets
     his wife's birthday
</DL>
```

might be rendered as follows:

```
Dweeb
        young excitable person who may mature into a Nerd or Geek
Cracker
        hacker on the Internet
Nerd
        male so into the Net that he forgets his wife's birthday
```

10.4 The DIR and MENU elements

DIR and MENU are deprecated.

See the Transitional DTD for the formal definition.

Attributes defined elsewhere

- id, class (document-wide identifiers)
- lang (language information), dir (text direction)
- title (element title)
- style (inline style information)
- onclick, ondblclick, onmousedown, onmouseup, onmouseover, onmousemove, onmouseout, onkeypress, onkeydown, onkeyup (intrinsic events)

The `DIR` element was designed to be used for creating multicolumn directory lists. The `MENU` element was designed to be used for single column menu lists. Both elements have the same structure as `UL`, just different rendering. In practice, a user agent will render a `DIR` or `MENU` list exactly as a `UL` list.

We strongly recommend using `UL` instead of these elements.

Chapter 11

Tables

Contents

1. Introduction to tables
2. Elements for constructing tables
   1. The `TABLE` element
      - Table directionality
   2. Table Captions: The `CAPTION` element
   3. Row groups: the `THEAD`, `TFOOT`, and `TBODY` elements
   4. Column groups: the `COLGROUP` and `COL` elements
      - The `COLGROUP` element
      - The `COL` element
      - Calculating the number of columns in a table
      - Calculating the width of columns
   5. Table rows: The `TR` element
   6. Table cells: The `TH` and `TD` elements
      - Cells that span several rows or columns
3. Table formatting by visual user agents
   1. Borders and rules
   2. Horizontal and vertical alignment
      - Inheritance of alignment specifications
   3. Cell margins
4. Table rendering by non-visual user agents
   1. Associating header information with data cells
   2. Categorizing cells
   3. Algorithm to find heading information
5. Sample table

11.1 Introduction to tables

The HTML table model allows authors to arrange data—text, preformatted text, images, links, forms, form fields, other tables, etc.—into rows and columns of cells.

Each table may have an associated caption (see the `CAPTION` element) that provides a short description of the table's purpose. A longer description may also be provided (via the summary attribute) for the benefit of people using speech or Braille-based user agents.

Table rows may be grouped into a head, foot, and body sections, (via the `THEAD`, `TFOOT` and `TBODY` elements, respectively). Row groups convey additional structural information and may be rendered by user agents in ways that emphasize this structure. User agents may exploit the head/body/foot division to support scrolling of body sections independently of the head and foot sections. When long tables are printed, the head and foot information may be repeated on each page that contains table data.

Authors may also group columns to provide additional structural information that may be exploited by user agents. Furthermore, authors may declare column properties at the start of a table definition (via the `COLGROUP` and `COL` elements) in a way that enables user agents to render the table incrementally rather than having to wait for all the table data to arrive before rendering.

Table cells may either contain "header" information (see the `TH` element) or "data" (see the `TD` element). Cells may span multiple rows and columns. The HTML 4.0 table model allows authors to label each cell so that non-visual user agents may more easily communicate heading information about the cell to the user. Not only do these mechanisms greatly assist users with visual disabilities, they make it possible for multi-modal wireless browsers with limited display capabilities (e.g., Web-enabled pagers and phones) to handle tables.

Tables should not be used purely as a means to layout document content as this may present problems when rendering to non-visual media. Additionally, when used with graphics, these tables may force users to scroll horizontally to view a table designed on a system with a larger display. To minimize these problems, authors should use style sheets to control layout rather than tables. ***Note***. *This specification includes more detailed information about tables in sections on table design* rationale and implementation issues. Here's a simple table that illustrates some of the features of the HTML table model. The following table definition:

```
<TABLE border="1"
          summary="This table gives some statistics about fruit
                   flies: average height and weight, and percentage
```

```
                    with red eyes (for both males and females)."
<CAPTION<EMA test table with merged cells</EM</CAPTION
<TR<TH rowspan="2"<TH colspan="2"Average
    <TH rowspan="2"Red<BReyes
<TR<THheight<THweight
<TR<THMales<TD1.9<TD0.003<TD40%
<TR<THFemales<TD1.7<TD0.002<TD43%
</TABLE
```

might be rendered something like this on a tty device:

```
             A test table with merged cells
    /---------------------------------------------\
    |           |      Average       |   Red     |
    |           |--------------------|   eyes    |
    |           |  height |  weight  |           |
    |-------------------------------------------- |
    |  Males    |  1.9    |  0.003   |    40%    |
    |-------------------------------------------- |
    |  Females  |  1.7    |  0.002   |    43%    |
    \---------------------------------------------/
```

or like this by a graphical user agent:

	A test table with merged cells		
	Average		Red eyes
	height	weight	
Males	1.9	0.003	40%
Females	1.7	0.002	43%

11.2 Elements for constructing tables

11.2.1 The TABLE element

```
<!ELEMENT TABLE - -
     (CAPTION?, (COL*|COLGROUP*), THEAD?, TFOOT?, TBODY+)
<!ATTLIST TABLE                       -- table element --
    %attrs;                           -- %coreattrs, %i18n, %events --
    summary      %Text;     #IMPLIED  -- purpose/structure for speech output--
    width        %Length;   #IMPLIED  -- table width --
    border       %Pixels;   #IMPLIED  -- controls frame width around table --
    frame        %TFrame;   #IMPLIED  -- which parts of frame to render --
    rules        %TRules;   #IMPLIED  -- rulings between rows and cols --
    cellspacing  %Length;   #IMPLIED  -- spacing between cells --
    cellpadding  %Length;   #IMPLIED  -- spacing within cells --
```

*Start tag: **required**, End tag: **required*** Attribute definitions

`summary` = text [CS]

This attribute provides a summary of the table's purpose and structure for user agents rendering to non-visual media such as speech and Braille.

`align` = left|center|right [CI]

Deprecated. This attribute specifies the position of the table with respect to the document. Permitted values:

- left: The table is to the left of the document.
- center: The table is to the center of the document.
- right: The table is to the right of the document.

`width` = length [CN]

This attribute specifies the desired width of the entire table and is intended for visual user agents. When the value is a percentage value, the value is relative to the user agent's available horizontal space. In the absence of any width specification, table width is determined by the user agent.

Attributes defined elsewhere

- id, class (document-wide identifiers)
- lang (language information), dir (text direction)
- title (element title)
- style (inline style information)
- onclick, ondblclick, onmousedown, onmouseup, onmouseover, onmousemove, onmouseout, onkeypress, onkeydown, onkeyup (intrinsic events)
- bgcolor (background color)
- frame, rules, border (borders and rules)
- cellspacing, cellpadding (cell margins)

The TABLE element contains all other elements that specify caption, rows, content, and formatting.

The following informative list describes what operations user agents may carry out when rendering a table:

- Make the table summary available to the user. Authors should provide a summary of a table's content and structure so that people using non-visual user agents may better understand it.
- Render the caption, if one is defined.
- Render the table header, if one is specified. Render the table footer, if one is specified. User agents must know where to render the header and footer. For instance, if the output medium is paged, user agents may put the header at the top of each page and the footer at the bottom. Similarly, if the user agent provides a mechanism to scroll the rows, the header may appear at the top of the scrolled area and the footer at the bottom.
- Calculate the number of columns in the table. Note that the number of rows in a table is equal to the number of TR elements contained by the TABLE element.
- Group the columns according to any column group specifications.
- Render the cells, row by row and grouped in appropriate columns, between the header and footer. Visual user agents should format the table according to HTML attributes and style sheet specification.

The HTML table model has been designed so that, with author assistance, user agents may render tables *incrementally* (i.e., as table rows arrive) rather than having to wait for all the data before beginning to render.

In order for a user agent to format a table in one pass, authors must tell the user agent:

- The number of columns in the table. Please consult the section on calculating the number of columns in a table for details on how to supply this information.
- The widths of these columns. Please consult the section on calculating the width of columns for details on how to supply this information.

More precisely, a user agent may render a table in a single pass when the column widths are specified using a combination of COLGROUP and COL elements. If any of the columns are specified in relative or percentage terms (see the section on calculating the width of columns), authors must also specify the width of the table itself.

Table directionality

The directionality of a table is either the inherited directionality (the default is left-to-right) or that specified by the dir attribute for the TABLE element.

For a left-to-right table, column zero is on the left side and row zero is at the top. For a right-to-left table, column zero is on the right side and row zero is at the top.

When a user agent allots extra cells to a row (see the section on calculating the number of columns in a table), extra row cells are added to the right of the table for left-to-right tables and to the left side for right-to-left tables.

Note that TABLE is the only element on which dir reverses the visual order of the columns; a single table row (TR) or a group of columns (COLGROUP) cannot be independently reversed.

When set for the TABLE element, the dir attribute also affects the direction of text within table cells (since the dir attribute is inherited by block-level elements). To specify a right-to-left table, set the dir attribute as follows:

```
<TABLE dir="RTL"
...the rest of the table...
</TABLE
```

The direction of text in individual cells can be changed by setting the dir attribute in an element that defines the cell. Please consult the section on bidirectional text for more information on text direction issues.

11.2.2 Table Captions: The CAPTION element

```
<!ELEMENT CAPTION   - - (%inline;)*        — table caption —
<!ENTITY % CAlign  "(top|bottom|left|right)"

<!ATTLIST CAPTION
   %attrs;                                 — %coreattrs, %i18n, %events —
```

*Start tag: **required**, End tag: **required** Attribute definitions*

```
align = top|bottom|left|right [CI]
```

Deprecated. For visual user agents, this attribute specifies the position of the caption with respect to the table. Possible values:

- `top`: The caption is at the top of the table. This is the default value.
- `bottom`: The caption is at the bottom of the table.
- `left`: The caption is at the left of the table.
- `right`: The caption is at the right of the table.

Attributes defined elsewhere

- id, class (document-wide identifiers)
- lang (language information), dir (text direction)
- title (element title)
- style (inline style information)
- onclick, ondblclick, onmousedown, onmouseup, onmouseover, onmousemove, onmouseout, onkeypress, onkeydown, onkeyup (intrinsic events)

When present, the CAPTION element's text should describe the nature of the table. The CAPTION element is only permitted immediately after the TABLE start tag. A TABLE element may only contain one CAPTION element.

Visual user agents allow sighted people to quickly grasp the structure of the table from the headings as well as the caption. A consequence of this is that captions will often be inadequate as a summary of the purpose and structure of the table from the perspective of people relying on non-visual user agents.

Authors should therefore take care to provide additional information summarizing the purpose and structure of the table using the summary attribute of the TABLE element. This is especially important for tables without captions. Examples below illustrate the use of the summary attribute.

Visual user agents should avoid clipping any part of the table including the caption, unless a means is provided to access all parts, e.g., by horizontal or vertical scrolling. We recommend that the caption text be wrapped to the same width as the table. (See also the section on recommended layout algorithms.)

11.2.3 Row groups: the THEAD, TFOOT, and TBODY elements

```
<!ELEMENT THEAD      - O (TR)+         —table header —
<!ELEMENT TFOOT      - O (TR)+         —table footer —
```

Start tag: **required**, *End tag:* **optional**

```
<!ELEMENT TBODY     O O (TR)+          —table body —
```

Start tag: **optional**, *End tag:* **optional**

```
<!ATTLIST (THEAD|TBODY|TFOOT)          — table section —
    %attrs;                            — %coreattrs, %i18n, %events —
    %cellhalign;                       — horizontal alignment in cells —
    %cellvalign;                       — vertical alignment in cells —
```

Attributes defined elsewhere

- id, class (document-wide identifiers)

- lang (language information), dir (text direction)

- title (element title)

- style (inline style information)

- onclick, ondblclick, onmousedown, onmouseup, onmouseover, onmousemove, onmouseout, onkeypress, onkeydown, onkeyup (intrinsic events)

- align, char, charoff, valign (cell alignment)

Table rows may be grouped into a table head, table foot, and one or more table body sections, using the THEAD, TFOOT and TBODY elements, respectively. This division enables user agents to support scrolling of table bodies independently of the table head and foot. When long tables are printed, the table head and foot information may be repeated on each page that contains table data.

The table head and table foot should contain information about the table's columns. The table body should contain rows of table data.

When present, each THEAD, TFOOT, and TBODY contains a *row group*. Each row group must contain at least one row, defined by the TR element. This example illustrates the order and structure of table heads, feet, and bodies.

```
<TABLE
<THEAD
     <TR ...header information...
</THEAD
<TFOOT
     <TR ...footer information...
</TFOOT
<TBODY
     <TR ...first row of block one data...
     <TR ...second row of block one data...
</TBODY
<TBODY
     <TR ...first row of block two data...
     <TR ...second row of block two data...
     <TR ...third row of block two data...
</TBODY
</TABLE
```

TFOOT must appear before TBODY within a TABLE definition so that user agents can render the foot before receiving all of the (potentially numerous) rows of data. The following summarizes which tags are required and which may be omitted:

- The TBODY start tag is always required except when the table contains only one table body and no table head or foot sections. The TBODY end tag may always be safely omitted.

- The start tags for THEAD and TFOOT are required when the table head and foot sections are present respectively, but the corresponding end tags may always be safely omitted.

Conforming user agent parsers must obey these rules for reasons of backward compatibility. The table of the previous example could be shortened by removing certain end tags, as in:

```
<TABLE
<THEAD
     <TR ...header information...
<TFOOT
     <TR ...footer information...
<TBODY
     <TR ...first row of block one data...
     <TR ...second row of block one data...
<TBODY
     <TR ...first row of block two data...
     <TR ...second row of block two data...
     <TR ...third row of block two data...
</TABLE
```

The THEAD, TFOOT, and TBODY sections must contain the same number of columns.

11.2.4 Column groups: the COLGROUP and COL elements

Column groups allow authors to create structural divisions within a table. Authors may highlight this structure through style sheets or HTML attributes (e.g., the rules attribute for the TABLE element). For an example of the visual presentation of column groups, please consult the sample table.

A table may either contain a single implicit column group (no COLGROUP element delimits the columns) or any number of explicit column groups (each delimited by an instance of the COLGROUP element).

The COL element allows authors to share attributes among several columns without implying any structural grouping. The "span" of the COL element is the number of columns that will share the element's attributes.

The COLGROUP element

```
<!ELEMENT COLGROUP - O (col)*          -- table column group --
<!ATTLIST COLGROUP
   %attrs;                             -- %coreattrs, %i18n, %events --
   span           NUMBER        1      -- default number of columns in group --
```

```
width          %MultiLength;   #IMPLIED  -- default width for enclosed COLs --
%cellhalign;                             -- horizontal alignment in cells --
%cellvalign;                             -- vertical alignment in cells --
```

*Start tag: **required**, End tag: **optional*** Attribute definitions

span = number [CN]

This attribute, which must be an integer 0, specifies the number of columns in a column group. Values mean the following:

- In the absence of a span attribute, each COLGROUP defines a column group containing one column.

- If the span attribute is set to N 0, the current COLGROUP element defines a column group containing N columns.

User agents must ignore this attribute if the COLGROUP element contains one or more COL elements.

width = multi-length [CN]

This attribute specifies a default width for each column in the current column group. In addition to the standard pixel, percentage, and relative values, this attribute allows the special form "0*" (zero asterisk) which means that the width of the each column in the group should be the minimum width necessary to hold the column's contents. This implies that a column's entire contents must be known before its width may be correctly computed. Authors should be aware that specifying "0*" will prevent visual user agents from rendering a table incrementally.

This attribute is overridden for any column in the column group whose width is specified via a COL element. *Attributes defined elsewhere*

- id, class (document-wide identifiers)

- lang (language information), dir (text direction)

- title (element title)

- style (inline style information)

- onclick, ondblclick, onmousedown, onmouseup, onmouseover, onmousemove, onmouseout, onkeypress, onkeydown, onkeyup (intrinsic events)

- align, char, charoff, valign (cell alignment)

The COLGROUP element creates an explicit column group. The number of columns in the column group may be specified in two, mutually exclusive ways:

1. The element's span attribute (default value 1) specifies the number of columns in the group.
2. Each COL element in the COLGROUP represents one or more columns in the group.

The advantage of using the span attribute is that authors may group together information about column widths. Thus, if a table contains forty columns, all of which have a width of 20 pixels, it is easier to write:

```
<COLGROUP span="40" width="20">
</COLGROUP>
```

than:

```
<COLGROUP
    <COL width="20"
    <COL width="20"
    ...a total of forty COL elements...
</COLGROUP>
```

When it is necessary to single out a column (e.g., for style information, to specify width information, etc.) within a group, authors must identify that column with a COL element. Thus, to apply special style information to the last column of the previous table, we single it out as follows:

```
<COLGROUP width="20"
    <COL span="39"
    <COL id="format-me-specially"
</COLGROUP>
```

The width attribute of the COLGROUP element is inherited by all 40 columns. The first COL element refers to the first 39 columns (doing nothing special to them) and the second one assigns an id value to the fortieth columns so that style sheets may refer to it. The table in the following example contains two column groups. The first column group contains 10 columns and the second contains 5 columns. The default width for each column in the first column group is 50 pixels. The width of each column in the second column group will be the minimum required for that column.

```
<TABLE
<COLGROUP span="10" width="50"
<COLGROUP span="5" width="0*"
```

```
<THEAD
<TR<TD ...
</TABLE
```

The COL element

```
<!ELEMENT COL   - O EMPTY                  -- table column --
<!ATTLIST COL                              -- column groups and properties --
  %attrs;                                  -- %coreattrs, %i18n, %events --
  span          NUMBER        1            -- COL attributes affect N columns --
  width         %MultiLength; #IMPLIED     -- column width specification --
  %cellhalign;                             -- horizontal alignment in cells --
  %cellvalign;                             -- vertical alignment in cells --
```

Start tag: **required**, End tag: **forbidden** Attribute definitions

span = number [CN]

This attribute, whose value must be an integer 0, specifies the number of columns "spanned" by the COL element; the COL element shares its attributes with all the columns it spans. The default value for this attribute is 1 (i.e., the COL element refers to a single column). If the span attribute is set to N 1, the current COL element shares its attributes with the next N-1 columns.

width = multi-length [CN]

This attribute specifies a default width for each column spanned by the current COL element. It has the same meaning as the width attribute for the COLGROUP element and overrides it.

Attributes defined elsewhere

- id, class (document-wide identifiers)
- lang (language information), dir (text direction)
- title (element title)
- style (inline style information)
- onclick, ondblclick, onmousedown, onmouseup, onmouseover, onmousemove, onmouseout, onkeypress, onkeydown, onkeyup (intrinsic events)
- align, char, charoff, valign (cell alignment)

The COL element allows authors to group together attribute specifications for table columns. The COL does **not** group columns together structurally—that is the role of the COLGROUP element. COL elements are empty and serve only as a support for attributes. They may appear inside or outside an explicit column group (i.e., COLGROUP element).

The width attribute for COL refers to the width of each column in the element's span.

Calculating the number of columns in a table

There are two ways to determine the number of columns in a table (in order of precedence):

1. If the TABLE element contains any COLGROUP or COL elements, user agents should calculate the number of columns by summing the following:

   - For each COL element, take the value of its span attribute (default value 1).

   - For each COLGROUP element containing at least one COL element, ignore the span attribute for the COLGROUP element. For each COL element, perform the calculation of step 1.

   - For each empty COLGROUP element, take the value of its span attribute (default value 1).

2. Otherwise, if the TABLE element contains no COLGROUP or COL elements, user agents should base the number of columns on what is required by the rows. The number of columns is equal to the number of columns required by the row with the most columns, including cells that span multiple columns. For any row that has fewer than this number of columns, the end of that row should be padded with empty cells. The "end" of a row depends on the table directionality.

It is an error if a table contains COLGROUP or COL elements and the two calculations do not result in the same number of columns.

Once the user agent has calculated the number of columns in the table, it may group them into column groups. For example, for each of the following tables, the two column calculation methods should result in three columns. The first three tables may be rendered incrementally.

```
<TABLE
<COLGROUP span="3"</COLGROUP
<TR<TD ...
...rows...
</TABLE

<TABLE
<COLGROUP
```

```
<COL
<COL span="2"
</COLGROUP
<TR<TD ...
...rows...
</TABLE

<TABLE
<COLGROUP
<COL
</COLGROUP
<COLGROUP span="2"
<TR<TD ...
...rows...
</TABLE

<TABLE
<TR
   <TD<TD<TD
</TR
</TABLE
```

Calculating the width of columns

Authors may specify column widths in three ways:

Fixed

A fixed width specification is given in pixels (e.g., width="30"). A fixed-width specification enables incremental rendering.

Percentage

A percentage specification (e.g., width="20%") is based on the percentage of the horizontal space available to the table (between the current left and right margins, including floats). Note that this space does not depend on the table itself, and thus percentage specifications enable incremental rendering.

Proportional

Proportional specifications (e.g., width="3*") refer to portions of the horizontal space required by a table. If the table width is given a fixed value via the width attribute of the TABLE element, user agents may render the table incrementally even with proportional columns.

However, if the table does not have a fixed width, user agents must receive all table data before they can determine the horizontal space required by the table. Only then may this space be allotted to proportional columns. If an author specifies no width information for a column, a user agent may not be able to incrementally format the table since it must wait for the entire column of data to arrive in order to allot an appropriate width.

If column widths prove to be too narrow for the contents of a particular table cell, user agents may choose to reflow the table. The table in this example contains six columns. The first one does not belong to an explicit column group. The next three belong to the first explicit column group and the last two belong to the second explicit column group. This table cannot be formatted incrementally since it contains proportional column width specifications and no value for the width attribute for the TABLE element.

Once the (visual) user agent has received the table's data: the available horizontal space will be allotted by the user agent as follows: First the user agent will allot 30 pixels to columns one and two. Then, the minimal space required for the third column will be reserved. The remaining horizontal space will be divided into six equal portions (since 2* + 1* + 3* = 6 portions). Column four (2*) will receive two of these portions, column five (1*) will receive one, and column six (3*) will receive three.

```
<TABLE
<COLGROUP
    <COL width="30"
<COLGROUP
    <COL width="30"
    <COL width="0*"
    <COL width="2*"
<COLGROUP align="center"
    <COL width="1*"
    <COL width="3*" align="char" char=":"
<THEAD
<TR<TD ...
...rows...
</TABLE
```

We have set the value of the align attribute in the third column group to "center". All cells in every column in this group will inherit this value, but may override it. In fact, the final COL does just that, by specifying that every cell in the column it governs will be aligned along the ":" character. In the following table, the column width specifications allow the user agent to format the table incrementally:

```
<TABLE width="200"
<COLGROUP span="10" width="15"
<COLGROUP width="*"
   <COL id="penultimate-column"
   <COL id="last-column"
<THEAD
<TR<TD ...
...rows...
</TABLE
```

The first ten columns will be 15 pixels wide each. The last two columns will each receive half of the remaining 50 pixels. Note that the COL elements appear only so that an id value may be specified for the last two columns. *Note. Although the width attribute on the TABLE element is not deprecated, authors are encouraged to use style sheets to specify table widths.*

11.2.5 Table rows: The TR element

```
<!ELEMENT TR        - O (TH|TD)+         —table row —
<!ATTLIST TR                             —table row —
  %attrs;                                —%coreattrs, %i18n, %events —
  %cellhalign;                           —horizontal alignment in cells —
  %cellvalign;                           —vertical alignment in cells —
```

Start tag: **required**, *End tag:* **optional** *Attributes defined elsewhere*

- id, class (document-wide identifiers)
- lang (language information), dir (text direction)
- title (element title)
- style (inline style information)
- onclick, ondblclick, onmousedown, onmouseup, onmouseover, onmousemove, onmouseout, onkeypress, onkeydown, onkeyup (intrinsic events)
- align, char, charoff, valign (cell alignment)

The TR elements acts as a container for a row of table cells. The end tag may be omitted. This sample table contains three rows, each begun by the TR element:

```
<TABLE summary="This table charts the number of cups
                of coffee consumed by each senator, the type
                of coffee (decaf or regular), and whether
                taken with sugar."
<CAPTIONCups of coffee consumed by each senator</CAPTION
<TR ...A header row...
<TR ...First row of data...
<TR ...Second row of data...
...the rest of the table...
</TABLE
```

11.2.6 Table cells: The TH and TD elements

```
<!ELEMENT (TH|TD)  - O (%flow;)*           —table header cell, table data cell—

<!— Scope is simpler than axes attribute for common tables —
<!ENTITY % Scope "(row|col|rowgroup|colgroup)"

<!— TH is for headers, TD for data, but for cells acting as both use TD —
<!ATTLIST (TH|TD)                          —header or data cell —
    %attrs;                                —%coreattrs, %i18n, %events —
    abbr        %Text;       #IMPLIED      —abbreviation for header cell —
    axis        CDATA        #IMPLIED      —names groups of related headers—
    headers     IDREFS       #IMPLIED      —list of id's for header cells —
    scope       %Scope;      #IMPLIED      —scope covered by header cells —
    rowspan     NUMBER       1             —number of rows spanned by cell —
    colspan     NUMBER       1             —number of cols spanned by cell —
    %cellhalign;                           —horizontal alignment in cells —
    %cellvalign;                           —vertical alignment in cells —
```

Start tag: **required**, *End tag:* **optional** *Attribute definitions*

headers = idrefs [CS]

This attribute specifies the list of header cells that provide header information for the current data cell. The value of this attribute is a space-separated list of cell names; those cells must be named by setting their id attribute. Authors generally use the headers attribute to help non-visual user agents render header information about data cells (e.g., header information is spoken prior to the cell data), but the attribute may also be used in conjunction with style sheets. See also the scope attribute.

scope = *scope-name* [CI]

This attribute specifies the set of data cells for which the current header cell provides header information. This attribute may be used in place of the headers attribute, particularly for simple tables. When specified, this attribute must have one of the following values:

- **row**: The current cell provides header information for the rest of the row that contains it (see also the section on table directionality).
- **col**: The current cell provides header information for the rest of the column that contains it.
- **rowgroup**: The header cell provides header information for the rest of the row group that contains it.
- **colgroup**: The header cell provides header information for the rest of the column group that contains it.

abbr = text [CS]

This attribute should be used to provide an abbreviated form of the cell's content, and may be rendered by user agents when appropriate in place of the cell's content. Abbreviated names should be short since user agents may render them repeatedly. For instance, speech synthesizers may render the abbreviated headers relating to a particular cell before rendering that cell's content.

axis = cdata [CI]

This attribute may be used to place a cell into conceptual categories that can be considered to form axes in an n-dimensional space. User agents may give users access to these categories (e.g., the user may query the user agent for all cells that belong to certain categories, the user agent may present a table in the form of a table of contents, etc.). Please consult the section on categorizing cells for more information. The value of this attribute is a comma-separated list of category names.

rowspan = number [CN]

This attribute specifies the number of rows spanned by the current cell. The default value of this attribute is one ("1"). The value zero ("0") means that the cell spans all rows from the current row to the last row of the table.

`colspan` = number [CN]

This attribute specifies the number of columns spanned by the current cell. The default value of this attribute is one ("1"). The value zero ("0") means that the cell spans all columns from the current column to the last column of the table.

`nowrap` [CI]

Deprecated. When present, this boolean attribute tells visual user agents to disable automatic text wrapping for this cell. Style sheets should be used instead of this attribute to achieve wrapping effects. Note. if used carelessly, this attribute may result in excessively wide cells.

`width` = pixels [CN]

Deprecated. This attribute supplies user agents with a recommended cell width.

`height` = pixels [CN]

Deprecated. This attribute supplies user agents with a recommended cell height.

Attributes defined elsewhere

- id, class (document-wide identifiers)
- lang (language information), dir (text direction)
- title (element title)
- style (inline style information)
- onclick, ondblclick, onmousedown, onmouseup, onmouseover, onmousemove, onmouseout, onkeypress, onkeydown, onkeyup (intrinsic events)
- bgcolor (background color)
- align, char, charoff, valign (cell alignment)

Table cells may contain two types of information: header information and data. This distinction enables user agents to render header and data cells distinctly, even in the absence of style sheets. For example, visual user agents may present header cell text with a bold font. Speech synthesizers may render header information with a distinct voice inflection.

The TH element defines a cell that contains header information. User agents have two pieces of header information available: the contents of the TH element and the value of the abbr attribute. User agents must render either the contents of the cell or the value of the abbr attribute. For visual media, the latter may be appropriate when there is insufficient space to render the full contents of the cell. For non-visual media abbr may be used as an abbreviation for table headers when these are rendered along with the contents of the cells to which they apply.

The headers and scope attributes also allow authors to help non-visual user agents process header information. Please consult the section on labeling cells for non-visual user agents for information and examples.

The TD element defines a cell that contains data.

Cells may be empty (i.e., contain no data). For example, the following table contains four columns of data, each headed by a column description.

```
<TABLE summary="This table charts the number of cups
                of coffee consumed by each senator, the type
                of coffee (decaf or regular), and whether
                taken with sugar."
<CAPTIONCups of coffee consumed by each senator</CAPTION
<TR
    <THName</TH
    <THCups</TH
    <THType of Coffee</TH
    <THSugar?</TH
<TR
    <TDT. Sexton</TD
    <TD10</TD
    <TDEspresso</TD
    <TDNo</TD
<TR
    <TDJ. Dinnen</TD
    <TD5</TD
    <TDDecaf</TD
    <TDYes</TD
</TABLE
```

A user agent rendering to a tty device might display this as follows:

```
Name            Cups        Type of Coffee      Sugar?
T. Sexton       10          Espresso            No
J. Dinnen       5           Decaf               Yes
```

Cells that span several rows or columns

Cells may span several rows or columns. The number of rows or columns spanned by a cell is set by the rowspan and colspan attributes for the TH and TD elements. In this table definition, we specify that the cell in row four, column two should span a total of three columns, including the current column.

```
<TABLE border="1"
<CAPTIONCups of coffee consumed by each senator</CAPTION
<TR<THName<THCups<THType of Coffee<THSugar?
<TR<TDT. Sexton<TD10<TDEspresso<TDNo
<TR<TDJ. Dinnen<TD5<TDDecaf<TDYes
<TR<TDA. Soria<TD colspan="3"<emNot available</em
</TABLE
```

This table might be rendered on a tty device by a visual user agent as follows:

```
Cups of coffee consumed by each senator
----------------------------------------
|    Name    |Cups|Type of Coffee |Sugar? |
----------------------------------------
|T. Sexton   |10  |Espresso       |No     |
----------------------------------------
|J. Dinnen   |5   |Decaf          |Yes    |
----------------------------------------
|A. Soria    |Not available              |
----------------------------------------
```

The next example illustrates (with the help of table borders) how cell definitions that span more than one row or column affect the definition of later cells. Consider the following table definition:

```
<TABLE border="1"
<TR<TD1  <TD rowspan="2"2  <TD3
<TR<TD4  <TD6
<TR<TD7  <TD8  <TD9
</TABLE
```

As cell "2" spans the first and second rows, the definition of the second row will take it into account. Thus, the second TD in row two actually defines the row's third cell. Visually, the table might be rendered to a tty device as:

```
 --------------
| 1 | 2 | 3 |
---- |   |----
| 4 |   | 6 |
---- |---|----
| 7 | 8 | 9 |
 --------------
```

while a graphical user agent might render this as:

Note that if the TD defining cell "6" had been omitted, an extra empty cell would have been added by the user agent to complete the row.

Similarly, in the following table definition:

```
<TABLE border="1"
<TR<TD1  <TD2  <TD3
<TR<TD colspan="2"4  <TD6
<TR<TD7  <TD8  <TD9
</TABLE
```

cell "4" spans two columns, so the second TD in the row actually defines the third cell ("6"):

```
 --------------
| 1 | 2 | 3 |
--------|----
| 4     | 6 |
--------|----
| 7 | 8 | 9 |
 --------------
```

A graphical user agent might render this as:

1	2	3
4		6
7	8	9

Defining overlapping cells is an error. User agents may vary in how they handle this error (e.g., rendering may vary). The following illegal example illustrates how one might create overlapping cells. In this table, cell "5" spans two rows and cell "7" spans two columns, so there is overlap in the cell between "7" and "9":

```
<TABLE border="1"
<TR<TD1 <TD2 <TD3
<TR<TD4 <TD rowspan="2"5 <TD6
<TR<TD colspan="2"7 <TD9
</TABLE
```

11.3 Table formatting by visual user agents

Note. *The following sections describe the HTML table attributes that concern visual formatting. Although style sheets will offer better control of visual table formatting, at the writing of this specification,* [CSS1] *did not offer mechanisms to control all aspects of visual table formatting.* HTML 4.0 includes mechanisms to control:

- border styles
- horizontal and vertical alignment of cell contents
- and cell margins

11.3.1 Borders and rules

The following attributes affect a table's external frame and internal rules. *Attribute definitions*

```
frame = void|above|below|hsides|lhs|rhs|vsides|box|border [CI]
```

This attribute specifies which sides of the frame that surrounds a table will be visible. Possible values:

- `void`: No sides. This is the default value.
- `above`: The top side only.
- `below`: The bottom side only.
- `hsides`: The top and bottom sides only.
- `vsides`: The right and left sides only.
- `lhs`: The left-hand side only.
- `rhs`: The right-hand side only.
- `box`: All four sides.
- `border`: All four sides.

`rules = none|groups|rows|cols|all [CI]`

This attribute specifies which rules will appear between cells within a table. The rendering of rules is user agent dependent. Possible values:

- none: No rules. This is the default value.
- groups: Rules will appear between row groups (see `THEAD`, `TFOOT`, and `TBODY`) and column groups (see `COLGROUP` and `COL`) only.
- rows: Rules will appear between rows only.
- cols: Rules will appear between columns only.
- all: Rules will appear between all rows and columns.

`border` = pixels [CN]

This attributes specifies the width (in pixels only) of the frame around a table (see the Note below for more information about this attribute).

To help distinguish the cells of a table, we can set the border attribute of the `TABLE` element. Consider a previous example:

```
<TABLE border="1"
       summary="This table charts the number of cups
```

```
                         of coffee consumed by each senator, the type
                         of coffee (decaf or regular), and whether
                         taken with sugar."
<CAPTIONCups of coffee consumed by each senator</CAPTION
<TR
    <THName</TH
    <THCups</TH
    <THType of Coffee</TH
    <THSugar?</TH
<TR
    <TDT. Sexton</TD
    <TD10</TD
    <TDEspresso</TD
    <TDNo</TD
<TR
    <TDJ. Dinnen</TD
    <TD5</TD
    <TDDecaf</TD
    <TDYes</TD
</TABLE
```

In the following example, the user agent should show borders five pixels thick on the left-hand and right-hand sides of the table, with rules drawn between each column.

```
<TABLE border="5" frame="vsides" rules="cols"
<TR <TD1 <TD2 <TD3
<TR <TD4 <TD5 <TD6
<TR <TD7 <TD8 <TD9
</TABLE
```

The following settings should be observed by user agents for backwards compatibility.

- Setting border="0" implies frame="void" and, unless otherwise specified, rules="none".

- Other values of border imply frame="border" and, unless otherwise specified, rules="all".

- The value "border" in the start tag of the TABLE element should be interpreted as the value of the frame attribute. It implies rules="all" and some default (non-zero) value for the border attribute.

For example, the following definitions are equivalent:

```
<TABLE border="2"
<TABLE border="2" frame="border" rules="all"
```

as are the following:

```
<TABLE border
<TABLE frame="border" rules="all"
```

Note. *The border attribute also defines the border behavior for the* OBJECT *and* IMG *elements, but takes different values for those elements.*

11.3.2 Horizontal and vertical alignment

The following attributes may be set for different table elements (see their definitions).

```
<!-- horizontal alignment attributes for cell contents -
<!ENTITY % cellhalign
  "align       (left|center|right|justify|char) #IMPLIED
   char        %Character;     #IMPLIED   -alignment char, e.g. char=':' -
   charoff     %Length;        #IMPLIED   -offset for alignment char -"

<!-- vertical alignment attributes for cell contents -
<!ENTITY % cellvalign
  "valign      (top|middle|bottom|baseline) #IMPLIED"
```

Attribute definitions

align = left|center|right|justify|char [CI]

This attribute specifies the alignment of data and the justification of text in a cell. Possible values:

- left: Left-flush data/Left-justify text. This is the default value for table data.
- center: Center data/Center-justify text. This is the default value for table headers.
- right: Right-flush data/Right-justify text.
- justify: Double-justify text.
- char: Align text around a specific character.

`valign = top|middle|bottom|baseline` [CI]

>This attribute specifies the vertical position of data within a cell. Possible values:
>- `top`: Cell data is flush with the top of the cell.
>- `middle`: Cell data is centered vertically within the cell. This is the default value.
>- `bottom`: Cell data is flush with the bottom of the cell.
>- `baseline`: All cells in the same row as a cell whose valign attribute has this value should have their textual data positioned so that the first text line occurs on a baseline common to all cells in the row. This constraint does not apply to subsequent text lines in these cells.

`char = character` [CN]

>This attribute specifies a single character within a text fragment to act as an axis for alignment. The default value for this attribute is the decimal point character for the current language as set by the lang attribute (e.g., the period (".") in English and the comma (",") in French). User agents are not required to support this attribute.

`charoff = length` [CN]

>When present, this attribute specifies the offset to the first occurrence of the alignment character on each line. If a line doesn't include the alignment character, it should be horizontally shifted to end at the alignment position.

When charoff is used to set the offset of an alignment character, the direction of offset is determined by the current text direction (set by the dir attribute). In left-to-right texts (the default), offset is from the left margin. In right-to-left texts, offset is from the right margin. User agents are not required to support this attribute. The table in this example aligns a row of currency values along a decimal point. We set the alignment character to "." explicitly.

```
<TABLE border="1"
<COLGROUP
<COL<COL align="char" char="."
<THEAD
<TR<THVegetable <THCost per kilo
<TBODY
<TR<TDLettuce        <TD$1
<TR<TDSilver carrots <TD$10.50
<TR<TDGolden turnips <TD$100.30
</TABLE
```

The formatted table may resemble the following:

```
---------------------------------
|   Vegetable    |Cost per kilo |
|----------------|------------- |
|Lettuce         |           $1 |
|----------------|------------- |
|Silver carrots  |       $10.50 |
|----------------|------------- |
|Golden turnips  |      $100.30 |
---------------------------------
```

When the contents of a cell contain more than one instance of the alignment character specified by char and the contents wrap, user agent behavior is undefined. Authors should therefore be attentive in their use of char. *Note. Visual user agents typically render TH elements vertically and horizontally centered within the cell and with a bold font weight.*

Inheritance of alignment specifications

The alignment of cell contents can be specified on a cell by cell basis, or inherited from enclosing elements, such as the row, column or the table itself.

The order of precedence (from highest to lowest) for the attributes align, char, and charoff is the following:

1. An alignment attribute set on an element within a cell's data (e.g., P).

2. An alignment attribute set on a cell (TH and TD).

3. An alignment attribute set on a column grouping element (COL and COLGROUP). When a cell is part of a multi-column span, the alignment property is inherited from the cell definition at the beginning of the span.

4. An alignment attribute set on a row or row grouping element (TR, THEAD, TFOOT, and TBODY). When a cell is part of a multi-row span, the alignment property is inherited from the cell definition at the beginning of the span.

5. An alignment attribute set on the table (TABLE).

6. The default alignment value.

The order of precedence (from highest to lowest) for the attribute valign (as well as the other inherited attributes lang, dir, and style) is the following:

1. An attribute set on an element within a cell's data (e.g., P).
2. An attribute set on a cell (TH and TD).
3. An attribute set on a row or row grouping element (TR, THEAD, TFOOT, and TBODY). When a cell is part of a multi-row span, the attribute value is inherited from the cell definition at the beginning of the span.
4. An attribute set on a column grouping element (COL and COLGROUP). When a cell is part of a multi-column span, the attribute value is inherited from the cell definition at the beginning of the span.
5. An attribute set on the table (TABLE).
6. The default attribute value.

Furthermore, when rendering cells, horizontal alignment is determined by columns in preference to rows, while for vertical alignment, rows are given preference over columns.

The default alignment for cells depends on the user agent. However, user agents should substitute the default attribute for the current directionality (i.e., not just "left" in all cases).

User agents that do not support the "justify" value of the align attribute should use the value of the inherited directionality in its place. ***Note.*** *Note that a cell may inherit an attribute not from its parent but from the first cell in a span. This is an exception to the general attribute inheritance rules.*

11.3.3 Cell margins

Attribute definitions

cellspacing = length [CN]

>This attribute specifies how much space the user agent should leave between the left side of the table and the left-hand side of the leftmost column, the top of the table and the top side of the topmost row, and so on for the right and bottom of the table. The attribute also specifies the amount of space to leave between cells.

`cellpadding` = length [CN]

This attribute specifies the amount of space between the border of the cell and its contents. If the value of this attribute is a pixel length, all four margins should be this distance from the contents. If the value of the attribute is a percentage length, the top and bottom margins should be equally separated from the content based on a percentage of the available vertical space, and the left and right margins should be equally separated from the content based on a percentage of the available horizontal space.

These two attributes control spacing between and within cells. The following illustration explains how they relate:

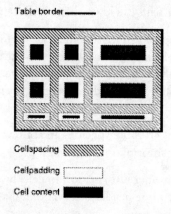

In the following example, the cellspacing attribute specifies that cells should be separated from each other and from the table frame by twenty pixels. The cellpadding attribute specifies that the top margin of the cell and the bottom margin of the cell will each be separated from the cell's contents by 10% of the available vertical space (the total being 20%). Similarly, the left margin of the cell and the right margin of the cell will each be separated from the cell's contents by 10% of the available horizontal space (the total being 20%).

```
<TABLE cellspacing="20" cellpadding="20%"
<TR <TDData1 <TDData2 <TDData3
</TABLE
```

If a table or given column has a fixed width, cellspacing and cellpadding may demand more space than assigned. User agents may give these attributes precedence over the width attribute when a conflict occurs, but are not required to.

11.4 Table rendering by non-visual user agents

11.4.1 Associating header information with data cells

Non-visual user agents such as speech synthesizers and Braille-based devices may use the following TD and TH element attributes to render table cells more intuitively:

- For a given data cell, the headers attribute lists which cells provide pertinent header information. For this purpose, each header cell must be named using the id attribute. Note that its not always possible to make a clean division of cells into headers or data. You should use the TD element for such cells together with the id or scope attributes as appropriate.

- For a given header cell, the scope attribute tells the user agent the data cells for which this header provides information. Authors may choose to use this attribute instead of headers according to which is more convenient; the two attributes fulfill the same function. The headers attribute is generally needed when headers are placed in irregular positions with respect to the data they apply to.

- The tables.html - adef-abbrabbr attribute specifies an abbreviated header for header cells so that user agents may render header information more rapidly.

In the following example, we assign header information to cells by setting the headers attribute. Each cell in the same column refers to the same header cell (via the id attribute).

```
<TABLE border="1"
       summary="This table charts the number of cups
                of coffee consumed by each senator, the type
                of coffee (decaf or regular), and whether
                taken with sugar."
<CAPTIONCups of coffee consumed by each senator</CAPTION
<TR
    <TH id="t1"Name</TH
    <TH id="t2"Cups</TH
    <TH id="t3" abbr="Type"Type of Coffee</TH
    <TH id="t4"Sugar?</TH
<TR
    <TD headers="t1"T. Sexton</TD
    <TD headers="t2"10</TD
```

```
        <TD headers="t3"Espresso</TD>
        <TD headers="t4"No</TD>
   <TR
        <TD headers="t1"J. Dinnen</TD>
        <TD headers="t2"5</TD>
        <TD headers="t3"Decaf</TD>
        <TD headers="t4"Yes</TD>
</TABLE>
```

A speech synthesizer might render this table as follows:

```
Caption: Cups of coffee consumed by each senator
Summary: This table charts the number of cups
         of coffee consumed by each senator, the type
         of coffee (decaf or regular), and whether
         taken with sugar.
Name: T. Sexton,    Cups: 10,    Type: Espresso,    Sugar: No
Name: J. Dinnen,    Cups: 5,     Type: Decaf,       Sugar: Yes
```

Note how the header "Type of Coffee" is abbreviated to "Type" using the abbr attribute. Here is the same example substituting the scope attribute for the headers attribute. Note the value "col" for the scope attribute, meaning "all cells in the current column":

```
<TABLE border="1"
       summary="This table charts the number of cups
                of coffee consumed by each senator, the type
                of coffee (decaf or regular), and whether
                taken with sugar."
<CAPTIONCups of coffee consumed by each senator</CAPTION>
<TR
    <TH scope="col"Name</TH>
    <TH scope="col"Cups</TH>
    <TH scope="col" abbr="Type"Type of Coffee</TH>
    <TH scope="col"Sugar?</TH>
<TR
    <TDT. Sexton</TD>
    <TD10</TD>
    <TDEspresso</TD>
    <TDNo</TD>
```

```
  <TR
    <TDJ. Dinnen</TD>
    <TD5</TD>
    <TDDecaf</TD>
    <TDYes</TD>
</TABLE>
```

Here's a somewhat more complex example illustrating other values for the scope attribute:

```
<TABLE border="1" cellpadding="5" cellspacing="2"
  summary="History courses offered in the community of
           Bath arranged by course name, tutor, summary,
           code, and fee"
  <TR
    <TH colspan="5" scope="colgroup"Community Courses—Bath Autumn 1997</TH>
  </TR
  <TR
    <TH scope="col" abbr="Name"Course Name</TH>
    <TH scope="col" abbr="Tutor"Course Tutor</TH>
    <TH scope="col"Summary</TH>
    <TH scope="col"Code</TH>
    <TH scope="col"Fee</TH>
  </TR
  <TR
    <TD scope="row"After the Civil War</TD>
    <TDDr. John Wroughton</TD>
    <TD
        The course will examine the turbulent years in England
        after 1646. <EM6 weekly meetings starting Monday 13th
        October.</EM
    </TD>
    <TDH27</TD>
    <TD&pound;32</TD>
  </TR
  <TR
    <TD scope="row"An Introduction to Anglo-Saxon England</TD>
    <TDMark Cottle</TD>
    <TD
```

```
            One day course introducing the early medieval
            period reconstruction the Anglo-Saxons and
            their society. <EMSaturday 18th October.</EM
        </TD>
        <TDH28</TD>
        <TD&pound;18</TD>
    </TR>
    <TR
        <TD scope="row"The Glory that was Greece</TD>
        <TDValerie Lorenz</TD>
        <TD
         Birthplace of democracy, philosophy, heartland of theater, home of
         argument. The Romans may have done it but the Greeks did it
         first. <EMSaturday day school 25th October 1997</EM
        </TD>
        <TDH30</TD>
        <TD&pound;18</TD>
    </TR>
</TABLE>
```

A graphical user agent might render this as:

Community Courses -- Bath Autumn 1997					
Course Name	Course Tutor	Summary	Code	Fee
After the Civil War	Dr. John Wroughton	The course will examine the turbulent years in England after 1646. *6 weekly meetings starting Monday 13th October.*	H27	£32
An Introduction to Anglo-Saxon England	Mark Cottle	One day course introducing the early medieval period reconstruction the Anglo-Saxons and their society. *Saturday 18th October.*	H28	£18
The Glory that was Greece	Valerie Lorenz	Birthplace of democracy, philosophy, heartland of theater, home of argument. The Romans may have done it but the Greeks did it first. *Saturday day school 25th October 1997*	H30	£18

Note the use of the scope attribute with the "row" value. Although the first cell in each row contains data, not header information, the scope attribute makes the data cell behave like a row header cell. This allows speech synthesizers to provide the relevant course name upon request or to state it immediately before each cell's content.

11.4.2 Categorizing cells

Users browsing a table with a speech-based user agent may wish to hear an explanation of a cell's contents in addition to the contents themselves. One way the user might provide an explanation is by speaking associated header information before speaking the data cell's contents (see the section on associating header information with data cells).

Users may also want information about more than one cell, in which case header information provided at the cell level (by headers, scope, and abbr) may not provide adequate context. Consider the following table, which classifies expenses for meals, hotels, and transport in two locations (San Jose and Seattle) over several days:

Users might want to extract information from the table in the form of queries:

- "What did I spend for all my meals?"
- "What did I spend for meals on 25 August?"
- "What did I spend for all expenses in San Jose?"

Each query involves a computation by the user agent that may involve zero or more cells. In order to determine, for example, the costs of meals on 25 August, the user agent must know which table cells refer to "Meals" (all of them) and which refer to "Dates" (specifically, 25 August), and find the intersection of the two sets.

To accommodate this type of query, the HTML 4.0 table model allows authors to place cell headers and data into categories. For example, for the travel expense table, an author could group the header cells "San Jose" and "Seattle" into the category "Location", the headers "Meals", "Hotels", and "Transport" in the category "Expenses", and the four days into the category "Date". The previous three questions would then have the following meanings:

- "What did I spend for all my meals?" means "What are all the data cells in the "Expenses=Meals" category?
- "What did I spend for meals on 25 August?" means "What are all the data cells in the "Expenses=Meals" and "Date=Aug-25-1997" categories?

- "What did I spend for all expenses in San Jose?" means "What are all the data cells in the "Expenses=Meals, Hotels, Transport" and "Location=San Jose" categories?

Authors categorize a header or data cell by setting the axis attribute for the cell. For instance, in the travel expense table, the cell containing the information "San Jose" could be placed in the "Location" category as follows:

```
<TH id="a6" axis="location"San Jose</TH>
```

Any cell containing information related to "San Jose" should refer to this header cell via either the headers or the scope attribute. Thus, meal expenses for 25-Aug-1997 should be marked up to refer to id attribute (whose value here is "a6") of the "San Jose" header cell:

```
<TD headers="a6"37.74</TD>
```

Each headers attribute provides a list of id references. Authors may thus categorize a given cell in any number of ways (or, along any number of "headers", hence the name).

Below we mark up the travel expense table with category information:

```
<TABLE border="1"
          summary="This table summarizes travel expenses
                   incurred during August trips to
                   San Jose and Seattle"
<CAPTION
  Travel Expense Report
</CAPTION>
<TR
  <TH</TH
  <TH id="a2" axis="expenses"Meals</TH
  <TH id="a3" axis="expenses"Hotels</TH
  <TH id="a4" axis="expenses"Transport</TH
  <TDsubtotals</TD
</TR
<TR
  <TH id="a6" axis="location"San Jose</TH
  <TH</TH
  <TH</TH
  <TH</TH
  <TD</TD
```

```
    </TR>
    <TR
      <TD id="a7" axis="date"25-Aug-97</TD
      <TD headers="a6 a7 a2"37.74</TD
      <TD headers="a6 a7 a3"112.00</TD
      <TD headers="a6 a7 a4"45.00</TD
      <TD</TD
    </TR
    <TR
      <TD id="a8" axis="date"26-Aug-97</TD
      <TD headers="a6 a8 a2"27.28</TD
      <TD headers="a6 a8 a3"112.00</TD
      <TD headers="a6 a8 a4"45.00</TD
      <TD</TD
    </TR
    <TR
      <TDsubtotals</TD
      <TD65.02</TD
      <TD224.00</TD
      <TD90.00</TD
      <TD379.02</TD
    </TR
    <TR
      <TH id="a10" axis="location"Seattle</TH
      <TH</TH
      <TH</TH
      <TH</TH
      <TD</TD
    </TR
    <TR
      <TD id="a11" axis="date"27-Aug-97</TD
      <TD headers="a10 a11 a2"96.25</TD
      <TD headers="a10 a11 a3"109.00</TD
      <TD headers="a10 a11 a4"36.00</TD
      <TD</TD
    </TR
    <TR
```

```
    <TD id="a12" axis="date"28-Aug-97</TD>
    <TD headers="a10 a12 a2"35.00</TD>
    <TD headers="a10 a12 a3"109.00</TD>
    <TD headers="a10 a12 a4"36.00</TD>
    <TD</TD>
  </TR>
  <TR
    <TDsubtotals</TD>
    <TD131.25</TD>
    <TD218.00</TD>
    <TD72.00</TD>
    <TD421.25</TD>
  </TR>
  <TR
    <THTotals</TH>
    <TD196.27</TD>
    <TD442.00</TD>
    <TD162.00</TD>
    <TD800.27</TD>
  </TR>
  </TABLE>
```

Note that marking up the table this way also allows user agents to avoid confusing the user with unwanted information. For instance, if a speech synthesizer were to speak all of the figures in the "Meals" column of this table in response to the query "What were all my meal expenses?", a user would not be able to distinguish a day's expenses from subtotals or totals. By carefully categorizing cell data, authors allow user agents to make important semantic distinctions when rendering.

Of course, there is no limit to how authors may categorize information in a table. In the travel expense table, for example, we could add the additional categories "subtotals" and "totals".

This specification does not require user agents to handle information provided by the axis attribute, nor does it make any recommendations about how user agents may present axis information to users or how users may query the user agent about this information.

However, user agents, particularly speech synthesizers, may want to factor out information common to several cells that are the result of a query. For instance, if the user asks "What did I spend for meals in San Jose?", the user agent would first determine the cells in question (25-Aug-1997: 37.74, 26-Aug-1997:27.28), then render this information. A user agent speaking this information might read it:

```
Location: San Jose. Date: 25-Aug-1997. Expenses, Meals: 37.74
Location: San Jose. Date: 26-Aug-1997. Expenses, Meals: 27.28
```

or, more compactly:

```
San Jose, 25-Aug-1997, Meals: 37.74
San Jose, 26-Aug-1997, Meals: 27.28
```

An even more economical rendering would factor the common information and reorder it:

```
San Jose, Meals, 25-Aug-1997: 37.74
                 26-Aug-1997: 27.28
```

User agents that support this type of rendering should allow user agents a means to customize rendering (e.g., through style sheets).

11.4.3 Algorithm to find heading information

In the absence of header information from either the scope or headers attribute, user agents may construct header information according to the following algorithm. The goal of the algorithm is to find an ordered list of headers. (In the following description of the algorithm the table directionality is assumed to be left-to-right.)

- First, search left from the cell's position to find row header cells. Then search upwards to find column header cells. The search in a given direction stops when the edge of the table is reached or when a data cell is found after a header cell.

- Row headers are inserted into the list in the order they appear in the table. For left-to-right tables, headers are inserted from left to right.

- Column headers are inserted after row headers, in the order they appear in the table, from top to bottom.

- If a header cell has the headers attribute set, then the headers referenced by this attribute are inserted into the list and the search stops for the current direction.

- TD cells that set the axis attribute are also treated as header cells.

11.5 Sample table

This sample illustrates grouped rows and columns. The example is adapted from "Developing International Software", by Nadine Kano. In "ascii art", the following table:

```
<TABLE border="2" frame="hsides" rules="groups"
         summary="Code page support in different versions
                  of MS Windows."
<CAPTIONCODE-PAGE SUPPORT IN MICROSOFT WINDOWS</CAPTION
<COLGROUP align="center"
<COLGROUP align="left"
<COLGROUP align="center" span="2"
<COLGROUP align="center" span="3"
<THEAD valign="top"
<TR
<THCode-Page<BRID
<THName
<THACP
<THOEMCP
<THWindows<BRNT 3.1
<THWindows<BRNT 3.51
<THWindows<BR95
<TBODY
<TR<TD1200<TDUnicode (BMP of ISO/IEC-10646)<TD<TD<TDX<TDX<TD*
<TR<TD1250<TDWindows 3.1 Eastern European<TDX<TD<TDX<TDX<TDX
<TR<TD1251<TDWindows 3.1 Cyrillic<TDX<TD<TDX<TDX<TDX
<TR<TD1252<TDWindows 3.1 US (ANSI)<TDX<TD<TDX<TDX<TDX
<TR<TD1253<TDWindows 3.1 Greek<TDX<TD<TDX<TDX<TDX
<TR<TD1254<TDWindows 3.1 Turkish<TDX<TD<TDX<TDX<TDX
<TR<TD1255<TDHebrew<TDX<TD<TD<TD<TDX
<TR<TD1256<TDArabic<TDX<TD<TD<TD<TDX
<TR<TD1257<TDBaltic<TDX<TD<TD<TD<TDX
<TR<TD1361<TDKorean (Johab)<TDX<TD<TD<TD**<TDX
<TBODY
<TR<TD437<TDMS-DOS United States<TD<TDX<TDX<TDX<TDX
<TR<TD708<TDArabic (ASMO 708)<TD<TDX<TD<TD<TDX
<TR<TD709<TDArabic (ASMO 449+, BCON V4)<TD<TDX<TD<TD<TDX
```

```
<TR<TD710<TDArabic (Transparent Arabic)<TD<TDX<TD<TD<TDX
<TR<TD720<TDArabic (Transparent ASMO)<TD<TDX<TD<TD<TDX
</TABLE
```

would be rendered something like this:

```
                    CODE-PAGE SUPPORT IN MICROSOFT WINDOWS

===============================================================================
Code-Page | Name                             | ACP  OEMCP | Windows Windows Windows
    ID    |                                  |            | NT 3.1  NT 3.51    95
----------|----------------------------------|------------|-------------------------
   1200   | Unicode (BMP of ISO 10646)       |            |   X       X        *
   1250   | Windows 3.1 Eastern European     |  X         |   X       X        X
   1251   | Windows 3.1 Cyrillic             |  X         |   X       X        X
   1252   | Windows 3.1 US (ANSI)            |  X         |   X       X        X
   1253   | Windows 3.1 Greek                |  X         |   X       X        X
   1254   | Windows 3.1 Turkish              |  X         |   X       X        X
   1255   | Hebrew                           |  X         |                    X
   1256   | Arabic                           |  X         |                    X
   1257   | Baltic                           |  X         |                    X
   1361   | Korean (Johab)                   |  X         |          **        X
----------|----------------------------------|------------|-------------------------
    437   | MS-DOS United States             |      X     |   X       X        X
    708   | Arabic (ASMO 708)                |      X     |                    X
    709   | Arabic (ASMO 449+, BCON V4)      |      X     |                    X
    710   | Arabic (Transparent Arabic)      |      X     |                    X
    720   | Arabic (Transparent ASMO)        |      X     |                    X
===============================================================================
```

A graphical user agent might render this as:

CODE-PAGE SUPPORT IN MICROSOFT WINDOWS						
Code-Page ID	Name	ACP	OEMCP	Windows NT 3.1	Windows NT 3.51	Windows 95
1200	Unicode (BMP of ISO/IEC-10646)			X	X	*
1250	Windows 3.1 Eastern European	X		X	X	X
1251	Windows 3.1 Cyrillic	X		X	X	X
1252	Windows 3.1 US (ANSI)	X		X	X	X
1253	Windows 3.1 Greek	X		X	X	X
1254	Windows 3.1 Turkish	X		X	X	X
1255	Hebrew	X				X
1256	Arabic	X				X
1257	Baltic	X				X
1361	Korean (Johab)	X			**	X
437	MS-DOS United States		X	X	X	X
708	Arabic (ASMO 708)		X			X
709	Arabic (ASMO 449+, BCON V4)		X			X
710	Arabic (Transparent Arabic)		X			X
720	Arabic (Transparent ASMO)		X			X

This example illustrates how COLGROUP can be used to group columns and set the default column alignment. Similarly, TBODY is used to group rows. The frame and rules attributes tell the user agent which borders and rules to render.

Chapter 12
Links

Contents

1. Introduction to links and anchors
   1. Visiting a linked resource
   2. Other link relationships
   3. Specifying anchors and links
   4. Link titles
   5. Internationalization and links
2. The `A` element
   1. Syntax of anchor names
   2. Nested links are illegal
   3. Anchors with the `id` attribute
   4. Unavailable and unidentifiable resources
3. Document relationships: the `LINK` element
   1. Forward and reverse links
   2. Links and external style sheets
   3. Links and search engines
4. Path information: the `BASE` element
   1. Resolving relative URIs

12.1 Introduction to links and anchors

HTML offers many of the conventional publishing idioms for rich text and structured documents, but what separates it from most other markup languages is its features for hypertext and interactive documents. This section introduces the *link* (or hyperlink, or Web link), the basic hypertext construct. A link is a connection from one Web resource to another. Although a simple concept, the link has been one of the primary forces driving the success of the Web.

A link has two ends—called anchors—and a direction. The link starts at the "source" anchor and points to the "destination" anchor, which may be any Web resource (e.g., an image, a video clip, a sound bite, a program, an HTML document, an element within an HTML document, etc.).

12.1.1 Visiting a linked resource

The default behavior associated with a link is the retrieval of another Web resource. This behavior is commonly and implicitly obtained by selecting the link (e.g., by clicking, through keyboard input, etc.).

The following HTML excerpt contains two links, one whose destination anchor is an HTML document named "chapter2.html" and the other whose destination anchor is a GIF image in the file "forest.gif":

```
<BODY>
...some text...
<P>You'll find a lot more in  <A href="chapter2.html">chapter two</A>.
See also this <A href="../images/forest.gif">map of the enchanted forest.</A>
</BODY>
```

By activating these links (by clicking with the mouse, through keyboard input, voice commands, etc.), users may visit these resources. Note that the href attribute in each source anchor specifies the address of the destination anchor with a URI.

The destination anchor of a link may be an element within an HTML document. The destination anchor must be given an anchor name and any URI addressing this anchor must include the name as its fragment identifier.

Destination anchors in HTML documents may be specified either by the A element (naming it with the name attribute), or by any other element (naming with the id attribute).

Thus, for example, an author might create a table of contents whose entries link to header elements H2, H3, etc., in the same document. Using the A element to create destination anchors, we would write:

```
<H1>Table of Contents</H1>
<P><A href="#section1">Introduction</A><BR>
<A href="#section2">Some background</A><BR>
<A href="#section2.1">On a more personal note</A><BR>
...the rest of the table of contents...
...the document body...
```

```
<H2><A name="section1">Introduction</A></H2>
...section 1...
<H2><A name="section2">Some background</A></H2>
...section 2...
<H3><A name="section2.1">On a more personal note</A></H3>
...section 2.1...
```

We may achieve the same effect by making the header elements themselves the anchors:

```
<H1>Table of Contents</H1>
<P><A href="#section1">Introduction</A><BR>
<A href="#section2">Some background</A><BR>
<A href="#section2.1">On a more personal note</A><BR>
...the rest of the table of contents...
...the document body...
<H2 id="section1">Introduction</H2>
...section 1...
<H2 id="section2">Some background</H2>
...section 2...
<H3 id="section2.1">On a more personal note</H3>
...section 2.1...
```

12.1.2 Other link relationships

By far the most common use of a link is to retrieve another Web resource, as illustrated in the previous examples. However, authors may insert links in their documents that express other relationships between resources than simply "activate this link to visit that related resource". Links that express other types of relationships have one or more link types specified in their source anchor.

The *roles* of a link defined by A or LINK are specified via the rel and rev attributes.

For instance, links defined by the LINK element may describe the position of a document within a series of documents. In the following excerpt, links within the document entitled "Chapter 5" point to the previous and next chapters:

```
<HEAD>
...other head information...
<TITLE>Chapter 5</TITLE>
<LINK rel="prev" href="chapter4.html">
```

```
<LINK rel="next" href="chapter6.html">
</HEAD>
```

The link type of the first link is "prev" and that of the second is "next" (two of several recognized link types). Links specified by LINK are **not** rendered with the document's contents, although user agents may render them in other ways (e.g., as navigation tools).

Even if they are not used for navigation, these links may be interpreted in interesting ways. For example, a user agent that prints a series of HTML documents as a single document may use this link information as the basis of forming a coherent linear document. Further information is given below of using links for the benefit of search engines

12.1.3 Specifying anchors and links

Although several HTML elements and attributes create links to other resources (e.g., the IMG element, the FORM element, etc.), this chapter discusses links and anchors created by the LINK and A elements. The LINK element may only appear in the head of a document. The A element may only appear in the body.

When the A element's href attribute is set, the element defines a source anchor for a link that may be activated by the user to retrieve a Web resource. The source anchor is the location of the A instance and the destination anchor is the Web resource.

The retrieved resource may be handled by the user agent in several ways: by opening a new HTML document in the same user agent window, opening a new HTML document in a different window, starting a new program to handle the resource, etc. Since the A element has content (text, images, etc.), user agents may render this content in such a way as to indicate the presence of a link (e.g., by underlining the content).

When the name or id attributes of the A element are set, the element defines an anchor that may be the destination of other links.

Authors may set the name and href attributes simultaneously in the same A instance.

The LINK element defines a relationship between the current document and another resource. Although LINK has no content, the relationships it defines may be rendered by some user agents.

12.1.4 Link titles

The title attribute may be set for both A and LINK to add information about the nature of a link. This information may be spoken by a user agent, rendered as a tool tip, cause a change in cursor image, etc.

Thus, we may augment a previous example by supplying a title for each link:

```
<BODY>
...some text...
<P>You'll find a lot more in <A href="chapter2.html"
        title="Go to chapter two">chapter two</A>.
<A href="./chapter2.html"
        title="Get chapter two.">chapter two</A>.
See also this <A href="../images/forest.gif"
        title="GIF image of enchanted forest">map of
the enchanted forest.</A>
</BODY>
```

12.1.5 Internationalization and links

Since links may point to documents encoded with different character encodings, the A and LINK elements support the charset attribute. This attribute allows authors to advise user agents about the encoding of data at the other end of the link.

The hreflang attribute provides user agents with information about the language of a resource at the end of a link, just as the lang attribute provides information about the language of an element's content or attribute values.

Armed with this additional knowledge, user agents should be able to avoid presenting "garbage" to the user. Instead, they may either locate resources necessary for the correct presentation of the document or, if they cannot locate the resources, they should at least warn the user that the document will be unreadable and explain the cause.

12.2 The A element

```
<!ELEMENT A - - (%inline;)* -(A)         -anchor ->
<!ATTLIST A
```

```
%attrs;                              -%coreattrs, %i18n, %events -
charset     %Charset;       #IMPLIED -char encoding of linked resource -
type        %ContentType;   #IMPLIED -advisory content type -
name        CDATA           #IMPLIED -named link end -
href        %URI;           #IMPLIED -URI for linked resource -
hreflang    %LanguageCode;  #IMPLIED - language code -
rel         %LinkTypes;     #IMPLIED - forward link types -
rev         %LinkTypes;     #IMPLIED - reverse link types -
accesskey   %Character;     #IMPLIED - accessibility key character -
shape       %Shape;         rect     - for use with client-side image maps -
coords      %Coords;        #IMPLIED - for use with client-side image maps -
tabindex    NUMBER          #IMPLIED - position in tabbing order -
onfocus     %Script;        #IMPLIED - the element got the focus -
onblur      %Script;        #IMPLIED - the element lost the focus -
>
```

*Start tag: **required**, End tag: **required***

Attribute definitions

name = *cdata* [CS]

This attribute names the current anchor so that it may be the destination of another link. The value of this attribute must be a unique anchor name. The scope of this name is the current document. Note that this attribute shares the same name space as the id attribute.

href = *uri* [CT]

This attribute specifies the location of a Web resource, thus defining a link between the current element (the source anchor) and the destination anchor defined by this attribute.

hreflang = *langcode* [CI]

This attribute specifies the base language of the resource designated by href and may only be used when href is specified.

type = *content-type* [CI]

When present, this attribute specifies the content type of a piece of content, for example, the result of dereferencing a URI. Content types are defined in [MIMETYPES].

rel = *link-types* [CI]

> This attribute describes the relationship from the current document to the anchor specified by the href attribute. The value of this attribute is a space-separated list of link types.

rev = *link-types* [CI]

> This attribute is used to describe a reverse link from the anchor specified by the href attribute to the current document. The value of this attribute is a space-separated list of link types.

charset = *charset* [CI]

> This attribute specifies the character encoding of the resource designated by the link. Please consult the section on character encodings for more details.

Attributes defined elsewhere

- id, class (document-wide identifiers)
- lang (language information), dir (text direction)
- title (element title)
- style (inline style information)
- shape and coords (image maps)
- onfocus, onblur, onclick, ondblclick, onmousedown, onmouseup, onmouseover, onmousemove, onmouseout, onkeypress, onkeydown, onkeyup (intrinsic events)
- target (target frame information)
- tabindex (tabbing navigation)
- accesskey (access keys)

Each A element defines an anchor

1. The A element's content defines the position of the anchor.
2. The name attribute names the anchor so that it may be the destination of zero or more links (see also anchors with `id`).
3. The href attribute makes this anchor the source anchor of exactly one link.

Authors may also create an A element that specifies no anchors, i.e., that doesn't specify href, name, or id. Values for these attributes may be set at a later time through scripts.

In the example that follows, the A element defines a link. The source anchor is the text "W3C Web site" and the destination anchor is "http://www.w3.org/":

```
For more information about W3C, please consult the
<A href="http://www.w3.org/">W3C Web site</A>.
```

This link designates the home page of the World Wide Web Consortium. When a user activates this link in a user agent, the user agent will retrieve the resource, in this case, an HTML document.

User agents generally render links in such a way as to make them obvious to users (underlining, reverse video, etc.). The exact rendering depends on the user agent. Rendering may vary according to whether the user has already visited the link or not. A possible visual rendering of the previous link might be:

```
For more information about W3C, please consult the W3C Web site.
                                                    ~~~~~~~~~~~~
```

To tell user agents explicitly what the character encoding of the destination page is, set the charset attribute:

```
For more information about W3C, please consult the
<A href="http://www.w3.org/" charset="ISO-8859-1">W3C Web site</A>
```

Suppose we define an anchor named "anchor-one" in the file "one.html".

```
...text before the anchor...
<A name="anchor-one">This is the location of anchor one.</A>
...text after the anchor...
```

This creates an anchor around the text "This is the location of anchor one.". Usually, the contents of A are not rendered in any special way when A defines an anchor only.

Having defined the anchor, we may link to it from the same or another document. URIs that designate anchors contain a "#" character followed by the anchor name (the fragment identifier). Here are some examples of such URIs:

- An absolute URI: `http://www.mycompany.com/one.html#anchor-one`

- A relative URI: `./one.html#anchor-one` or `one.html#anchor-one`

- When the link is defined in the same document: `#anchor-one`

Thus, a link defined in the file "two.html" in the same directory as "one.html" would refer to the anchor as follows:

```
...text before the link...
For more information, please consult <A href="./one.html#anchor-one"> anchor
one</A>.
...text after the link...
```

The A element in the following example specifies a link (with href) and creates a named anchor (with name) simultaneously:

```
I just returned from vacation! Here's a
<A name="anchor-two"
    href="http://www.somecompany.com/People/Ian/vacation/family.png">
photo of my family at the lake.</A>.
```

This example contains a link to a different type of Web resource (a PNG image). Activating the link should cause the image resource to be retrieved from the Web (and possibly displayed if the system has been configured to do so).

Note. *User agents should be able to find anchors created by empty A elements, but some fail to do so. For example, some user agents may not find the "empty-anchor" in the following HTML fragment:*

```
<A name="empty-anchor"></A>
<EM>...some HTML...</EM>
<A href="#empty-anchor">Link to empty anchor</A>
```

12.2.1 Syntax of anchor names

An anchor name is the value of either the name or id attribute when used in the context of anchors. Anchor names must observe the following rules:

- **Uniqueness:** Anchor names must be unique within a document. Anchor names that differ only in case may not appear in the same document.
- **String matching:** Comparisons between fragment identifiers and anchor names must be done by exact (case-sensitive) match.

Thus, the following example is correct with respect to string matching and must be considered a match by user agents:

```
<P><A href="#xxx">...</A>
...more document...
<P><A name="xxx">...</A>
```

ILLEGAL EXAMPLE:
The following example is illegal with respect to uniqueness since the two names are the same except for case:

```
<P><A name="xxx">...</A>
<P><A name="XXX">...</A>
```

Although the following excerpt is legal HTML, the behavior of the user agent is not defined; some user agents may (incorrectly) consider this a match and others may not.

```
<P><A href="#xxx">...</A>
...more document...
<P><A name="XXX">...</A>
```

Anchor names should be restricted to ASCII characters. Please consult the appendix for more information about non-ASCII characters in URI attribute values.

12.2.2 Nested links are illegal

Links and anchors defined by the A element must not be nested; an A element must not contain any other A elements.

Since the DTD defines `LINK` element to be empty, `LINK` elements may not be nested either.

12.2.3 Anchors with the `id` attribute

The id attribute may be used to create an anchor at the start tag of any element (including the A element).

This example illustrates the use of the id attribute to position an anchor in an H2 element. The anchor is linked to via the A element.

```
You may read more about this in <A href="#section2">Section Two</A>.
...later in the document
<H2 id="section2">Section Two</H2>
...later in the document
```

```
<P>Please refer to <A href="#section2">Section Two</A> above
for more details.
```

The following example names a destination anchor with the id attribute:

```
I just returned from vacation! Here's a
<A id="anchor-two">photo of my family at the lake.</A>.
```

The id and name attributes share the same name space. This means that they cannot both define an anchor with the same name in the same document.

ILLEGAL EXAMPLE:
The following excerpt is illegal HTML since these attributes declare the same name twice in the same document.

```
<A href="#a1">...</A>
...
<H1 id="a1">
...pages and pages...
<A name="a1"></A>
```

Because of its specification in the HTML DTD, the name attribute may contain character references. Thus, the value Dürst is a valid name attribute value, as is Dürst . The id attribute, on the other hand, may not contain character references.

Use id *or* name? *Authors should consider the following issues when deciding whether to use* id *or* name *for an anchor name:*

- *The* id *attribute can act as more than just an anchor name (e.g., style sheet selector, processing identifier, etc.).*

- *Some older user agents don't support anchors created with the* id *attribute.*

- *The* name *attribute allows richer anchors names (with* entities*).*

12.2.4 Unavailable and unidentifiable resources

A reference to an unavailable or unidentifiable resource is an error. Although user agents may vary in how they handle such an error, we recommend the following behavior:

- If a user agent cannot locate a linked resource, it should alert the user.

- If a user agent cannot identify the type of a linked resource, it should still attempt to process it. It should alert the user and may allow the user to intervene and identify the document type.

12.3 Document relationships: the `LINK` element

```
<!ELEMENT LINK - O EMPTY              -- a media-independent link -->
<!ATTLIST LINK
  %attrs;                             -- %coreattrs, %i18n, %events --
  charset     %Charset;      #IMPLIED --char encoding of linked resource --
  href        %URI;          #IMPLIED --URI for linked resource --
  hreflang    %LanguageCode; #IMPLIED --language code --
  type        %ContentType;  #IMPLIED --advisory content type --
  rel         %LinkTypes;    #IMPLIED --forward link types --
  rev         %LinkTypes;    #IMPLIED --reverse link types --
  media       %MediaDesc;    #IMPLIED --for rendering on these media --
  >
```

*Start tag: **required**, End tag: **forbidden***

Attributes defined elsewhere

- id, class (document-wide identifiers)
- lang (language information), dir (text direction)
- title (element title)
- style (inline style information)
- onclick, ondblclick, onmousedown, onmouseup, onmouseover, onmousemove, onmouseout, onkeypress, onkeydown, onkeyup (intrinsic events)
- href, hreflang, type, rel, rev (links and anchors)
- target (target frame information)
- media (header style information)
- charset(character encodings)

This element defines a link. Unlike A, it may only appear in the HEAD section of a document, although it may appear any number of times. Although LINK has no content, it conveys relationship information that may be rendered by user agents in a variety of ways (e.g., a tool-bar with a drop-down menu of links).

This example illustrates how several LINK definitions may appear in the HEAD section of a document. The current document is "Chapter2.html". The rel attribute specifies the relationship of the linked document with the current document. The values "Index", "Next", and "Prev" are explained in the section on link types.

```
<!DOCTYPE HTML PUBLIC "-//W3C//DTD HTML 4.0//EN"
   "http://www.w3.org/TR/REC-html40/strict.dtd">
<HTML>
<HEAD>
  <TITLE>Chapter 2</TITLE>
  <LINK rel="Index" href="../index.html">
  <LINK rel="Next"  href="Chapter3.html">
  <LINK rel="Prev"  href="Chapter1.html">
</HEAD>
...the rest of the document...
```

12.3.1 Forward and reverse links

The rel and rev attributes play complementary roles—the rel attribute specifies a forward link and the rev attribute specifies a reverse link.

Consider two documents A and B.

```
Document A:         <LINK href="docB" rel="foo">
```

Has exactly the same meaning as:

```
Document B:         <LINK href="docA" rev="foo">
```

Both attributes may be specified simultaneously.

12.3.2 Links and external style sheets

When the LINK element links an external style sheet to a document, the type attribute specifies the style sheet language and the media attribute specifies the intended rendering medium or media. User agents may save time by retrieving from the network only those style sheets that apply to the current device.

Media types are further discussed in the section on style sheets.

12.3.3 Links and search engines

Authors may use the LINK element to provide a variety of information to search engines, including:

- Links to alternate versions of a document, written in another human language.
- Links to alternate versions of a document, designed for different media, for instance a version especially suited for printing.
- Links to the starting page of a collection of documents.

The examples below illustrate how language information, media types, and link types may be combined to improve document handling by search engines.

In the following example, we use the hreflang attribute to tell search engines where to find Dutch, Portuguese, and Arabic versions of a document. Note the use of the dir and charset attributes for the Arabic manual, and the use of the lang attribute to indicate that the value of the title attribute for the LINK element designating the French manual is in French.

```
<HEAD>
<TITLE>The manual in English</TITLE>
<LINK title="The manual in Dutch"
      type="text/html"
      rel="alternate"
      hreflang="nl"
      href="http://someplace.com/manual/dutch.html">
<LINK title="The manual in Portuguese"
      type="text/html"
      rel="alternate"
      hreflang="pt"
      href="http://someplace.com/manual/portuguese.html">
<LINK title="The manual in Arabic"
      dir="rtl"
      type="text/html"
      rel="alternate"
      charset="ISO-8859-6"
      hreflang="ar"
      href="http://someplace.com/manual/arabic.html">
<LINK lang="fr" title="La documentation en Fran&ccedil;ais"
      type="text/html"
```

```
        rel="alternate"
        hreflang="fr"
        href="http://someplace.com/manual/french.html">
</HEAD>
```

In the following example, we tell search engines where to find the printed version of a manual.

```
<HEAD>
<TITLE>Reference manual</TITLE>
<LINK media="print" title="The manual in postscript"
        type="application/postscript"
        rel="alternate"
        href="http://someplace.com/manual/postscript.ps">
</HEAD>
```

In the following example, we tell search engines where to find the front page of a collection of documents.

```
<HEAD>
<TITLE>Reference manual—Page 5</TITLE>
<LINK rel="Start" title="The first page of the manual"
        type="text/html"
        href="http://someplace.com/manual/start.html">
</HEAD>
```

Further information is given in the notes in the appendix on helping search engines index your Web site.

12.4 Path information: the BASE element

```
<!ELEMENT BASE - O EMPTY             —document base URI —>
<!ATTLIST BASE
  href          %URI;         #REQUIRED—URI that acts as base URI —
  >
```

Start tag: **required**, End tag: **forbidden**

Attribute definitions

href = *uri* [CT]

This attribute specifies an absolute URI that acts as the base URI for resolving relative URIs.

Attributes defined elsewhere

- target (target frame information)

In HTML, links and references to external images, applets, form-processing programs, style sheets, etc. are always specified by a URI. Relative URIs are resolved according to a base URI, which may come from a variety of sources. The BASE element allows authors to specify a document's base URI explicitly.

When present, the BASE element must appear in the HEAD section of an HTML document, before any element that refers to an external source. The path information specified by the BASE element only affects URIs in the document where the element appears.

For example, given the following BASE declaration and A declaration:

```
<!DOCTYPE HTML PUBLIC "-//W3C//DTD HTML 4.0//EN"
    "http://www.w3.org/TR/REC-html40/strict.dtd">
<HTML>
 <HEAD>
    <TITLE>Our Products</TITLE>
    <BASE href="http://www.aviary.com/products/intro.html">
 </HEAD>

 <BODY>
    <P>Have you seen our <A href="../cages/birds.gif">Bird Cages</A>?
 </BODY>
</HTML>
```

the relative URI "../cages/birds.gif" would resolve to:

```
http://www.aviary.com/cages/birds.gif
```

12.4.1 Resolving relative URIs

User agents must calculate the base URI for resolving relative URIs according to [RFC1808], section 3. The following describes how [RFC1808] applies specifically to HTML.

User agents must calculate the base URI according to the following precedences (highest priority to lowest):

- The base URI is set by the BASE element.
- The base URI is given by meta data discovered during a protocol interaction, such as an HTTP header (see [RFC2068]).
- By default, the base URI is that of the current document. Not all HTML documents have a base URI (e.g., a valid HTML document may appear in an email and may not be designated by a URI). Such HTML documents are considered erroneous if they contain relative URIs and rely on a default base URI.

Additionally, the OBJECT and APPLET elements define attributes that take precedence over the value set by the BASE element. Please consult the definitions of these elements for more information about URI issues specific to them.

Link elements specified by HTTP headers are handled exactly as LINK elements that appear explicitly in a document.

Chapter 13

Objects, Images, and Applets

Contents

1. Introduction to objects, images, and applets
2. Including an image: the `IMG` element
3. Generic inclusion: the `OBJECT` element
    1. Rules for rendering objects
    2. Object initialization: the `PARAM` element
    3. Global naming schemes for objects
    4. Object declarations and instantiations
4. Including an applet: the `APPLET` element
5. Notes on embedded documents
6. Image maps
    1. Client-side image maps: the `MAP` and `AREA` elements
        - Client-side image map examples
    2. Server-side image maps
7. Visual presentation of images, objects, and applets
    1. Width and height
    2. White space around images and objects
    3. Borders
    4. Alignment
8. How to specify alternate text

13.1 Introduction to objects, images, and applets

HTML's multimedia features allow authors to include images, applets (programs that are automatically downloaded and run on the user's machine), video clips, and other HTML documents in their pages. For example, to include a PNG image in a document, authors may write:

```
<BODY
<PHere's a closeup of the Grand Canyon:
<OBJECT data="canyon.png" type="image/png">
This is a <EMcloseup</EM of the Grand Canyon.
</OBJECT>
</BODY>
```

Previous versions of HTML allowed authors to include images (via IMG) and applets (via APPLET). These elements have several limitations:

- They fail to solve the more general problem of how to include new and future media types.
- The APPLET element only works with Java-based applets. This element is deprecated in favor of OBJECT.
- They pose accessibility problems.

To address these issues, HTML 4.0 introduces the OBJECT element, which offers an all-purpose solution to generic object inclusion. The OBJECT element allows HTML authors to specify everything required by an object for its presentation by a user agent: source code, initial values, and run-time data. In this specification, the term "object" is used to describe the things that people want to place in HTML documents; other commonly used terms for these things are: applets, plug-ins, media handlers, etc.

The new OBJECT element thus subsumes some of the tasks carried out by existing elements. Consider the following chart of functionalities:

Type of inclusion	Specific element	Generic element
Image	IMG	OBJECT
Applet	APPLET (Deprecated.)	OBJECT
Another HTML document	IFRAME	OBJECT

The chart indicates that each type of inclusion has a specific and a general solution. The generic OBJECT element will serve as the solution for implementing future media types.

To include images, authors may use the OBJECT element or the IMG element.

To include applets, authors should use the OBJECT element as the APPLET element is deprecated.

To include one HTML document in another, authors may use either the new IFRAME element or the OBJECT element. In both cases, the embedded document remains independent of the main document. Visual user agents may present the embedded document in a distinct window within the main document. Please consult the notes on embedded documents for a comparison of `OBJECT` and `IFRAME` for document inclusion.

Images and other included objects may have hyperlinks associated with them, both through the standard linking mechanisms, but also via image maps. An image map specifies active geometric regions of an included object and assigns a link to each region. When activated, these links may cause a document to be retrieved, may run a program on the server, etc.

In the following sections, we discuss the various mechanisms available to authors for multimedia inclusions and creating image maps for those inclusions.

13.2 Including an image: the `IMG` element

```
<!-- To avoid problems with text-only UAs as well as
    to make image content understandable and navigable
    to users of non-visual UAs, you need to provide
    a description with ALT, and avoid server-side image maps -->
<!ELEMENT IMG - O EMPTY                  -- Embedded image -->
<!ATTLIST IMG
  %attrs;                                -- %coreattrs, %i18n, %events --
  src         %URI;          #REQUIRED  -- URI of image to embed --
  alt         %Text;         #REQUIRED  -- short description --
  longdesc    %URI;          #IMPLIED   -- link to long description
                                          (complements alt) --
  height      %Length;       #IMPLIED   -- override height --
  width       %Length;       #IMPLIED   -- override width --
  usemap      %URI;          #IMPLIED   -- use client-side image map --
  ismap       (ismap)        #IMPLIED   -- use server-side image map --
```

Start tag: **required**, *End tag:* **forbidden** Attribute definitions

src = *uri* [CT]

This attribute specifies the location of the image resource. Examples of widely recognized image formats include GIF, JPEG, and PNG.

`longdesc = uri` [CT]

> This attribute specifies a link to a long description of the image. This description should supplement the short description provided using the alt attribute. When the image has an associated image map, this attribute should provide information about the image map's contents. This is particularly important for server-side image maps.

Attributes defined elsewhere

- id, class (document-wide identifiers)
- alt (alternate text)
- lang (language information), dir (text direction)
- title (element title)
- style (inline style information)
- onclick, ondblclick, onmousedown, onmouseup, onmouseover, onmousemove, onmouseout, onkeypress, onkeydown, onkeyup (intrinsic events)
- ismap, usemap (client side image maps)
- align, width, height, border, hspace, vspace (visual presentation of objects, images, and applets)

The `IMG` element embeds an image in the current document at the location of the element's definition. The `IMG` element has no content; it is usually replaced inline by the image designated by the src attribute, the exception being for left or right-aligned images that are "floated" out of line. In an earlier example, we defined a link to a family photo. Here, we insert the photo directly into the current document:

```
<BODY
<P I just returned from vacation! Here's a photo of my family at the lake:
<IMG src="http://www.somecompany.com/People/Ian/vacation/family.png"
     alt="A photo of my family at the lake."
</BODY>
```

This inclusion may also be achieved with the `OBJECT` element as follows:

```
<BODY
<P I just returned from vacation! Here's a photo of my family at the lake:
<OBJECT data="http://www.somecompany.com/People/Ian/vacation/family.png"
```

```
        type="image/png"
A photo of my family at the lake.
</OBJECT>
</BODY>
```

The alt attribute specifies alternate text that is rendered when the image cannot be displayed (see below for information on how to specify alternate text). User agents must render alternate text when they cannot support images, they cannot support a certain image type or when they are configured not to display images. The following example shows how the `longdesc` attribute can be used to link to a richer description:

```
<BODY
<P
<IMG src="sitemap.gif"
     alt="HP Labs Site Map"
     longdesc="sitemap.html"
</BODY>
```

The alt attribute provides a short description of the image. This should be sufficient to allow users to decide whether they want to follow the link given by the `longdesc` attribute to the longer description, here "sitemap.html". Please consult the section on the visual presentation of objects, images, and applets for information about image size, alignment, and borders.

13.3 Generic inclusion: the OBJECT element

```
<!ELEMENT OBJECT - - (PARAM | %flow;)*
—generic embedded object —
<!ATTLIST OBJECT
  %attrs;                                 —%coreattrs, %i18n, %events —
  declare     (declare)       #IMPLIED    —declare but don't instantiate flag —
  classid     %URI;           #IMPLIED    —identifies an implementation —
  codebase    %URI;           #IMPLIED    —base URI for classid, data, archive—
  data        %URI;           #IMPLIED    —reference to object's data —
  type        %ContentType;   #IMPLIED    —content type for data —
  codetype    %ContentType;   #IMPLIED    —content type for code —
  archive     %URI;           #IMPLIED    —space separated archive list —
  standby     %Text;          #IMPLIED    —message to show while loading —
```

```
height      %Length;    #IMPLIED   -override height -
width       %Length;    #IMPLIED   -override width -
usemap      %URI;       #IMPLIED   -use client-side image map -
name        CDATA       #IMPLIED   -submit as part of form -
tabindex    NUMBER      #IMPLIED   -position in tabbing order -
```

Start tag: **required**, *End tag:* **required** *Attribute definitions*

classid = uri [CT]

This attribute may be used to specify the location of an object's implementation via a URI. It may be used together with, or as an alternative to the data attribute, depending on the type of object involved.

codebase = uri [CT]

This attribute specifies the base path used to resolve relative URIs specified by the classid, data, and archive attributes. When absent, its default value is the base URI of the current document.

codetype = content-type [CI]

This attribute specifies the content type of data expected when downloading the object specified by classid. This attribute is optional but recommended when classid is specified since it allows the user agent to avoid loading information for unsupported content types. When absent, it defaults to the value of the type attribute.

data = uri [CT]

This attribute may be used to specify the location of the object's data, for instance image data for objects defining images, or more generally, a serialized form of an object which can be used to recreate it. If given as a relative URI, it should be interpreted relative to the codebase attribute.

type = content-type [CI]

This attribute specifies the content type for the data specified by data. This attribute is optional but recommended when data is specified since it allows the user agent to avoid loading information for unsupported content types.

archive = uri list [CT]

This attribute may be used to specify a space-separated list of URIs for archives containing resources relevant to the object, which may include the resources specified by the classid and data attributes. Preloading archives will generally result in reduced load times for objects. Archives specified as relative URIs should be interpreted relative to the `codebase` attribute.

`declare` [CI]

When present, this boolean attribute makes the current OBJECT definition a declaration only. The object must be instantiated by a subsequent OBJECT definition referring to this declaration.

`standby` = text [CS]

This attribute specifies a message that a user agent may render while loading the object's implementation and data.

Attributes defined elsewhere

- id, class (document-wide identifiers)
- lang (language information), dir (text direction)
- title (element title)
- style (inline style information)
- onclick, ondblclick, onmousedown, onmouseup, onmouseover, onmousemove, onmouseout, onkeypress, onkeydown, onkeyup (intrinsic events)
- tabindex (tabbing navigation)
- usemap (client side image maps)
- name (form submission)
- align, width, height, border, hspace, vspace (visual presentation of objects, images, and applets)

Most user agents have built-in mechanisms for rendering common data types such as text, GIF images, colors, fonts, and a handful of graphic elements. To render data types they don't support natively, user agents generally run external applications. The OBJECT element allows authors to control whether data should be rendered externally or by some program, specified by the author, that renders the data within the user agent.

In the most general case, an author may need to specify three types of information:

- The implementation of the included object. For instance, if the included object is a clock applet, the author must indicate the location of the applet's executable code.

- The data to be rendered. For instance, if the included object is a program that renders font data, the author must indicate the location of that data.

- Additional values required by the object at run-time. For example, some applets may require initial values for parameters.

The OBJECT element allows authors to specify all three types of data, but authors may not have to specify all three at once. For example, some objects may not require data (e.g., a self-contained applet that performs a small animation). Others may not require run-time initialization. Still others may not require additional implementation information, i.e., the user agent itself may already know how to render that type of data (e.g., GIF images).

Authors specify an object's implementation and the location of the data to be rendered via the OBJECT element. To specify run-time values, however, authors use the PARAM element, which is discussed in the section on object initialization.

The objects.html—edef-OBJECTOBJECT element may also appear in the content of the HEAD element. Since user agents generally do not render elements in the HEAD, authors should ensure that any OBJECT elements in the HEAD do not specify content that may be rendered. Please consult the section on sharing frame data for an example of including the OBJECT element in the HEAD element.

Please consult the section on form controls for information about OBJECT elements in forms.

13.3.1 Rules for rendering objects

A user agent must interpret an OBJECT element according to the following precedence rules:

1. The user agent must first try to render the object. It should not render the element's contents, but it must examine them in case the element contains any direct children that are PARAM elements (see object initialization) or MAP elements (see client-side image maps).

2. If the user agent is not able to render the object for whatever reason (configured not to, lack of resources, wrong architecture, etc.), it must try to render its contents.

Authors should not include content in OBJECT elements that appear in the HEAD element. In the following example, we insert an analog clock applet in a document via the OBJECT element. The applet, written in the Python language, requires no additional data or run-time values. The classid attribute specifies the location of the applet:

```
<P<OBJECT classid="http://www.miamachina.it/analogclock.py"
</OBJECT
```

Objects, Images, and Applets 191

Note that the clock will be rendered as soon as the user agent interprets this `OBJECT` declaration. It is possible to delay rendering of an object by first declaring the object (described below).

Authors should complete this declaration by including alternate text as the contents of `OBJECT` in case the user agent cannot render the clock.

```
<P<OBJECT classid="http://www.miamachina.it/analogclock.py"
An animated clock.
</OBJECT
```

One significant consequence of the `OBJECT` element's design is that it offers a mechanism for specifying alternate object renderings; each embedded `OBJECT` declaration may specify alternate content types. If a user agent cannot render the outermost `OBJECT`, it tries to render the contents, which may be another `OBJECT` element, etc. In the following example, we embed several `OBJECT` declarations to illustrate how alternate renderings work. A user agent will attempt to render the first `OBJECT` element it can, in the following order: (1) an Earth applet written in the Python language, (2) an MPEG animation of the Earth, (3) a GIF image of the Earth, (4) alternate text.

```
<P                    <!-- First, try the Python applet -
<OBJECT title="The Earth as seen from space"
        classid="http://www.observer.mars/TheEarth.py"
                    <!-- Else, try the MPEG video -
  <OBJECT data="TheEarth.mpeg" type="application/mpeg">
                    <!-- Else, try the GIF image -
    <OBJECT data="TheEarth.gif" type="image/gif">
                    <!-- Else render the text -
      The <STRONGEarth</STRONG as seen from space.
    </OBJECT
  </OBJECT
</OBJECT
```

The outermost declaration specifies an applet that requires no data or initial values. The second declaration specifies an MPEG animation and, since it does not define the location of an implementation to handle MPEG, relies on the user agent to handle the animation. We also set the type attribute so that a user agent that knows it cannot render MPEG will not bother to retrieve "TheEarth.mpeg" from the network. The third declaration specifies the location of a GIF file and furnishes alternate text in case all other mechanisms fail. ***Inline vs. external data.*** *Data to be rendered may be supplied in two ways: inline and from an external resource. While the former method will generally lead to faster rendering, it is not convenient when rendering large quantities of data.*

Here's an example that illustrates how inline data may be fed to an OBJECT:

```
<P
<OBJECT id="clock1"
        classid="clsid:663C8FEF-1EF9-11CF-A3DB-080036F12502"
        data="data:application/x-oleobject;base64, ...base64 data...">
    A clock.
</OBJECT
```

Please consult the section on the visual presentation of objects, images, and applets for information about object size, alignment, and borders.

13.3.2 Object initialization: the PARAM element

```
<!ELEMENT PARAM - O EMPTY              -- named property value --
<!ATTLIST PARAM
    id          ID                 #IMPLIED   -- document-wide unique id --
    name        CDATA              #REQUIRED  -- property name --
    value       CDATA              #IMPLIED   -- property value --
    valuetype   (DATA|REF|OBJECT)  DATA       -- How to interpret value --
    type        %ContentType;      #IMPLIED   -- content type for value
                                                 when valuetype=ref --
```

*Start tag: **required**, End tag: **forbidden** Attribute definitions*

name = cdata

This attribute defines the name of a run-time parameter, assumed to be known by the inserted object. Whether the property name is case-sensitive depends on the specific object implementation.

value = cdata

This attribute specifies the value of a run-time parameter specified by name. Property values have no meaning to HTML; their meaning is determined by the object in question.

valuetype = data|ref|object [CI]

This attribute specifies the type of the value attribute. Possible values:

- `data`: This is default value for the attribute. It means that the value specified by value will be evaluated and passed to the object's implementation as a string.

- `ref`: The value specified by value is a URI that designates a resource where run-time values are stored. This allows support tools to identify URIs given as parameters. The URI must be passed to the object **as is**, i.e., unresolved.

- `object`: The value specified by `value` is an identifier that refers to an `OBJECT` declaration in the same document. The identifier must be the value of the id attribute set for the declared `OBJECT` element.

`type` = content-type [CI]

This attribute specifies the content type of the resource designated by the `value` attribute **only** in the case where valuetype is set to "ref". This attribute thus specifies for the user agent, the type of values that will be found at the URI designated by `value`.

Attributes defined elsewhere

- id (document-wide identifiers)

`PARAM` elements specify a set of values that may be required by an object at run-time. Any number of `PARAM` elements may appear in the content of an `OBJECT` or `APPLET` element, in any order, but must be placed at the start of the content of the enclosing `OBJECT` or `APPLET` element.

The syntax of names and values is assumed to be understood by the object's implementation. This document does not specify how user agents should retrieve name/value pairs nor how they should interpret parameter names that appear twice. We return to the clock example to illustrate the use of `PARAM`: suppose that the applet is able to handle two run-time parameters that define its initial height and width. We can set the initial dimensions to 40x40 pixels with two `PARAM` elements.

```
<P<OBJECT classid="http://www.miamachina.it/analogclock.py"
<PARAM name="height" value="40" valuetype="data"
<PARAM name="width" value="40" valuetype="data"
This user agent cannot render Python applications.
</OBJECT
```

In the following example, run-time data for the object's "Init_values" parameter is specified as an external resource (a GIF file). The value of the valuetype attribute is thus set to "ref" and the `value` is a URI designating the resource.

```
<P<OBJECT classid="http://www.gifstuff.com/gifappli"
        standby="Loading Elvis..."
<PARAM name="Init_values"
       value="./images/elvis.gif"
       valuetype="ref"
</OBJECT>
```

Note that we have also set the standby attribute so that the user agent may display a message while the rendering mechanism loads. When an OBJECT element is rendered, user agents must search the content for only those PARAM elements that are direct children and "feed" them to the OBJECT. Thus, in the following example, if "obj1" is rendered, "param1" applies to "obj1" (and not "obj2"). If "obj1" is not rendered and "obj2" is, "param1" is ignored, and "param2" applies to "obj2". If neither OBJECT is rendered, neither PARAM applies.

```
<P
<OBJECT id="obj1"
    <PARAM name="param1"
    <OBJECT id="obj2"
        <PARAM name="param2"
    </OBJECT>
</OBJECT>
```

13.3.3 Global naming schemes for objects

The location of an object's implementation is given by a URI. As we discussed in the introduction to URIs, the first segment of an absolute URI specifies the naming scheme used to transfer the data designated by the URI. For HTML documents, this scheme is frequently "http". Some applets might employ other naming schemes. For instance, when specifying a Java applet, authors may use URIs that begin with "java" and for ActiveX applets, authors may use "clsid". In the following example, we insert a Java applet into an HTML document.

```
<P<OBJECT classid="java:program.start"
</OBJECT>
```

By setting the codetype attribute, a user agent can decide whether to retrieve the Java application based on its ability to do so.

```
<OBJECT codetype="application/java-archive"
        classid="java:program.start"
</OBJECT>
```

Some rendering schemes require additional information to identify their implementation and must be told where to find that information. Authors may give path information to the object's implementation via the codebase attribute.

```
<OBJECT codetype="application/java-archive"
        classid="java:program.start"
        codebase="http://foooo.bar.com/java/myimplementation/"
</OBJECT>
```

The following example specifies (with the classid attribute) an ActiveX object via a URI that begins with the naming scheme "clsid". The data attribute locates the data to render (another clock).

```
<P<OBJECT classid="clsid:663C8FEF-1EF9-11CF-A3DB-080036F12502"
        data="http://www.acme.com/ole/clock.stm"
This application is not supported.
</OBJECT>
```

13.3.4 Object declarations and instantiations

The preceding examples have only illustrated isolated object definitions. When a document is to contain more than one instance of the same object, it is possible to separate the declaration of the object from its instantiations. Doing so has several advantages:

- Data may be retrieved from the network by the user agent one time (during the declaration) and reused for each instantiation.
- It is possible to instantiate an object from a location other than the object's declaration, for example, from a link.
- It is possible to specify objects as run-time data for other objects.

To declare an object so that it is not executed when read by the user agent, set the boolean declare attribute in the OBJECT element. At the same time, authors must identify the declaration by setting the id attribute in the OBJECT element to a unique value. Later instantiations of the object will refer to this identifier.

A declared OBJECT must appear in a document before the first instance of that OBJECT.

An object defined with the declare attribute is instantiated every time an element that refers to that object requires it to be rendered (e.g., a link that refers to it is activated, an object that refers to it is activated, etc.). In the following example, we declare an OBJECT and cause it so be instantiated by referring to it from a link. Thus, the object can be activated by clicking on some highlighted text, for example.

```
<P<OBJECT declare
        id="earth.declaration"
        data="TheEarth.mpeg"
        type="application/mpeg"
   The <STRONGEarth</STRONG as seen from space.
</OBJECT
...later in the document...
<PA neat <A href="#earth.declaration" animation of The Earth!</A
```

The following example illustrates how to specify run-time values that are other objects. In this example, we send text (a poem, in fact) to a hypothetical mechanism for viewing poems. The object recognizes a run-time parameter named "font" (say, for rendering the poem text in a certain font). The value for this parameter is itself an object that inserts (but does not render) the font object. The relationship between the font object and the poem viewer object is achieved by (1) assigning the id "tribune" to the font object declaration and (2) referring to it from the PARAM element of the poem viewer object (with valuetype and value).

```
<P<OBJECT declare
      id="tribune"
      type="application/x-webfont"
      data="tribune.gif"
</OBJECT
...view the poem in KublaKhan.txt here...
<P<OBJECT classid="http://foo.bar.com/poem_viewer"
          data="KublaKhan.txt"
<PARAM name="font" valuetype="object" value="#tribune"
<PYou're missing a really cool poem viewer ...
</OBJECT
```

User agents that don't support the declare attribute must render the contents of the OBJECT declaration.

13.4 Including an applet: the `APPLET` element

`APPLET` is deprecated (with all its attributes) **in favor of** `OBJECT`.

See the Transitional DTD for the formal definition.

Attribute definitions

`codebase` = uri [CT]

> This attribute specifies the base URI for the applet. If this attribute is not specified, then it defaults the same base URI as for the current document. Values for this attribute may only refer to subdirectories of the directory containing the current document.

`code` = cdata [CS]

> This attribute specifies either the name of the class file that contains the applet's compiled applet subclass or the path to get the class, including the class file itself. It is interpreted with respect to the applet's codebase. One of code or object must be present.

`name` = cdata [CS]

> This attribute specifies a name for the applet instance, which makes it possible for applets on the same page to find (and communicate with) each other.

`archive` = uri-list [CT]

> This attribute specifies a comma-separated list of URIs for archives containing classes and other resources that will be "preloaded". The classes are loaded using an instance of an AppletClassLoader with the given codebase. Relative URIs for archives are interpreted with respect to the applet's codebase. Preloading resources can significantly improve the performance of applets.

`object` = cdata [CS]

> This attribute names a resource containing a serialized representation of an applet's state. It is interpreted relative to the applet's codebase. The serialized data contains the applet's class name but not the implementation. The class name is used to retrieve the implementation from a class file or archive.

When the applet is "deserialized" the `start()` method is invoked but not the `init()` method. Attributes valid when the original object was serialized are **not** restored. Any attributes passed to this

`APPLET` instance will be available to the applet. Authors should use this feature with extreme caution. An applet should be stopped before it is serialized.

Either code or object must be present. If both code and object are given, it is an error if they provide different class names.

`width` = length [CI]

> This attribute specifies the initial width of the applet's display area (excluding any windows or dialogs that the applet creates).

`height` = length [CI]

> This attribute specifies the initial height of the applet's display area (excluding any windows or dialogs that the applet creates).

Attributes defined elsewhere

- id, class (document-wide identifiers)
- title (element title)
- style (inline style information)
- alt (alternate text)
- align, hspace, vspace (visual presentation of objects, images, and applets)

This element, supported by all Java-enabled browsers, allows designers to embed a Java applet in an HTML document. It has been deprecated in favor of the `OBJECT` element.

The content of the `APPLET` acts as alternate information for user agents that don't support this element or are currently configured not to support applets. User agents must ignore the content otherwise. DEPRECATED EXAMPLE:
In the following example, the `APPLET` element includes a Java applet in the document. Since no codebase is supplied, the applet is assumed to be in the same directory as the current document.

```
<APPLET code="Bubbles.class" width="500" height="500"
Java applet that draws animated bubbles.
</APPLET
```

This example may be rewritten as follows with OBJECT as follows:

```
<P<OBJECT codetype="application/java"
        classid="java:Bubbles.class"
        width="500" height="500">
Java applet that draws animated bubbles.
</OBJECT
```

Initial values may be supplied to the applet via the PARAM element. DEPRECATED EXAMPLE: The following sample Java applet:

```
<APPLET code="AudioItem" width="15" height="15"
<PARAM name="snd" value="Hello.au|Welcome.au"
Java applet that plays a welcoming sound.
</APPLET>
```

may be rewritten as follows with OBJECT:

```
<OBJECT codetype="application/java"
        classid="AudioItem"
        width="15" height="15"
<PARAM name="snd" value="Hello.au|Welcome.au"
Java applet that plays a welcoming sound.
</OBJECT
```

13.5 Notes on embedded documents

Sometimes, rather than linking to a document, an author may want to embed it directly into a primary HTML document. Authors may use either the IFRAME element or the OBJECT element for this purpose, but the elements differ in some ways. Not only do the two elements have different content models, the IFRAME element may be a target frame (see the section on specifying target frame information for details) and may be "selected" by a user agent as the focus for printing, viewing HTML source, etc. User agents may render selected frames elements in ways that distinguish them from unselected frames (e.g., by drawing a border around the selected frame).

An embedded document is entirely independent of the document in which it is embedded. For instance, relative URIs within the embedded document resolve according to the base URI of the embedded document, not that of the main document. An embedded document is only rendered within another document (e.g., in a subwindow); it remains otherwise independent. For instance, the following line embeds the contents of embed_me.html at the location where the OBJECT definition occurs.

```
...text before...
<OBJECT data="embed_me.html"
Warning: embed_me.html could not be embedded.
</OBJECT>
...text after...
```

Recall that the contents of OBJECT must only be rendered if the file specified by the data attribute cannot be loaded. The behavior of a user agent in cases where a file includes itself is not defined.

13.6 Image maps

Image maps allow authors to specify regions of an image or object and assign a specific action to each region (e.g., retrieve a document, run a program, etc.) When the region is activated by the user, the action is executed.

An image map is created by associating an object with a specification of sensitive geometric areas on the object.

There are two types of image maps:

- *Client-side*. When a user activates a region of a client-side image map with a mouse, the pixel coordinates are interpreted by the user agent. The user agent selects a link that was specified for the activated region and follows it.

- *Server-side*. When a user activates a region of a server-side image map with a mouse, the pixel coordinates of the click are sent to the server-side agent specified by the href attribute of the A element. The server-side agent interprets the coordinates and performs some action.

Client-side image maps are preferred over server-side image maps for at least two reasons: they are accessible to people browsing with non-graphical user agents and they offer immediate feedback as to whether or not the pointer is over an active region.

13.6.1 Client-side image maps: the MAP and AREA elements

```
<!ELEMENT MAP - - ((%block;)+ | AREA+)—client-side image map —
<!ATTLIST MAP
    %attrs;                          —%coreattrs, %i18n, %events —
    name         CDATA               #REQUIRED—for reference by usemap —
```
*Start tag: **required**, End tag: **required***

```
<!ELEMENT AREA - O EMPTY              — client-side image map area —
<!ATTLIST AREA
    %attrs;                           — %coreattrs, %i18n, %events —
    shape        %Shape;      rect    — controls interpretation of coords —
    coords       %Coords;     #IMPLIED — comma separated list of lengths —
    href         %URI;        #IMPLIED — URI for linked resource —
    nohref       (nohref)     #IMPLIED — this region has no action —
    alt          %Text;       #REQUIRED — short description —
    tabindex     NUMBER       #IMPLIED — position in tabbing order —
    accesskey    %Character;  #IMPLIED — accessibility key character —
    onfocus      %Script;     #IMPLIED — the element got the focus —
    onblur       %Script;     #IMPLIED — the element lost the focus —
```
*Start tag: **required**, End tag: **forbidden***

MAP attribute definitions

name = cdata [CI]

This attribute assigns a name to the image map defined by a MAP element.

AREA attribute definitions

shape = default|rect|circle|poly [CI]

This attribute specifies the shape of a region. Possible values:

- `default`: Specifies the entire region.
- `rect`: Define a rectangular region.
- `circle`: Define a circular region.
- `poly`: Define a polygonal region.

`coords` = *coordinates* [CN]

This attribute specifies the position a shape on the screen. The number and order of values depends on the shape being defined. Possible combinations:

- `rect`: left-x, top-y, right-x, bottom-y.
- `circle`: center-x, center-y, radius. Note. When the radius value is a percentage value, user agents should calculate the final radius value based on the associated object's width and height. The radius should be the smaller value of the two.
- `poly`: x1, y1, x2, y2, ..., xN, yN.

Coordinates are relative to the top, left corner of the object. All values are lengths. All values are separated by commas.

`nohref` [CI]

When set, this boolean attribute specifies that a region has no associated link.

Attribute to associate an image map with an element

`usemap` = uri [CT]

This attribute associates an image map with an element. The image map is defined by a `MAP` element. The value of `usemap` must match the value of the `name` attribute of the associated `MAP` element.

Attributes defined elsewhere

- id, class (document-wide identifiers)
- lang (language information), dir (text direction)
- title (element title)
- style (inline style information)
- name (submitting objects with forms)
- alt (alternate text)
- href (anchor reference) target (frame target information)
- tabindex (tabbing navigation)

- accesskey (access keys)
- shape (image maps)
- onclick, ondblclick, onmousedown, onmouseup, onmouseover, onmousemove, onmouseout, onkeypress, onkeydown, onkeyup, onfocus, onblur (intrinsic events)

The MAP element specifies a client-side image map that may be associated with one or more elements (IMG, OBJECT, or INPUT). An image map is associated with an element via the element's usemap attribute.

The presence of the usemap attribute for an OBJECT implies that the object being included is an image. Furthermore, when the OBJECT element has an associated client-side image map, user agents may implement user interaction with the OBJECT solely in terms of the client-side image map. This allows user agents (such as an audio browser or robot) to interact with the OBJECT without having to process it; the user agent may even elect not to retrieve (or process) the object. When an OBJECT has an associated image map, authors should not expect that the object will be retrieved or processed by every user agent.

Each objects.html—edef-MAPMAP element may contain either one of the following:

- One or more AREA elements. These elements have no content but specify the geometric regions of the image map and the link associated with each region. Note that when this method is used, the MAP has no rendered content. Therefore, authors must provide alternate text for each AREA with the alt attribute (see below for information on how to specify alternate text).
- Block-level content. This content should include A elements that specify the geometric regions of the image map and the link associated with each region. Note that when this method is used, the MAP element content may be rendered by the user agent. Authors should use this method to create more accessible documents.

If two or more defined regions overlap, the region-defining element that appears earliest in the document takes precedence (i.e., responds to user input).

User agents and authors should offer textual alternates to graphical image maps for cases when graphics are not available or the user cannot access them. For example, user agents may use alt text to create textual links in place of a graphical image map. Such links may be activated in a variety of ways (keyboard, voice activation, etc.).

Note. MAP *is not backwards compatible with HTML 2.0 user agents.*

Client-side image map examples

In the following example, we create a client-side image map for the OBJECT element. We do not want to render the image map's contents when the OBJECT is rendered, so we "hide" the MAP element within the OBJECT element's content. Consequently, the MAP element's contents will only be rendered if the OBJECT cannot be rendered.

```
<HTML>
   <HEAD>
      <TITLEThe cool site!</TITLE>
   </HEAD>
   <BODY>
      <P<OBJECT data="navbar1.gif" type="image/gif" usemap="#map1"
      <MAP name="map1"
         <PNavigate the site:
         <A href="guide.html" shape="rect" coords="0,0,118,28"Access Guide</a |
         <A href="shortcut.html" shape="rect" coords="118,0,184,28"Go</A |
         <A href="search.html" shape="circle" coords="184,200,60"Search</A |
         <A href="top10.html" shape="poly" coords="276,0,373,28,50,50,100,120"Top Ten</A<
      </MAP>
      </OBJECT
   </BODY>
</HTML>
```

We may want to render the image map's contents even when a user agent can render the OBJECT. For instance, we may want to associate an image map with an OBJECT element and include a text navigation bar at the bottom of the page. To do so, we define the MAP element outside the OBJECT:

```
<HTML>
   <HEAD>
      <TITLEThe cool site!</TITLE>
   </HEAD>
   <BODY>
      <P<OBJECT data="navbar1.gif" type="image/gif" usemap="#map1"
      </OBJECT

      ...the rest of the page here...

      <MAP name="map1"
```

```
        <PNavigate the site:
        <A href="guide.html" shape="rect" coords="0,0,118,28"Access Guide</a |
        <A href="shortcut.html" shape="rect" coords="118,0,184,28"Go</A |
        <A href="search.html" shape="circle" coords="184,200,60"Search</A |
        <A href="top10.html" shape="poly" coords="276,0,373,28,50,50,100,120"Top Ten</A
     </MAP
  </BODY
</HTML
```

In the following example, we create a similar image map, this time using the AREA element. Note the use of alt text:

```
<P<OBJECT data="navbar1.gif" type="image/gif" usemap="#map1"
    <PThis is a navigation bar.
    </OBJECT

<MAP name="map1"
 <AREA href="guide.html"
         alt="Access Guide"
         shape="rect"
         coords="0,0,118,28"
 <AREA href="search.html"
         alt="Search"
         shape="rect"
         coords="184,0,276,28"
 <AREA href="shortcut.html"
         alt="Go"
         shape="circle"
         coords="184,200,60"
 <AREA href="top10.html"
         alt="Top Ten"
         shape="poly"
         coords="276,0,373,28,50,50,100,120"
</MAP
```

Here is a similar version using the IMG element instead of OBJECT (with the same MAP declaration):

```
<P<IMG src="navbar1.gif" usemap="#map1" alt="navigation bar"
```

The following example illustrates how image maps may be shared.

Nested OBJECT elements are useful for providing fallbacks in case a user agent doesn't support certain formats. For example:

```
<P
<OBJECT data="navbar.png" type="image/png"
  <OBJECT data="navbar.gif" type="image/gif"
    text describing the image...
  </OBJECT
</OBJECT
```

If the user agent doesn't support the PNG format, it tries to render the GIF image. If it doesn't support GIF (e.g., it's a speech-based user agent), it defaults to the text description provided as the content of the inner OBJECT element. When OBJECT elements are nested this way, authors may share image maps among them:

```
<P
<OBJECT data="navbar.png" type="image/png" usemap="#map1"
  <OBJECT data="navbar.gif" type="image/gif" usemap="#map1"
      <MAP name="map1"
      <PNavigate the site:
        <A href="guide.html" shape="rect" coords="0,0,118,28"Access Guide</a |
        <A href="shortcut.html" shape="rect" coords="118,0,184,28"Go</A |
        <A href="search.html" shape="circle" coords="184,200,60"Search</A |
        <A href="top10.html" shape="poly" coords="276,0,373,28,50,50,100,120"Top Ten</A
      </MAP
  </OBJECT
</OBJECT
```

The following example illustrates how anchors may be specified to create inactive zones within an image map. The first anchor specifies a small circular region with no associated link. The second anchor specifies a larger circular region with the same center coordinates. Combined, the two form a ring whose center is inactive and whose rim is active. The order of the anchor definitions is important, since the smaller circle must override the larger circle.

```
<MAP name="map1"
<P
<A shape="circle" coords="100,200,50"I'm inactive.</A
```

```
<A href="outer-ring-link.html" shape="circle" coords="100,200,250"I'm active.</A
</MAP>
```

Similarly, the nohref attribute for the AREA element declares that geometric region has no associated link.

13.6.2 Server-side image maps

Server-side image maps may be interesting in cases where the image map is too complicated for a client-side image map.

It is only possible to define a server-side image map for the IMG and INPUT elements. In the case of IMG, the IMG must be inside an A element and the boolean attribute ismap ([CI]) must be set. In the case of INPUT, the INPUT must be of type "image".

When the user activates the link by clicking on the image, the screen coordinates are sent directly to the server where the document resides. Screen coordinates are expressed as screen pixel values relative to the image. For normative information about the definition of a pixel and how to scale it, please consult [CSS1]. In the following example, the active region defines a server-side link. Thus, a click anywhere on the image will cause the click's coordinates to be sent to the server.

```
<P<A href="http://www.acme.com/cgi-bin/competition"
     <IMG src="game.gif" ismap alt="target"</A
```

The location clicked is passed to the server as follows. The user agent derives a new URI from the URI specified by the href attribute of the A element, by appending `?' followed by the x and y coordinates, separated by a comma. The link is then followed using the new URI. For instance, in the given example, if the user clicks at the location x=10, y=27 then the derived URI is "http://www.acme.com/cgi-bin/competition?10,27".

User agents that do not offer the user a means to select specific coordinates (e.g., non-graphical user agents that rely on keyboard input, speech-based user agents, etc.) should send the coordinates "0,0" to the server when the link is activated.

13.7 Visual presentation of images, objects, and applets

All IMG *and* OBJECT *attributes that concern visual alignment and presentation have been* deprecated *in favor of style sheets.*

13.7.1 Width and height

Attribute definitions

width = length [CN]

    Image and object width override.

height = length [CN]

    Image and object override.

When specified, the width and height attributes tell user agents to override the natural image or object size in favor of these values.

When the object is an image, it is scaled. User agents should do their best to scale an object or image to match the width and height specified by the author. Note that lengths expressed as percentages are based on the horizontal or vertical space currently available, not on the natural size of the image, object, or applet.

The height and width attributes give user agents an idea of the size of an image or object so that they may reserve space for it and continue rendering the document while waiting for the image data.

13.7.2 White space around images and objects

The vspace and hspace attributes specify the amount of white space to be inserted to the left and right (hspace) and above and below (vspace) an IMG, APPLET, OBJECT. The default value for these attributes is not specified, but is generally a small, non-zero length. Both attributes take values of type length.

13.7.3 Borders

An image or object may be surrounded by a border (e.g., when a border is specified by the user or when the image is the content of an A element).

Attribute definitions

border = pixels

    Deprecated. The border attribute specifies the width of this border in pixels. The default value for this attribute depends on the user agent.

13.7.4 Alignment

The align attribute specifies the position of an IMG, OBJECT, or APPLET with respect to its context.

The following values for align concern the object's position with respect to surrounding text:

- bottom: means that the bottom of the object should be vertically aligned with the current baseline. This is the default value.
- middle: means that the center of the object should be vertically aligned with the current baseline.
- top: means that the top of the object should be vertically aligned with the top of the current text line.

Two other values, left and right, cause the image to float to the current left or right margin. They are discussed in the section on floating objects.

Differing interpretations of align. User agents vary in their interpretation of the align attribute. Some only take into account what has occurred on the text line prior to the element, some take into account the text on both sides of the element.

13.8 How to specify alternate text

Attribute definitions

alt = text [CS]

> For user agents that cannot display images, forms, or applets, this attribute specifies alternate text. The language of the alternate text is specified by the lang attribute.

Several non-textual elements (IMG, AREA, APPLET, and INPUT) let authors specify alternate text to serve as content when the element cannot be rendered normally. Specifying alternate text assists users without graphic display terminals, users whose browsers don't support forms, visually impaired users, those who use speech synthesizers, those who have configured their graphical user agents not to display images, etc.

The alt attribute must be specified for the IMG and AREA elements. It is optional for the INPUT and APPLET elements.

While alternate text may be very helpful, it must be handled with care. Authors should observe the following guidelines:

- Do not specify irrelevant alternate text when including images intended to format a page, for instance, alt="red ball" would be inappropriate for an image that adds a red ball for decorating a heading or paragraph. In such cases, the alternate text should be the empty string (""). Authors are in any case advised to avoid using images to format pages; style sheets should be used instead.

- Do not specify meaningless alternate text (e.g., "dummy text"). Not only will this frustrate users, it will slow down user agents that must convert text to speech or braille output.

Implementors should consult the section on generating alternate text for information about how to handle cases of omitted alternate text.

Note. *For more information about designing accessible HTML documents, please consult* [WAIGUIDE].

Chapter 14

Style Sheets

Contents

1. Introduction to style sheets
2. Adding style to HTML
   1. Setting the default style sheet language
   2. Inline style information
   3. Header style information: the STYLE element
   4. Media types
3. External style sheets
   1. Preferred and alternate style sheets
   2. Specifying external style sheets
4. Cascading style sheets
   1. Media-dependent cascades
   2. Inheritance and cascading
5. Hiding style data from user agents
6. Linking to style sheets with HTTP headers

14.1 Introduction to style sheets

Style sheets represent a major breakthrough for Web page designers, expanding their ability to improve the appearance of their pages. In the scientific environments in which the Web was conceived, people are more concerned with the content of their documents than the presentation. As people from wider walks of life discovered the Web, the limitations of HTML became a source of continuing frustration and authors were forced to sidestep HTML's stylistic limitations. While the intentions have been good—to improve the presentation of Web pages—the techniques for doing so have had unfortunate side effects. These techniques work for some of the people, some of the time, but not for all of the people, all of the time. They include:

- Using proprietary HTML extensions
- Converting text into images
- Using images for white space control
- Use of tables for page layout
- Writing a program instead of using HTML

These techniques considerably increase the complexity of Web pages, offer limited flexibility, suffer from interoperability problems, and create hardships for people with disabilities.

Style sheets solve these problems at the same time they supersede the limited range of presentation mechanisms in HTML. Style sheets make it easy to specify the amount of white space between text lines, the amount lines are indented, the colors used for the text and the backgrounds, the font size and style, and a host of other details.

For example, the following short CSS style sheet (stored in the file "special.css"), sets the text color of a paragraph to green and surrounds it with a solid red border:

```
P.special {
color : green;
border: solid red;
}
```

Authors may link this style sheet to their source HTML document with the LINK element:

```
<!DOCTYPE HTML PUBLIC "-//W3C//DTD HTML 4.0//EN"
    "http://www.w3.org/TR/REC-html40">
<HTML>
  <HEAD>
    <LINK href="special.css" rel="stylesheet" type="text/css">
  </HEAD>
  <BODY>
    <P class="special">This paragraph should have special green text.
  </BODY>
</HTML>
```

HTML 4.0 provides support for the following style sheet features:

Flexible placement of style information

Placing style sheets in separate files makes them easy to reuse. Sometimes it's useful to include rendering instructions within the document to which they apply, either grouped at the start of the document, or in attributes of the elements throughout the body of the document. To make it easier to manage style on a site basis, this specification describes how to use HTTP headers to set the style sheets to be applied to a document.

Independence from specific style sheet languages

This specification doesn't tie HTML to any particular style sheet language. This allows for a range of such languages to be used, for instance simple ones for the majority of users and much more complex ones for the minority of users with highly specialized needs. The examples included below all use the CSS (Cascading Style Sheets) language [CSS1], but other style sheet languages would be possible.

Cascading

This is the capability provided by some style sheet languages such as CSS to allow style information from several sources to be blended together. These could be, for instance, corporate style guidelines, styles common to a group of documents, and styles specific to a single document. By storing these separately, style sheets can be reused, simplifying authoring and making more effective use of network caching. The cascade defines an ordered sequence of style sheets where rules in later sheets have greater precedence than earlier ones. Not all style sheet languages support cascading.

Media dependencies

HTML allows authors to specify documents in a media-independent way. This allows users to access Web pages using a wide variety of devices and media, e.g., graphical displays for computers running Windows, Macintosh OS, and X11, devices for television sets, specially adapted phones and PDA-based portable devices, speech-based browsers, and braille-based tactile devices.

Style sheets, by contrast, apply to specific media or media groups. A style sheet intended for screen use may be applicable when printing, but is of little use for speech-based browsers. This specification allows you to define the broad categories of media a given style sheet is applicable to. This allows user agents to avoid retrieving inappropriate style sheets. Style sheet languages may include features for describing media dependencies within the same style sheet.

Alternate styles

Authors may wish to offer readers several ways to view a document. For instance, a style sheet for rendering compact documents with small fonts, or one that specifies larger fonts for increased legibility. This specification allows authors to specify a preferred style sheet as well as alternates that target specific users or media. User agents should give users the opportunity to select from among alternate style sheets or to switch off style sheets altogether.

Performance concerns

Some people have voiced concerns over performance issues for style sheets. For instance, retrieving an external style sheet may delay the full presentation for the user. A similar situation arises if the document head includes a lengthy set of style rules.

The current proposal addresses these issues by allowing authors to include rendering instructions within each HTML element. The rendering information is then always available by the time the user agent wants to render each element.

In many cases, authors will take advantage of a common style sheet for a group of documents. In this case, distributing style rules throughout the document will actually lead to worse performance than using a linked style sheet, since for most documents, the style sheet will already be present in the local cache. The public availability of good style sheets will encourage this effect.

14.2 Adding style to HTML

Note. *The sample default style sheet for HTML 4.0 that is included in* [CSS2] *expresses generally accepted default style information for each element. Authors and implementors alike might find this a useful resource.*

HTML documents may contain style sheet rules directly in them or they may import style sheets.

Any style sheet language may be used with HTML. A simple style sheet language may suffice for the needs of most users, but other languages may be more suited to highly specialized needs. This specification uses the style language "Cascading Style Sheets" ([CSS1]), abbreviated CSS, for examples.

The syntax of style data depends on the style sheet language.

14.2.1 Setting the default style sheet language

Authors must specify the style sheet language of style information associated with an HTML document.

Authors should use the `META` element to set the default style sheet language for a document. For example, to set the default to CSS, authors should put the following declaration in the HEAD of their documents:

```
<META http-equiv="Content-Style-Type" content="text/css">
```

The default style sheet language may also be set with HTTP headers. The above META declaration is equivalent to the HTTP header:

```
Content-Style-Type: text/css
```

User agents should determine the default style sheet language for a document according to the following steps (highest to lowest priority):

1. If any `META` declarations specify the "Content-Style-Type", the last one in the character stream determines the default style sheet language.

2. Otherwise, if any HTTP headers specify the "Content-Style-Type", the last one in the character stream determines the default style sheet language.

3. Otherwise, the default style sheet language is "text/css".

Documents that include elements that set the style attribute but which don't define a default style sheet language are incorrect. Authoring tools should generate default style sheet language information (typically a `META` declaration) so that user agents do not have to rely on a default of "text/css".

14.2.2 Inline style information

Attribute definitions

style = *style* [CN]

This attribute specifies style information for the current element.

The style attribute specifies style information for a single element. The style sheet language of inline style rules is given by the default style sheet language. The syntax of style data depends on the style sheet language.

This example sets color and font size information for the text in a specific paragraph.

```
<P style="font-size: 12pt; color: fuchsia">Aren't style sheets wonderful?
```

In CSS, property declarations have the form "name : value" and are separated by a semi-colon.

The style attribute may be used to apply a particular style to an individual HTML element. If the style will be reused for several elements, authors should use the STYLE element to regroup that information. For optimal flexibility, authors should define styles in external style sheets.

14.2.3 Header style information: the STYLE element

```
<!ELEMENT STYLE - - %StyleSheet          -- style info -->
<!ATTLIST STYLE
  %i18n;                                 -- lang, dir, for use with title --
  type       %ContentType;  #REQUIRED    -- content type of style language --
  media      %MediaDesc;    #IMPLIED     -- designed for use with these media --
  title      %Text;         #IMPLIED     -- advisory title --
  >
```

*Start tag: **required**, End tag: **required***

Attribute definitions

type = *content-type* [CI]

> This attribute specifies the style sheet language of the element's contents and overrides the default style sheet language. The style sheet language is specified as a content type (e.g., "text/css"). Authors must supply a value for this attribute; there is no default value for this attribute.

media = *media-descriptors* [CI]

> This attribute specifies the intended destination medium for style information. It may be a single media descriptor or a comma-separated list. The default value for this attribute is "screen".

Attributes defined elsewhere

- lang (language information), dir (text direction)
- title (element title)

The STYLE element allows authors to put style sheet rules in the head of the document. HTML permits any number of STYLE elements in the HEAD section of a document.

User agents that don't support style sheets, or don't support the specific style sheet language used by a STYLE element, must hide the contents of the STYLE element. It is an error to render the content as part of the document's text. Some style sheet languages support syntax for hiding the content from non-conforming user agents.

The syntax of style data depends on the style sheet language.

Some style sheet implementations may allow a wider variety of rules in the STYLE element than in the style attribute. For example, with CSS, rules may be declared within a STYLE element for:

- All instances of a specific HTML element (e.g., all P elements, all H1 elements, etc.)
- All instances of an HTML element belonging to a specific class (i.e., whose class attribute is set to some value).
- Single instances of an HTML element (i.e., whose id attribute is set to some value).

Rules for style rule precedences and inheritance depend on the style sheet language.

The following CSS STYLE declaration puts a border around every H1 element in the document and centers it on the page.

```
<HEAD>
 <STYLE type="text/css">
   H1 {border-width: 1; border: solid; text-align: center}
 </STYLE>
</HEAD>
```

To specify that this style information should only apply to H1 elements of a specific class, we modify it as follows:

```
<HEAD>
 <STYLE type="text/css">
   H1.myclass {border-width: 1; border: solid; text-align: center}
 </STYLE>
</HEAD>
<BODY>
 <H1 class="myclass"> This H1 is affected by our style </H1>
 <H1> This one is not affected by our style </H1>
</BODY>
```

Finally, to limit the scope of the style information to a single instance of H1, set the id attribute:

```
<HEAD>
 <STYLE type="text/css">
   #myid {border-width: 1; border: solid; text-align: center}
 </STYLE>
</HEAD>
<BODY>
 <H1 class="myclass"> This H1 is not affected </H1>
 <H1 id="myid"> This H1 is affected by style </H1>
 <H1> This H1 is not affected </H1>
</BODY>
```

Although style information may be set for almost every HTML element, two elements, DIV and SPAN, are particularly useful in that they do not impose any presentation semantics (besides block-level vs. inline). When combined with style sheets, these elements allow users to extend HTML indefinitely, particularly when used with the class and id attributes.

In the following example, we use the SPAN element to set the font style of the first few words of a paragraph to small caps.

```
<HEAD>
 <STYLE type="text/css">
  SPAN.sc-ex { font-variant: small-caps }
 </STYLE>
</HEAD>
<BODY>
  <P><SPAN class="sc-ex">The first</SPAN> few words of
  this paragraph are in small-caps.
</BODY>
```

In the following example, we use DIV and the class attribute to set the text justification for a series of paragraphs that make up the abstract section of a scientific article. This style information could be reused for other abstract sections by setting the class attribute elsewhere in the document.

```
<HEAD>
 <STYLE type="text/css">
   DIV.Abstract { text-align: justify }
 </STYLE>
```

```
</HEAD>
<BODY>
 <DIV class="Abstract">
   <P>The Chieftain product range is our market winner for
      the coming year. This report sets out how to position
      Chieftain against competing products.

   <P>Chieftain replaces the Commander range, which will
      remain on the price list until further notice.
 </DIV>
</BODY>
```

14.2.4 Media types

HTML allows authors to design documents that take advantage of the characteristics of the media where the document is to be rendered (e.g., graphical displays, television screens, handheld devices, speech-based browsers, braille-based tactile devices, etc.). By specifying the media attribute, authors allow user agents to load and apply style sheets selectively. Please consult the list of recognized media descriptors.

The following sample declarations apply to H1 elements. When projected in a business meeting, all instances will be blue. When printed, all instances will be centered.

```
<HEAD>
  <STYLE type="text/css" media="projection">
     H1 { color: blue}
  </STYLE>

  <STYLE type="text/css" media="print">
    H1 { text-align: center }
  </STYLE>
```

This example adds sound effects to anchors for use in speech output:

```
  <STYLE type="text/css" media="aural">
     A { cue-before: uri(bell.aiff); cue-after: uri(dong.wav)}
  </STYLE>
</HEAD>
```

Media control is particularly interesting when applied to external style sheets since user agents can save time by retrieving from the network only those style sheets that apply to the current device. For instance, speech-based browsers can avoid downloading style sheets designed for visual rendering. See the section on media-dependent cascades for more information.

14.3 External style sheets

Authors may separate style sheets from HTML documents. This offers several benefits:

- Authors and Web site managers may share style sheets across a number of documents (and sites).
- Authors may change the style sheet without requiring modifications to the document.
- User agents may load style sheets selectively (based on media descriptions).

14.3.1 Preferred and alternate style sheets

HTML allows authors to associate any number of external style sheets with a document. The style sheet language defines how multiple external style sheets interact (for example, the CSS "cascade" rules).

Authors may specify a number of mutually exclusive style sheets called *alternate* style sheets. Users may select their favorite among these depending on their preferences. For instance, an author may specify one style sheet designed for small screens and another for users with weak vision (e.g., large fonts). User agents should allow users to select from alternate style sheets.

The author may specify that one of the alternates is a *preferred* style sheet. User agents should apply the author's preferred style sheet unless the user has selected a different alternate.

Authors may group several alternate style sheets (including the author's preferred style sheets) under a single *style name*. When a user selects a named style, the user agent must apply all style sheets with that name. User agents must not apply alternate style sheets with a different style name. The section on specifying external style sheets explains how to name a group of style sheets.

Authors may also specify *persistent* style sheets that user agents must apply in addition to any alternate style sheet.

User agents must respect media descriptors when applying any style sheet.

User agents should also allow users to disable the author's style sheets entirely, in which case the user agent must not apply any persistent or alternate style sheets.

14.3.2 Specifying external style sheets

Authors specify external style sheets with the following attributes of the LINK element:

- Set the value of href to the location of the style sheet file. The value of href is a URI.
- Set the value of the type attribute to indicate the language of the linked (style sheet) resource. This allows the user agent to avoid downloading a style sheet for an unsupported style sheet language.
- Specify that the style sheet is persistent, preferred, or alternate:
  - To make a style sheet persistent, set the rel attribute to "stylesheet" and don't set the title attribute.
  - To make a style sheet preferred, set the rel attribute to "stylesheet" and name the style sheet with the title attribute.
  - To specify an alternate style sheet, set the rel attribute to "alternate stylesheet" and name the style sheet with the title attribute.

User agents should provide a means for users to view and pick from the list of alternate styles. The value of the title attribute is recommended as the name of each choice.

In this example, we first specify a persistent style sheet located in the file mystyle.css:

```
<LINK href="mystyle.css" rel="stylesheet" type="text/css">
```

Setting the title attribute makes this the author's preferred style sheet:

```
<LINK href="mystyle.css" title="compact" rel="stylesheet" type="text/css">
```

Adding the keyword "alternate" to the rel attribute makes it an alternate style sheet:

```
<LINK    href="mystyle.css"    title="Medium"    rel="alternate    stylesheet"
type="text/css">
```

For more information on external style sheets, please consult the section on links and external style sheets.

Authors may also use the META element to set the document's preferred style sheet. For example, to set the preferred style sheet to "compact" (see the preceding example), authors may include the following line in the HEAD:

```
<META http-equiv="Default-Style" content="compact">
```

The preferred style sheet may also be specified with HTTP headers. The above META declaration is equivalent to the HTTP header:

```
Default-Style: "compact"
```

If two or more META declarations or HTTP headers specify the preferred style sheet, the last one takes precedence. HTTP headers are considered to occur earlier than the document HEAD for this purpose.

If two or more LINK elements specify a preferred style sheet, the first one takes precedence.

Preferred style sheets specified with META or HTTP headers have precedence over those specified with the LINK element.

14.4 Cascading style sheets

Cascading style sheet languages such as CSS allow style information from several sources to be blended together. However, not all style sheet languages support cascading. To define a cascade, authors specify a sequence of LINK and/or STYLE elements. The style information is cascaded in the order the elements appear in the HEAD.

Note. *This specification does not specify how style sheets from different style languages cascade. Authors should avoid mixing style sheet languages.*

In the following example, we specify two alternate style sheets named "compact". If the user selects the "compact" style, the user agent must apply both external style sheets, as well as the persistent "common.css" style sheet. If the user selects the "big print" style, only the alternate style sheet "bigprint.css" and the persistent "common.css" will be applied.

```
<LINK rel="alternate stylesheet" title="compact"  href="small-base.css"   type="text/css">
<LINK rel="alternate stylesheet" title="compact"  href="small-extras.css" type="text/css">
<LINK rel="alternate stylesheet" title="big print" href="bigprint.css"    type="text/css">
<LINK rel="stylesheet" href="common.css" type="text/css">
```

Here is a cascade example that involves both the LINK and STYLE elements.

```
<LINK rel="stylesheet" href="corporate.css" type="text/css">
<LINK rel="stylesheet" href="techreport.css" type="text/css">
<STYLE type="text/css">
    p.special { color: rgb(230, 100, 180) }
</STYLE>
```

14.4.1 Media-dependent cascades

A cascade may include style sheets applicable to different media. Both LINK and STYLE may be used with the media attribute. The user agent is then responsible for filtering out those style sheets that do not apply to the current medium.

In the following example, we define a cascade where the "corporate" style sheet is provided in several versions: one suited to printing, one for screen use and one for speech-based browsers (useful, say, when reading email in the car). The "techreport" stylesheet applies to all media. The color rule defined by the STYLE element is used for print and screen but not for aural rendering.

```
<LINK rel="stylesheet" media="aural"  href="corporate-aural.css"  type="text/css">
<LINK rel="stylesheet" media="screen" href="corporate-screen.css" type="text/css">
<LINK rel="stylesheet" media="print"  href="corporate-print.css"  type="text/css">
<LINK rel="stylesheet" href="techreport.css" type="text/css">
<STYLE type="text/css">
    p.special { color: rgb(230, 100, 180) }
</STYLE>
```

14.4.2 Inheritance and cascading

When the user agent wants to render a document, it needs to find values for style properties, e.g. the font family, font style, size, line height, text color and so on. The exact mechanism depends on the style sheet language, but the following description is generally applicable:

The cascading mechanism is used when a number of style rules all apply directly to an element. The mechanism allows the user agent to sort the rules by specificity, to determine which rule to apply. If no rule can be found, the next step depends on whether the style property can be inherited or not. Not all properties can be inherited. For these properties the style sheet language provides default values for use when there are no explicit rules for a particular element.

If the property can be inherited, the user agent examines the immediately enclosing element to see if a rule applies to that. This process continues until an applicable rule is found. This mechanism allows style sheets to be specified compactly. For instance, authors may specify the font family for all elements within the BODY by a single rule that applies to the BODY element.

14.5 Hiding style data from user agents

Some style sheet languages support syntax intended to allow authors to hide the content of STYLE elements from non-conforming user agents.

This example illustrates for CSS how to comment out the content of STYLE elements to ensure that older non-conforming user agents will not render them as text.

```
<STYLE type="text/css">
<!--
    H1 { color: red }
    P  { color: blue}
    -->
</STYLE>
```

14.6 Linking to style sheets with HTTP headers

Web server managers may find it convenient to configure a server so that a style sheet will be applied to a group of pages. The HTTP Link header described in [RFC2068], section 19.6.1.2, has the same effect as a LINK element with the same attributes and values. Multiple Link headers correspond to multiple LINK elements occurring in the same order. For instance,

```
Link: <http://www.acme.com/corporate.css>; REL=stylesheet
```

corresponds to:

```
<LINK rel="stylesheet" href="http://www.acme.com/corporate.css">
```

It is possible to specify several alternate styles using multiple Link headers, and then use the rel attribute to determine the default style.

In the following example, "compact" is applied by default since it omits the "alternate" keyword for the rel attribute.

```
Link: <compact.css>; rel="stylesheet"; title="compact"
Link: <bigprint.css>; rel="alternate stylesheet"; title="big print"
```

This should also work when HTML documents are sent by email. Some email agents can alter the ordering of [RFC822] headers. To protect against this affecting the cascading order for style sheets specified by Link headers, authors can use header concatenation to merge several instances of the same header field. The quote marks are only needed when the attribute values include whitespace. Use SGML entities to reference characters that are otherwise not permitted within HTTP or email headers, or that are likely to be affected by transit through gateways.

`LINK` and `META` elements implied by HTTP headers are defined as occurring before any explicit `LINK` and `META` elements in the document's `HEAD`.

Chapter 15

Alignment, Font Styles, and Horizontal Rules

Contents

1. Formatting
    1. Background color
    2. Alignment
    3. Floating objects
        - Float an object
        - Float text around an object
2. Fonts
    1. Font style elements: the TT, I, B, BIG, SMALL, STRIKE, S, and U elements
    2. Font modifier elements: FONT and BASEFONT
3. Rules: the HR element

This section of the specification discusses some HTML elements and attributes that may be used for visual formatting of elements. Many of them are deprecated.

15.1 Formatting

15.1.1 Background color

Attribute definitions

bgcolor = *color* [CI]

   Deprecated. This attribute sets the background color for the document body or table cells.

This attribute sets the background color of the canvas for the document body (the BODY element) or for tables (the TABLE, TR, TH, and TD elements). Additional attributes for specifying text color can be used with the BODY element.

This attribute has been deprecated in favor of style sheets for specifying background color information.

15.1.2 Alignment

It is possible to align block elements (tables, images, objects, paragraphs, etc.) on the canvas with the `align` attribute. Although this attribute may be set for many HTML elements, its range of possible values sometimes differs from element to element. Here we only discuss the meaning of the align attribute for text.

Attribute definitions

align = left|center|right|justify [CI]

> **Deprecated.** This attribute specifies the horizontal alignment of its element with respect to the surrounding context. Possible values:
> - `left`: text lines are rendered flush left.
> - `center`: text lines are centered.
> - `right`: text lines are rendered flush right.
> - `justify`: text lines are justified to both margins.

The default depends on the base text direction. For left to right text, the default is `align=left`, while for right to left text, the default is `align=right`.

DEPRECATED EXAMPLE:
This example centers a heading on the canvas.

```
<H1 align="center"> How to Carve Wood </H1>
```

Using CSS, for example, you could achieve the same effect as follows:

```
<HEAD>
  <TITLE>How to Carve Wood</TITLE>
  <STYLE type="text/css">
```

```
  H1 { text-align: center}
  </STYLE>
<BODY>
  <H1> How to Carve Wood </H1>
```

Note that this would center all H1 declarations. You could reduce the scope of the style by setting the class attribute on the element:

```
<HEAD>
  <TITLE>How to Carve Wood</TITLE>
  <STYLE type="text/css">
   H1.wood {text-align: center}
  </STYLE>
<BODY>
  <H1 class="wood"> How to Carve Wood </H1>
```

DEPRECATED EXAMPLE:
Similarly, to right align a paragraph on the canvas with HTML's align attribute you could have:

```
<P align="right">...Lots of paragraph text...
```

which, with CSS, would be:

```
<HEAD>
  <TITLE>How to Carve Wood</TITLE>
  <STYLE type="text/css">
   P.mypar {text-align: right}
  </STYLE>
<BODY>
  <P class="mypar">...Lots of paragraph text...
```

DEPRECATED EXAMPLE:
To right align a series of paragraphs, group them with the DIV element:

```
<DIV align="right">
  <P>...text in first paragraph...
  <P>...text in second paragraph...
  <P>...text in third paragraph...
</DIV>
```

With CSS, the text-align property is inherited from the parent element, you can therefore use:

```
<HEAD>
 <TITLE>How to Carve Wood</TITLE>
 <STYLE type="text/css">
  DIV.mypars {text-align: right}
 </STYLE>
<BODY>
 <DIV class="mypars">
  <P>...text in first paragraph...
  <P>...text in second paragraph...
  <P>...text in third paragraph...
 </DIV>
```

To center the entire document with CSS:

```
<HEAD>
 <TITLE>How to Carve Wood</TITLE>
 <STYLE type="text/css">
  BODY {text-align: center}
 </STYLE>
<BODY>
 ...the body is centered...
</BODY>
```

The CENTER element is exactly equivalent to specifying the DIV element with the align attribute set to "center". **The CENTER element is** deprecated.

15.1.3 Floating objects

Images and objects may appear directly "in-line" or may be floated to one side of the page, temporarily altering the margins of text that may flow on either side of the object.

Float an object

The align attribute for object, images, tables, frames, etc., causes the object to float to the left or right margin. Floating objects generally begin a new line. This attribute takes the following values:

- left: Floats the object to the current left margin. Subsequent text flows along the image's right side.

- `right`: Floats the object to the current right margin. Subsequent text flows along the image's left side.

DEPRECATED EXAMPLE:
The following example shows how to float an `IMG` element to the current left margin of the canvas.

```
<IMG align="left" src="http://foo.com/animage.gif" alt="my boat">
```

Some alignment attributes also permit the "center" value, which does not cause floating, but centers the object within the current margins. However, for `P` and `DIV`, the value "center" causes the contents of the element to be centered.

Float text around an object

Another attribute, defined for the `BR` element, controls text flow around floating objects.

Attribute definitions

clear = none|left|right|all [CI]

Deprecated. Specifies where the next line should appear in a visual browser after the line break caused by this element. This attribute takes into account floating objects (images, tables, etc.). Possible values:

- `none`: The next line will begin normally. This is the default value.
- `left`: The next line will begin at nearest line below any floating objects on the left-hand margin.
- `right`: The next line will begin at nearest line below any floating objects on the right-hand margin.
- `all`: The next line will begin at nearest line below any floating objects on either margin.

Consider the following visual scenario, where text flows to the right of an image until a line is broken by a BR:

If the clear attribute is set to none, the line following BR will begin immediately below it at the right margin of the image:

```
*********   -----
|       |   ----
| image |   -<BR>
|       |   ----
*********
```

DEPRECATED EXAMPLE:
If the clear attribute is set to `left` or `all`, next line will appear as follows:

```
*********   -----
|       |   ----
| image |   -<BR clear="left">
|       |
*********
---------------
```

Using style sheets, you could specify that all line breaks should behave this way for objects (images, tables, etc.) floating against the left margin. With CSS, you could achieve this as follows:

```
<STYLE type="text/css">
BR { clear: left }
</STYLE>
```

To specify this behavior for a specific instance of the BR element, you could combine style information and the id attribute:

```
<HEAD>
...
<STYLE type="text/css">
BR#mybr { clear: left }
</STYLE>
</HEAD>
<BODY>
<P>...
*********   -----
|       |   ----
| table |   -<BR id="mybr">
|       |
*********
---------------
...
</BODY>
```

15.2 Fonts

The following HTML elements specify font information. Although they are not all deprecated, their use is discouraged in favor of style sheets.

15.2.1 Font style elements: the TT, I, B, BIG, SMALL, STRIKE, S, and U elements

```
<!ENTITY % fontstyle
 "TT | I | B | BIG | SMALL">
<!ELEMENT (%fontstyle;|%phrase;) - - (%inline;)*>
<!ATTLIST (%fontstyle;|%phrase;)
   %attrs;                                   —%coreattrs, %i18n, %events —
   >
```

Start tag: **required**, *End tag:* **required**

Attributes defined elsewhere

- id, class (document-wide identifiers)
- lang (language information), dir (text direction)
- title (element title)
- style (inline style information)
- onclick, ondblclick, onmousedown, onmouseup, onmouseover, onmousemove, onmouseout, onkeypress, onkeydown onkeyup (intrinsic events)

Rendering of font style elements depends on the user agent. The following is an informative description only.

TT: Renders as teletype or monospaced text.

I: Renders as italic text style.

B: Renders as bold text style.

BIG: Renders text in a "large" font.

SMALL: Renders text in a "small" font.

STRIKE and **S: Deprecated.** Render strike-through style text.

U: Deprecated. Renders underlined text.

The following sentence shows several types of text:

```
<P><b>bold</b>,
<i>italic</i>, <b><i>bold italic</i></b>, <tt>teletype text</tt>, and
<big>big</big> and <small>small</small> text.
```

These words might be rendered as follows:

bold, *italic*, ***bold italic***, `teletype text`, and big and small text.

It is possible to achieve a much richer variety of font effects using style sheets. To specify blue, italic text in a paragraph with CSS:

```
<HEAD>
<STYLE type="text/css">
P.mypar {font-style: italic; color: blue}
</STYLE>
</HEAD>
<P id="mypar">...Lots of blue italic text...
```

Font style elements must be properly nested. Rendering of nested font style elements depends on the user agent.

15.2.2 Font modifier elements: FONT and BASEFONT

FONT and BASEFONT are deprecated.

See the Transitional DTD for the formal definition.

Attribute definitions

size = *cdata* [CN]

Deprecated. This attribute sets the size of the font. Possible values:

- An integer between 1 and 7. This sets the font to some fixed size, whose rendering depends on the user agent. Not all user agents may render all seven sizes.

- A relative increase in font size. The value "+1" means one size larger. The value "-3" means three sizes smaller. All sizes belong to the scale of 1 to 7.

color = *color* [CI]

Deprecated. This attribute sets the text color.

face = *cdata* [CI]

Deprecated. This attribute defines a comma-separated list of font names the user agent should search for in order of preference.

Attributes defined elsewhere

- id, class (document-wide identifiers)
- lang (language information), dir (text direction)
- title (element title)
- style (inline style information)

The FONT element changes the font size and color for text in its contents.

The BASEFONT element sets the base font size (using the size attribute). Font size changes achieved with FONT are relative to the base font size set by BASEFONT. If BASEFONT is not used, the default base font size is 3.

DEPRECATED EXAMPLE:
The following example will show the difference between the seven font sizes available with FONT:

```
<P><font size=1>size=1</font>
<font size=2>size=2</font>
<font size=3>size=3</font>
<font size=4>size=4</font>
<font size=5>size=5</font>
<font size=6>size=6</font>
<font size=7>size=7</font>
```

This might be rendered as:

size=1 size=2 size=3 size=4 size=5 size=6 size=7

The following shows an example of the effect of relative font sizes using a base font size of 3:

size=-4 size=-3 size=-2 size=-1 size=+1 size=+2 size=+3 size=+4

The base font size does not apply to headings, except where these are modified using the FONT element with a relative font size change.

15.3 Rules: the HR element

```
<!ELEMENT HR - O EMPTY-horizontal rule -->
<!ATTLIST HR
  %coreattrs;                          -id, class, style, title -
  %events;
  >
```

*Start tag: **required**, End tag: **forbidden***

Attribute definitions

align = left|center|right [CI]

> **Deprecated.** This attribute specifies the horizontal alignment of the rule with respect to the surrounding context. Possible values:
>
> - left: the rule is rendered flush left.
> - center: the rule is centered.
> - right: the rule is rendered flush right.
>
> The default is align=center.

noshade [CI]

> **Deprecated.** When set, this boolean attribute requests that the user agent render the rule in a solid color rather than as the traditional two-color "groove".

size = *pixels* [CI]

> **Deprecated.** This attribute specifies the height of the rule. The default value for this attribute depends on the user agent.

width = *length* [CI]

> **Deprecated.** This attribute specifies the width of the rule. The default width is 100%, i.e., the rule extends across the entire canvas.

Attributes defined elsewhere

- id, class (document-wide identifiers)
- lang (language information), dir (text direction)
- title (element title)
- style (inline style information)
- onclick, ondblclick, onmousedown, onmouseup, onmouseover, onmousemove, onmouseout, onkeypress, onkeydown, onkeyup (intrinsic events)
- align (alignment)

The HR element causes a horizontal rule to be rendered by visual user agents.

The amount of vertical space inserted between a rule and the content that surrounds it depends on the user agent.

DEPRECATED EXAMPLE:
This example centers the rules, sizing them to half the available width between the margins. The top rule has the default thickness while the bottom two are set to 5 pixels. The bottom rule should be rendered in a solid color without shading:

```
<HR width="50%" align="center">
<HR size="5" width="50%" align="center">
<HR noshade size="5" width="50%" align="center">
```

These rules might be rendered as follows:

Chapter 16

Frames

Contents

1. Introduction to frames
2. Layout of frames
   1. The FRAMESET element
      - Rows and columns
      - Nested frame sets
      - Sharing data among frames
   2. The FRAME element
      - Setting the initial contents of a frame
      - Visual rendering of a frame
3. Specifying target frame information
   1. Setting the default target for links
   2. Target semantics
4. Alternate content
   1. The NOFRAMES element
   2. Long descriptions of frames
5. Inline frames: the IFRAME element

16.1 Introduction to frames

HTML frames allow authors to present documents in multiple views, which may be independent windows or subwindows. Multiple views offer designers a way to keep certain information visible, while other views are scrolled or replaced. For example, within the same window, one frame might display a static banner, a second a navigation menu, and a third the main document that can be scrolled though or replaced by navigating in the second frame.

Here is a simple frame document:

```
<!DOCTYPE HTML PUBLIC "-//W3C//DTD HTML 4.0 Frameset//EN"
    "http://www.w3.org/TR/REC-html40/frameset.dtd">
<HTML>
<HEAD>
<TITLE>A simple frameset document</TITLE>
</HEAD>
<FRAMESET cols="20%, 80%">
  <FRAMESET rows="100, 200">
      <FRAME src="contents_of_frame1.html">
      <FRAME src="contents_of_frame2.gif">
  </FRAMESET>
  <FRAME src="contents_of_frame3.html">
  <NOFRAMES>
      <P>This frameset document contains:
      <UL>
          <LI><A href="contents_of_frame1.html">Some neat contents</A>
          <LI><IMG src="contents_of_frame2.gif" alt="A neat image">
          <LI><A href="contents_of_frame3.html">Some other neat contents</A>
      </UL>
  </NOFRAMES>
</FRAMESET>
</HTML>
```

that might create a frame layout something like this:

```
 -------------------------------------------
|         |                                 |
|         |                                 |
| Frame 1 |                                 |
|         |                                 |
|         |                                 |
|---------|                                 |
|         |                                 |
|         |          Frame 3                |
|         |                                 |
|         |                                 |
| Frame 2 |                                 |
|         |                                 |
|         |                                 |
|         |                                 |
|         |                                 |
 -------------------------------------------
```

If the user agent can't display frames or is configured not to, it will render the contents of the NOFRAMES element.

16.2 Layout of frames

An HTML document that describes frame layout (called a *frameset document*) has a different makeup than an HTML document without frames. A standard document has one HEAD section and one BODY. A frameset document has a HEAD, and a FRAMESET in place of the BODY.

The FRAMESET section of a document specifies the layout of views in the main user agent window. In addition, the FRAMESET section can contain a NOFRAMES element to provide alternate content for user agents that do not support frames or are configured not to display frames.

Elements that might normally be placed in the BODY element must not appear before the first FRAMESET element or the FRAMESET will be ignored.

16.2.1 The FRAMESET element

```
<![ %HTML.Frameset; [
<!ELEMENT FRAMESET - - ((FRAMESET|FRAME)+ & NOFRAMES?)—window subdivision—>
<!ATTLIST FRAMESET
  %coreattrs;                              — id, class, style, title —
  rows         %MultiLengths; #IMPLIED     — list of lengths,
                                             default: 100% (1 row) —
  cols         %MultiLengths; #IMPLIED     — list of lengths,
                                             default: 100% (1 col) —
  onload       %Script;       #IMPLIED     — all the frames have been loaded —
  onunload     %Script;       #IMPLIED     — all the frames have been removed—
  >
]]>
```

Attribute definitions

rows = *multi-length-list* [CN]

This attribute specifies the layout of horizontal frames. It is a comma-separated list of pixels, percentages, and relative lengths. The default value is 100%, meaning one row.

cols = *multi-length-list* [CN]

This attribute specifies the layout of vertical frames. It is a comma-separated list of pixels, percentages, and relative lengths. The default value is 100%, meaning one column.

Attributes defined elsewhere

- id, class (document-wide identifiers)
- title (element title)
- style (inline style information)
- onload, onunload (intrinsic events)

The FRAMESET element specifies the layout of the main user window in terms of rectangular subspaces.

Rows and columns

Setting the rows attribute defines the number of horizontal subspaces in a frameset. Setting the cols attribute defines the number of vertical subspaces. Both attributes may be set simultaneously to create a grid.

If the rows attribute is not set, each column extends the entire length of the page. If the cols attribute is not set, each row extends the entire width of the page. If neither attribute is set, the frame takes up exactly the size of the page.

Frames are created left-to-right for columns and top-to-bottom for rows. When both attributes are specified, views are created left-to-right in the top row, left-to-right in the second row, etc.

The first example divides the screen vertically in two (i.e., creates a top half and a bottom half).

```
<FRAMESET rows="50%, 50%">
...the rest of the definition...
</FRAMESET>
```

The next example creates three columns: the second has a fixed width of 250 pixels (useful, for example, to hold an image with a known size). The first receives 25% of the remaining space and the third 75% of the remaining space.

```
<FRAMESET cols="1*,250,3*">
...the rest of the definition...
</FRAMESET>
```

The next example creates a 2x3 grid of subspaces.

```
<FRAMESET rows="30%,70%" cols="33%,34%,33%">
...the rest of the definition...
</FRAMESET>
```

For the next example, suppose the browser window is currently 1000 pixels high. The first view is allotted 30% of the total height (300 pixels). The second view is specified to be exactly 400 pixels high. This leaves 300 pixels to be divided between the other two frames. The fourth frame's height is specified as "2*", so it is twice as high as the third frame, whose height is only "*" (equivalent to 1*). Therefore the third frame will be 100 pixels high and the fourth will be 200 pixels high.

```
<FRAMESET rows="30%,400,*,2*">
...the rest of the definition...
</FRAMESET>
```

Absolute lengths that do not sum to 100% of the real available space should be adjusted by the user agent. When underspecified, remaining space should be allotted proportionally to each view. When overspecified, each view should be reduced according to its specified proportion of the total space.

Nested frame sets

Framesets may be nested to any level.

In the following example, the outer FRAMESET divides the available space into three equal columns. The inner FRAMESET then divides the second area into two rows of unequal height.

```
<FRAMESET cols="33%, 33%, 34%">
     ...contents of first frame...
     <FRAMESET rows="40%, 50%">
          ...contents of second frame, first row...
          ...contents of second frame, second row...
     </FRAMESET>
     ...contents of third frame...
</FRAMESET>
```

Sharing data among frames

Authors may share data among several frames by including this data via an OBJECT element. Authors should include the OBJECT element in the HEAD element of a frameset document and name it with the id attribute. Any document that is the contents of a frame in the frameset may refer to this identifier.

The following example illustrates how a script might refer to an OBJECT element defined for an entire frameset:

```
<!DOCTYPE HTML PUBLIC "-//W3C//DTD HTML 4.0 Frameset//EN"
    "http://www.w3.org/TR/REC-html40/frameset.dtd">
<HTML>
<HEAD>
<TITLE>This is a frameset with OBJECT in the HEAD</TITLE>
<!- This OBJECT is not rendered! ->
<OBJECT id="myobject" data="data.bar"></OBJECT>
</HEAD>
<FRAMESET>
    <FRAME src="bianca.html" name="bianca">
</FRAMESET>
</HTML>

<!- In bianca.html ->
<HTML>
<HEAD>
<TITLE>Bianca's page</TITLE>
</HEAD>
<BODY>
...the beginning of the document...
<P>
<SCRIPT type="text/javascript">
parent.myobject.myproperty
</SCRIPT>
...the rest of the document...
</BODY>
</HTML>
```

16.2.2 The FRAME element

```
<![ %HTML.Frameset; [
<!- reserved frame names start with "_" otherwise starts with letter ->
<!ELEMENT FRAME - O EMPTY              - subwindow ->
<!ATTLIST FRAME
```

```
        %coreattrs;                            - id, class, style, title -
        longdesc     %URI;         #IMPLIED    - link to long description
                                                 (complements title) -
        name         CDATA         #IMPLIED    - name of frame for targetting -
        src          %URI;         #IMPLIED    - source of frame content -
        frameborder  (1|0)         1           - request frame borders? -
        marginwidth  %Pixels;      #IMPLIED    - margin widths in pixels -
        marginheight %Pixels;      #IMPLIED    - margin height in pixels -
        noresize     (noresize)    #IMPLIED    - allow users to resize frames? -
        scrolling    (yes|no|auto) auto        - scrollbar or none -
        >
]]>
```

Attribute definitions

name = *cdata* [CI]

This attribute assigns a name to the current frame. This name may be used as the target of subsequent links.

longdesc = *uri* [CT]

This attribute specifies a link to a long description of the frame. This description should supplement the short description provided using the title attribute, and may be particularly useful for nonvisual user agents.

src = *uri* [CT]

This attribute specifies the location of the initial contents to be contained in the frame.

noresize [CI]

When present, this boolean attribute tells the user agent that the frame window must not be resizeable.

scrolling = auto|yes|no [CI]

This attribute specifies scroll information for the frame window. Possible values

- auto: This value tells the user agent to provide scrolling devices for the frame window when necessary. This is the default value.

- **yes**: This value tells the user agent to always provide scrolling devices for the frame window.
- **no**: This value tells the user agent not to provide scrolling devices for the frame window.

frameborder = 1 | 0 [CN]

This attribute provides the user agent with information about the frame border. Possible values:

- **1**: This value tells the user agent to draw a separator between this frame and every adjoining frame. This is the default value.
- **0**: This value tells the user agent not to draw a separator between this frame and every adjoining frame. Note that separators may be drawn next to this frame nonetheless if specified by other frames.

marginwidth = *pixels* [CN]

This attribute specifies the amount of space to be left between the frame's contents in its left and right margins. The value must be greater than one pixel. The default value depends on the user agent.

marginheight = *pixels* [CN]

This attribute specifies the amount of space to be left between the frame's contents in its top and bottom margins. The value must be greater than one pixel. The default value depends on the user agent.

Attributes defined elsewhere

- id, class (document-wide identifiers)
- title (element title)
- style (inline style information)
- target (target frame information)

The FRAME element defines the contents and appearance of a single frame.

Setting the initial contents of a frame

The src attribute specifies the initial document the frame will contain.

The following example HTML document:

```
<!DOCTYPE HTML PUBLIC "-//W3C//DTD HTML 4.0 Frameset//EN"
    "http://www.w3.org/TR/REC-html40/frameset.dtd">
<HTML>
<HEAD>
<TITLE>A frameset document</TITLE>
</HEAD>
<FRAMESET cols="33%,33%,33%">
  <FRAMESET rows="*,200">
      <FRAME src="contents_of_frame1.html">
      <FRAME src="contents_of_frame2.gif">
  </FRAMESET>
  <FRAME src="contents_of_frame3.html">
  <FRAME src="contents_of_frame4.html">
</FRAMESET>
</HTML>
```

should create a frame layout something like this:

```
-----------------------------------------------
|Frame 1         |Frame 3        |Frame 4       |
|                |               |              |
|                |               |              |
|                |               |              |
|                |               |              |
|                |               |              |
|                |               |              |
|                |               |              |
|                |               |              |
----------------|                |              |
|Frame 2         |               |              |
|                |               |              |
|                |               |              |
-----------------------------------------------
```

and cause the user agent to load each file into a separate view.

The contents of a frame must not be in the same document as the frame's definition.

ILLEGAL EXAMPLE:
The following frameset definition is not legal HTML since the contents of the second frame are in the same document as the frameset.

```
<!DOCTYPE HTML PUBLIC "-//W3C//DTD HTML 4.0 Frameset//EN"
    "http://www.w3.org/TR/REC-html40/frameset.dtd">
<HTML>
<HEAD>
<TITLE>A frameset document</TITLE>
</HEAD>
<FRAMESET cols="50%,50%">
  <FRAME src="contents_of_frame1.html">
  <FRAME src="#anchor_in_same_document">
  <NOFRAMES>
  ...some text...
  <H2><A name="anchor_in_same_document">Important section</A></H2>
  ...some text...
  </NOFRAMES>
</FRAMESET>
</HTML>
```

Visual rendering of a frame

The following example illustrates the usage of the decorative FRAME attributes. We specify that frame 1 will allow no scroll bars. Frame 2 will leave white space around its contents (initially, an image file) and the frame will not be resizeable. No border will be drawn between frames 3 and 4. Borders will be drawn (by default) between frames 1, 2, and 3.

```
<!DOCTYPE HTML PUBLIC "-//W3C//DTD HTML 4.0 Frameset//EN"
    "http://www.w3.org/TR/REC-html40/frameset.dtd">
<HTML>
<HEAD>
<TITLE>A frameset document</TITLE>
</HEAD>
<FRAMESET cols="33%,33%,33%">
  <FRAMESET rows="*,200">
      <FRAME src="contents_of_frame1.html" scrolling="no">
      <FRAME src="contents_of_frame2.gif"
             marginwidth="10" marginheight="15"
```

```
            noresize>
   </FRAMESET>
   <FRAME src="contents_of_frame3.html" frameborder="0">
   <FRAME src="contents_of_frame4.html" frameborder="0">
</FRAMESET>
</HTML>
```

16.3 Specifying target frame information

Note. For information about current practice in determining the target of a frame, please consult the notes on frames in the appendix.

Attribute definitions

target = *frame-target* [CI]

This attribute specifies the name of a frame where a document is to be opened.

By assigning a name to a frame via the name attribute, authors can refer to it as the "target" of links defined by other elements. The target attribute may be set for elements that create links (A, LINK), image maps (AREA), and forms (FORM).

Please consult the section on target frame names for information about recognized frame names.

This example illustrates how targets allow the dynamic modification of a frame's contents. First we define a frameset in the document frameset.html, shown here:

```
<!DOCTYPE HTML PUBLIC "-//W3C//DTD HTML 4.0 Frameset//EN"
    "http://www.w3.org/TR/REC-html40/frameset.dtd">
<HTML>
<HEAD>
<TITLE>A frameset document</TITLE>
</HEAD>
<FRAMESET rows="50%,50%">
    <FRAME name="fixed" src="init_fixed.html">
    <FRAME name="dynamic" src="init_dynamic.html">
</FRAMESET>
</HTML>
```

Then, in `init_dynamic.html`, we link to the frame named "dynamic".

```
<!DOCTYPE HTML PUBLIC "-//W3C//DTD HTML 4.0 Transitional//EN"
    "http://www.w3.org/TR/REC-html40/loose.dtd">
<HTML>
<HEAD>
<TITLE>A document with anchors with specific targets</TITLE>
</HEAD>
<BODY>
...beginning of the document...
<P>Now you may advance to
    <A href="slide2.html" target="dynamic">slide 2.</A>
...more document...
<P>You're doing great. Now on to
    <A href="slide3.html" target="dynamic">slide 3.</A>
</BODY>
</HTML>
```

Activating either link opens a new document in the frame named "dynamic" while the other frame, "fixed", maintains its initial contents.

Note. *A frameset definition never changes, but the contents of one of its frames can. Once the initial contents of a frame change, the frameset definition no longer reflects the current state of its frames.*

There is currently no way to encode the entire state of a frameset in a URI. Therefore, many user agents do not allow users to assign a bookmark to a frameset.

Framesets may make navigation forward and backward through your user agent's history more difficult for users.

16.3.1 Setting the default target for links

When many links in the same document designate the same target, it is possible to specify the target once and dispense with the target attribute of each element. This is done by setting the target attribute of the `BASE` element.

We return to the previous example, this time factorizing the target information by defining it in the `BASE` element and removing it from the `A` elements.

```
<!DOCTYPE HTML PUBLIC "-//W3C//DTD HTML 4.0 Transitional//EN"
    "http://www.w3.org/TR/REC-html40/loose.dtd">
<HTML>
<HEAD>
<TITLE>A document with BASE with a specific target</TITLE>
<BASE href="http://www.mycom.com/Slides" target="dynamic">
</HEAD>
<BODY>
...beginning of the document...
<P>Now you may advance to <A href="slide2.html">slide 2.</A>
...more document...
<P>You're doing great. Now on to
        <A href="slide3.html">slide 3.</A>
</BODY>
</HTML>
```

16.3.2 Target semantics

User agents should determine the target frame in which to load a linked resource according to the following precedences (highest priority to lowest):

1. If an element has its target attribute set to a known frame, when the element is activated (i.e., a link is followed or a form is processed), the resource designated by the element should be loaded into the target frame.

2. If an element does not have the target attribute set but the BASE element does, the BASE element's target attribute determines the frame.

3. If neither the element nor the BASE element refers to a target, the resource designated by the element should be loaded into the frame containing the element.

4. If any target attribute refers to an unknown frame F, the user agent should create a new window and frame, assign the name F to the frame, and load the resource designated by the element in the new frame.

User agents may provide users with a mechanism to override the target attribute.

16.4 Alternate content

Authors should supply alternate content for those user agents that do not support frames or are configured not to display frames.

16.4.1 The NOFRAMES element

```
<![ %HTML.Frameset; [
<!ENTITY % noframes.content "(BODY) -(NOFRAMES)">
]]>

<!ENTITY % noframes.content "(%flow;)*">

<!ELEMENT NOFRAMES - - %noframes.content;
—alternate content container for non frame-based rendering —>
<!ATTLIST NOFRAMES
    %attrs;                          —%coreattrs, %i18n, %events —
    >
```

The NOFRAMES element specifies content that should be displayed only when frames are not being displayed. User agents that support frames must only display the contents of a NOFRAMES declaration when configured not to display frames. User agents that do not support frames must display the contents of NOFRAMES in any case.

NOFRAMES can be used in the FRAMESET section of a frameset document.

For example:

```
<!DOCTYPE HTML PUBLIC "-//W3C//DTD HTML 4.0 Frameset//EN"
    "http://www.w3.org/TR/REC-html40">
<HTML>
<HEAD>
<TITLE>A frameset document with NOFRAMES</TITLE>
</HEAD>
<FRAMESET cols="50%, 50%">
    <FRAME src="main.html">
    <FRAME src="table_of_contents.html">
    <NOFRAMES>
    <P>Here is the <A href="main-noframes.html">
```

```
                    non-frame based version of the document.</A>
        </NOFRAMES>
</FRAMESET>
</HTML>
```

16.4.2 Long descriptions of frames

The longdesc attribute allows authors to make frame documents more accessible to people using non-visual user agents. This attribute designates a resource that provides a long description of the frame. Authors should note that long descriptions associated with frames are attached to the *frame*, not the frame's contents. Since the contents may vary over time, the initial long description is likely to become inappropriate for the frame's later contents. In particular, authors should not include an image as the sole content of a frame.

The following frameset document describes two frames. The left frame contains a table of contents and the right frame initially contains an image of an ostrich:

```
<!DOCTYPE HTML PUBLIC "-//W3C//DTD HTML 4.0 Frameset//EN"
    "http://www.w3.org/TR/REC-html40">
<HTML>
<HEAD>
<TITLE>A poorly-designed frameset document</TITLE>
</HEAD>
<FRAMESET cols="20%, 80%">
    <FRAME src="table_of_contents.html">
    <FRAME src="ostrich.gif" longdesc="ostrich-desc.html">
</FRAMESET>
</HTML>
```

Note that the image has been included in the frame independently of any HTML element, so the author has no means of specifying alternate text other than via the longdesc attribute. If the contents of the right frame change (e.g., the user selects a rattlesnake from the table of contents), users will have no textual access to the frame's new content.

Thus, authors should not put an image directly in a frame. Instead, the image should be specified in a separate HTML document, and therein annotated with the appropriate alternate text:

```
<!DOCTYPE HTML PUBLIC "-//W3C//DTD HTML 4.0 Frameset//EN"
    "http://www.w3.org/TR/REC-html40">
```

```
<HTML>
<HEAD>
<TITLE>A well-designed frameset document</TITLE>
</HEAD>
<FRAMESET cols="20%, 80%">
   <FRAME src="table_of_contents.html">
   <FRAME src="ostrich-container.html">
</FRAMESET>
</HTML>

<!-- In ostrich-container.html: -->
<HTML>
<HEAD>
<TITLE>The fast and powerful ostrich</TITLE>
</HEAD>
<P>
<OBJECT data="ostrich.gif" type="image/gif">
These ostriches sure taste good!
</OBJECT>
</HTML>
```

16.5 Inline frames: the IFRAME element

```
<!ELEMENT IFRAME - - (%flow;)*        -- inline subwindow -->
<!ATTLIST IFRAME
  %coreattrs;                         -- id, class, style, title --
  longdesc    %URI;       #IMPLIED    -- link to long description
                                         (complements title) --
  name        CDATA       #IMPLIED    -- name of frame for targetting --
  src         %URI;       #IMPLIED    -- source of frame content --
  frameborder (1|0)       1           -- request frame borders? --
  marginwidth %Pixels;    #IMPLIED    -- margin widths in pixels --
  marginheight %Pixels;   #IMPLIED    -- margin height in pixels --
  scrolling   (yes|no|auto) auto      -- scrollbar or none --
  align       %IAlign;    #IMPLIED    -- vertical or horizontal alignment --
  height      %Length;    #IMPLIED    -- frame height --
  width       %Length;    #IMPLIED    -- frame width --
  >
```

Attribute definitions

`longdesc` = *uri* [CT]

> This attribute specifies a link to a long description of the frame. This description should supplement the short description provided using the title attribute, and is particularly useful for non-visual user agents.

name = *cdata* [CI]

> This attribute assigns a name to the current frame. This name may be used as the target of subsequent links.

width = *length* [CN]

> The width of the inline frame.

height = *length* [CN]

> The height of the inline frame.

Attributes defined elsewhere

- id, class (document-wide identifiers)
- title (element title)
- style (inline style information)
- name, src, frameborder, marginwidth, marginheight, scrolling (frame controls and decoration)
- target (target frame information)
- align (alignment)

The `IFRAME` element allows authors to insert a frame within a block of text. Inserting an inline frame within a section of text is much like inserting an object via the `OBJECT` element: they both allow you to insert an HTML document in the middle of another, they may both be aligned with surrounding text, etc.

The information to be inserted inline is designated by the src attribute of this element. The contents of the `IFRAME` element, on the other hand, should only be displayed by user agents that do not support frames or are configured not to display frames.

For user agents that support frames, the following example will place an inline frame surrounded by a border in the middle of the text.

```
<IFRAME src="foo.html" width="400" height="500"
        scrolling="auto" frameborder="1">
[Your user agent does not support frames or is currently configured
not to display frames. However, you may visit
<A href="foo.html">the related document.</A>]
</IFRAME>
```

Inline frames may not be resized (and thus, they do not take the noresize attribute).

Note. *HTML documents may also be embedded in other HTML documents with the* OBJECT *element. See the section on* embedded documents *for details.*

Chapter 17

Forms

Contents

1. Introduction to forms
2. Controls
   1. Control types
3. The `FORM` element
4. The `INPUT` element
   1. Control types created with `INPUT`
   2. Examples of forms containing `INPUT` controls
5. The `BUTTON` element
6. The `SELECT`, `OPTGROUP`, and `OPTION` elements
   1. Preselected options
7. The `TEXTAREA` element
8. The `ISINDEX` element
9. Labels
   1. The `LABEL` element
10. Adding structure to forms: the `FIELDSET` and `LEGEND` elements
11. Giving focus to an element
    1. Tabbing navigation
    2. Access keys
12. Disabled and read-only controls
    1. Disabled controls
    2. Read-only controls
13. Form submission
    1. Form submission method
    2. Successful controls
    3. Processing form data
       - Step one: Identify the successful controls
       - Step two: Build a form data set

- Step three: Encode the form data set
- Step four: Submit the encoded form data set
4. Form content types
   - application/x-www-form-urlencoded
   - multipart/form-data

17.1 Introduction to forms

An HTML form is a section of a document containing normal content, markup, special elements called controls (checkboxes, radio buttons, menus, etc.), and labels on those controls. Users generally "complete" a form by modifying its controls (entering text selecting menu items, etc.), before submitting the form to an agent for processing (e.g., to a Web server, to a mail server, etc.) Here's a simple form that includes labels, radio buttons, and push buttons (reset the form or submit it):

```
<FORM action="http://somesite.com/prog/adduser" method="post">
    <P
    <LABEL for="firstname"First name: </LABEL>
            <INPUT type="text" id="firstname"<BR
    <LABEL for="lastname"Last name: </LABEL>
            <INPUT type="text" id="lastname"<BR
    <LABEL for="email"email: </LABEL>
            <INPUT type="text" id="email"<BR
    <INPUT type="radio" name="sex" value="Male" Male<BR
    <INPUT type="radio" name="sex" value="Female" Female<BR
    <INPUT type="submit" value="Send" <INPUT type="reset">
    </P
</FORM
```

Note. *This specification includes more detailed information about forms in the subsections on* form display issues.

17.2 Controls

Users interact with forms through named *controls*.

A control's *"control name"* is given by its name attribute. The scope of the name attribute for a control within a FORM element is the FORM element.

Each control has both an initial value and a current value, both of which are character strings. Please consult the definition of each control for information about initial values and possible constraints on values imposed by the control. In general, a control's *"initial value"* may be specified with the control element's `value` attribute. However, the initial value of a `TEXTAREA` element is given by its contents, and the initial value of an `OBJECT` element in a form is determined by the object implementation (i.e., it lies outside the scope of this specification).

The control's *"current value"* is first set to the initial value. Thereafter, the control's current value may be modified through user interaction and scripts.

A control's initial value does not change. Thus, when a form is reset, each control's current value is reset to its initial value. If a control does not have an initial value, the effect of a form reset on that control is undefined.

When a form is submitted for processing, some controls have their name paired with their current value and these pairs are submitted with the form. Those controls for which name/value pairs are submitted are called successful controls.

17.2.1 Control types

HTML defines the following control types:

buttons

Authors may create three types of buttons:

- submit buttons: When activated, a submit button submits a form. A form may contain more than one submit button.

- reset buttons: When activated, a reset button resets all controls to their initial values.

- push buttons: Push buttons have no default behavior. Each push button may have client-side scripts associated with the element's event attributes. When an event occurs (e.g., the user presses the button, releases it, etc.), the associated script is triggered.

Authors should specify the scripting language of a push button script through a default script declaration (with the `META` element).

Authors create buttons with the `BUTTON` element or the `INPUT` element. Please consult the definitions of these elements for details about specifying different button types. ***Note.*** *Authors should note that the* `BUTTON` *element offers richer rendering capabilities than the* `INPUT` *element.*

checkboxes

Checkboxes (and radio buttons) are on/off switches that may be toggled by the user. A switch is "on" when the control element's selected attribute is set.

When a form is submitted, only "on" checkbox controls can become successful. Several checkboxes in a form may share the same control name. Thus, for example, checkboxes allow users to select several values for the same property. The INPUT element is used to create a checkbox control.

radio buttons

Radio buttons are like checkboxes except that when several share the same control name, they are mutually exclusive: when one is switched "on", all others with the same name are switched "off". The INPUT element is used to create a radio button control.

menus

Menus offer users options from which to choose. The SELECT element creates a menu, in combination with the OPTGROUP and OPTION elements.

text input

Authors may create two types of controls that allow users to input text. The INPUT element creates a single-line input control and the TEXTAREA element creates a multi-line input control. In both cases, the input text becomes the control's current value.

file select

This control type allows the user to select files so that their contents may be submitted with a form. The INPUT element is used to create a file select control.

hidden controls

Authors may create controls that are not rendered but whose values are submitted with a form. Authors generally use this control type to store information between client/server exchanges that would otherwise be lost due to the stateless nature of HTTP (see [RFC2068]). The INPUT element is used to create a hidden control.

object controls

Authors may insert generic objects in forms such that associated values are submitted along with other controls. Authors create object controls with the OBJECT element.

The elements used to create controls generally appear inside a FORM element, but may also appear outside of a FORM element declaration when they are used to build user interfaces. This is discussed in the section on intrinsic events. Note that controls outside a form cannot be successful controls.

17.3 The FORM element

```
<!ELEMENT FORM - - (%block;|SCRIPT)+ -(FORM)—interactive form —
<!ATTLIST FORM
  %attrs;                              — %coreattrs, %i18n, %events —
  action         %URI;         #REQUIRED — server-side form handler —
  method         (GET|POST)    GET       — HTTP method used to submit the form—
  enctype        %ContentType; "application/x-www-form-urlencoded"
  onsubmit       %Script;      #IMPLIED  —the form was submitted —
  onreset        %Script;      #IMPLIED  —the form was reset —
  accept-charset %Charsets;    #IMPLIED  —list of supported charsets —
```

*Start tag: **required**, End tag: **required*** *Attribute definitions*

action = uri [CT]

This attribute specifies a form processing agent. For example, the value might be a HTTP URI (to submit the form to a program) or a mailto URI (to email the form).

method = get|post [CI]

This attribute specifies which HTTP method will be used to submit the form data set. Possible (case-insensitive) values are "get" (the default) and "post". See the section on form submission for usage information.

enctype = content-type [CI]

This attribute specifies the content type used to submit the form to the server (when the value of method is "post"). The default value for this attribute is "application/x-www-form-urlencoded". The value "multipart/form-data" should be used in combination with the INPUT element, type="file".

accept-charset = charset list [CI]

This attribute specifies the list of ..\charset.html - doc-char-setcharacter encodings for input data that must be accepted by the server processing this form. The value is a space- and/or comma-delimited list of charset values. The server must interpret this list as an exclusive-or list, i.e., the server must be able to accept any single character encoding per entity received.

The default value for this attribute is the reserved string "UNKNOWN". User agents may interpret this value as the character encoding that was used to transmit the document containing this FORM element.

accept = content-type-list [CI]

This attribute specifies a comma-separated list of content types that a server processing this form will handle correctly. User agents may use this information to filter out non-conforming files when prompting a user to select files to be sent to the server (cf. the INPUT element when type="file").

Attributes defined elsewhere

- id, class (document-wide identifiers)
- lang (language information), dir (text direction)
- style (inline style information)
- title (element title)
- target (target frame information)
- onsubmit, onreset, onclick, ondblclick, onmousedown, onmouseup, onmouseover, onmousemove, onmouseout, onkeypress, onkeydown, onkeyup (intrinsic events)

The FORM element acts as a container for controls. It specifies:

- The layout of the form (given by the contents of the element).
- The program that will handle the completed and submitted form (the action attribute). The receiving program must be able to parse name/value pairs in order to make use of them.
- The method by which user data will be sent to the server (the method attribute).
- A character encoding that must be accepted by the server in order to handle this form (the accept-charset attribute). User agents may advise the user of the value of the accept-charset attribute and/or restrict the user's ability to enter unrecognized characters.

A form can contain text and markup (paragraphs, lists, etc.) in addition to form controls. The following example shows a form that is to be processed by the "adduser" program when submitted. The form will be sent to the program using the HTTP "post" method.

```
<FORM action="http://somesite.com/prog/adduser" method="post"
...form contents...
</FORM>
```

The next example shows how to send a submitted form to an email address:

```
<FORM action="mailto:Kligor.T@gee.whiz.com" method="post"
...form contents...
</FORM>
```

Please consult the section on form submission for information about how user agents must prepare form data for servers and how user agents should handle expected responses. ***Note.*** *Further discussion on the behavior of servers that receive form data is beyond the scope of this specification.*

17.4 The INPUT element

```
<!ENTITY % InputType
  "(TEXT | PASSWORD | CHECKBOX |
    RADIO | SUBMIT | RESET |
    FILE | HIDDEN | IMAGE | BUTTON)"

<!- attribute name required for all but submit & reset -
  <!ELEMENT INPUT - O EMPTY            - form control -
  <!ATTLIST INPUT
    %attrs;                            - %coreattrs, %i18n, %events -
    type         %InputType;    TEXT   - what kind of widget is needed -
    name         CDATA          #IMPLIED - submit as part of form -
    value        CDATA          #IMPLIED - required for radio and checkboxes -
    checked      (checked)      #IMPLIED - for radio buttons and check boxes -
    disabled     (disabled)     #IMPLIED - unavailable in this context -
    readonly     (readonly)     #IMPLIED - for text and passwd -
    size         CDATA          #IMPLIED - specific to each type of field -
    maxlength    NUMBER         #IMPLIED - max chars for text fields -
    src          %URI;          #IMPLIED - for fields with images -
    alt          CDATA          #IMPLIED -short description -
    usemap       %URI;          #IMPLIED -use client-side image map -
    tabindex     NUMBER         #IMPLIED -position in tabbing order -
    accesskey    %Character;    #IMPLIED -accessibility key character -
```

```
        onfocus      %Script;                #IMPLIED   -the element got the focus -
        onblur       %Script;                #IMPLIED   -the element lost the focus -
        onselect     %Script;                #IMPLIED   -some text was selected -
        onchange     %Script;                #IMPLIED   -the element value was changed -
        accept       %ContentTypes;          #IMPLIED   -list of MIME types for file upload -
```

Start tag: **required**, End tag: **forbidden** Attribute definitions

```
type = text|password|checkbox|radio|submit|reset|file|hidden|image|button [CI]
```

This attribute specifies the type of control to create. The default value for this attribute is "text".

name = cdata [CI]

This attribute assigns the control name.

value = cdata [CA]

This attribute specifies the initial value of the control. It is optional except when the type attribute has the value "radio".

size = cdata [CN]

This attribute tells the user agent the initial width of the control. The width is given in pixels except when type attribute has the value "text" or "password". In that case, its value refers to the (integer) number of characters.

maxlength = number [CN]

When the type attribute has the value "text" or "password", this attribute specifies the maximum number of characters the user may enter. This number may exceed the specified size, in which case the user agent should offer a scrolling mechanism. The default value for this attribute is an unlimited number.

checked [CI]

When the type attribute has the value "radio" or "checkbox", this boolean attribute specifies that the button is on. User agents must ignore this attribute for other control types.

src = uri [CT]

When the type attribute has the value "image", this attribute specifies the location of the image to be used to decorate the graphical submit button.

Attributes defined elsewhere

- id, class (document-wide identifiers)
- lang (language information), dir (text direction)
- title (element title)
- style (inline style information)
- alt (alternate text)
- align (alignment)
- accept (legal content types for a server)
- readonly (read-only input controls)
- disabled (disabled input controls)
- tabindex (tabbing navigation)
- accesskey (access keys)
- usemap (client-side image maps)
- onfocus, onblur, onselect, onchange, onclick, ondblclick, onmousedown, onmouseup, onmouseover, onmousemove, onmouseout, onkeypress, onkeydown, onkeyup (intrinsic events)

17.4.1 Control types created with INPUT

The control type defined by the INPUT element depends on the value of the type attribute:

text

Creates a single-line text-inputtext input control.

password

Like "text", but the input text is rendered in such a way as to hide the characters (e.g., a series of asterisks). This control type is often used for sensitive input such as passwords. Note that the current value is the text *entered* by the user, not the text rendered by the user agent.

Note. *Application designers should note that this mechanism affords only light security protection. Although the password is masked by user agents from casual observers, it is transmitted to the server in clear text, and may be read by anyone with low-level access to the network.*

checkbox

    Creates a checkbox.

radio

    Creates a radio button.

submit

    Creates a submit button.

image

    Creates a graphical submit button. The value of the src attribute specifies the URI of the image that will decorate the button. For accessibility reasons, authors should provide alternate text for the image via the alt attribute.

When a pointing device is used to click on the image, the form is submitted and the click coordinates passed to the server. The x value is measured in pixels from the left of the image, and the y value in pixels from the top of the image. The submitted data includes *name*.x=*x-value* and *name*.y=*y-value* where *"name"* is the value of the name attribute, and *x-value* and *y-value* are the x and y coordinate values, respectively.

If the server takes different actions depending on the location clicked, users of non-graphical browsers will be disadvantaged. For this reason, authors should consider alternate approaches:

- Use multiple submit buttons (each with its own image) in place of a single graphical submit button. Authors may use style sheets to control the positioning of these buttons.
- Use a client-side image map together with scripting.

reset

    Creates a reset button.

button

    Creates a push button. User agents should use the value of the `value` attribute as the button's label.

hidden

Creates a hidden control.

file

Creates a file select control. User agents may use the value of the value attribute as the initial file name.

17.4.2 Examples of forms containing INPUT controls

The following sample HTML fragment defines a simple form that allows the user to enter a first name, last name, email address, and gender. When the submit button is activated, the form will be sent to the program specified by the action attribute.

```
<FORM action="http://somesite.com/prog/adduser" method="post"
   <P
   First name: <INPUT type="text" name="firstname"<BR
   Last name: <INPUT type="text" name="lastname"<BR
   email: <INPUT type="text" name="email"<BR
   <INPUT type="radio" name="sex" value="Male" Male<BR
   <INPUT type="radio" name="sex" value="Female" Female<BR
   <INPUT type="submit" value="Send" <INPUT type="reset"
   </P
</FORM
```

This form might be rendered as follows:

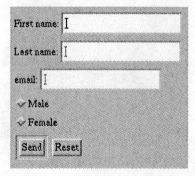

In the section on the LABEL element, we discuss marking up labels such as "First name". In this next example, the JavaScript function name `verify` is triggered when the "onclick" event occurs:

```
<HEAD
<META http-equiv="Content-Script-Type" content="text/javascript"
</HEAD
<BODY
 <FORM action="..." method="post"
    <P
    <INPUT type="button" value="Click Me" onclick="verify()"
 </FORM
</BODY
```

Please consult the section on intrinsic events for more information about scripting and events. The following example shows how the contents of a user-specified file may be submitted with a form. The user is prompted for his or her name and a list of file names whose contents should be submitted with the form. By specifying the enctype value of "multipart/form-data", each file's contents will be packaged for submission in a separate section of a multipart document.

```
<FORM action="http://server.dom/cgi/handle"
     enctype="multipart/form-data"
     method="post"
 <P
 What is your name? <INPUT type="text" name="name_of_sender"
 What files are you sending? <INPUT type="file" name="name_of_files"
 </P
</FORM
```

17.5 The BUTTON element

```
<!ELEMENT BUTTON - -
     (%flow;)* -(A|%formctrl;|FORM|FIELDSET)
   —push button —
<!ATTLIST BUTTON
   %attrs;                              — %coreattrs, %i18n, %events —
   name         CDATA         #IMPLIED
   value        CDATA         #IMPLIED  — sent to server when submitted —
```

```
type        (button|submit|reset) submit–for use as form button –
disabled    (disabled)    #IMPLIED  – unavailable in this context –
tabindex    NUMBER        #IMPLIED  – position in tabbing order –
accesskey   %Character;   #IMPLIED  – accessibility key character –
onfocus     %Script;      #IMPLIED  – the element got the focus –
onblur      %Script;      #IMPLIED  – the element lost the focus –
```

*Start tag: **required**, End tag: **required*** *Attribute definitions*

name = cdata [CI]

This attribute assigns the control name.

value = cdata [CS]

This attribute assigns the initial value to the button.

type = submit|button|reset [CI]

This attribute declares the type of the button. Possible values:

- submit: Creates a submit button. This is the default value.
- reset: Creates a reset button.
- button: Creates a push button.

Attributes defined elsewhere

- id, class (document-wide identifiers)
- lang (language information), dir (text direction)
- title (element title)
- style (inline style information)
- disabled (disabled input controls)
- accesskey (access keys)
- tabindex (tabbing navigation)
- onfocus, onblur, onclick, ondblclick, onmousedown, onmouseup, onmouseover, onmousemove, onmouseout, onkeypress, onkeydown, onkeyup (intrinsic events)

Buttons created with the BUTTON element function just like buttons created with the INPUT element, but they offer richer rendering possibilities: the BUTTON element may have content. For example, a BUTTON element that contains an image functions like and may resemble an INPUT element whose type is set to "image", but the BUTTON element type allows content.

Visual user agents may render BUTTON buttons with relief and an up/down motion when clicked, while they may render INPUT buttons as a "flat" images. The following example expands a previous example, but creates submit and reset buttons with BUTTON instead of INPUT. The buttons contain images by way of the IMG element.

```
<FORM action="http://somesite.com/prog/adduser" method="post"
   <P
   First name: <INPUT type="text" name="firstname"<BR
   Last name: <INPUT type="text" name="lastname"<BR
   email: <INPUT type="text" name="email"<BR
   <INPUT type="radio" name="sex" value="Male" Male<BR
   <INPUT type="radio" name="sex" value="Female" Female<BR
   <BUTTON name="submit" value="submit" type="submit">
   Send<IMG src="/icons/wow.gif" alt="wow"></BUTTON>
   <BUTTON name="reset" type="reset">
   Reset<IMG src="/icons/oops.gif" alt="oops"></BUTTON>
   </P>
</FORM>
```

Recall that authors must provide alternate text for an IMG element.

It is illegal to associate an image map with an IMG that appears as the contents of a BUTTON element.
ILLEGAL EXAMPLE:
The following is not legal HTML.

```
<BUTTON
<IMG src="foo.gif" usemap="...">
</BUTTON>
```

17.6 The SELECT, OPTGROUP, and OPTION elements

```
<!ELEMENT SELECT - - (OPTGROUP|OPTION)+ -- option selector --
<!ATTLIST SELECT
```

```
%attrs;                                  - %coreattrs, %i18n, %events -
name       CDATA        #IMPLIED         - field name -
size       NUMBER       #IMPLIED         - rows visible -
multiple   (multiple)   #IMPLIED         - default is single selection -
disabled   (disabled)   #IMPLIED         - unavailable in this context -
tabindex   NUMBER       #IMPLIED         - position in tabbing order -
onfocus    %Script;     #IMPLIED         - the element got the focus -
onblur     %Script;     #IMPLIED         - the element lost the focus -
onchange   %Script;     #IMPLIED         - the element value was changed -
```

*Start tag: **required**, End tag: **required** SELECT Attribute definitions*

name = cdata [CI]

This attribute assigns the control name.

size = number [CN]

If a SELECT element is presented as a scrolled list box, this attribute specifies the number of rows in the list that should be visible at the same time. Visual user agents are not required to present a SELECT element as a list box; they may use any other mechanism, such as a drop-down menu.

multiple [CI]

If set, this boolean attribute allows multiple selections. If not set, the SELECT element only permits single selections.

Attributes defined elsewhere

- id, class (document-wide identifiers)
- lang (language information), dir (text direction)
- title (element title)
- style (inline style information)
- disabled (disabled input controls)
- tabindex (tabbing navigation)
- onclick, ondblclick, onmousedown, onmouseup, onmouseover, onmousemove, onmouseout, onkeypress, onkeydown, onkeyup (intrinsic events)

The SELECT element creates a menu. Each choice offered by the menu is represented by an OPTION element. A SELECT element must contain at least one OPTION element.

The forms.html—edef-OPTGROUPOPTGROUP element allows authors to group choices logically. This is particularly helpful when the user must choose from a long list of options; groups of related choices are easier to grasp and remember than a single long list of options. In HTML 4.0, all OPTGROUP elements must be specified directly within a SELECT element (i.e., groups may not be nested).

17.6.1 Preselected options

Zero or more choices may be pre-selected for the user. User agents should determine which choices are pre-selected as follows:

- If no OPTION element has the selected attribute set, no options should be pre-selected.
- If one OPTION element has the selected attribute set, it should be pre-selected.
- If the SELECT element has the multiple attribute set and more than one OPTION element has the selected attribute set, they should all be pre-selected.
- It is considered an error if more than one OPTION element has the selected attribute set and the SELECT element does not have the multiple attribute set. User agents may vary in how they handle this error, but should not pre-select more than one choice.

```
<!ELEMENT OPTGROUP - - (OPTION)+—option group —
<!ATTLIST OPTGROUP
    %attrs;                                 — %coreattrs, %i18n, %events —
    disabled    (disabled)    #IMPLIED      — unavailable in this context —
    label       %Text;        #REQUIRED     — for use in hierarchical menus —
```

Start tag: **required**, *End tag:* **required** OPTGROUP *Attribute definitions*

label = text [CS]

This attribute specifies the label for the option group.

Attributes defined elsewhere

- id, class (document-wide identifiers)
- lang (language information), dir (text direction)

- title (element title)
- style (inline style information)
- disabled (disabled input controls)
- onfocus, onblur, onchange, onclick, ondblclick, onmousedown, onmouseup, onmouseover, onmousemove, onmouseout, onkeypress, onkeydown, onkeyup (intrinsic events)

Note. *Implementors are advised that future versions of HTML may extend the grouping mechanism to allow for nested groups (i.e.,* OPTGROUP *elements may nest). This will allow authors to represent a richer hierarchy of choices.*

```
<!ELEMENT OPTION - O (#PCDATA)         — selectable choice —
<!ATTLIST OPTION
  %attrs;                              — %coreattrs, %i18n, %events —
  selected     (selected)    #IMPLIED
  disabled     (disabled)    #IMPLIED  — unavailable in this context —
  label        %Text;        #IMPLIED  — for use in hierarchical menus —
  value        CDATA         #IMPLIED  — defaults to element content —
```

Start tag: ***required****, End tag:* ***optional*** *OPTION Attribute definitions*

`selected` [CI]

When set, this boolean attribute specifies that this option is pre-selected.

`value` = cdata [CS]

This attribute specifies the initial value of the control. If this attribute is not set, the initial value is set to the contents of the OPTION element.

`label` = text [CS]

This attribute allows authors to specify a shorter label for an option than the content of the OPTION element. When specified, user agents should use the value of this attribute rather than the content of the OPTION element as the option label.

Attributes defined elsewhere

- id, class (document-wide identifiers)
- lang (language information), dir (text direction)

- title (element title)
- style (inline style information)
- disabled (disabled input controls)
- onclick, ondblclick, onmousedown, onmouseup, onmouseover, onmousemove, onmouseout, onkeypress, onkeydown, onkeyup (intrinsic events)

When rendering a menu choice, user agents should use the value of the label attribute of the OPTION element as the choice. If this attribute is not specified, user agents should use the contents of the OPTION element.

The label attribute of the OPTGROUP element specifies the label for a group of choices. In this example, we create a menu that allows the user to select which of seven software components to install. The first and second components are pre-selected but may be deselected by the user. The remaining components are not pre-selected. The size attribute states that the menu should only have 4 rows even though the user may select from among 7 options. The other options should be made available through a scrolling mechanism.

The SELECT is followed by submit and reset buttons.

```
<FORM action="http://somesite.com/prog/component-select" method="post"
    <P
    <SELECT multiple size="4" name="component-select">
        <OPTION selected value="Component_1_a"Component_1</OPTION>
        <OPTION selected value="Component_1_b"Component_2</OPTION>
        <OPTIONComponent_3</OPTION>
        <OPTIONComponent_4</OPTION>
        <OPTIONComponent_5</OPTION>
        <OPTIONComponent_6</OPTION>
        <OPTIONComponent_7</OPTION>
    </SELECT>
    <INPUT type="submit" value="Send"<INPUT type="reset">
    </P>
</FORM>
```

Only selected options will be successful (using the control name "component-select"). Note that where the value attribute is set, it determines the control's initial value, otherwise it's the element's contents. In this example we use the OPTGROUP element to group choices. The following markup:

```
<FORM action="http://somesite.com/prog/someprog" method="post"
 <P
 <SELECT name="ComOS">
      <OPTGROUP label="PortMaster 3"
         <OPTION label="3.7.1" value="pm3_3.7.1"PortMaster 3 with ComOS 3.7.1
         <OPTION label="3.7" value="pm3_3.7"PortMaster 3 with ComOS 3.7
         <OPTION label="3.5" value="pm3_3.5"PortMaster 3 with ComOS 3.5
      </OPTGROUP>
      <OPTGROUP label="PortMaster 2"
         <OPTION label="3.7" value="pm2_3.7"PortMaster 2 with ComOS 3.7
         <OPTION label="3.5" value="pm2_3.5"PortMaster 2 with ComOS 3.5
      </OPTGROUP>
      <OPTGROUP label="IRX"
         <OPTION label="3.7R" value="IRX_3.7R"IRX with ComOS 3.7R
         <OPTION label="3.5R" value="IRX_3.5R"IRX with ComOS 3.5R
      </OPTGROUP>
 </SELECT>
</FORM>
```

represents the following grouping:

```
PortMaster 3
     3.7.1
     3.7
     3.5
PortMaster 2
     3.7
     3.5
IRX
     3.7R
     3.5R
```

Visual user agents may allow users to select from option groups through a hierarchical menu or some other mechanism that reflects the structure of choices.

A graphical user agent might render this as:

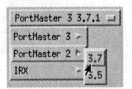

This image shows a SELECT element rendered as cascading menus. The top label of the menu displays the currently selected value (PortMaster 3, 3.7.1). The user has unfurled two cascading menus, but has not yet selected the new value (PortMaster 2, 3.7). Note that each cascading menu displays the label of an OPTGROUP or OPTION element.

17.7 The TEXTAREA element

```
<!ELEMENT TEXTAREA - - (#PCDATA)         — multi-line text field —
<!ATTLIST TEXTAREA
    %attrs;                              — %coreattrs, %i18n, %events —
    name        CDATA        #IMPLIED
    rows        NUMBER       #REQUIRED
    cols        NUMBER       #REQUIRED
    disabled    (disabled)   #IMPLIED    — unavailable in this context —
    readonly    (readonly)   #IMPLIED
    tabindex    NUMBER       #IMPLIED    —position in tabbing order —
    accesskey   %Character;  #IMPLIED    —accessibility key character —
    onfocus     %Script;     #IMPLIED    —the element got the focus —
    onblur      %Script;     #IMPLIED    —the element lost the focus —
    onselect    %Script;     #IMPLIED    —some text was selected —
    onchange    %Script;     #IMPLIED    —the element value was changed —
```

Start tag: **required**, End tag: **required** Attribute definitions

name = cdata [CI]

This attribute assigns the control name.

`rows = number` [CN]

> This attribute specifies the number of visible text lines. Users should be able to enter more lines than this, so user agents should provide some means to scroll through the contents of the control when the contents extend beyond the visible area.

`cols = number` [CN]

> This attribute specifies the visible width in average character widths. Users should be able to enter longer lines than this, so user agents should provide some means to scroll through the contents of the control when the contents extend beyond the visible area. User agents may wrap visible text lines to keep long lines visible without the need for scrolling.

Attributes defined elsewhere

- id, class (document-wide identifiers)
- lang (language information), dir (text direction)
- title (element title)
- style (inline style information)
- readonly (read-only input controls)
- disabled (disabled input controls)
- tabindex (tabbing navigation)
- onfocus, onblur, onselect, onchange, onclick, ondblclick, onmousedown, onmouseup, onmouseover, onmousemove, onmouseout, onkeypress, onkeydown, onkeyup (intrinsic events)

The `TEXTAREA` element creates a multi-line text input control. User agents should use the contents of this element as the initial value of the control and should render this text initially. This example creates a `TEXTAREA` control that is 20 rows by 80 columns and contains two lines of text initially. The `TEXTAREA` is followed by submit and reset buttons.

```
<FORM action="http://somesite.com/prog/text-read" method="post"
    <P
    <TEXTAREA name="thetext" rows="20" cols="80"
    First line of initial text.
    Second line of initial text.
    </TEXTAREA
```

```
        <INPUT type="submit" value="Send"<INPUT type="reset"
        </P>
</FORM>
```

Setting the readonly attribute allows authors to display unmodifiable text in a TEXTAREA. This differs from using standard marked-up text in a document because the value of TEXTAREA is submitted with the form.

17.8 The ISINDEX element

ISINDEX is deprecated. This element creates a single-line text input control. Authors should use the INPUT element to create text input controls.

See the Transitional DTD for the formal definition. *Attribute definitions*

prompt = text [CS]

Deprecated. This attribute specifies a prompt string for the input field.

Attributes defined elsewhere

- id, class (document-wide identifiers)
- lang (language information), dir (text direction)
- title (element title)
- style (inline style information)

The ISINDEX element creates a single-line text input control that allows any number of characters. User agents may use the value of the prompt attribute as a title for the prompt. DEPRECATED EXAMPLE:
The following ISINDEX declaration:

```
<ISINDEX prompt="Enter your search phrase: "
```

could be rewritten with INPUT as follows:

```
<FORM action="..." method="post"
<PEnter your search phrase: <INPUT type="text"</P>
</FORM>
```

Semantics of `ISINDEX`. *Currently, the semantics for* `ISINDEX` *are only well-defined when the base URI for the enclosing document is an HTTP URI. In practice, the input string is restricted to Latin-1 as there is no mechanism for the URI to specify a different character set.*

17.9 Labels

Some form controls automatically have labels associated with them (press buttons) while most do not (text fields, checkboxes and radio buttons, and menus).

For those controls that have implicit labels, user agents should use the value of the `value` attribute as the label string.

The LABEL element is used to specify labels for controls that do not have implicit labels,

17.9.1 The `LABEL` element

```
<!ELEMENT LABEL - - (%inline;)* -(LABEL)—form field label text —
<!ATTLIST LABEL
  %attrs;                             — %coreattrs, %i18n, %events —
  for         IDREF       #IMPLIED    — matches field ID value —
  accesskey   %Character; #IMPLIED    — accessibility key character —
  onfocus     %Script;    #IMPLIED    — the element got the focus —
  onblur      %Script;    #IMPLIED    — the element lost the focus —
```

Start tag: **required**, *End tag:* **required** Attribute definitions

for = idref [CS]

>This attribute explicitly associates the label being defined with another control. When present, the value of this attribute must be the same as the value of the id attribute of some other control in the same document. When absent, the label being defined is associated with the element's contents.

Attributes defined elsewhere

- id, class (document-wide identifiers)
- lang (language information), dir (text direction)
- title (element title)

- style (inline style information)
- accesskey (access keys)
- onfocus, onblur, onclick, ondblclick, onmousedown, onmouseup, onmouseover, onmousemove, onmouseout, onkeypress, onkeydown, onkeyup (intrinsic events)

The LABEL element may be used to attach information to controls. Each LABEL element is associated with exactly one form control.

The forms.html—adef-forfor attribute associates a label with another control explicitly: the value of the for attribute must be the same as the value of the id attribute of the associated control element. More than one LABEL may be associated with the same control by creating multiple references via the for attribute. This example creates a table that is used to align two text input controls and their associated labels. Each label is associated explicitly with one text input:

```
<FORM action="..." method="post"
<TABLE
  <TR
    <TD<LABEL for="fname"First Name</LABEL
    <TD<INPUT type="text" name="firstname" id="fname"
  <TR
    <TD<LABEL for="lname"Last Name</LABEL
    <TD<INPUT type="text" name="lastname" id="lname"
</TABLE
</FORM
```

This example extends a previous example form to include LABEL elements.

```
<FORM action="http://somesite.com/prog/adduser" method="post"
  <P
  <LABEL for="firstname"First name: </LABEL
       <INPUT type="text" id="firstname"<BR
  <LABEL for="lastname"Last name: </LABEL
       <INPUT type="text" id="lastname"<BR
  <LABEL for="email"email: </LABEL
       <INPUT type="text" id="email"<BR
  <INPUT type="radio" name="sex" value="Male" Male<BR
  <INPUT type="radio" name="sex" value="Female" Female<BR
  <INPUT type="submit" value="Send" <INPUT type="reset"
```

```
      </P>
   </FORM>
```

To associate a label with another control implicitly, the control element must be within the contents of the LABEL element. In this case, the LABEL may only contain one control element. The label itself may be positioned before or after the associated control. In this example, we implicitly associate two labels with two text input controls:

```
<FORM action="..." method="post"
<P
<LABEL
    First Name
    <INPUT type="text" name="firstname">
</LABEL>
<LABEL
    <INPUT type="text" name="lastname">
    Last Name
</LABEL>
</P>
</FORM>
```

Note that this technique cannot be used when a table is being used for layout, with the label in one cell and its associated control in another cell. When a forms.html—edef-LABELLABEL element receives focus, it passes the focus on to its associated control. See the section below on access keys for examples.

Labels may be rendered by user agents in a number of ways (e.g., visually, read by speech synthesizers, etc.)

17.10 Adding structure to forms: the FIELDSET and LEGEND elements

```
<!—
   #PCDATA is to solve the mixed content problem,
   per specification only whitespace is allowed there!
   —
<!ELEMENT FIELDSET - - (#PCDATA,LEGEND,(%flow;)*)—form control group —
<!ATTLIST FIELDSET
   %attrs;                              —%coreattrs, %i18n, %events —
```

```
<!ELEMENT LEGEND - - (%inline;)*        -fieldset legend -
<!ENTITY % LAlign "(top|bottom|left|right)"

<!ATTLIST LEGEND
  %attrs;                               -%coreattrs, %i18n, %events -
  accesskey    %Character;  #IMPLIED    -accessibility key character -
```

*Start tag: **required**, End tag: **required*** LEGEND *Attribute definitions*

`align = top|bottom|left|right [CI]`

Deprecated. This attribute specifies the position of the legend with respect to the fieldset. Possible values:

- `top`: The legend is at the top of the fieldset. This is the default value.
- `bottom`: The legend is at the bottom of the fieldset.
- `left`: The legend is at the left side of the fieldset.
- `right`: The legend is at the right side of the fieldset.

Attributes defined elsewhere

- id, class (document-wide identifiers)
- lang (language information), dir (text direction)
- title (element title)
- style (inline style information)
- accesskey (access keys)
- onclick, ondblclick, onmousedown, onmouseup, onmouseover, onmousemove, onmouseout, onkeypress, onkeydown, onkeyup (intrinsic events)

The forms.html—edef-FIELDSETFIELDSET element allows authors to group thematically related controls and labels. Grouping controls makes it easier for users to understand their purpose while simultaneously facilitating tabbing navigation for visual user agents and speech navigation for speech-oriented user agents. The proper use of this element makes documents more accessible.

The `LEGEND` element allows authors to assign a caption to a `FIELDSET`. The legend improves accessibility when the `FIELDSET` is rendered non-visually. In this example, we create a form that one might fill out at the doctor's office. It is divided into three sections: personal information, medical history, and current medication. Each section contains controls for inputting the appropriate information.

```
<FORM action="..." method="post"
 <P
 <FIELDSET
  <LEGENDPersonal Information</LEGEND
  Last Name: <INPUT name="personal_lastname" type="text" tabindex="1"
  First Name: <INPUT name="personal_firstname" type="text" tabindex="2"
  Address: <INPUT name="personal_address" type="text" tabindex="3"
  ...more personal information...
 </FIELDSET>
 <FIELDSET
  <LEGENDMedical History</LEGEND
  <INPUT name="history_illness"
         type="checkbox"
         value="Smallpox" tabindex="20" Smallpox
  <INPUT name="history_illness"
         type="checkbox"
         value="Mumps" tabindex="21" Mumps
  <INPUT name="history_illness"
         type="checkbox"
         value="Dizziness" tabindex="22" Dizziness
  <INPUT name="history_illness"
         type="checkbox"
         value="Sneezing" tabindex="23" Sneezing
  ...more medical history...
 </FIELDSET>
 <FIELDSET
  <LEGENDCurrent Medication</LEGEND
  Are you currently taking any medication?
  <INPUT name="medication_now"
         type="radio"
         value="Yes" tabindex="35"Yes
  <INPUT name="medication_now"
         type="radio"
         value="No" tabindex="35"No
```

```
   If you are currently taking medication, please indicate
   it in the space below:
   <TEXTAREA name="current_medication"
             rows="20" cols="50"
             tabindex="40">
   </TEXTAREA>
  </FIELDSET>
 </FORM>
```

Note that in this example, we might improve the visual presentation of the form by aligning elements within each FIELDSET (with style sheets), adding color and font information (with style sheets), adding scripting (say, to only open the "current medication" text area if the user indicates he or she is currently on medication), etc.

17.11 Giving focus to an element

In an HTML document, an element must receive *focus* from the user in order to become active and perform its tasks. For example, users must activate a link specified by the A element in order to follow the specified link. Similarly, users must give a TEXTAREA focus in order to enter text into it.

There are several ways to give focus to an element:

- Designate the element with a pointing device.

- Navigate from one element to the next with the keyboard. The document's author may define a *tabbing order* that specifies the order in which elements will receive focus if the user navigates the document with the keyboard (see tabbing navigation). Once selected, an element may be activated by some other key sequence.

- Select an element through an access key (sometimes called "keyboard shortcut" or "keyboard accelerator").

17.11.1 Tabbing navigation

Attribute definitions

`tabindex` = number [CN]

> This attribute specifies the position of the current element in the tabbing order for the current document. This value must be a number between 0 and 32767. User agents should ignore leading zeros.

The *tabbing order* defines the order in which elements will receive focus when navigated by the user via the keyboard. The tabbing order may include elements nested within other elements.

Elements that may receive focus should be navigated by user agents according to the following rules:

1. Those elements that support the tabindex attribute and assign a positive value to it are navigated first. Navigation proceeds from the element with the lowest tabindex value to the element with the highest value. Values need not be sequential nor must they begin with any particular value. Elements that have identical tabindex values should be navigated in the order they appear in the character stream.

2. Those elements that do not support the tabindex attribute or support it and assign it a value of "0" are navigated next. These elements are navigated in the order they appear in the character stream.

3. Elements that are disabled do not participate in the tabbing order.

The following elements support the tabindex attribute: `A`, `AREA`, `BUTTON`, `INPUT`, `OBJECT`, `SELECT`, and `TEXTAREA`. In this example, the tabbing order will be the `BUTTON`, the `INPUT` elements in order (note that "field1" and the button share the same tabindex, but "field1" appears later in the character stream), and finally the link created by the A element.

```
<!DOCTYPE HTML PUBLIC "-//W3C//DTD HTML 4.0//EN"
    "http://www.w3.org/TR/REC-html40/strict.dtd">
<HTML>
<HEAD>
<TITLEA document with FORM</TITLE
</HEAD>
<BODY>
...some text...
<PGo to the
```

```
<A tabindex="10" href="http://www.w3.org/"W3C Web site.</A
...some more...
<BUTTON type="button" name="get-database"
        tabindex="1" onclick="get-database"
Get the current database.
</BUTTON
...some more...
<FORM action="..." method="post"
<P
<INPUT tabindex="1" type="text" name="field1"
<INPUT tabindex="2" type="text" name="field2"
<INPUT tabindex="3" type="submit" name="submit"
</P
</FORM
</BODY
</HTML
```

Tabbing keys. *The actual key sequence that causes tabbing navigation or element activation depends on the configuration of the user agent (e.g., the "tab" key is used for navigation and the "enter" key is used to activate a selected element).*

User agents may also define key sequences to navigate the tabbing order in reverse. When the end (or beginning) of the tabbing order is reached, user agents may circle back to the beginning (or end).

17.11.2 Access keys

Attribute definitions

accesskey = character [CN]

> This attribute assigns an access key to an element. An access key is a single character from the document character set.**Note.** Authors should consider the input method of the expected reader when specifying an accesskey.

Pressing an access key assigned to an element gives focus to the element. The action that occurs when an element receives focus depends on the element. For example, when a user activates a link defined by the A element, the user agent generally follows the link. When a user activates a radio button, the user agent changes the value of the radio button. When the user activates a text field, it allows input, etc.

The following elements support the accesskey attribute: A, AREA, BUTTON, INPUT, LABEL, and LEGEND, and TEXTAREA. This example assigns the access key "U" to a label associated with an INPUT control. Typing the access key gives focus to the label which in turn gives it to the associated control. The user may then enter text into the INPUT area.

```
<FORM action="..." method="post"
<P
<LABEL for="fuser" accesskey="U"
User Name
</LABEL
<INPUT type="text" name="user" id="fuser"
</P
</FORM
```

In this example, we assign an access key to a link defined by the A element. Typing this access key takes the user to another document, in this case, a table of contents.

```
<P<A accesskey="C"
     rel="contents"
     href="http://someplace.com/specification/contents.html"
   Table of Contents</A
```

The invocation of access keys depends on the underlying system. For instance, on machines running MS Windows, one generally has to press the "alt" key in addition to the access key. On Apple systems, one generally has to press the "cmd" key in addition to the access key.

The rendering of access keys depends on the user agent. We recommend that authors include the access key in label text or wherever the access key is to apply. User agents should render the value of an access key in such a way as to emphasize its role and to distinguish it from other characters (e.g., by underlining it).

17.12 Disabled and read-only controls

In contexts where user input is either undesirable or irrelevant, it is important to be able to disable a control or render it read-only. For example, one may want to disable a form's submit button until the user has entered some required data. Similarly, an author may want to include a piece of read-only text that must be submitted as a value along with the form. The following sections describe disabled and read-only controls.

17.12.1 Disabled controls

Attribute definitions

`disabled` [CI]

When set for a form control, this boolean attribute disables the control for user input.

When set, the disabled attribute has the following effects on an element:

- Disabled controls do not receive focus.
- Disabled controls are skipped in tabbing navigation.
- Disabled controls cannot be successful.

The following elements support the disabled attribute: `BUTTON` `INPUT`, `OPTGROUP`, `OPTION`, `SELECT`, and `TEXTAREA`.

This attribute is inherited but local declarations override the inherited value.

How disabled elements are rendered depends on the user agent. For example, some user agents "gray out" disabled menu items, button labels, etc. In this example, the `INPUT` element is disabled. Therefore, it cannot receive user input nor will its value be submitted with the form.

```
<INPUT disabled name="fred" value="stone"
```

Note. *The only way to modify dynamically the value of the* disabled *attribute is through a* script.

17.12.2 Read-only controls

Attribute definitions

`readonly` [CI]

When set for a form control, this boolean attribute prohibits changes to the control.

The readonly attribute specifies whether the control may be modified by the user.

When set, the readonly attribute has the following effects on an element:

- Read-only elements receive focus but cannot be modified by the user.
- Read-only elements are included in tabbing navigation.

- Read-only elements may be successful.

The following elements support the readonly attribute: INPUT and TEXTAREA.

How read-only elements are rendered depends on the user agent. *Note.* *The only way to modify dynamically the value of the* readonly *attribute is through a script.*

17.13 Form submission

The following sections explain how user agents submit form data to form processing agents.

17.13.1 Form submission method

The method attribute of the FORM element specifies the HTTP method used to send the form to the processing agent. This attribute may take two values:

- get: With the HTTP "get" method, the form data set is appended to the URI specified by the action attribute (with a question-mark ("?") as separator) and this new URI is sent to the processing agent.
- post: With the HTTP "post" method, the form data set is included in the body of the form and sent to the processing agent.

The "get" method should be used when the form is idempotent (i.e., causes no side-effects). Many database searches have no visible side-effects and make ideal applications for the "get" method.

If the service associated with the processing of a form causes side effects (for example, if the form modifies a database or subscription to a service), the "post" method should be used. *Note.* *The "get" method restricts* form data set *values to ASCII characters. Only the "post" method (with* enctype="multipart/form-data") *is specified to cover the entire* [ISO10646] *character set.*

17.13.2 Successful controls

A *successful control* is "valid" for submission. Every successful control has its control name paired with its current value as part of the submitted form data set. A successful control must be defined within a FORM element and must have a control name.

However:

- Controls that are disabled cannot be successful.
- If a form contains more than one submit button, only the activated submit button is successful.
- All "on" checkboxes may be successful.
- For radio buttons that share the same value of the name attribute, only the "on" radio button may be successful.
- For menus, the control name is provided by a SELECT element and values are provided by OPTION elements. Only selected options may be successful.
- The current-valuecurrent value of a file select is a list of one or more file names. Upon submission of the form, the contents of each file are submitted with the rest of the form data. The file contents are packaged according to the form's content type.
- The current value of an object control is determined by the object's implementation.

If a control doesn't have a current value when the form is submitted, user agents are not required to treat it as a successful control.

Furthermore, user agents should not consider the following controls successful:

- Reset buttons.
- ..\struct/objects.html—edef-OBJECTOBJECT elements whose declare attribute has been set.

hidden-controlHidden controls and controls that are not rendered because of style sheet settings may still be successful. For example:

```
<FORM action="..." method="post"
<P
<INPUT type="password" style="display:none"
        name="invisible-password"
        value="mypassword"
</FORM
```

will still cause a value to be paired with the name "invisible-password" and submitted with the form.

17.13.3 Processing form data

When the user submits a form (e.g., by activating a submit button), the user agent processes it as follows.

Step one: Identify the successful controls

Step two: Build a form data set

A *form data set* is a sequence of control-name/current-value pairs constructed from successful controls

Step three: Encode the form data set

The form data set is then encoded according to the content type specified by the enctype attribute of the FORM element.

Step four: Submit the encoded form data set

Finally, the encoded data is sent to the processing agent designated by the action attribute using the protocol specified by the method attribute.

This specification does not specify all valid submission methods or content types that may be used with forms. However, HTML 4.0 user agents must support the established conventions in the following cases:

- If the method is "get" and the action is an HTTP URI, the user agent takes the value of action, appends a `?` to it, then appends the form data set, encoded using the "application/x-www-form-urlencoded" content type. The user agent then traverses the link to this URI. In this scenario, form data are restricted to ASCII codes.

- If the method is "post" and the action is an HTTP URI, the user agent conducts an HTTP "post" transaction using the value of the action attribute and a message created according to the content type specified by the enctype attribute.

For any other value of action or method, behavior is unspecified.

User agents should render the response from the HTTP "get" and "post" transactions.

17.13.4 Form content types

The enctype attribute of the FORM element specifies the content type used to encode the form data set for submission to the server. User agents must support the content types listed below. Behavior for other content types is unspecified.

Please also consult the section on escaping ampersands in URI attribute values.

application/x-www-form-urlencoded

This is the default content type. Forms submitted with this content type must be encoded as follows:

1. Control names and values are escaped. Space characters are replaced by `+`, and then reserved characters are escaped as described in [RFC1738], section 2.2: Non-alphanumeric characters are replaced by `%HH`, a percent sign and two hexadecimal digits representing the ASCII code of the character. Line breaks are represented as "CR LF" pairs (i.e., `%0D%0A`).
2. The control names/values are listed in the order they appear in the document. The name is separated from the value by `=` and name/value pairs are separated from each other by `&`.

multipart/form-data

Note. *Please consult [RFC1867] for additional information about file uploads, including backwards compatibility issues, the relationship between "multipart/form-data" and other content types, performance issues, etc.*

Please consult the appendix for information about security issues for forms. The content type "application/x-www-form-urlencoded" is inefficient for sending large quantities of binary data or text containing non-ASCII characters. The content type "multipart/form-data" should be used for submitting forms that contain files, non-ASCII data, and binary data.

The content "multipart/form-data" follows the rules of all multipart MIME data streams as outlined in [RFC2045]. The definition of "multipart/form-data" is available at the [IANA] registry.

A "multipart/form-data" message contains a series of parts, each representing a successful control. The parts are sent to the processing agent in the same order the corresponding controls appear in the document stream. Part boundaries should not occur in any of the data; how this is done lies outside the scope of this specification.

As with all multipart MIME types, each part has an optional "Content-Type" header that defaults to "text/plain". User agents should supply the "Content-Type" header, accompanied by a "charset" parameter.

Each part is expected to contain:

1. a "Content-Disposition" header whose value is "form-data".
2. a name attribute specifying the control name of the corresponding control. Control names originally encoded in non-ASCII character sets may be encoded using the method outlined in [RFC2045].

Thus, for example, for a control named "mycontrol", the corresponding part would be specified:

```
Content-Disposition: form-data; name="mycontrol"
```

As with all MIME transmissions, "CR LF" (i.e., `%0D%0A`) is used to separate lines of data.

Each part may be encoded and the "Content-Transfer-Encoding" header supplied if the value of that part does not conform to the default (7BIT) encoding (see [RFC2045], section 6)

If the contents of a file are submitted with a form, the file input should be identified by the appropriate content type (e.g., "application/octet-stream"). If multiple files are to be returned as the result of a single form entry, they should be returned as "multipart/mixed" embedded within the "multipart/form-data".

The user agent should attempt to supply a file name for each submitted file. The file name may be specified with the "filename" parameter of the 'Content-Disposition: form-data' header, or, in the case of multiple files, in a 'Content-Disposition: file' header of the subpart. If the file name of the client's operating system is not in US-ASCII, the file name might be approximated or encoded using the method of [RFC2045]. This is convenient for those cases where, for example, the uploaded files might contain references to each other (e.g., a TeX file and its ".sty" auxiliary style description).

The following example illustrates "multipart/form-data" encoding. Suppose we have the following form:

```
<FORM action="http://server.dom/cgi/handle"
      enctype="multipart/form-data"
      method="post"
  <P
  What is your name? <INPUT type="text" name="submit-name"<BR
  What files are you sending? <INPUT type="file" name="files"<BR
  <INPUT type="submit" value="Send" <INPUT type="reset"
</FORM>
```

If the user enters "Larry" in the text input, and selects the text file "file1.txt", the user agent might send back the following data:

```
Content-Type: multipart/form-data; boundary=AaB03x

—AaB03x
Content-Disposition: form-data; name="submit-name"

Larry
—AaB03x
Content-Disposition: form-data; name="files"; filename="file1.txt"
Content-Type: text/plain

... contents of file1.txt ...
—AaB03x—
```

If the user selected a second (image) file "file2.gif", the user agent might construct the parts as follows:

```
Content-Type: multipart/form-data; boundary=AaB03x

—AaB03x
Content-Disposition: form-data; name="submit-name"

Larry
—AaB03x
Content-Disposition: form-data; name="files"
Content-Type: multipart/mixed; boundary=BbC04y

—BbC04y
Content-Disposition: attachment; filename="file1.txt"
Content-Type: text/plain

... contents of file1.txt ...
—BbC04y
Content-Disposition: attachment; filename="file2.gif"
Content-Type: image/gif
Content-Transfer-Encoding: binary

...contents of file2.gif...
—BbC04y—
—AaB03x—
```

Chapter 18

Scripts

Contents

1. Introduction to scripts
2. Designing documents for user agents that support scripting
   1. The SCRIPT element
   2. Specifying the scripting language
      - The default scripting language
      - Local declaration of a scripting language
      - References to HTML elements from a script
   3. Intrinsic events
   4. Dynamic modification of documents
3. Designing documents for user agents that don't support scripting
   1. The NOSCRIPT element
   2. Hiding script data from user agents

18.1 Introduction to scripts

A client-side *script* is a program that may accompany an HTML document or be embedded directly in it. The program executes on the client's machine when the document loads, or at some other time such as when a link is activated. HTML's support for scripts is independent of the scripting language.

Scripts offer authors a means to extend HTML documents in highly active and interactive ways. For example:

- Scripts may be evaluated as a document loads to modify the contents of the document dynamically.

- Scripts may accompany a form to process input as it is entered. Designers may dynamically fill out parts of a form based on the values of other fields. They may also ensure that input data conforms to predetermined ranges of values, that fields are mutually consistent, etc.

- Scripts may be triggered by events that affect the document, such as loading, unloading, element focus, mouse movement, etc.
- Scripts may be linked to form controls (e.g., buttons) to produce graphical user interface elements.

There are two types of scripts authors may attach to an HTML document:

- Those that are executed one time when the document is loaded by the user agent. Scripts that appear within a SCRIPT element are executed when the document is loaded. For user agents that cannot or will not handle scripts, authors may include alternate content via the NOSCRIPT element.
- Those that are executed every time a specific event occurs. These scripts may be assigned to a number of elements via the intrinsic event attributes.

Note. This specification includes more detailed information about scripting in sections on script macros.

18.2 Designing documents for user agents that support scripting

The following sections discuss issues that concern user agents that support scripting.

18.2.1 The SCRIPT element

```
<!ELEMENT SCRIPT - - %Script;          -- script statements -->
<!ATTLIST SCRIPT
  charset     %Charset;      #IMPLIED  -- char encoding of linked resource --
  type        %ContentType;  #REQUIRED -- content type of script language --
  src         %URI;          #IMPLIED  -- URI for an external script --
  defer       (defer)        #IMPLIED  -- UA may defer execution of script --
  >
```

Start tag: **required**, End tag: **required**

Attribute definitions

src = *uri* [CT]

This attribute specifies the location of an external script.

type = *content-type* [CI]

    This attribute specifies the scripting language of the element's contents and overrides the default scripting language. The scripting language is specified as a content type (e.g., "text/javascript"). Authors must supply a value for this attribute. There is no default value for this attribute.

language = *cdata* [CI]

    Deprecated. This attribute specifies the scripting language of the contents of this element. Its value is an identifier for the language, but since these identifiers are not standard, this attribute has been deprecated in favor of type.

defer [CI]

    When set, this boolean attribute provides a hint to the user agent that the script is not going to generate any document content (e.g., no "document.write" in javascript) and thus, the user agent can continue parsing and rendering.

Attributes defined elsewhere

- charset(character encodings)

The SCRIPT element places a script within a document. This element may appear any number of times in the HEAD or BODY of an HTML document.

The script may be defined within the contents of the SCRIPT element or in an external file. If the src attribute is not set, user agents must interpret the contents of the element as the script. If the src has a URI value, user agents must ignore the element's contents and retrieve the script via the URI. Note that the charset attribute refers to the character encoding of the script designated by the src attribute; it does not concern the content of the SCRIPT element.

Scripts are evaluated by *script engines* that must be known to a user agent.

The syntax of script data depends on the scripting language.

18.2.2 Specifying the scripting language

As HTML does not rely on a specific scripting language, document authors must explicitly tell user agents the language of each script. This may be done either through a default declaration or a local declaration.

The default scripting language

Authors should specify the default scripting language for all scripts in a document by including the following META declaration in the HEAD:

```
<META http-equiv="Content-Script-Type" content="type">
```

where "type" is an content type naming the scripting language. Examples of values include "text/tcl", "text/javascript", "text/vbscript".

In the absence of a META declaration, the default can be set by a "Content-Script-Type" HTTP header.

```
Content-Script-Type: type
```

where "type" is again an content type naming the scripting language.

User agents should determine the default scripting language for a document according to the following steps (highest to lowest priority):

1. If any META declarations specify the "Content-Script-Type", the last one in the character stream determines the default scripting language.

2. Otherwise, if any HTTP headers specify the "Content-Script-Type", the last one in the character stream determines the default scripting language.

Documents that do not specify a default scripting language information and that contain elements that specify an intrinsic event script are incorrect. User agents may still attempt to interpret incorrectly specified scripts but are not required to. Authoring tools should generate default scripting language information to help authors avoid creating incorrect documents.

Local declaration of a scripting language

The type attribute must be specified for each SCRIPT element instance in a document. The value of the type attribute for a SCRIPT element overrides the default scripting language for that element.

In this example, we declare the default scripting language to be "text/tcl". We include one SCRIPT in the header, whose script is located in an external file and is in the scripting language "text/vbscript". We also include one SCRIPT in the body, which contains its own script written in "text/javascript".

```
<!DOCTYPE HTML PUBLIC "-//W3C//DTD HTML 4.0//EN"
     "http://www.w3.org/TR/REC-html40/strict.dtd">
<HTML>
<HEAD>
```

```
<TITLE>A document with SCRIPT</TITLE>
<META http-equiv="Content-Script-Type" content="text/tcl">
<SCRIPT type="text/vbscript" src="http://someplace.com/progs/vbcalc">
</SCRIPT>
</HEAD>
<BODY>
<SCRIPT type="text/javascript">
...some JavaScript...
</SCRIPT>
</BODY>
</HTML>
```

References to HTML elements from a script

Each scripting language has its own conventions for referring to HTML objects from within a script. This specification does not define a standard mechanism for referring to HTML objects.

However, scripts should refer to an element according to its assigned name. Scripting engines should observe the following precedence rules when identifying an element: a name attribute takes precedence over an id if both are set. Otherwise, one or the other may be used.

18.2.3 Intrinsic events

Note. Authors of HTML documents are advised that changes are likely to occur in realm of intrinsic events (e.g., how scripts are bound to events). Research in this realm is carried on by members of the W3C Document Object Model Working Group (see the W3C Web Site at http://www.w3.org/ *for more information).*

Attribute definitions

onload = *script* [CT]

> The onload event occurs when the user agent finishes loading a window or all frames within a FRAMESET. This attribute may be used with BODY and FRAMESET elements.

onunload = *script* [CT]

> The onunload event occurs when the user agent removes a document from a window or frame. This attribute may be used with BODY and FRAMESET elements.

onclick = *script* [CT]

The `onclick` event occurs when the pointing device button is clicked over an element. This attribute may be used with most elements.

ondblclick = *script* [CT]

The `ondblclick` event occurs when the pointing device button is double clicked over an element. This attribute may be used with most elements.

onmousedown = *script* [CT]

The `onmousedown` event occurs when the pointing device button is pressed over an element. This attribute may be used with most elements.

onmouseup = *script* [CT]

The `onmouseup` event occurs when the pointing device button is released over an element. This attribute may be used with most elements.

onmouseover = *script* [CT]

The `onmouseover` event occurs when the pointing device is moved onto an element. This attribute may be used with most elements.

onmousemove = *script* [CT]

The `onmousemove` event occurs when the pointing device is moved while it is over an element. This attribute may be used with most elements.

onmouseout = *script* [CT]

The `onmouseout` event occurs when the pointing device is moved away from an element. This attribute may be used with most elements.

onfocus = *script* [CT]

The `onfocus` event occurs when an element receives focus either by the pointing device or by tabbing navigation. This attribute may be used with the following elements: `LABEL`, `INPUT`, `SELECT`, `TEXTAREA`, and `BUTTON`.

onblur = *script* [CT]

The `onblur` event occurs when an element loses focus either by the pointing device or by tabbing navigation. It may be used with the same elements as onfocus.

onkeypress = *script* [CT]

The `onkeypress` event occurs when a key is pressed and released over an element. This attribute may be used with most elements.

onkeydown = *script* [CT]

The `onkeydown` event occurs when a key is pressed down over an element. This attribute may be used with most elements.

onkeyup = *script* [CT]

The `onkeyup` event occurs when a key is released over an element. This attribute may be used with most elements.

onsubmit = *script* [CT]

The `onsubmit` event occurs when a form is submitted. It only applies to the FORM element.

onreset = *script* [CT]

The `onreset` event occurs when a form is reset. It only applies to the FORM element.

onselect = *script* [CT]

The `onselect` event occurs when a user selects some text in a text field. This attribute may be used with the INPUT and TEXTAREA elements.

onchange = *script* [CT]

The `onchange` event occurs when a control loses the input focus and its value has been modified since gaining focus. This attribute applies to the following elements: INPUT, SELECT, and TEXTAREA.

It is possible to associate an action with a certain number of events that occur when a user interacts with a user agent. Each of the "intrinsic events" listed above takes a value that is a script. The script is executed whenever the event occurs for that element. The syntax of script data depends on the scripting language.

Control elements such as INPUT, SELECT, BUTTON, TEXTAREA, and LABEL all respond to certain intrinsic events. When these elements do not appear within a form, they may be used to augment the graphical user interface of the document.

For instance, authors may want to include press buttons in their documents that do not submit a form but still communicate with a server when they are activated.

The following examples show some possible control and user interface behavior based on intrinsic events.

In the following example, userName is a required text field. When a user attempts to leave the field, the onblur event calls a JavaScript function to confirm that userName has an acceptable value.

```
<INPUT NAME="userName" onblur="validUserName(this.value)">
```

Here is another JavaScript example:

```
<INPUT NAME="num"
    onchange="if (!checkNum(this.value, 1, 10))
        {this.focus();this.select();} else {thanks()}"
    VALUE="0">
```

Here is a VBScript example of an event handler for a text field:

```
<INPUT name="edit1" size="50">
<SCRIPT type="text/vbscript">
  Sub edit1_changed()
    If edit1.value = "abc" Then
      button1.enabled = True
    Else
      button1.enabled = False
    End If
  End Sub
</SCRIPT>
```

Here is the same example using Tcl:

```
<INPUT name="edit1" size="50">
<SCRIPT type="text/tcl">
  proc edit1_changed {} {
    if {[edit value] == abc} {
      button1 enable 1
    } else {
      button1 enable 0
    }
```

```
        }
        edit1 onChange edit1_changed
    </SCRIPT>
```

Here is a JavaScript example for event binding within a script. First, here's a simple click handler:

```
<BUTTON type="button" name="mybutton" value="10">
<SCRIPT type="text/javascript">
    function my_onclick() {
        . . .
    }
    document.form.mybutton.onclick = my_onclick
</SCRIPT>
</BUTTON>
```

Here's a more interesting window handler:

```
<SCRIPT type="text/javascript">
    function my_onload() {
        . . .
    }

    var win = window.open("some/other/URI")
    if (win) win.onload = my_onload
</SCRIPT>
```

In Tcl this looks like:

```
<SCRIPT type="text/tcl">
    proc my_onload {} {
       . . .
    }
    set win [window open "some/other/URI"]
    if {$win != ""} {
        $win onload my_onload
    }
</SCRIPT>
```

Note that "document.write" or equivalent statements in intrinsic event handlers create and write to a new document rather than modifying the current one.

18.2.4 Dynamic modification of documents

Scripts that are executed when a document is loaded may be able to modify the document's contents dynamically. The ability to do so depends on the scripting language itself (e.g., the "document.write" statement in the HTML object model supported by some vendors).

The dynamic modification of a document may be modeled as follows:

1. All SCRIPT elements are evaluated in order as the document is loaded.

2. All script constructs within a given SCRIPT element that generate SGML CDATA are evaluated. Their combined generated text is inserted in the document in place of the SCRIPT element.

3. The generated CDATA is re-evaluated.

HTML documents are constrained to conform to the HTML DTD both before and after processing any SCRIPT elements.

The following example illustrates how scripts may modify a document dynamically. The following script:

```
<TITLE>Test Document</TITLE>
<SCRIPT type="text/javascript">
    document.write("<p><b>Hello World!<\/b>")
</SCRIPT>
```

Has the same effect as this HTML markup:

```
<TITLE>Test Document</TITLE>
<P><B>Hello World!</B>
```

18.3 Designing documents for user agents that don't support scripting

The following sections discuss how authors may create documents that work for user agents that don't support scripting.

18.3.1 The NOSCRIPT element

```
<!ELEMENT NOSCRIPT - - (%block;)+
  -alternate content container for non script-based rendering -->
```

```
<!ATTLIST NOSCRIPT
  %attrs;                                    -%coreattrs, %i18n, %events -
  >
```

*Start tag: **required**, End tag: **required***

The NOSCRIPT element allows authors to provide alternate content when a script is not executed. The content of a NOSCRIPT element should only rendered by a script-aware user agent in the following cases:

- The user agent is configured not to evaluate scripts.
- The user agent doesn't support a scripting language invoked by a SCRIPT element earlier in the document.

User agents that do not support client-side scripts must render this element's contents.

In the following example, a user agent that executes the SCRIPT will include some dynamically created data in the document. If the user agent doesn't support scripts, the user may still retrieve the data through a link.

```
<SCRIPT type="text/tcl">
 ...some Tcl script to insert data...
</SCRIPT>
<NOSCRIPT>
 <P>Access the <A href="http://someplace.com/data">data.</A>
</NOSCRIPT>
```

18.3.2 Hiding script data from user agents

User agents that don't recognize the SCRIPT element will likely render that element's contents as text. Some scripting engines, including those for languages JavaScript, VBScript, and Tcl allow the script statements to be enclosed in an SGML comment. User agents that don't recognize the SCRIPT element will thus ignore the comment while smart scripting engines will understand that the script in comments should be executed.

Another solution to the problem is to keep scripts in external documents and refer to them with the src attribute.

Commenting scripts in JavaScript

The JavaScript engine allows the string "<!—" to occur at the start of a SCRIPT element, and ignores further characters until the end of the line. JavaScript interprets "//" as starting a comment extending to the end of the current line. This is needed to hide the string "—>" from the JavaScript parser.

```
<SCRIPT type="text/javascript">
<!-- to hide script contents from old browsers
  function square(i) {
    document.write("The call passed ", i ," to the function.","<BR>")
    return i * i
  }
  document.write("The function returned ",square(5),".")
// end hiding contents from old browsers -->
</SCRIPT>
```

Commenting scripts in VBScript

In VBScript, a single quote character causes the rest of the current line to be treated as a comment. It can therefore be used to hide the string "—>" from VBScript, for instance:

```
<SCRIPT type="text/vbscript">
  <!--
    Sub foo()
      ...
    End Sub
  ' -->
</SCRIPT>
```

Commenting scripts in TCL

In Tcl, the "#" character comments out the rest of the line:

```
<SCRIPT type="text/tcl">
<!-- to hide script contents from old browsers
  proc square {i} {
    document write "The call passed $i to the function.<BR>"
    return [expr $i * $i]
  }
  document write "The function returned [square 5]."
# end hiding contents from old browsers -->
</SCRIPT>
```

Note. *Some browsers close comments on the first ">" character, so to hide script content from such browsers, you can transpose operands for relational and shift operators (e.g., use "y < x" rather than "x > y") or use scripting language-dependent escapes for ">".*

Chapter 19

SGML Reference Information for HTML

Contents

1. Document Validation
2. Sample SGML catalog

The following sections contain the formal SGML definition of HTML 4.0. It includes the SGML declaration, the Document Type Definition (DTD), and the Character entity references, as well as a sample SGML catalog.

These files are also available in ASCII format as listed below:

Default DTD:

http://www.w3.org/TR/REC-html40/strict.dtd

Transitional DTD:

http://www.w3.org/TR/REC-html40/loose.dtd

Frameset DTD:

http://www.w3.org/TR/REC-html40/frameset.dtd

SGML declaration:

http://www.w3.org/TR/REC-html40/HTML4.decl

Entity definition files:

http://www.w3.org/TR/REC-html40/HTMLspecial.ent
http://www.w3.org/TR/REC-html40/HTMLsymbol.ent
http://www.w3.org/TR/REC-html40/HTMLlat1.ent

A sample catalog:

http://www.w3.org/TR/REC-html40/HTML4.cat

19.1 Document Validation

Many authors rely on a limited set of browsers to check on the documents they produce, assuming that if the browsers can render their documents they are valid. Unfortunately, this is a very ineffective means of verifying a document's validity precisely because browsers are designed to cope with invalid documents by rendering them as well as they can to avoid frustrating users.

For better validation, you should check your document against an SGML parser such as nsgmls (see [SP]), to verify that HTML documents conform to the HTML 4.0 DTD. If the document type declaration of your document includes a URI and your SGML parser supports this type of system identifier, it will get the DTD directly. Otherwise you can use the following sample SGML catalog. It assumes that the DTD has been saved as the file "strict.dtd" and that the entities are in the files "HTMLlat1.ent", "HTMLsymbol.ent" and "HTMLspecial.ent". In any case, make sure your SGML parser is capable of handling Unicode. See your validation tool documentation for further details.

Beware that such validation, although useful and highly recommended, does not guarantee that a document fully conforms to the HTML 4.0 specification. This is because an SGML parser relies solely on the given SGML DTD which does not express all aspects of a valid HTML 4.0 document. Specifically, an SGML parser ensures that the syntax, the structure, the list of elements, and their attributes are valid. But for instance, it cannot catch errors such as setting the width attribute of an IMG element to an invalid value (i.e., "foo" or "12.5"). Although the specification restricts the value for this attribute to an "integer representing a length in pixels," the DTD only defines it to be CDATA, which actually allows any value. Only a specialized program could capture the complete specification of HTML 4.0.

Nevertheless, this type of validation is still highly recommended since it permits the detection of a large set of errors that make documents invalid.

19.2 Sample SGML catalog

This catalog includes the override directive to ensure that processing software such as nsgmls uses public identifiers in preference to system identifiers. This means that users do not have to be connected to the Web when retrieving URI-based system identifiers.

```
OVERRIDE YES

PUBLIC "-//W3C//DTD HTML 4.0//EN" strict.dtd
PUBLIC "-//W3C//DTD HTML 4.0 Transitional//EN" loose.dtd
PUBLIC "-//W3C//DTD HTML 4.0 Frameset//EN" frameset.dtd
PUBLIC "-//W3C//ENTITIES Latin1//EN//HTML" HTMLlat1.ent
PUBLIC "-//W3C//ENTITIES Special//EN//HTML" HTMLspecial.ent
PUBLIC "-//W3C//ENTITIES Symbols//EN//HTML" HTMLsymbol.ent
```

Chapter 20

SGML Declaration of HTML 4.0

Note. *The total number of codepoints allowed in the document character set of this SGML declaration includes the first 17 planes of* [ISO10646] *(17 times 65536). This limitation has been made because this number is limited to a length of 8 digits in the current version of the SGML standard. It does not imply any statement about the feasibility of a long-term restriction of characters in UCS to the first 17 planes. Chances are very high that the limitation to 8 digits in SGML will be removed before, and that this specification will be updated before, the first assignment of a character beyond the first 17 planes.*

Note. *Strictly speaking, ISO Registration Number 177 refers to the original state of* [ISO10646] *in 1993, while in this specification, we always refer to the most up-to-date form of ISO 10646. Changes since 1993 have been the addition of characters and a one-time operation reallocating a large number of codepoints for Korean Hangul (Amendment 5).*

20.1 SGML Declaration

```
<!SGML    "ISO 8879:1986"
    --

        SGML Declaration for HyperText Markup Language version 4.0

        With support for the first 17 planes of ISO 10646 and
        increased limits for tag and literal lengths etc.

    --

    CHARSET
        BASESET    "ISO Registration Number 177//CHARSET
                   ISO/IEC 10646-1:1993 UCS-4 with
                   implementation level 3//ESC 2/5 2/15 4/6"
        DESCSET    0      9      UNUSED
                   9      2      9
                   11     2      UNUSED
```

```
                        13         1          13
                        14         18         UNUSED
                        32         95         32
                        127        1          UNUSED
                        128        32         UNUSED
                        160        55136      160
                        55296      2048       UNUSED  —SURROGATES—
                        57344      1056768    57344

CAPACITY          SGMLREF
                  TOTALCAP              150000
                  GRPCAP                150000
                  ENTCAP                150000

SCOPE      DOCUMENT
SYNTAX
           SHUNCHAR CONTROLS 0 1 2 3 4 5 6 7 8 9 10 11 12 13 14 15 16
              17 18 19 20 21 22 23 24 25 26 27 28 29 30 31 127
           BASESET  "ISO 646IRV:1991//CHARSET
                    International Reference Version
                    (IRV)//ESC 2/8 4/2"
           DESCSET  0 128 0

           FUNCTION
                    RE              13
                    RS              10
                    SPACE           32
                    TAB SEPCHAR      9

           NAMING   LCNMSTRT      ""
                    UCNMSTRT      ""
                    LCNMCHAR      ".-_:"
                    UCNMCHAR      ".-_:"
                    NAMECASE  GENERAL  YES
                              ENTITY   NO
           DELIM    GENERAL   SGMLREF
                    SHORTREF  SGMLREF
           NAMES    SGMLREF
           QUANTITY SGMLREF
```

```
            ATTCNT    60        -- increased --
            ATTSPLEN  65536     -- These are the largest values --
            LITLEN    65536     -- permitted in the declaration --
            NAMELEN   65536     -- Avoid fixed limits in actual --
            PILEN     65536     -- implementations of HTML UA's --
            TAGLVL    100
            TAGLEN    65536
            GRPGTCNT  150
            GRPCNT    64

FEATURES
   MINIMIZE
      DATATAG   NO
      OMITTAG   YES
      RANK      NO
      SHORTTAG  YES
   LINK
      SIMPLE    NO
      IMPLICIT  NO
      EXPLICIT  NO
   OTHER
      CONCUR    NO
      SUBDOC    NO
      FORMAL    YES
   APPINFO NONE
>
```

Chapter 21

Document Type Definition

```
<!--
    This is HTML 4.0 Strict DTD, which excludes the presentation
    attributes and elements that W3C expects to phase out as
    support for style sheets matures. Authors should use the Strict
    DTD when possible, but may use the Transitional DTD when support
    for presentation attribute and elements is required.

    HTML 4.0 includes mechanisms for style sheets, scripting,
    embedding objects, improved support for right to left and mixed
    direction text, and enhancements to forms for improved
    accessibility for people with disabilities.

        Draft: $Date: 1998/04/02 00:17:00 $

        Authors:
            Dave Raggett <dsr@w3.org>
            Arnaud Le Hors <lehors@w3.org>
            Ian Jacobs <ij@w3.org>

    Further information about HTML 4.0 is available at:

        http://www.w3.org/TR/REC-html40
-->
<!--
    Typical usage:

    <!DOCTYPE HTML PUBLIC "-//W3C//DTD HTML 4.0//EN"
            "http://www.w3.org/TR/REC-html40/strict.dtd">
    <html>
    <head>
    ...
```

```
</head>
<body
...
</body>
</html>
```

The URI used as a system identifier with the public identifier allows the user agent to download the DTD and entity sets as needed.

The FPI for the Transitional HTML 4.0 DTD is:

"-//W3C//DTD HTML 4.0 Transitional//EN"

and its URI is:

http://www.w3.org/TR/REC-html40/loose.dtd

If you are writing a document that includes frames, use the following FPI:

"-//W3C//DTD HTML 4.0 Frameset//EN"

with the URI:

http://www.w3.org/TR/REC-html40/frameset.dtd

The following URIs are supported in relation to HTML 4.0

"http://www.w3.org/TR/REC-html40/strict.dtd" (Strict DTD)
"http://www.w3.org/TR/REC-html40/loose.dtd" (Loose DTD)
"http://www.w3.org/TR/REC-html40/frameset.dtd" (Frameset DTD)
"http://www.w3.org/TR/REC-html40/HTMLlat1.ent" (Latin-1 entities)
"http://www.w3.org/TR/REC-html40/HTMLsymbol.ent" (Symbol entities)
"http://www.w3.org/TR/REC-html40/HTMLspecial.ent" (Special entities)

These URIs point to the latest version of each file. To reference this specific revision use the following URIs:

"http://www.w3.org/TR/1998/REC-html40-19980424/strict.dtd"
"http://www.w3.org/TR/1998/REC-html40-19980424/loose.dtd"
"http://www.w3.org/TR/1998/REC-html40-19980424/frameset.dtd"
"http://www.w3.org/TR/1998/REC-html40-19980424/HTMLlat1.ent"
"http://www.w3.org/TR/1998/REC-html40-19980424/HTMLsymbol.ent"

"http://www.w3.org/TR/1998/REC-html40-19980424/HTMLspecial.ent"
--

<!--================== Imported Names ======================================-->
<!ENTITY % ContentType "CDATA"
    --media type, as per [RFC2045]
    -->

<!ENTITY % ContentTypes "CDATA"
    --comma-separated list of media types, as per [RFC2045]
    -->

<!ENTITY % Charset "CDATA"
    --a character encoding, as per [RFC2045]
    -->

<!ENTITY % Charsets "CDATA"
    --a space separated list of character encodings, as per [RFC2045]
    -->

<!ENTITY % LanguageCode "NAME"
    --a language code, as per [RFC1766]
    -->

<!ENTITY % Character "CDATA"
    --a single character from [ISO10646]
    -->

<!ENTITY % LinkTypes "CDATA"
    --space-separated list of link types
    -->

<!ENTITY % MediaDesc "CDATA"
    --single or comma-separated list of media descriptors
    -->

<!ENTITY % URI "CDATA"
    --a Uniform Resource Identifier,
        see [URI]
    -->

```
<!ENTITY % Datetime "CDATA"--date and time information. ISO date format --

<!ENTITY % Script "CDATA"--script expression --

<!ENTITY % StyleSheet "CDATA"--style sheet data --

<!ENTITY % Text "CDATA"

<!-- Parameter Entities --

<!ENTITY % head.misc "SCRIPT|STYLE|META|LINK|OBJECT"--repeatable head elements
 --

<!ENTITY % heading "H1|H2|H3|H4|H5|H6"

<!ENTITY % list "UL | OL"

<!ENTITY % preformatted "PRE"

<!--================ Character mnemonic entities ==========================--

<!ENTITY % HTMLlat1 PUBLIC
    "-//W3C//ENTITIES Latin1//EN//HTML"
    "http://www.w3.org/TR/1998/REC-html40-19980424/HTMLlat1.ent">
%HTMLlat1;

<!ENTITY % HTMLsymbol PUBLIC
    "-//W3C//ENTITIES Symbols//EN//HTML"
    "http://www.w3.org/TR/1998/REC-html40-19980424/HTMLsymbol.ent">
%HTMLsymbol;

<!ENTITY % HTMLspecial PUBLIC
    "-//W3C//ENTITIES Special//EN//HTML"
    "http://www.w3.org/TR/1998/REC-html40-19980424/HTMLspecial.ent">
%HTMLspecial;
<!--=================== Generic Attributes ===============================--

<!ENTITY % coreattrs
    "id          ID              #IMPLIED  -- document-wide unique id --
     class       CDATA           #IMPLIED  -- space separated list of classes --
     style       %StyleSheet;    #IMPLIED  -- associated style info --
     title       %Text;          #IMPLIED  -- advisory title/amplification --"
```

```
<!ENTITY % i18n
 "lang        %LanguageCode;  #IMPLIED   - language code -
  dir         (ltr|rtl)       #IMPLIED   - direction for weak/neutral text -"
<!ENTITY % events
 "onclick     %Script;        #IMPLIED -a pointer button was clicked -
  ondblclick  %Script;        #IMPLIED -a pointer button was double clicked-
  onmousedown %Script;        #IMPLIED -a pointer button was pressed down -
  onmouseup   %Script;        #IMPLIED -a pointer button was released -
  onmouseover %Script;        #IMPLIED -a pointer was moved onto -
  onmousemove %Script;        #IMPLIED -a pointer was moved within -
  onmouseout  %Script;        #IMPLIED -a pointer was moved away -
  onkeypress  %Script;        #IMPLIED -a key was pressed and released -
  onkeydown   %Script;        #IMPLIED -a key was pressed down -
  onkeyup     %Script;        #IMPLIED -a key was released -"

<!- Reserved Feature Switch -
<!ENTITY % HTML.Reserved "IGNORE"

<!- The following attributes are reserved for possible future use -
<![ %HTML.Reserved; [
<!ENTITY % reserved
 "datasrc     %URI;           #IMPLIED -a single or tabular Data Source -
  datafld     CDATA           #IMPLIED -the property or column name -
  dataformatas (plaintext|html) plaintext-text or html -"

]]

<!ENTITY % reserved ""

<!ENTITY % attrs "%coreattrs; %i18n; %events;"

<!-=================== Text Markup ========================================-

<!ENTITY % fontstyle
  "TT | I | B | BIG | SMALL"

<!ENTITY % phrase "EM | STRONG | DFN | CODE |
                   SAMP | KBD | VAR | CITE | ABBR | ACRONYM"

<!ENTITY % special
    "A | IMG | OBJECT | BR | SCRIPT | MAP | Q | SUB | SUP | SPAN | BDO"
```

```
<!ENTITY % formctrl "INPUT | SELECT | TEXTAREA | LABEL | BUTTON"

<!-- %inline; covers inline or "text-level" elements -->
<!ENTITY % inline "#PCDATA | %fontstyle; | %phrase; | %special; | %formctrl;"

<!ELEMENT (%fontstyle;|%phrase;) - - (%inline;)*
<!ATTLIST (%fontstyle;|%phrase;)
  %attrs;                             -- %coreattrs, %i18n, %events --

<!ELEMENT (SUB|SUP) - - (%inline;)*   -- subscript, superscript --
<!ATTLIST (SUB|SUP)
  %attrs;                             -- %coreattrs, %i18n, %events --

<!ELEMENT SPAN - - (%inline;)*        -- generic language/style container --
<!ATTLIST SPAN
  %attrs;                             -- %coreattrs, %i18n, %events --
  %reserved;                          -- reserved for possible future use --

<!ELEMENT BDO - - (%inline;)*         -- I18N BiDi over-ride --
<!ATTLIST BDO
  %coreattrs;                         -- id, class, style, title --
  lang        %LanguageCode;  #IMPLIED -- language code --
  dir         (ltr|rtl)       #REQUIRED -- directionality --

<!ELEMENT BR - O EMPTY                -- forced line break --
<!ATTLIST BR
  %coreattrs;                         -- id, class, style, title --

<!--================== HTML content models ================================-->

<!--
    HTML has two basic content models:

        %inline;     character level elements and text strings
        %block;      block-like elements e.g. paragraphs and lists
-->

<!ENTITY % block
    "P | %heading; | %list; | %preformatted; | DL | DIV | NOSCRIPT |
     BLOCKQUOTE | FORM | HR | TABLE | FIELDSET | ADDRESS"

<!ENTITY % flow "%block; | %inline;"
```

```
<!--==================== Document Body ====================-->

<!ELEMENT BODY O O (%block;|SCRIPT)+ +(INS|DEL) -document body -
<!ATTLIST BODY
  %attrs;                               - %coreattrs, %i18n, %events -
  onload          %Script;   #IMPLIED   - the document has been loaded -
  onunload        %Script;   #IMPLIED   - the document has been removed -

<!ELEMENT ADDRESS - - (%inline;)* -information on author -
<!ATTLIST ADDRESS
  %attrs;                               - %coreattrs, %i18n, %events -

<!ELEMENT DIV - - (%flow;)*             - generic language/style container -
<!ATTLIST DIV
  %attrs;                               - %coreattrs, %i18n, %events -
  %reserved;                            - reserved for possible future use -

<!--================== The Anchor Element ====================-->

<!ENTITY % Shape "(rect|circle|poly|default)"
<!ENTITY % Coords "CDATA" -comma separated list of lengths -

<!ELEMENT A - - (%inline;)* -(A)        - anchor -
<!ATTLIST A
  %attrs;                               - %coreattrs, %i18n, %events -
  charset     %Charset;      #IMPLIED   - char encoding of linked resource -
  type        %ContentType;  #IMPLIED   - advisory content type -
  name        CDATA          #IMPLIED   - named link end -
  href        %URI;          #IMPLIED   - URI for linked resource -
  hreflang    %LanguageCode; #IMPLIED   - language code -
  rel         %LinkTypes;    #IMPLIED   - forward link types -
  rev         %LinkTypes;    #IMPLIED   - reverse link types -
  accesskey   %Character;    #IMPLIED   - accessibility key character -
  shape       %Shape;        rect       - for use with client-side image maps -
  coords      %Coords;       #IMPLIED   - for use with client-side image maps -
  tabindex    NUMBER         #IMPLIED   - position in tabbing order -
  onfocus     %Script;       #IMPLIED   - the element got the focus -
  onblur      %Script;       #IMPLIED   - the element lost the focus -
```

```
<!--================== Client-side image maps ============================-->

<!-- These can be placed in the same document or grouped in a
     separate document although this isn't yet widely supported -->

<!ELEMENT MAP - - ((%block;)+ | AREA+)-client-side image map -->
<!ATTLIST MAP
  %attrs;                              -- %coreattrs, %i18n, %events --
  name        CDATA        #REQUIRED   -- for reference by usemap --
  >

<!ELEMENT AREA - O EMPTY              -- client-side image map area -->
<!ATTLIST AREA
  %attrs;                              -- %coreattrs, %i18n, %events --
  shape       %Shape;      rect        -- controls interpretation of coords --
  coords      %Coords;     #IMPLIED    -- comma separated list of lengths --
  href        %URI;        #IMPLIED    -- URI for linked resource --
  nohref      (nohref)     #IMPLIED    -- this region has no action --
  alt         %Text;       #REQUIRED   -- short description --
  tabindex    NUMBER       #IMPLIED    -- position in tabbing order --
  accesskey   %Character;  #IMPLIED    -- accessibility key character --
  onfocus     %Script;     #IMPLIED    -- the element got the focus --
  onblur      %Script;     #IMPLIED    -- the element lost the focus --
  >

<!--================== The LINK Element ==================================-->

<!--
  Relationship values can be used in principle:

    a) for document specific toolbars/menus when used
       with the LINK element in document head e.g.
         start, contents, previous, next, index, end, help
    b) to link to a separate style sheet (rel=stylesheet)
    c) to make a link to a script (rel=script)
    d) by stylesheets to control how collections of
       html nodes are rendered into printed documents
    e) to make a link to a printable version of this document
       e.g. a postscript or pdf version (rel=alternate media=print)
  -->
```

```
<!ELEMENT LINK - O EMPTY              -- a media-independent link --
<!ATTLIST LINK
   %attrs;                            -- %coreattrs, %i18n, %events --
   charset     %Charset;      #IMPLIED  -- char encoding of linked resource --
   href        %URI;          #IMPLIED  -- URI for linked resource --
   hreflang    %LanguageCode; #IMPLIED  -- language code --
   type        %ContentType;  #IMPLIED  -- advisory content type --
   rel         %LinkTypes;    #IMPLIED  -- forward link types --
   rev         %LinkTypes;    #IMPLIED  -- reverse link types --
   media       %MediaDesc;    #IMPLIED  -- for rendering on these media --

<!--==================== Images =======================================-->

<!-- Length defined in strict DTD for cellpadding/cellspacing --
<!ENTITY % Length "CDATA"--nn for pixels or nn% for percentage length --
<!ENTITY % MultiLength "CDATA"--pixel, percentage, or relative --

<!ENTITY % MultiLengths "CDATA"--comma-separated list of MultiLength --

<!ENTITY % Pixels "CDATA"--integer representing length in pixels --

<!-- To avoid problems with text-only UAs as well as
     to make image content understandable and navigable
     to users of non-visual UAs, you need to provide
     a description with ALT, and avoid server-side image maps --
<!ELEMENT IMG - O EMPTY               -- Embedded image --
<!ATTLIST IMG
   %attrs;                            -- %coreattrs, %i18n, %events --
   src         %URI;          #REQUIRED -- URI of image to embed --
   alt         %Text;         #REQUIRED -- short description --
   longdesc    %URI;          #IMPLIED  -- link to long description
                                           (complements alt) --
   height      %Length;       #IMPLIED  -- override height --
   width       %Length;       #IMPLIED  -- override width --
   usemap      %URI;          #IMPLIED  -- use client-side image map --
   ismap       (ismap)        #IMPLIED  -- use server-side image map --

<!-- USEMAP points to a MAP element which may be in this document
     or an external document, although the latter is not widely supported --
```

```
<!--==================== OBJECT ========================================-->
<!--
  OBJECT is used to embed objects as part of HTML pages
  PARAM elements should precede other content. SGML mixed content
  model technicality precludes specifying this formally ...
-->

<!ELEMENT OBJECT - - (PARAM | %flow;)*
--generic embedded object -->
<!ATTLIST OBJECT
  %attrs;                                 -- %coreattrs, %i18n, %events --
  declare     (declare)       #IMPLIED    -- declare but don't instantiate flag --
  classid     %URI;           #IMPLIED    -- identifies an implementation --
  codebase    %URI;           #IMPLIED    -- base URI for classid, data, archive--
  data        %URI;           #IMPLIED    -- reference to object's data --
  type        %ContentType;   #IMPLIED    -- content type for data --
  codetype    %ContentType;   #IMPLIED    -- content type for code --
  archive     %URI;           #IMPLIED    -- space separated archive list --
  standby     %Text;          #IMPLIED    -- message to show while loading --
  height      %Length;        #IMPLIED    -- override height --
  width       %Length;        #IMPLIED    -- override width --
  usemap      %URI;           #IMPLIED    -- use client-side image map --
  name        CDATA           #IMPLIED    -- submit as part of form --
  tabindex    NUMBER          #IMPLIED    -- position in tabbing order --
  %reserved;                              -- reserved for possible future use --
  >
<!ELEMENT PARAM - O EMPTY                 -- named property value --
<!ATTLIST PARAM
  id          ID              #IMPLIED    -- document-wide unique id --
  name        CDATA           #REQUIRED   -- property name --
  value       CDATA           #IMPLIED    -- property value --
  valuetype   (DATA|REF|OBJECT) DATA      -- How to interpret value --
  type        %ContentType;   #IMPLIED    -- content type for value
                                             when valuetype=ref --
  >

<!--==================== Horizontal Rule ================================-->

<!ELEMENT HR - O EMPTY--horizontal rule -->
<!ATTLIST HR
```

```
    %coreattrs;                           — id, class, style, title —
    %events;

<!—================== Paragraphs =======================================—

<!ELEMENT P - O (%inline;)*            — paragraph —
<!ATTLIST P
    %attrs;                               — %coreattrs, %i18n, %events —

<!—================== Headings ========================================—

<!—
    There are six levels of headings from H1 (the most important)
    to H6 (the least important).
—

<!ELEMENT (%heading;)  - - (%inline;)*    — heading —
<!ATTLIST (%heading;)
    %attrs;                               — %coreattrs, %i18n, %events —

<!—================== Preformatted Text ================================—

<!— excludes markup for images and changes in font size —
<!ENTITY % pre.exclusion "IMG|OBJECT|BIG|SMALL|SUB|SUP"

<!ELEMENT PRE - - (%inline;)* -(%pre.exclusion;)—preformatted text —
<!ATTLIST PRE
    %attrs;                              —%coreattrs, %i18n, %events —

<!—==================== Inline Quotes ===================================—

<!ELEMENT Q - - (%inline;)*           — short inline quotation —
<!ATTLIST Q
    %attrs;                               — %coreattrs, %i18n, %events —
    cite        %URI;      #IMPLIED       — URI for source document or msg —

<!—================== Block-like Quotes =================================—

<!ELEMENT BLOCKQUOTE - - (%block;|SCRIPT)+—long quotation —
<!ATTLIST BLOCKQUOTE
    %attrs;                               — %coreattrs, %i18n, %events —
    cite        %URI;      #IMPLIED       — URI for source document or msg —
```

```
<!--================== Inserted/Deleted Text ============================-->
<!-- INS/DEL are handled by inclusion on BODY -->
<!ELEMENT (INS|DEL) - - (%flow;)*       -- inserted text, deleted text -->
<!ATTLIST (INS|DEL)
   %attrs;                              -- %coreattrs, %i18n, %events -->
   cite         %URI;          #IMPLIED -- info on reason for change -->
   datetime     %Datetime;     #IMPLIED -- date and time of change -->

<!--================== Lists =============================================-->

<!-- definition lists - DT for term, DD for its definition -->

<!ELEMENT DL - - (DT|DD)+               -- definition list -->
<!ATTLIST DL
   %attrs;                              -- %coreattrs, %i18n, %events -->

<!ELEMENT DT - O (%inline;)*            -- definition term -->
<!ELEMENT DD - O (%flow;)*              -- definition description -->
<!ATTLIST (DT|DD)
   %attrs;                              -- %coreattrs, %i18n, %events -->

<!ELEMENT OL - - (LI)+                  -- ordered list -->
<!ATTLIST OL
   %attrs;                              -- %coreattrs, %i18n, %events -->

<!-- Unordered Lists (UL) bullet styles -->
<!ELEMENT UL - - (LI)+                  -- unordered list -->
<!ATTLIST UL
   %attrs;                              -- %coreattrs, %i18n, %events -->

<!ELEMENT LI - O (%flow;)*              -- list item -->
<!ATTLIST LI
   %attrs;                              -- %coreattrs, %i18n, %events -->

<!--=============== Forms ================================================-->
<!ELEMENT FORM - - (%block;|SCRIPT)+ -(FORM)--interactive form -->
<!ATTLIST FORM
   %attrs;                              -- %coreattrs, %i18n, %events -->
   action       %URI;          #REQUIRED -- server-side form handler -->
```

```
    method          (GET|POST)          GET         — HTTP method used to submit the form—
    enctype         %ContentType;       "application/x-www-form-urlencoded"
    onsubmit        %Script;            #IMPLIED    — the form was submitted —
    onreset         %Script;            #IMPLIED    — the form was reset —
    accept-charset  %Charsets;          #IMPLIED    — list of supported charsets —
<!— Each label must not contain more than ONE field —
<!ELEMENT LABEL - - (%inline;)* -(LABEL)—form field label text —
<!ATTLIST LABEL
    %attrs;                                         — %coreattrs, %i18n, %events —
    for             IDREF               #IMPLIED    — matches field ID value —
    accesskey       %Character;         #IMPLIED    — accessibility key character —
    onfocus         %Script;            #IMPLIED    — the element got the focus —
    onblur          %Script;            #IMPLIED    — the element lost the focus —

<!ENTITY % InputType
    "(TEXT | PASSWORD | CHECKBOX |
      RADIO | SUBMIT | RESET |
      FILE | HIDDEN | IMAGE | BUTTON)"

<!— attribute name required for all but submit & reset —
<!ELEMENT INPUT - O EMPTY                  —form control —
<!ATTLIST INPUT
    %attrs;                                         —%coreattrs, %i18n, %events —
    type            %InputType;         TEXT        — what kind of widget is needed —
    name            CDATA               #IMPLIED    — submit as part of form —
    value           CDATA               #IMPLIED    — required for radio and checkboxes —
    checked         (checked)           #IMPLIED    — for radio buttons and check boxes —
    disabled        (disabled)          #IMPLIED    — unavailable in this context —
    readonly        (readonly)          #IMPLIED    — for text and passwd —
    size            CDATA               #IMPLIED    — specific to each type of field —
    maxlength       NUMBER              #IMPLIED    — max chars for text fields —
    src             %URI;               #IMPLIED    — for fields with images —
    alt             CDATA               #IMPLIED    — short description —
    usemap          %URI;               #IMPLIED    — use client-side image map —
    tabindex        NUMBER              #IMPLIED    — position in tabbing order —
    accesskey       %Character;         #IMPLIED    — accessibility key character —
    onfocus         %Script;            #IMPLIED    — the element got the focus —
```

```
  onblur      %Script;           #IMPLIED   -- the element lost the focus --
  onselect    %Script;           #IMPLIED   -- some text was selected --
  onchange    %Script;           #IMPLIED   -- the element value was changed --
  accept      %ContentTypes;     #IMPLIED   -- list of MIME types for file upload --
  %reserved;                                -- reserved for possible future use --

<!ELEMENT SELECT - - (OPTGROUP|OPTION)+ -- option selector -->
<!ATTLIST SELECT
  %attrs;                                   -- %coreattrs, %i18n, %events --
  name        CDATA              #IMPLIED   -- field name --
  size        NUMBER             #IMPLIED   -- rows visible --
  multiple    (multiple)         #IMPLIED   -- default is single selection --
  disabled    (disabled)         #IMPLIED   -- unavailable in this context --
  tabindex    NUMBER             #IMPLIED   -- position in tabbing order --
  onfocus     %Script;           #IMPLIED   -- the element got the focus --
  onblur      %Script;           #IMPLIED   -- the element lost the focus --
  onchange    %Script;           #IMPLIED   -- the element value was changed --
  %reserved;                                -- reserved for possible future use --

<!ELEMENT OPTGROUP - - (OPTION)+ -- option group -->
<!ATTLIST OPTGROUP
  %attrs;                                   -- %coreattrs, %i18n, %events --
  disabled    (disabled)         #IMPLIED   -- unavailable in this context --
  label       %Text;             #REQUIRED  -- for use in hierarchical menus --

<!ELEMENT OPTION - O (#PCDATA)              -- selectable choice -->
<!ATTLIST OPTION
  %attrs;                                   -- %coreattrs, %i18n, %events --
  selected    (selected)         #IMPLIED
  disabled    (disabled)         #IMPLIED   -- unavailable in this context --
  label       %Text;             #IMPLIED   -- for use in hierarchical menus --
  value       CDATA              #IMPLIED   -- defaults to element content --

<!ELEMENT TEXTAREA - - (#PCDATA)            -- multi-line text field -->
<!ATTLIST TEXTAREA
  %attrs;                                   -- %coreattrs, %i18n, %events --
  name        CDATA              #IMPLIED
  rows        NUMBER             #REQUIRED
  cols        NUMBER             #REQUIRED
```

```
  disabled    (disabled)    #IMPLIED   -- unavailable in this context --
  readonly    (readonly)    #IMPLIED
  tabindex    NUMBER        #IMPLIED   -- position in tabbing order --
  accesskey   %Character;   #IMPLIED   -- accessibility key character --
  onfocus     %Script;      #IMPLIED   -- the element got the focus --
  onblur      %Script;      #IMPLIED   -- the element lost the focus --
  onselect    %Script;      #IMPLIED   -- some text was selected --
  onchange    %Script;      #IMPLIED   -- the element value was changed --
  %reserved;                           -- reserved for possible future use --
<!--
   #PCDATA is to solve the mixed content problem,
   per specification only whitespace is allowed there!
   -->
<!ELEMENT FIELDSET - - (#PCDATA,LEGEND,(%flow;)*)—form control group --
<!ATTLIST FIELDSET
  %attrs;                              -- %coreattrs, %i18n, %events --

<!ELEMENT LEGEND - - (%inline;)*       --fieldset legend --
<!ENTITY % LAlign "(top|bottom|left|right)"

<!ATTLIST LEGEND
  %attrs;                              -- %coreattrs, %i18n, %events --
  accesskey   %Character;   #IMPLIED   -- accessibility key character --

<!ELEMENT BUTTON - -
      (%flow;)* -(A|%formctrl;|FORM|FIELDSET)
    --push button --
<!ATTLIST BUTTON
  %attrs;                              -- %coreattrs, %i18n, %events --
  name        CDATA         #IMPLIED
  value       CDATA         #IMPLIED   -- sent to server when submitted --
  type        (button|submit|reset) submit--for use as form button --
  disabled    (disabled)    #IMPLIED   -- unavailable in this context --
  tabindex    NUMBER        #IMPLIED   -- position in tabbing order --
  accesskey   %Character;   #IMPLIED   -- accessibility key character --
  onfocus     %Script;      #IMPLIED   -- the element got the focus --
  onblur      %Script;      #IMPLIED   -- the element lost the focus --
  %reserved;                           -- reserved for possible future use --
```

```
<!--======================= Tables ========================-->

<!-- IETF HTML table standard, see [RFC1942] -->

<!--
    The BORDER attribute sets the thickness of the frame around the
    table. The default units are screen pixels.

    The FRAME attribute specifies which parts of the frame around
    the table should be rendered. The values are not the same as
    CALS to avoid a name clash with the VALIGN attribute.

    The value "border" is included for backwards compatibility with
    <TABLE BORDER> which yields frame=border and border=implied
    For <TABLE BORDER=1> you get border=1 and frame=implied. In this
    case, it is appropriate to treat this as frame=border for backwards
    compatibility with deployed browsers.
-->

<!ENTITY % TFrame "(void|above|below|hsides|lhs|rhs|vsides|box|border)">

<!--
    The RULES attribute defines which rules to draw between cells:

    If RULES is absent then assume:
        "none" if BORDER is absent or BORDER=0 otherwise "all"
-->

<!ENTITY % TRules "(none | groups | rows | cols | all)">

<!-- horizontal placement of table relative to document -->
<!ENTITY % TAlign "(left|center|right)">

<!-- horizontal alignment attributes for cell contents -->
<!ENTITY % cellhalign
    "align       (left|center|right|justify|char) #IMPLIED
     char        %Character;   #IMPLIED  -- alignment char, e.g. char=':' --
     charoff     %Length;      #IMPLIED  -- offset for alignment char --"

<!-- vertical alignment attributes for cell contents -->
<!ENTITY % cellvalign
    "valign      (top|middle|bottom|baseline) #IMPLIED"
```

```
<!ELEMENT TABLE - -
        (CAPTION?, (COL*|COLGROUP*), THEAD?, TFOOT?, TBODY+)
<!ELEMENT CAPTION  - - (%inline;)*     -- table caption --
<!ELEMENT THEAD    - O (TR)+           -- table header --
<!ELEMENT TFOOT    - O (TR)+           -- table footer --
<!ELEMENT TBODY    O O (TR)+           -- table body --
<!ELEMENT COLGROUP - O (col)*          -- table column group --
<!ELEMENT COL      - O EMPTY           -- table column --
<!ELEMENT TR       - O (TH|TD)+        -- table row --
<!ELEMENT (TH|TD)  - O (%flow;)*       -- table header cell, table data cell--

<!ATTLIST TABLE                        -- table element --
   %attrs;                             -- %coreattrs, %i18n, %events --
   summary      %Text;      #IMPLIED   -- purpose/structure for speech output--
   width        %Length;    #IMPLIED   -- table width --
   border       %Pixels;    #IMPLIED   -- controls frame width around table --
   frame        %TFrame;    #IMPLIED   -- which parts of frame to render --
   rules        %TRules;    #IMPLIED   -- rulings between rows and cols --
   cellspacing  %Length;    #IMPLIED   -- spacing between cells --
   cellpadding  %Length;    #IMPLIED   -- spacing within cells --
   %reserved;                          -- reserved for possible future use --
   datapagesize CDATA       #IMPLIED   -- reserved for possible future use --

<!ENTITY % CAlign "(top|bottom|left|right)"

<!ATTLIST CAPTION
   %attrs;                             --%coreattrs, %i18n, %events --

<!--
COLGROUP groups a set of COL elements. It allows you to group
several semantically related columns together.
-->
<!ATTLIST COLGROUP
   %attrs;                             -- %coreattrs, %i18n, %events --
   span         NUMBER      1          -- default number of columns in group --
   width        %MultiLength; #IMPLIED -- default width for enclosed COLs --
   %cellhalign;                        -- horizontal alignment in cells --
   %cellvalign;                        -- vertical alignment in cells --
```

```
<!--
COL elements define the alignment properties for cells in
one or more columns.

The WIDTH attribute specifies the width of the columns, e.g.
    width=64          width in screen pixels
    width=0.5*        relative width of 0.5

The SPAN attribute causes the attributes of one
COL element to apply to more than one column.
-->
<!ATTLIST COL                         -- column groups and properties --
  %attrs;                             -- %coreattrs, %i18n, %events --
  span        NUMBER       1          -- COL attributes affect N columns --
  width       %MultiLength; #IMPLIED  -- column width specification --
  %cellhalign;                        -- horizontal alignment in cells --
  %cellvalign;                        -- vertical alignment in cells --

<!--
    Use THEAD to duplicate headers when breaking table
    across page boundaries, or for static headers when
    TBODY sections are rendered in scrolling panel.

    Use TFOOT to duplicate footers when breaking table
    across page boundaries, or for static footers when
    TBODY sections are rendered in scrolling panel.

    Use multiple TBODY sections when rules are needed
    between groups of table rows.
-->
<!ATTLIST (THEAD|TBODY|TFOOT)         -- table section --
  %attrs;                             -- %coreattrs, %i18n, %events --
  %cellhalign;                        -- horizontal alignment in cells --
  %cellvalign;                        -- vertical alignment in cells --

<!ATTLIST TR                          -- table row --
  %attrs;                             -- %coreattrs, %i18n, %events --
  %cellhalign;                        -- horizontal alignment in cells --
  %cellvalign;                        -- vertical alignment in cells --
```

```
<!-- Scope is simpler than axes attribute for common tables -->
<!ENTITY % Scope "(row|col|rowgroup|colgroup)"

<!-- TH is for headers, TD for data, but for cells acting as both use TD -->
<!ATTLIST (TH|TD)                          -- header or data cell --
  %attrs;                                  -- %coreattrs, %i18n, %events --
  abbr        %Text;        #IMPLIED       -- abbreviation for header cell --
  axis        CDATA         #IMPLIED       -- names groups of related headers--
  headers     IDREFS        #IMPLIED       -- list of id's for header cells --
  scope       %Scope;       #IMPLIED       -- scope covered by header cells --
  rowspan     NUMBER        1              -- number of rows spanned by cell --
  colspan     NUMBER        1              -- number of cols spanned by cell --
  %cellhalign;                             -- horizontal alignment in cells --
  %cellvalign;                             -- vertical alignment in cells --

<!--================ Document Head =========================================-->
<!-- %head.misc; defined earlier on as "SCRIPT|STYLE|META|LINK|OBJECT" -->
<!ENTITY % head.content "TITLE & BASE?"

<!ELEMENT HEAD O O (%head.content;) +(%head.misc;)--document head --
<!ATTLIST HEAD
  %i18n;                                   -- lang, dir --
  profile     %URI;         #IMPLIED       -- named dictionary of meta info --

<!-- The TITLE element is not considered part of the flow of text.
     It should be displayed, for example as the page header or
     window title. Exactly one title is required per document.
  -->
<!ELEMENT TITLE - - (#PCDATA) -(%head.misc;)--document title --
<!ATTLIST TITLE %i18n

<!ELEMENT BASE - O EMPTY                   -- document base URI --
<!ATTLIST BASE
  href        %URI;         #REQUIRED      -- URI that acts as base URI --

<!ELEMENT META - O EMPTY                   --generic metainformation --
<!ATTLIST META
  %i18n;                                   --lang, dir, for use with content --
  http-equiv  NAME          #IMPLIED       -- HTTP response header name --
  name        NAME          #IMPLIED       -- metainformation name --
```

```
        content      CDATA          #REQUIRED    — associated information —
        scheme       CDATA          #IMPLIED     — select form of content —
<!ELEMENT STYLE - - %StyleSheet                  — style info —
<!ATTLIST STYLE
        %i18n;                                   — lang, dir, for use with title —
        type         %ContentType;  #REQUIRED    — content type of style language —
        media        %MediaDesc;    #IMPLIED     — designed for use with these media —
        title        %Text;         #IMPLIED     — advisory title —

<!ELEMENT SCRIPT - - %Script;                    —script statements —
<!ATTLIST SCRIPT
        charset      %Charset;      #IMPLIED     — char encoding of linked resource —
        type         %ContentType;  #REQUIRED    — content type of script language —
        src          %URI;          #IMPLIED     — URI for an external script —
        defer        (defer)        #IMPLIED     — UA may defer execution of script —
        event        CDATA          #IMPLIED     — reserved for possible future use —
        for          %URI;          #IMPLIED     — reserved for possible future use —

<!ELEMENT NOSCRIPT - - (%block;)+
  —alternate content container for non script-based rendering —
<!ATTLIST NOSCRIPT
        %attrs;                                  — %coreattrs, %i18n, %events —

<!--================ Document Structure ====================================-->
<!ENTITY % html.content "HEAD, BODY">
<!ELEMENT HTML O O (%html.content;)              — document root element —
<!ATTLIST HTML
        %i18n;                                   — lang, dir —
```

Chapter 22

Transitional Document Type Definition

```
<!--
    This is the HTML 4.0 Transitional DTD, which includes
    presentation attributes and elements that W3C expects to phase out
    as support for style sheets matures. Authors should use the Strict
    DTD when possible, but may use the Transitional DTD when support
    for presentation attribute and elements is required.

    HTML 4.0 includes mechanisms for style sheets, scripting,
    embedding objects, improved support for right to left and mixed
    direction text, and enhancements to forms for improved
    accessibility for people with disabilities.

        Draft: $Date: 1998/04/02 00:17:00 $

        Authors:
            Dave Raggett <dsr@w3.org>
            Arnaud Le Hors <lehors@w3.org>
            Ian Jacobs <ij@w3.org>

    Further information about HTML 4.0 is available at:

        http://www.w3.org/TR/REC-html40
-->
<!ENTITY % HTML.Version "-//W3C//DTD HTML 4.0 Transitional//EN"
  --Typical usage:

    <!DOCTYPE HTML PUBLIC "-//W3C//DTD HTML 4.0 Transitional//EN"
            "http://www.w3.org/TR/REC-html40/loose.dtd">
    <html
```

```
<head
...
</head>
<body
...
</body>
</html>
```

The URI used as a system identifier with the public identifier allows the user agent to download the DTD and entity sets as needed.

The FPI for the Strict HTML 4.0 DTD is:

"-//W3C//DTD HTML 4.0//EN"

and its URI is:

http://www.w3.org/TR/REC-html40/strict.dtd

Authors should use the Strict DTD unless they need the presentation control for user agents that don't (adequately) support style sheets.

If you are writing a document that includes frames, use the following FPI:

"-//W3C//DTD HTML 4.0 Frameset//EN"

with the URI:

http://www.w3.org/TR/REC-html40/frameset.dtd

The following URIs are supported in relation to HTML 4.0

"http://www.w3.org/TR/REC-html40/strict.dtd" (Strict DTD)
"http://www.w3.org/TR/REC-html40/loose.dtd" (Loose DTD)
"http://www.w3.org/TR/REC-html40/frameset.dtd" (Frameset DTD)
"http://www.w3.org/TR/REC-html40/HTMLlat1.ent" (Latin-1 entities)
"http://www.w3.org/TR/REC-html40/HTMLsymbol.ent" (Symbol entities)
"http://www.w3.org/TR/REC-html40/HTMLspecial.ent" (Special entities)

These URIs point to the latest version of each file. To reference this specific revision use the following URIs:

```
          "http://www.w3.org/TR/1998/REC-html40-19980424/strict.dtd"
          "http://www.w3.org/TR/1998/REC-html40-19980424/loose.dtd"
          "http://www.w3.org/TR/1998/REC-html40-19980424/frameset.dtd"
          "http://www.w3.org/TR/1998/REC-html40-19980424/HTMLlat1.ent"
          "http://www.w3.org/TR/1998/REC-html40-19980424/HTMLsymbol.ent"
          "http://www.w3.org/TR/1998/REC-html40-19980424/HTMLspecial.ent"
—

<!--================== Imported Names ======================================-->
<!ENTITY % ContentType "CDATA"
    --media type, as per [RFC2045]
    —
<!ENTITY % ContentTypes "CDATA"
    --comma-separated list of media types, as per [RFC2045]
    —
<!ENTITY % Charset "CDATA"
    --a character encoding, as per [RFC2045]
    —
<!ENTITY % Charsets "CDATA"
    --a space separated list of character encodings, as per [RFC2045]
    —
<!ENTITY % LanguageCode "NAME"
    --a language code, as per [RFC1766]
    —
<!ENTITY % Character "CDATA"
    --a single character from [ISO10646]
    —
<!ENTITY % LinkTypes "CDATA"
    --space-separated list of link types
    —
<!ENTITY % MediaDesc "CDATA"
    --single or comma-separated list of media descriptors
    —
```

```
<!ENTITY % URI "CDATA"
    -- a Uniform Resource Identifier,
        see [URI]
    --
<!ENTITY % Datetime "CDATA" -- date and time information. ISO date format --
<!ENTITY % Script "CDATA" -- script expression --
<!ENTITY % StyleSheet "CDATA" -- style sheet data --
<!ENTITY % FrameTarget "CDATA" -- render in this frame --
<!ENTITY % Text "CDATA">
<!-- Parameter Entities -->
<!ENTITY % head.misc "SCRIPT|STYLE|META|LINK|OBJECT" -- repeatable head elements --
<!ENTITY % heading "H1|H2|H3|H4|H5|H6">
<!ENTITY % list "UL | OL | DIR | MENU">
<!ENTITY % preformatted "PRE">
<!ENTITY % Color "CDATA" -- a color using sRGB: #RRGGBB as Hex values --
<!-- There are also 16 widely known color names with their sRGB values:

    Black   = #000000    Green  = #008000
    Silver  = #C0C0C0    Lime   = #00FF00
    Gray    = #808080    Olive  = #808000
    White   = #FFFFFF    Yellow = #FFFF00
    Maroon  = #800000    Navy   = #000080
    Red     = #FF0000    Blue   = #0000FF
    Purple  = #800080    Teal   = #008080
    Fuchsia = #FF00FF    Aqua   = #00FFFF
    -->
<!ENTITY % bodycolors "
    bgcolor     %Color;     #IMPLIED  -- document background color --
    text        %Color;     #IMPLIED  -- document text color --
```

```
  link         %Color;       #IMPLIED —color of links —
  vlink        %Color;       #IMPLIED —color of visited links —
  alink        %Color;       #IMPLIED —color of selected links —
  "

<!—=============== Character mnemonic entities ==========================—
<!ENTITY % HTMLlat1 PUBLIC
   "-//W3C//ENTITIES Latin1//EN//HTML"
   "http://www.w3.org/TR/1998/REC-html40-19980424/HTMLlat1.ent"
%HTMLlat1;

<!ENTITY % HTMLsymbol PUBLIC
   "-//W3C//ENTITIES Symbols//EN//HTML"
   "http://www.w3.org/TR/1998/REC-html40-19980424/HTMLsymbol.ent"
%HTMLsymbol;

<!ENTITY % HTMLspecial PUBLIC
   "-//W3C//ENTITIES Special//EN//HTML"
   "http://www.w3.org/TR/1998/REC-html40-19980424/HTMLspecial.ent"
%HTMLspecial;
<!—=================== Generic Attributes ================================—

<!ENTITY % coreattrs
 "id          ID             #IMPLIED  — document-wide unique id —
  class       CDATA          #IMPLIED  — space separated list of classes —
  style       %StyleSheet;   #IMPLIED  — associated style info —
  title       %Text;         #IMPLIED  — advisory title/amplification —"

<!ENTITY % i18n
 "lang        %LanguageCode; #IMPLIED  — language code —
  dir         (ltr|rtl)      #IMPLIED  — direction for weak/neutral text —"

<!ENTITY % events
 "onclick     %Script;       #IMPLIED  — a pointer button was clicked —
  ondblclick  %Script;       #IMPLIED  — a pointer button was double clicked—
  onmousedown %Script;       #IMPLIED  — a pointer button was pressed down —
  onmouseup   %Script;       #IMPLIED  — a pointer button was released —
  onmouseover %Script;       #IMPLIED  — a pointer was moved onto —
  onmousemove %Script;       #IMPLIED  — a pointer was moved within —
  onmouseout  %Script;       #IMPLIED  — a pointer was moved away —
```

```
         onkeypress    %Script;         #IMPLIED   - a key was pressed and released -
         onkeydown     %Script;         #IMPLIED   - a key was pressed down -
         onkeyup       %Script;         #IMPLIED   - a key was released -"

<!- Reserved Feature Switch -
<!ENTITY % HTML.Reserved "IGNORE"

<!- The following attributes are reserved for possible future use -
<![ %HTML.Reserved; [
<!ENTITY % reserved
 "datasrc       %URI;           #IMPLIED    - a single or tabular Data Source -
  datafld       CDATA           #IMPLIED    - the property or column name -
  dataformatas (plaintext|html) plaintext-text or html -"

]]

<!ENTITY % reserved ""

<!ENTITY % attrs "%coreattrs; %i18n; %events;"

<!ENTITY % align "align (left|center|right|justify)  #IMPLIED"
                   -default is left for ltr paragraphs, right for rtl -

<!-=================== Text Markup ==========================-
<!ENTITY % fontstyle
 "TT | I | B | U | S | STRIKE | BIG | SMALL"

<!ENTITY % phrase "EM | STRONG | DFN | CODE |
                   SAMP | KBD | VAR | CITE | ABBR | ACRONYM"

<!ENTITY % special
   "A | IMG | APPLET | OBJECT | FONT | BASEFONT | BR | SCRIPT |
    MAP | Q | SUB | SUP | SPAN | BDO | IFRAME"

<!ENTITY % formctrl "INPUT | SELECT | TEXTAREA | LABEL | BUTTON"

<!- %inline; covers inline or "text-level" elements -
<!ENTITY % inline "#PCDATA | %fontstyle; | %phrase; | %special; | %formctrl;"

<!ELEMENT (%fontstyle;|%phrase;) - - (%inline;)*
<!ATTLIST (%fontstyle;|%phrase;)
    %attrs;                              -%coreattrs, %i18n, %events -
```

```
<!ELEMENT (SUB|SUP) - - (%inline;)*       — subscript, superscript —
<!ATTLIST (SUB|SUP)
  %attrs;                                 — %coreattrs, %i18n, %events —

<!ELEMENT SPAN - - (%inline;)*            — generic language/style container —
<!ATTLIST SPAN
  %attrs;                                 — %coreattrs, %i18n, %events —
  %reserved;                              — reserved for possible future use —

<!ELEMENT BDO - - (%inline;)*             — I18N BiDi over-ride —
<!ATTLIST BDO
  %coreattrs;                             — id, class, style, title —
  lang        %LanguageCode;   #IMPLIED   — language code —
  dir         (ltr|rtl)        #REQUIRED  — directionality —

<!ELEMENT BASEFONT - O EMPTY              —base font size —
<!ATTLIST BASEFONT
  id          ID               #IMPLIED   — document-wide unique id —
  size        CDATA            #REQUIRED  — base font size for FONT elements —
  color       %Color;          #IMPLIED   — text color —
  face        CDATA            #IMPLIED   — comma separated list of font names —

<!ELEMENT FONT - - (%inline;)*            — local change to font —
<!ATTLIST FONT
  %coreattrs;                             — id, class, style, title —
  %i18n;                                  — lang, dir —
  size        CDATA            #IMPLIED   — [+|-]nn e.g. size="+1", size="4" —
  color       %Color;          #IMPLIED   — text color —
  face        CDATA            #IMPLIED   — comma separated list of font names —

<!ELEMENT BR - O EMPTY                    — forced line break —
<!ATTLIST BR
  %coreattrs;                             — id, class, style, title —
  clear       (left|all|right|none) none  — control of text flow —

<!—================== HTML content models ==================—

<!—
    HTML has two basic content models:
```

```
              %inline;      character level elements and text strings
              %block;       block-like elements e.g. paragraphs and lists

<!ENTITY % block
     "P | %heading; | %list; | %preformatted; | DL | DIV | CENTER |
      NOSCRIPT | NOFRAMES | BLOCKQUOTE | FORM | ISINDEX | HR |
      TABLE | FIELDSET | ADDRESS"

<!ENTITY % flow "%block; | %inline;"

<!================== Document Body ====================================-

<!ELEMENT BODY O O (%flow;)* +(INS|DEL) -document body -
<!ATTLIST BODY
    %attrs;                              - %coreattrs, %i18n, %events -
    onload          %Script;   #IMPLIED  - the document has been loaded -
    onunload        %Script;   #IMPLIED  - the document has been removed -
    background      %URI;      #IMPLIED  - texture tile for document
                                           background -
    %bodycolors;                         - bgcolor, text, link, vlink, alink -

<!ELEMENT ADDRESS - - ((%inline;)|P)*   - information on author -
<!ATTLIST ADDRESS
    %attrs;                              - %coreattrs, %i18n, %events -

<!ELEMENT DIV - - (%flow;)*              - generic language/style container -
<!ATTLIST DIV
    %attrs;                              - %coreattrs, %i18n, %events -
    %align;                              - align, text alignment -
    %reserved;                           - reserved for possible future use -

<!ELEMENT CENTER - - (%flow;)*           - shorthand for DIV align=center -
<!ATTLIST CENTER
    %attrs;                              - %coreattrs, %i18n, %events -

<!================== The Anchor Element ===============================-

<!ENTITY % Shape "(rect|circle|poly|default)"
<!ENTITY % Coords "CDATA" -comma separated list of lengths -
```

```
<!ELEMENT A - - (%inline;)* -(A)        -- anchor --
<!ATTLIST A
  %attrs;                               -- %coreattrs, %i18n, %events --
  charset     %Charset;     #IMPLIED    -- char encoding of linked resource --
  type        %ContentType; #IMPLIED    -- advisory content type --
  name        CDATA         #IMPLIED    -- named link end --
  href        %URI;         #IMPLIED    -- URI for linked resource --
  hreflang    %LanguageCode; #IMPLIED   -- language code --
  target      %FrameTarget; #IMPLIED    -- render in this frame --
  rel         %LinkTypes;   #IMPLIED    -- forward link types --
  rev         %LinkTypes;   #IMPLIED    -- reverse link types --
  accesskey   %Character;   #IMPLIED    -- accessibility key character --
  shape       %Shape;       rect        -- for use with client-side image maps --
  coords      %Coords;      #IMPLIED    -- for use with client-side image maps --
  tabindex    NUMBER        #IMPLIED    -- position in tabbing order --
  onfocus     %Script;      #IMPLIED    -- the element got the focus --
  onblur      %Script;      #IMPLIED    -- the element lost the focus --
  >

<!--================== Client-side image maps ============================-->

<!-- These can be placed in the same document or grouped in a
     separate document although this isn't yet widely supported --

<!ELEMENT MAP - - ((%block;)+ | AREA+)-- client-side image map --
<!ATTLIST MAP
  %attrs;                               -- %coreattrs, %i18n, %events --
  name        CDATA         #REQUIRED   -- for reference by usemap --
  >

<!ELEMENT AREA - O EMPTY                -- client-side image map area --
<!ATTLIST AREA
  %attrs;                               -- %coreattrs, %i18n, %events --
  shape       %Shape;       rect        -- controls interpretation of coords --
  coords      %Coords;      #IMPLIED    -- comma separated list of lengths --
  href        %URI;         #IMPLIED    -- URI for linked resource --
  target      %FrameTarget; #IMPLIED    -- render in this frame --
  nohref      (nohref)      #IMPLIED    -- this region has no action --
  alt         %Text;        #REQUIRED   -- short description --
  tabindex    NUMBER        #IMPLIED    -- position in tabbing order --
  accesskey   %Character;   #IMPLIED    -- accessibility key character --
```

```
    onfocus     %Script;            #IMPLIED    - the element got the focus -
    onblur      %Script;            #IMPLIED    - the element lost the focus -

<!-=================== The LINK Element =====================================-

<!-
    Relationship values can be used in principle:

    a) for document specific toolbars/menus when used
        with the LINK element in document head e.g.
            start, contents, previous, next, index, end, help
    b) to link to a separate style sheet (rel=stylesheet)
    c) to make a link to a script (rel=script)
    d) by stylesheets to control how collections of
        html nodes are rendered into printed documents
    e) to make a link to a printable version of this document
        e.g. a postscript or pdf version (rel=alternate media=print)
-

<!ELEMENT LINK - O EMPTY                        - a media-independent link -
<!ATTLIST LINK
    %attrs;                                     - %coreattrs, %i18n, %events -
    charset     %Charset;           #IMPLIED    - char encoding of linked resource -
    href        %URI;               #IMPLIED    - URI for linked resource -
    hreflang    %LanguageCode;      #IMPLIED    - language code -
    type        %ContentType;       #IMPLIED    - advisory content type -
    rel         %LinkTypes;         #IMPLIED    - forward link types -
    rev         %LinkTypes;         #IMPLIED    - reverse link types -
    media       %MediaDesc;         #IMPLIED    - for rendering on these media -
    target      %FrameTarget;       #IMPLIED    - render in this frame -

<!-=================== Images ===============================================-

<!- Length defined in strict DTD for cellpadding/cellspacing -
<!ENTITY % Length "CDATA"-nn for pixels or nn% for percentage length -
<!ENTITY % MultiLength "CDATA"-pixel, percentage, or relative -

<!ENTITY % MultiLengths "CDATA"-comma-separated list of MultiLength -

<!ENTITY % Pixels "CDATA"-integer representing length in pixels -

<!ENTITY % IAlign "(top|middle|bottom|left|right)"-center? -
```

```
<!-- To avoid problems with text-only UAs as well as
     to make image content understandable and navigable
     to users of non-visual UAs, you need to provide
     a description with ALT, and avoid server-side image maps -->
<!ELEMENT IMG - O EMPTY                -- Embedded image -->
<!ATTLIST IMG
  %attrs;                              -- %coreattrs, %i18n, %events --
  src         %URI;         #REQUIRED  -- URI of image to embed --
  alt         %Text;        #REQUIRED  -- short description --
  longdesc    %URI;         #IMPLIED   -- link to long description
                                          (complements alt) --
  height      %Length;      #IMPLIED   -- override height --
  width       %Length;      #IMPLIED   -- override width --
  usemap      %URI;         #IMPLIED   -- use client-side image map --
  ismap       (ismap)       #IMPLIED   -- use server-side image map --
  align       %IAlign;      #IMPLIED   -- vertical or horizontal alignment --
  border      %Length;      #IMPLIED   -- link border width --
  hspace      %Pixels;      #IMPLIED   -- horizontal gutter --
  vspace      %Pixels;      #IMPLIED   -- vertical gutter --
  >
<!-- USEMAP points to a MAP element which may be in this document
     or an external document, although the latter is not widely supported -->

<!--==================== OBJECT ========================================-->
<!--
  OBJECT is used to embed objects as part of HTML pages
  PARAM elements should precede other content. SGML mixed content
  model technicality precludes specifying this formally ...
-->

<!ELEMENT OBJECT - - (PARAM | %flow;)*
 -- generic embedded object --
<!ATTLIST OBJECT
  %attrs;                              -- %coreattrs, %i18n, %events --
  declare     (declare)     #IMPLIED   -- declare but don't instantiate flag --
  classid     %URI;         #IMPLIED   -- identifies an implementation --
  codebase    %URI;         #IMPLIED   -- base URI for classid, data, archive--
  data        %URI;         #IMPLIED   -- reference to object's data --
```

```
  type          %ContentType;  #IMPLIED   -- content type for data --
  codetype      %ContentType;  #IMPLIED   -- content type for code --
  archive       %URI;          #IMPLIED   -- space separated archive list --
  standby       %Text;         #IMPLIED   -- message to show while loading --
  height        %Length;       #IMPLIED   -- override height --
  width         %Length;       #IMPLIED   -- override width --
  usemap        %URI;          #IMPLIED   -- use client-side image map --
  name          CDATA          #IMPLIED   -- submit as part of form --
  tabindex      NUMBER         #IMPLIED   -- position in tabbing order --
  align         %IAlign;       #IMPLIED   -- vertical or horizontal alignment --
  border        %Length;       #IMPLIED   -- link border width --
  hspace        %Pixels;       #IMPLIED   -- horizontal gutter --
  vspace        %Pixels;       #IMPLIED   -- vertical gutter --
  %reserved;                              -- reserved for possible future use --

<!ELEMENT PARAM - O EMPTY               -- named property value --
<!ATTLIST PARAM
  id            ID             #IMPLIED   -- document-wide unique id --
  name          CDATA          #REQUIRED  -- property name --
  value         CDATA          #IMPLIED   -- property value --
  valuetype     (DATA|REF|OBJECT) DATA    -- How to interpret value --
  type          %ContentType;  #IMPLIED   -- content type for value
                                             when valuetype=ref --

<!--================== Java APPLET ===================================-->
<!--
  One of code or object attributes must be present.
  Place PARAM elements before other content.
-->
<!ELEMENT APPLET - - (PARAM | %flow;)* -- Java applet --
<!ATTLIST APPLET
  %coreattrs;                             -- id, class, style, title --
  codebase      %URI;          #IMPLIED   -- optional base URI for applet --
  archive       CDATA          #IMPLIED   -- comma separated archive list --
  code          CDATA          #IMPLIED   -- applet class file --
  object        CDATA          #IMPLIED   -- serialized applet file --
  alt           %Text;         #IMPLIED   -- short description --
  name          CDATA          #IMPLIED   -- allows applets to find each other --
```

```
  width        %Length;          #REQUIRED    -- initial width --
  height       %Length;          #REQUIRED    -- initial height --
  align        %IAlign;          #IMPLIED     -- vertical or horizontal alignment --
  hspace       %Pixels;          #IMPLIED     -- horizontal gutter --
  vspace       %Pixels;          #IMPLIED     -- vertical gutter --

<!--================== Horizontal Rule ==================================-->

<!ELEMENT HR - O EMPTY--horizontal rule -->
<!ATTLIST HR
  %coreattrs;                                 --id, class, style, title --
  %events;
  align        (left|center|right) #IMPLIED
  noshade      (noshade)         #IMPLIED
  size         %Pixels;          #IMPLIED
  width        %Length;          #IMPLIED

<!--================== Paragraphs ======================================-->

<!ELEMENT P - O (%inline;)*                   -- paragraph --
<!ATTLIST P
  %attrs;                                     -- %coreattrs, %i18n, %events --
  %align;                                     -- align, text alignment --

<!--================== Headings ========================================-->

<!--
  There are six levels of headings from H1 (the most important)
  to H6 (the least important).
-->

<!ELEMENT (%heading;) - - (%inline;)*         -- heading --
<!ATTLIST (%heading;)
  %attrs;                                     -- %coreattrs, %i18n, %events --
  %align;                                     -- align, text alignment --

<!--================== Preformatted Text ================================-->

<!-- excludes markup for images and changes in font size -->
<!ENTITY % pre.exclusion "IMG|OBJECT|APPLET|BIG|SMALL|SUB|SUP|FONT|BASEFONT">
```

```
<!ELEMENT PRE - - (%inline;)* -(%pre.exclusion;) -preformatted text -
<!ATTLIST PRE
  %attrs;                            -- %coreattrs, %i18n, %events --
  width       NUMBER       #IMPLIED
  >

<!-- ===================== Inline Quotes ===================================-->

<!ELEMENT Q - - (%inline;)*          -- short inline quotation --
<!ATTLIST Q
  %attrs;                            -- %coreattrs, %i18n, %events --
  cite        %URI;        #IMPLIED  -- URI for source document or msg --
  >

<!-- =================== Block-like Quotes =================================-->

<!ELEMENT BLOCKQUOTE - - (%flow;)*   -- long quotation --
<!ATTLIST BLOCKQUOTE
  %attrs;                            -- %coreattrs, %i18n, %events --
  cite        %URI;        #IMPLIED  -- URI for source document or msg --
  >

<!-- =================== Inserted/Deleted Text =============================-->

<!-- INS/DEL are handled by inclusion on BODY -->
<!ELEMENT (INS|DEL) - - (%flow;)*    -- inserted text, deleted text --
<!ATTLIST (INS|DEL)
  %attrs;                            -- %coreattrs, %i18n, %events --
  cite        %URI;        #IMPLIED  -- info on reason for change --
  datetime    %Datetime;   #IMPLIED  -- date and time of change --
  >

<!-- =================== Lists =============================================-->

<!-- definition lists - DT for term, DD for its definition -->

<!ELEMENT DL - - (DT|DD)+            -- definition list --
<!ATTLIST DL
  %attrs;                            -- %coreattrs, %i18n, %events --
  compact     (compact)    #IMPLIED  -- reduced interitem spacing --
  >

<!ELEMENT DT - O (%inline;)*         -- definition term --
<!ELEMENT DD - O (%flow;)*           -- definition description --
<!ATTLIST (DT|DD)
  %attrs;                            -- %coreattrs, %i18n, %events --
```

```
<!-- Ordered lists (OL) Numbering style

    1    arabic numbers      1, 2, 3, ...
    a    lower alpha         a, b, c, ...
    A    upper alpha         A, B, C, ...
    i    lower roman         i, ii, iii, ...
    I    upper roman         I, II, III, ...

The style is applied to the sequence number which by default
is reset to 1 for the first list item in an ordered list.

This can't be expressed directly in SGML due to case folding.
-->

<!ENTITY % OLStyle "CDATA"              -- constrained to: "(1|a|A|i|I)" -->

<!ELEMENT OL - - (LI)+                  -- ordered list -->
<!ATTLIST OL
  %attrs;                               -- %coreattrs, %i18n, %events --
  type          %OLStyle;   #IMPLIED    -- numbering style --
  compact       (compact)   #IMPLIED    -- reduced interitem spacing --
  start         NUMBER      #IMPLIED    -- starting sequence number --
  >

<!-- Unordered Lists (UL) bullet styles -->
<!ENTITY % ULStyle "(disc|square|circle)">

<!ELEMENT UL - - (LI)+                  -- unordered list -->
<!ATTLIST UL
  %attrs;                               -- %coreattrs, %i18n, %events --
  type          %ULStyle;   #IMPLIED    -- bullet style --
  compact       (compact)   #IMPLIED    -- reduced interitem spacing --
  >

<!ELEMENT (DIR|MENU) - - (LI)+ -(%block;) -- directory list, menu list --
<!ATTLIST DIR
  %attrs;                               -- %coreattrs, %i18n, %events --
  compact       (compact)   #IMPLIED
  >

<!ATTLIST MENU
  %attrs;                               -- %coreattrs, %i18n, %events --
  compact       (compact)   #IMPLIED
  >
```

```
<!ENTITY % LIStyle "CDATA"—constrained to: "(%ULStyle;|%OLStyle;)" —

<!ELEMENT LI - O (%flow;)*           — list item —
<!ATTLIST LI
  %attrs;                            — %coreattrs, %i18n, %events —
  type         %LIStyle;   #IMPLIED  — list item style —
  value        NUMBER      #IMPLIED  — reset sequence number —

<!—================ Forms ================================================—
<!ELEMENT FORM - - (%flow;)* -(FORM) — interactive form —
<!ATTLIST FORM
  %attrs;                            — %coreattrs, %i18n, %events —
  action         %URI;        #REQUIRED — server-side form handler —
  method         (GET|POST)   GET       — HTTP method used to submit the form—
  enctype        %ContentType; "application/x-www-form-urlencoded"
  onsubmit       %Script;     #IMPLIED  — the form was submitted —
  onreset        %Script;     #IMPLIED  — the form was reset —
  target         %FrameTarget; #IMPLIED — render in this frame —
  accept-charset %Charsets;   #IMPLIED  — list of supported charsets —

<!— Each label must not contain more than ONE field —
<!ELEMENT LABEL - - (%inline;)* -(LABEL) — form field label text —
<!ATTLIST LABEL
  %attrs;                            — %coreattrs, %i18n, %events —
  for          IDREF        #IMPLIED  — matches field ID value —
  accesskey    %Character;  #IMPLIED  — accessibility key character —
  onfocus      %Script;     #IMPLIED  — the element got the focus —
  onblur       %Script;     #IMPLIED  — the element lost the focus —

<!ENTITY % InputType
  "(TEXT | PASSWORD | CHECKBOX |
    RADIO | SUBMIT | RESET |
    FILE | HIDDEN | IMAGE | BUTTON)"

<!— attribute name required for all but submit & reset —
<!ELEMENT INPUT - O EMPTY            — form control —
<!ATTLIST INPUT
  %attrs;                            — %coreattrs, %i18n, %events —
  type         %InputType;  TEXT     — what kind of widget is needed —
```

```
  name        CDATA          #IMPLIED    -- submit as part of form --
  value       CDATA          #IMPLIED    -- required for radio and checkboxes --
  checked     (checked)      #IMPLIED    -- for radio buttons and check boxes --
  disabled    (disabled)     #IMPLIED    -- unavailable in this context --
  readonly    (readonly)     #IMPLIED    -- for text and passwd --
  size        CDATA          #IMPLIED    -- specific to each type of field --
  maxlength   NUMBER         #IMPLIED    -- max chars for text fields --
  src         %URI;          #IMPLIED    -- for fields with images --
  alt         CDATA          #IMPLIED    -- short description --
  usemap      %URI;          #IMPLIED    -- use client-side image map --
  tabindex    NUMBER         #IMPLIED    -- position in tabbing order --
  accesskey   %Character;    #IMPLIED    -- accessibility key character --
  onfocus     %Script;       #IMPLIED    -- the element got the focus --
  onblur      %Script;       #IMPLIED    -- the element lost the focus --
  onselect    %Script;       #IMPLIED    -- some text was selected --
  onchange    %Script;       #IMPLIED    -- the element value was changed --
  accept      %ContentTypes; #IMPLIED    -- list of MIME types for file upload --
  align       %IAlign;       #IMPLIED    -- vertical or horizontal alignment --
  %reserved;                             -- reserved for possible future use --

<!ELEMENT SELECT - - (OPTGROUP|OPTION)+ -- option selector --
<!ATTLIST SELECT
  %attrs;                                -- %coreattrs, %i18n, %events --
  name        CDATA          #IMPLIED    -- field name --
  size        NUMBER         #IMPLIED    -- rows visible --
  multiple    (multiple)     #IMPLIED    -- default is single selection --
  disabled    (disabled)     #IMPLIED    -- unavailable in this context --
  tabindex    NUMBER         #IMPLIED    -- position in tabbing order --
  onfocus     %Script;       #IMPLIED    -- the element got the focus --
  onblur      %Script;       #IMPLIED    -- the element lost the focus --
  onchange    %Script;       #IMPLIED    -- the element value was changed --
  %reserved;                             -- reserved for possible future use --

<!ELEMENT OPTGROUP - - (OPTION)+ -- option group --
<!ATTLIST OPTGROUP
  %attrs;                                -- %coreattrs, %i18n, %events --
  disabled    (disabled)     #IMPLIED    -- unavailable in this context --
  label       %Text;         #REQUIRED   -- for use in hierarchical menus --
```

```
<!ELEMENT OPTION - O (#PCDATA)          -- selectable choice --
<!ATTLIST OPTION
   %attrs;                              -- %coreattrs, %i18n, %events --
   selected     (selected)    #IMPLIED
   disabled     (disabled)    #IMPLIED  -- unavailable in this context --
   label        %Text;        #IMPLIED  -- for use in hierarchical menus --
   value        CDATA         #IMPLIED  -- defaults to element content --

<!ELEMENT TEXTAREA - - (#PCDATA)        --multi-line text field --
<!ATTLIST TEXTAREA
   %attrs;                              -- %coreattrs, %i18n, %events --
   name         CDATA         #IMPLIED
   rows         NUMBER        #REQUIRED
   cols         NUMBER        #REQUIRED
   disabled     (disabled)    #IMPLIED  -- unavailable in this context --
   readonly     (readonly)    #IMPLIED
   tabindex     NUMBER        #IMPLIED  -- position in tabbing order --
   accesskey    %Character;   #IMPLIED  -- accessibility key character --
   onfocus      %Script;      #IMPLIED  -- the element got the focus --
   onblur       %Script;      #IMPLIED  -- the element lost the focus --
   onselect     %Script;      #IMPLIED  -- some text was selected --
   onchange     %Script;      #IMPLIED  -- the element value was changed --
   %reserved;                           -- reserved for possible future use --

<!--
   #PCDATA is to solve the mixed content problem,
   per specification only whitespace is allowed there!
  -->

<!ELEMENT FIELDSET - - (#PCDATA,LEGEND,(%flow;)*)--form control group --
<!ATTLIST FIELDSET
   %attrs;                              --%coreattrs, %i18n, %events --

<!ELEMENT LEGEND - - (%inline;)*        --fieldset legend --
<!ENTITY % LAlign "(top|bottom|left|right)"

<!ATTLIST LEGEND
   %attrs;                              -- %coreattrs, %i18n, %events --
   accesskey    %Character;   #IMPLIED  -- accessibility key character --
   align        %LAlign;      #IMPLIED  -- relative to fieldset --
```

```
<!ELEMENT BUTTON - -
     (%flow;)* -(A|%formctrl;|FORM|ISINDEX|FIELDSET|IFRAME)
     —push button —
<!ATTLIST BUTTON
    %attrs;                                — %coreattrs, %i18n, %events —
    name          CDATA             #IMPLIED
    value         CDATA             #IMPLIED   — sent to server when submitted —
    type          (button|submit|reset) submit—for use as form button —
    disabled      (disabled)        #IMPLIED   — unavailable in this context —
    tabindex      NUMBER            #IMPLIED   — position in tabbing order —
    accesskey     %Character;       #IMPLIED   — accessibility key character —
    onfocus       %Script;          #IMPLIED   — the element got the focus —
    onblur        %Script;          #IMPLIED   — the element lost the focus —
    %reserved;                                 — reserved for possible future use —

<!—======================= Tables =========================================—

<!— IETF HTML table standard, see [RFC1942] —

<!—
  The BORDER attribute sets the thickness of the frame around the
  table. The default units are screen pixels.

  The FRAME attribute specifies which parts of the frame around
  the table should be rendered. The values are not the same as
  CALS to avoid a name clash with the VALIGN attribute.

  The value "border" is included for backwards compatibility with
  <TABLE BORDER which yields frame=border and border=implied
  For <TABLE BORDER=1 you get border=1 and frame=implied. In this
  case, it is appropriate to treat this as frame=border for backwards
  compatibility with deployed browsers.
—
<!ENTITY % TFrame "(void|above|below|hsides|lhs|rhs|vsides|box|border)"

<!—
  The RULES attribute defines which rules to draw between cells:

  If RULES is absent then assume:
      "none" if BORDER is absent or BORDER=0 otherwise "all"
—
```

```
<!ENTITY % TRules "(none | groups | rows | cols | all)"

<!-- horizontal placement of table relative to document -->
<!ENTITY % TAlign "(left|center|right)"

<!-- horizontal alignment attributes for cell contents -->
<!ENTITY % cellhalign
   "align       (left|center|right|justify|char) #IMPLIED
    char        %Character;    #IMPLIED  -- alignment char, e.g. char=':' --
    charoff     %Length;       #IMPLIED  -- offset for alignment char --"

<!-- vertical alignment attributes for cell contents -->
<!ENTITY % cellvalign
   "valign      (top|middle|bottom|baseline) #IMPLIED"

<!ELEMENT TABLE - -
         (CAPTION?, (COL*|COLGROUP*), THEAD?, TFOOT?, TBODY+)>
<!ELEMENT CAPTION      - - (%inline;)*   -- table caption --
<!ELEMENT THEAD        - O (TR)+         -- table header --
<!ELEMENT TFOOT        - O (TR)+         -- table footer --
<!ELEMENT TBODY        O O (TR)+         -- table body --
<!ELEMENT COLGROUP     - O (col)*        -- table column group --
<!ELEMENT COL          - O EMPTY         -- table column --
<!ELEMENT TR           - O (TH|TD)+      -- table row --
<!ELEMENT (TH|TD)      - O (%flow;)*     -- table header cell, table data cell--

<!ATTLIST TABLE                          -- table element --
    %attrs;                              -- %coreattrs, %i18n, %events --
    summary     %Text;      #IMPLIED     -- purpose/structure for speech output--
    width       %Length;    #IMPLIED     -- table width --
    border      %Pixels;    #IMPLIED     -- controls frame width around table --
    frame       %TFrame;    #IMPLIED     -- which parts of frame to render --
    rules       %TRules;    #IMPLIED     -- rulings between rows and cols --
    cellspacing %Length;    #IMPLIED     -- spacing between cells --
    cellpadding %Length;    #IMPLIED     -- spacing within cells --
    align       %TAlign;    #IMPLIED     -- table position relative to window --
    bgcolor     %Color;     #IMPLIED     -- background color for cells --
    %reserved;                           -- reserved for possible future use --
    datapagesize CDATA      #IMPLIED     -- reserved for possible future use --
```

```
<!ENTITY % CAlign "(top|bottom|left|right)"

<!ATTLIST CAPTION
  %attrs;                             -- %coreattrs, %i18n, %events --
  align         %CAlign;    #IMPLIED  -- relative to table --

<!--
COLGROUP groups a set of COL elements. It allows you to group
several semantically related columns together.
-->

<!ATTLIST COLGROUP
  %attrs;                             -- %coreattrs, %i18n, %events --
  span          NUMBER      1         -- default number of columns in group --
  width         %MultiLength; #IMPLIED -- default width for enclosed COLs --
  %cellhalign;                        -- horizontal alignment in cells --
  %cellvalign;                        -- vertical alignment in cells --

<!--
 COL elements define the alignment properties for cells in
 one or more columns.

 The WIDTH attribute specifies the width of the columns, e.g.

     width=64        width in screen pixels
     width=0.5*      relative width of 0.5

 The SPAN attribute causes the attributes of one
 COL element to apply to more than one column.
-->

<!ATTLIST COL                         -- column groups and properties --
  %attrs;                             -- %coreattrs, %i18n, %events --
  span          NUMBER      1         -- COL attributes affect N columns --
  width         %MultiLength; #IMPLIED -- column width specification --
  %cellhalign;                        -- horizontal alignment in cells --
  %cellvalign;                        -- vertical alignment in cells --

<!--
    Use THEAD to duplicate headers when breaking table
    across page boundaries, or for static headers when
    TBODY sections are rendered in scrolling panel.
```

Use TFOOT to duplicate footers when breaking table
across page boundaries, or for static footers when
TBODY sections are rendered in scrolling panel.

Use multiple TBODY sections when rules are needed
between groups of table rows.

```
<!ATTLIST (THEAD|TBODY|TFOOT)            -- table section --
  %attrs;                                -- %coreattrs, %i18n, %events --
  %cellhalign;                           -- horizontal alignment in cells --
  %cellvalign;                           -- vertical alignment in cells --

<!ATTLIST TR                             -- table row --
  %attrs;                                -- %coreattrs, %i18n, %events --
  %cellhalign;                           -- horizontal alignment in cells --
  %cellvalign;                           -- vertical alignment in cells --
  bgcolor     %Color;      #IMPLIED      -- background color for row --

<!-- Scope is simpler than axes attribute for common tables -->
<!ENTITY % Scope "(row|col|rowgroup|colgroup)"

<!-- TH is for headers, TD for data, but for cells acting as both use TD -->
<!ATTLIST (TH|TD)                        -- header or data cell --
  %attrs;                                -- %coreattrs, %i18n, %events --
  abbr        %Text;       #IMPLIED      -- abbreviation for header cell --
  axis        CDATA        #IMPLIED      -- names groups of related headers--
  headers     IDREFS       #IMPLIED      -- list of id's for header cells --
  scope       %Scope;      #IMPLIED      -- scope covered by header cells --
  rowspan     NUMBER       1             -- number of rows spanned by cell --
  colspan     NUMBER       1             -- number of cols spanned by cell --
  %cellhalign;                           -- horizontal alignment in cells --
  %cellvalign;                           -- vertical alignment in cells --
  nowrap      (nowrap)     #IMPLIED      -- suppress word wrap --
  bgcolor     %Color;      #IMPLIED      -- cell background color --
  width       %Pixels;     #IMPLIED      -- width for cell --
  height      %Pixels;     #IMPLIED      -- height for cell --
```

```
<!--================ Document Frames ======================-->
<!--
  The content model for HTML documents depends on whether the HEAD is
  followed by a FRAMESET or BODY element. The widespread omission of
  the BODY start tag makes it impractical to define the content model
  without the use of a marked section.
-->

<!-- Feature Switch for frameset documents -->
<!ENTITY % HTML.Frameset "IGNORE">

<![ %HTML.Frameset; [
<!ELEMENT FRAMESET - - ((FRAMESET|FRAME)+ & NOFRAMES?)--window subdivision-->
<!ATTLIST FRAMESET
  %coreattrs;                            -- id, class, style, title --
  rows        %MultiLengths; #IMPLIED    -- list of lengths,
                                            default: 100% (1 row) --
  cols        %MultiLengths; #IMPLIED    -- list of lengths,
                                            default: 100% (1 col) --
  onload      %Script;       #IMPLIED    -- all the frames have been loaded --
  onunload    %Script;       #IMPLIED    -- all the frames have been removed--
  >
]]>

<![ %HTML.Frameset; [
<!-- reserved frame names start with "_" otherwise starts with letter -->
<!ELEMENT FRAME - O EMPTY              -- subwindow --
<!ATTLIST FRAME
  %coreattrs;                            -- id, class, style, title --
  longdesc    %URI;          #IMPLIED    -- link to long description
                                            (complements title) --
  name        CDATA          #IMPLIED    -- name of frame for targetting --
  src         %URI;          #IMPLIED    -- source of frame content --
  frameborder (1|0)          1           -- request frame borders? --
  marginwidth %Pixels;       #IMPLIED    -- margin widths in pixels --
  marginheight %Pixels;      #IMPLIED    -- margin height in pixels --
  noresize    (noresize)     #IMPLIED    -- allow users to resize frames? --
  scrolling   (yes|no|auto)  auto        -- scrollbar or none --
  >
]]>
```

```
<!ELEMENT IFRAME - - (%flow;)*         -- inline subwindow --
<!ATTLIST IFRAME
  %coreattrs;                          -- id, class, style, title --
  longdesc      %URI;       #IMPLIED   -- link to long description
                                          (complements title) --
  name          CDATA       #IMPLIED   -- name of frame for targeting --
  src           %URI;       #IMPLIED   -- source of frame content --
  frameborder   (1|0)       1          -- request frame borders? --
  marginwidth   %Pixels;    #IMPLIED   -- margin widths in pixels --
  marginheight  %Pixels;    #IMPLIED   -- margin height in pixels --
  scrolling     (yes|no|auto) auto     -- scrollbar or none --
  align         %IAlign;    #IMPLIED   -- vertical or horizontal alignment --
  height        %Length;    #IMPLIED   -- frame height --
  width         %Length;    #IMPLIED   -- frame width --

<![ %HTML.Frameset; [
<!ENTITY % noframes.content "(BODY) -(NOFRAMES)"
]]>

<!ENTITY % noframes.content "(%flow;)*"

<!ELEMENT NOFRAMES - - %noframes.content;
 --alternate content container for non frame-based rendering --
<!ATTLIST NOFRAMES
  %attrs;                              -- %coreattrs, %i18n, %events --

<!--================ Document Head =======================================-->
<!-- %head.misc; defined earlier on as "SCRIPT|STYLE|META|LINK|OBJECT" --
<!ENTITY % head.content "TITLE & ISINDEX? & BASE?">

<!ELEMENT HEAD O O (%head.content;) +(%head.misc;)--document head --
<!ATTLIST HEAD
  %i18n;                               -- lang, dir --
  profile       %URI;       #IMPLIED   -- named dictionary of meta info --

<!-- The TITLE element is not considered part of the flow of text.
       It should be displayed, for example as the page header or
       window title. Exactly one title is required per document.
       -->
<!ELEMENT TITLE - - (#PCDATA) -(%head.misc;)--document title --
<!ATTLIST TITLE %i18n
```

```
<!ELEMENT ISINDEX - O EMPTY             -- single line prompt --
<!ATTLIST ISINDEX
  %coreattrs;                           -- id, class, style, title --
  %i18n;                                -- lang, dir --
  prompt      %Text;        #IMPLIED    -- prompt message --

<!ELEMENT BASE - O EMPTY                -- document base URI --
<!ATTLIST BASE
  href        %URI;         #IMPLIED    -- URI that acts as base URI --
  target      %FrameTarget; #IMPLIED    -- render in this frame --

<!ELEMENT META - O EMPTY                -- generic metainformation --
<!ATTLIST META
  %i18n;                                -- lang, dir, for use with content --
  http-equiv  NAME          #IMPLIED    -- HTTP response header name --
  name        NAME          #IMPLIED    -- metainformation name --
  content     CDATA         #REQUIRED   -- associated information --
  scheme      CDATA         #IMPLIED    -- select form of content --

<!ELEMENT STYLE - - %StyleSheet         -- style info --
<!ATTLIST STYLE
  %i18n;                                -- lang, dir, for use with title --
  type        %ContentType; #REQUIRED   -- content type of style language --
  media       %MediaDesc;   #IMPLIED    -- designed for use with these media --
  title       %Text;        #IMPLIED    -- advisory title --

<!ELEMENT SCRIPT - - %Script;           -- script statements --
<!ATTLIST SCRIPT
  charset     %Charset;     #IMPLIED    -- char encoding of linked resource --
  type        %ContentType; #REQUIRED   -- content type of script language --
  language    CDATA         #IMPLIED    -- predefined script language name --
  src         %URI;         #IMPLIED    -- URI for an external script --
  defer       (defer)       #IMPLIED    -- UA may defer execution of script --
  event       CDATA         #IMPLIED    -- reserved for possible future use --
  for         %URI;         #IMPLIED    -- reserved for possible future use --

<!ELEMENT NOSCRIPT - - (%flow;)*
 --alternate content container for non script-based rendering --
<!ATTLIST NOSCRIPT
  %attrs;                               -- %coreattrs, %i18n, %events --
```

```
<!-================ Document Structure ====================================-
<!ENTITY % version "version CDATA #FIXED '%HTML.Version;'"

<![ %HTML.Frameset; [
<!ENTITY % html.content "HEAD, FRAMESET"
]]>

<!ENTITY % html.content "HEAD, BODY"

<!ELEMENT HTML O O (%html.content;)    -- document root element --
<!ATTLIST HTML
  %i18n;                               -- lang, dir --
  %version;
```

Chapter 23

Frameset Document Type Definition

```
<!--
    This is the HTML 4.0 Frameset DTD, which should be
    used for documents with frames. This DTD is identical
    to the HTML 4.0 Transitional DTD except for the
    content model of the "HTML" element: in frameset
    documents, the "FRAMESET" element replaces the "BODY"
    element.

        Draft: $Date: 1997/12/11 15:31:11 $

        Authors:
            Dave Raggett <dsr@w3.org>
            Arnaud Le Hors <lehors@w3.org>
            Ian Jacobs <ij@w3.org>

    Further information about HTML 4.0 is available at:

        http://www.w3.org/TR/REC-html40.
-->
<!ENTITY % HTML.Version "-//W3C//DTD HTML 4.0 Frameset//EN"
    --Typical usage:

        <!DOCTYPE HTML PUBLIC "-//W3C//DTD HTML 4.0 Frameset//EN"
                "http://www.w3.org/TR/REC-html40/frameset.dtd">
        <html>
        <head>
        ...
        </head>
        <frameset>
```

```
     ...
     </frameset>
     </html>
-->

<!ENTITY % HTML.Frameset "INCLUDE">
<!ENTITY % HTML4.dtd PUBLIC "-//W3C//DTD HTML 4.0 Transitional//EN">
%HTML4.dtd;
```

Chapter 24

Character entity references in HTML 4.0

Contents

1. Introduction to character entity references
2. Character entity references for ISO 8859-1 characters
   1. The list of characters
3. Character entity references for symbols, mathematical symbols, and Greek letters
   1. The list of characters
4. Character entity references for markup-significant and internationalization characters
   1. The list of characters

24.1 Introduction to character entity references

A character entity reference is an SGML construct that references a character of the document character set.

This version of HTML supports several sets of character entity references:

- ISO 8859-1 (Latin-1) characters In accordance with section 14 of [RFC1866], the set of Latin-1 entities has been extended by this specification to cover the whole right part of ISO-8859-1 (all code positions with the high-order bit set), including the already commonly used , © and ®. The names of the entities are taken from the appendices of SGML (defined in [ISO8879]).

- symbols, mathematical symbols, and Greek letters. These characters may be represented by glyphs in the Adobe font "Symbol".

- markup-significant and internationalization characters (e.g., for bidirectional text).

The following sections present the complete lists of character entity references. Although, by convention, [ISO10646] the comments following each entry are usually written with uppercase letters, we have converted them to lowercase in this specification for reasons of readability.

24.2 Character entity references for ISO 8859-1 characters

The character entity references in this section produce characters whose numeric equivalents should already be supported by conforming HTML 2.0 user agents. Thus, the character entity reference ÷ is a more convenient form than ÷ for obtaining the division sign (÷).

To support these named entities, user agents need only recognize the entity names and convert them to characters that lie within the repertoire of [ISO88591].

Character 65533 (FFFD hexadecimal) is the last valid character in UCS-2. 65534 (FFFE hexadecimal) is unassigned and reserved as the byte-swapped version of ZERO WIDTH NON-BREAKING SPACE for byte-order detection purposes. 65535 (FFFF hexadecimal) is unassigned.

24.2.1 The list of characters

```
<!-- Portions © International Organization for Standardization 1986
     Permission to copy in any form is granted for use with
     conforming SGML systems and applications as defined in
     ISO 8879, provided this notice is included in all copies.
-->
<!-- Character entity set. Typical invocation:
     <!ENTITY % HTMLlat1 PUBLIC
        "-//W3C//ENTITIES Latin 1//EN//HTML">
     %HTMLlat1;
-->

<!ENTITY nbsp    CDATA " "--no-break space = non-breaking space,
                                 U+00A0 ISOnum -->
<!ENTITY iexcl   CDATA "&#161;"--inverted exclamation mark, U+00A1 ISOnum -->
<!ENTITY cent    CDATA "&#162;"--cent sign, U+00A2 ISOnum -->
<!ENTITY pound   CDATA "&#163;"--pound sign, U+00A3 ISOnum -->
<!ENTITY curren  CDATA "&#164;"--currency sign, U+00A4 ISOnum -->
<!ENTITY yen     CDATA "&#165;"--yen sign = yuan sign, U+00A5 ISOnum -->
```

```
<!ENTITY brvbar  CDATA "&#166;" -- broken bar = broken vertical bar,
                                   U+00A6 ISOnum -->
<!ENTITY sect    CDATA "&#167;" -- section sign, U+00A7 ISOnum -->
<!ENTITY uml     CDATA "&#168;" -- diaeresis = spacing diaeresis,
                                   U+00A8 ISOdia -->
<!ENTITY copy    CDATA "&#169;" -- copyright sign, U+00A9 ISOnum -->
<!ENTITY ordf    CDATA "&#170;" -- feminine ordinal indicator, U+00AA ISOnum -->
<!ENTITY laquo   CDATA "&#171;" -- left-pointing double angle quotation mark
                                   = left pointing guillemet, U+00AB ISOnum -->
<!ENTITY not     CDATA "&#172;" -- not sign, U+00AC ISOnum -->
<!ENTITY shy     CDATA "&#173;" -- soft hyphen = discretionary hyphen,
                                   U+00AD ISOnum -->
<!ENTITY reg     CDATA "&#174;" -- registered sign = registered trade mark sign,
                                   U+00AE ISOnum -->
<!ENTITY macr    CDATA "&#175;" -- macron = spacing macron = overline
                                   = APL overbar, U+00AF ISOdia -->
<!ENTITY deg     CDATA "&#176;" -- degree sign, U+00B0 ISOnum -->
<!ENTITY plusmn  CDATA "&#177;" -- plus-minus sign = plus-or-minus sign,
                                   U+00B1 ISOnum -->
<!ENTITY sup2    CDATA "&#178;" -- superscript two = superscript digit two
                                   = squared, U+00B2 ISOnum -->
<!ENTITY sup3    CDATA "&#179;" -- superscript three = superscript digit three
                                   = cubed, U+00B3 ISOnum -->
<!ENTITY acute   CDATA "&#180;" -- acute accent = spacing acute,
                                   U+00B4 ISOdia -->
<!ENTITY micro   CDATA "&#181;" -- micro sign, U+00B5 ISOnum -->
<!ENTITY para    CDATA "&#182;" -- pilcrow sign = paragraph sign,
                                   U+00B6 ISOnum -->
<!ENTITY middot  CDATA "&#183;" -- middle dot = Georgian comma
                                   = Greek middle dot, U+00B7 ISOnum -->
<!ENTITY cedil   CDATA "&#184;" -- cedilla = spacing cedilla, U+00B8 ISOdia -->
<!ENTITY sup1    CDATA "&#185;" -- superscript one = superscript digit one,
                                   U+00B9 ISOnum -->
<!ENTITY ordm    CDATA "&#186;" -- masculine ordinal indicator,
                                   U+00BA ISOnum -->
<!ENTITY raquo   CDATA "&#187;" -- right-pointing double angle quotation mark
                                   = right pointing guillemet, U+00BB ISOnum -->
```

```
<!ENTITY frac14  CDATA "&#188;" -- vulgar fraction one quarter
                                   = fraction one quarter, U+00BC ISOnum -->
<!ENTITY frac12  CDATA "&#189;" -- vulgar fraction one half
                                   = fraction one half, U+00BD ISOnum -->
<!ENTITY frac34  CDATA "&#190;" -- vulgar fraction three quarters
                                   = fraction three quarters, U+00BE ISOnum -->
<!ENTITY iquest  CDATA "&#191;" -- inverted question mark
                                   = turned question mark, U+00BF ISOnum -->
<!ENTITY Agrave  CDATA "&#192;" -- latin capital letter A with grave
                                   = latin capital letter A grave,
                                   U+00C0 ISOlat1 -->
<!ENTITY Aacute  CDATA "&#193;" -- latin capital letter A with acute,
                                   U+00C1 ISOlat1 -->
<!ENTITY Acirc   CDATA "&#194;" -- latin capital letter A with circumflex,
                                   U+00C2 ISOlat1 -->
<!ENTITY Atilde  CDATA "&#195;" -- latin capital letter A with tilde,
                                   U+00C3 ISOlat1 -->
<!ENTITY Auml    CDATA "&#196;" -- latin capital letter A with diaeresis,
                                   U+00C4 ISOlat1 -->
<!ENTITY Aring   CDATA "&#197;" -- latin capital letter A with ring above
                                   = latin capital letter A ring,
                                   U+00C5 ISOlat1 -->
<!ENTITY AElig   CDATA "&#198;" -- latin capital letter AE
                                   = latin capital ligature AE,
                                   U+00C6 ISOlat1 -->
<!ENTITY Ccedil  CDATA "&#199;" -- latin capital letter C with cedilla,
                                   U+00C7 ISOlat1 -->
<!ENTITY Egrave  CDATA "&#200;" -- latin capital letter E with grave,
                                   U+00C8 ISOlat1 -->
<!ENTITY Eacute  CDATA "&#201;" -- latin capital letter E with acute,
                                   U+00C9 ISOlat1 -->
<!ENTITY Ecirc   CDATA "&#202;" -- latin capital letter E with circumflex,
                                   U+00CA ISOlat1 -->
<!ENTITY Euml    CDATA "&#203;" -- latin capital letter E with diaeresis,
                                   U+00CB ISOlat1 -->
<!ENTITY Igrave  CDATA "&#204;" -- latin capital letter I with grave,
                                   U+00CC ISOlat1 -->
```

```
<!ENTITY Iacute  CDATA "&#205;" -- latin capital letter I with acute,
                                   U+00CD ISOlat1 -->
<!ENTITY Icirc   CDATA "&#206;" -- latin capital letter I with circumflex,
                                   U+00CE ISOlat1 -->
<!ENTITY Iuml    CDATA "&#207;" -- latin capital letter I with diaeresis,
                                   U+00CF ISOlat1 -->
<!ENTITY ETH     CDATA "&#208;" -- latin capital letter ETH, U+00D0 ISOlat1 -->
<!ENTITY Ntilde  CDATA "&#209;" -- latin capital letter N with tilde,
                                   U+00D1 ISOlat1 -->
<!ENTITY Ograve  CDATA "&#210;" -- latin capital letter O with grave,
                                   U+00D2 ISOlat1 -->
<!ENTITY Oacute  CDATA "&#211;" -- latin capital letter O with acute,
                                   U+00D3 ISOlat1 -->
<!ENTITY Ocirc   CDATA "&#212;" -- latin capital letter O with circumflex,
                                   U+00D4 ISOlat1 -->
<!ENTITY Otilde  CDATA "&#213;" -- latin capital letter O with tilde,
                                   U+00D5 ISOlat1 -->
<!ENTITY Ouml    CDATA "&#214;" -- latin capital letter O with diaeresis,
                                   U+00D6 ISOlat1 -->
<!ENTITY times   CDATA "&#215;" -- multiplication sign, U+00D7 ISOnum -->
<!ENTITY Oslash  CDATA "&#216;" -- latin capital letter O with stroke
                                   = latin capital letter O slash,
                                   U+00D8 ISOlat1 -->
<!ENTITY Ugrave  CDATA "&#217;" -- latin capital letter U with grave,
                                   U+00D9 ISOlat1 -->
<!ENTITY Uacute  CDATA "&#218;" -- latin capital letter U with acute,
                                   U+00DA ISOlat1 -->
<!ENTITY Ucirc   CDATA "&#219;" -- latin capital letter U with circumflex,
                                   U+00DB ISOlat1 -->
<!ENTITY Uuml    CDATA "&#220;" -- latin capital letter U with diaeresis,
                                   U+00DC ISOlat1 -->
<!ENTITY Yacute  CDATA "&#221;" -- latin capital letter Y with acute,
                                   U+00DD ISOlat1 -->
<!ENTITY THORN   CDATA "&#222;" -- latin capital letter THORN,
                                   U+00DE ISOlat1 -->
<!ENTITY szlig   CDATA "&#223;" -- latin small letter sharp s = ess-zed,
                                   U+00DF ISOlat1 -->
```

```
<!ENTITY agrave  CDATA "&#224;" -- latin small letter a with grave
                                   = latin small letter a grave,
                                   U+00E0 ISOlat1 -->
<!ENTITY aacute  CDATA "&#225;" -- latin small letter a with acute,
                                   U+00E1 ISOlat1 -->
<!ENTITY acirc   CDATA "&#226;" -- latin small letter a with circumflex,
                                   U+00E2 ISOlat1 -->
<!ENTITY atilde  CDATA "&#227;" -- latin small letter a with tilde,
                                   U+00E3 ISOlat1 -->
<!ENTITY auml    CDATA "&#228;" -- latin small letter a with diaeresis,
                                   U+00E4 ISOlat1 -->
<!ENTITY aring   CDATA "&#229;" -- latin small letter a with ring above
                                   = latin small letter a ring,
                                   U+00E5 ISOlat1 -->
<!ENTITY aelig   CDATA "&#230;" -- latin small letter ae
                                   = latin small ligature ae, U+00E6 ISOlat1 -->
<!ENTITY ccedil  CDATA "&#231;" -- latin small letter c with cedilla,
                                   U+00E7 ISOlat1 -->
<!ENTITY egrave  CDATA "&#232;" -- latin small letter e with grave,
                                   U+00E8 ISOlat1 -->
<!ENTITY eacute  CDATA "&#233;" -- latin small letter e with acute,
                                   U+00E9 ISOlat1 -->
<!ENTITY ecirc   CDATA "&#234;" -- latin small letter e with circumflex,
                                   U+00EA ISOlat1 -->
<!ENTITY euml    CDATA "&#235;" -- latin small letter e with diaeresis,
                                   U+00EB ISOlat1 -->
<!ENTITY igrave  CDATA "&#236;" -- latin small letter i with grave,
                                   U+00EC ISOlat1 -->
<!ENTITY iacute  CDATA "&#237;" -- latin small letter i with acute,
                                   U+00ED ISOlat1 -->
<!ENTITY icirc   CDATA "&#238;" -- latin small letter i with circumflex,
                                   U+00EE ISOlat1 -->
<!ENTITY iuml    CDATA "&#239;" -- latin small letter i with diaeresis,
                                   U+00EF ISOlat1 -->
<!ENTITY eth     CDATA "&#240;" -- latin small letter eth, U+00F0 ISOlat1 -->
<!ENTITY ntilde  CDATA "&#241;" -- latin small letter n with tilde,
                                   U+00F1 ISOlat1 -->
```

```
<!ENTITY ograve CDATA "&#242;" -- latin small letter o with grave,
                                  U+00F2 ISOlat1 -->
<!ENTITY oacute CDATA "&#243;" -- latin small letter o with acute,
                                  U+00F3 ISOlat1 -->
<!ENTITY ocirc  CDATA "&#244;" -- latin small letter o with circumflex,
                                  U+00F4 ISOlat1 -->
<!ENTITY otilde CDATA "&#245;" -- latin small letter o with tilde,
                                  U+00F5 ISOlat1 -->
<!ENTITY ouml   CDATA "&#246;" -- latin small letter o with diaeresis,
                                  U+00F6 ISOlat1 -->
<!ENTITY divide CDATA "&#247;" -- division sign, U+00F7 ISOnum -->
<!ENTITY oslash CDATA "&#248;" -- latin small letter o with stroke,
                                = latin small letter o slash,
                                  U+00F8 ISOlat1 -->
<!ENTITY ugrave CDATA "&#249;" -- latin small letter u with grave,
                                  U+00F9 ISOlat1 -->
<!ENTITY uacute CDATA "&#250;" -- latin small letter u with acute,
                                  U+00FA ISOlat1 -->
<!ENTITY ucirc  CDATA "&#251;" -- latin small letter u with circumflex,
                                  U+00FB ISOlat1 -->
<!ENTITY uuml   CDATA "&#252;" -- latin small letter u with diaeresis,
                                  U+00FC ISOlat1 -->
<!ENTITY yacute CDATA "&#253;" -- latin small letter y with acute,
                                  U+00FD ISOlat1 -->
<!ENTITY thorn  CDATA "&#254;" -- latin small letter thorn with,
                                  U+00FE ISOlat1 -->
<!ENTITY yuml   CDATA "&#255;" -- latin small letter y with diaeresis,
                                  U+00FF ISOlat1 -->
```

24.3 Character entity references for symbols, mathematical symbols, and Greek letters

The character entity references in this section produce characters that may be represented by glyphs in the widely available Adobe Symbol font, including Greek characters, various bracketing symbols, and a selection of mathematical operators such as gradient, product, and summation symbols.

To support these entities, user agents may support full [ISO10646] or use other means. Display of glyphs for these characters may be obtained by being able to display the relevant [ISO10646] characters or by other means, such as internally mapping the listed entities, numeric character references, and characters to the appropriate position in some font that contains the requisite glyphs.

When to use Greek entities. This entity set contains all the letters used in modern Greek. However, it does not include Greek punctuation, precomposed accented characters nor the non-spacing accents (tonos, dialytika) required to compose them. There are no archaic letters, Coptic-unique letters, or precomposed letters for Polytonic Greek. The entities defined here are not intended for the representation of modern Greek text and would not be an efficient representation; rather, they are intended for occasional Greek letters used in technical and mathematical works.

24.3.1 The list of characters

```
<!-- Mathematical, Greek and Symbolic characters for HTML -->

<!-- Character entity set. Typical invocation:
     <!ENTITY % HTMLsymbol PUBLIC
       "-//W3C//ENTITIES Symbols//EN//HTML">
     %HTMLsymbol; -->

<!-- Portions © International Organization for Standardization 1986:
     Permission to copy in any form is granted for use with
     conforming SGML systems and applications as defined in
     ISO 8879, provided this notice is included in all copies.
-->

<!-- Relevant ISO entity set is given unless names are newly introduced.
     New names (i.e., not in ISO 8879 list) do not clash with any
     existing ISO 8879 entity names. ISO 10646 character numbers
     are given for each character, in hex. CDATA values are decimal
     conversions of the ISO 10646 values and refer to the document
     character set. Names are Unicode 2.0 names.

-->

<!-- Latin Extended-B -->
<!ENTITY fnof      CDATA "&#402;"--latin small f with hook = function
                                    = florin, U+0192 ISOtech -->
```

```
<!-- Greek -->
<!ENTITY Alpha    CDATA "&#913;" -- greek capital letter alpha, U+0391 -->
<!ENTITY Beta     CDATA "&#914;" -- greek capital letter beta, U+0392 -->
<!ENTITY Gamma    CDATA "&#915;" -- greek capital letter gamma,
                                    U+0393 ISOgrk3 -->
<!ENTITY Delta    CDATA "&#916;" -- greek capital letter delta,
                                    U+0394 ISOgrk3 -->
<!ENTITY Epsilon  CDATA "&#917;" -- greek capital letter epsilon, U+0395 -->
<!ENTITY Zeta     CDATA "&#918;" -- greek capital letter zeta, U+0396 -->
<!ENTITY Eta      CDATA "&#919;" -- greek capital letter eta, U+0397 -->
<!ENTITY Theta    CDATA "&#920;" -- greek capital letter theta,
                                    U+0398 ISOgrk3 -->
<!ENTITY Iota     CDATA "&#921;" -- greek capital letter iota, U+0399 -->
<!ENTITY Kappa    CDATA "&#922;" -- greek capital letter kappa, U+039A -->
<!ENTITY Lambda   CDATA "&#923;" -- greek capital letter lambda,
                                    U+039B ISOgrk3 -->
<!ENTITY Mu       CDATA "&#924;" -- greek capital letter mu, U+039C -->
<!ENTITY Nu       CDATA "&#925;" -- greek capital letter nu, U+039D -->
<!ENTITY Xi       CDATA "&#926;" -- greek capital letter xi, U+039E ISOgrk3 -->
<!ENTITY Omicron  CDATA "&#927;" -- greek capital letter omicron, U+039F -->
<!ENTITY Pi       CDATA "&#928;" -- greek capital letter pi, U+03A0 ISOgrk3 -->
<!ENTITY Rho      CDATA "&#929;" -- greek capital letter rho, U+03A1 -->
<!-- there is no Sigmaf, and no U+03A2 character either -->
<!ENTITY Sigma    CDATA "&#931;" -- greek capital letter sigma,
                                    U+03A3 ISOgrk3 -->
<!ENTITY Tau      CDATA "&#932;" -- greek capital letter tau, U+03A4 -->
<!ENTITY Upsilon  CDATA "&#933;" -- greek capital letter upsilon,
                                    U+03A5 ISOgrk3 -->
<!ENTITY Phi      CDATA "&#934;" -- greek capital letter phi,
                                    U+03A6 ISOgrk3 -->
<!ENTITY Chi      CDATA "&#935;" -- greek capital letter chi, U+03A7 -->
<!ENTITY Psi      CDATA "&#936;" -- greek capital letter psi,
                                    U+03A8 ISOgrk3 -->
<!ENTITY Omega    CDATA "&#937;" -- greek capital letter omega,
                                    U+03A9 ISOgrk3 -->
```

```
<!ENTITY alpha    CDATA "&#945;" -- greek small letter alpha,
                                    U+03B1 ISOgrk3 -->
<!ENTITY beta     CDATA "&#946;" -- greek small letter beta, U+03B2 ISOgrk3 -->
<!ENTITY gamma    CDATA "&#947;" -- greek small letter gamma,
                                    U+03B3 ISOgrk3 -->
<!ENTITY delta    CDATA "&#948;" -- greek small letter delta,
                                    U+03B4 ISOgrk3 -->
<!ENTITY epsilon  CDATA "&#949;" -- greek small letter epsilon,
                                    U+03B5 ISOgrk3 -->
<!ENTITY zeta     CDATA "&#950;" -- greek small letter zeta, U+03B6 ISOgrk3 -->
<!ENTITY eta      CDATA "&#951;" -- greek small letter eta, U+03B7 ISOgrk3 -->
<!ENTITY theta    CDATA "&#952;" -- greek small letter theta,
                                    U+03B8 ISOgrk3 -->
<!ENTITY iota     CDATA "&#953;" -- greek small letter iota, U+03B9 ISOgrk3 -->
<!ENTITY kappa    CDATA "&#954;" -- greek small letter kappa,
                                    U+03BA ISOgrk3 -->
<!ENTITY lambda   CDATA "&#955;" -- greek small letter lambda,
                                    U+03BB ISOgrk3 -->
<!ENTITY mu       CDATA "&#956;" -- greek small letter mu, U+03BC ISOgrk3 -->
<!ENTITY nu       CDATA "&#957;" -- greek small letter nu, U+03BD ISOgrk3 -->
<!ENTITY xi       CDATA "&#958;" -- greek small letter xi, U+03BE ISOgrk3 -->
<!ENTITY omicron  CDATA "&#959;" -- greek small letter omicron, U+03BF NEW -->
<!ENTITY pi       CDATA "&#960;" -- greek small letter pi, U+03C0 ISOgrk3 -->
<!ENTITY rho      CDATA "&#961;" -- greek small letter rho, U+03C1 ISOgrk3 -->
<!ENTITY sigmaf   CDATA "&#962;" -- greek small letter final sigma,
                                    U+03C2 ISOgrk3 -->
<!ENTITY sigma    CDATA "&#963;" -- greek small letter sigma,
                                    U+03C3 ISOgrk3 -->
<!ENTITY tau      CDATA "&#964;" -- greek small letter tau, U+03C4 ISOgrk3 -->
<!ENTITY upsilon  CDATA "&#965;" -- greek small letter upsilon,
                                    U+03C5 ISOgrk3 -->
<!ENTITY phi      CDATA "&#966;" -- greek small letter phi, U+03C6 ISOgrk3 -->
<!ENTITY chi      CDATA "&#967;" -- greek small letter chi, U+03C7 ISOgrk3 -->
<!ENTITY psi      CDATA "&#968;" -- greek small letter psi, U+03C8 ISOgrk3 -->
<!ENTITY omega    CDATA "&#969;" -- greek small letter omega,
                                    U+03C9 ISOgrk3 -->
```

```
<!ENTITY thetasym CDATA "&#977;" -- greek small letter theta symbol,
                                    U+03D1 NEW -->
<!ENTITY upsih    CDATA "&#978;" -- greek upsilon with hook symbol,
                                    U+03D2 NEW -->
<!ENTITY piv      CDATA "&#982;" -- greek pi symbol, U+03D6 ISOgrk3 -->

<!-- General Punctuation -->
<!ENTITY bull     CDATA "&#8226;" -- bullet = black small circle,
                                     U+2022 ISOpub  -->
<!-- bullet is NOT the same as bullet operator, U+2219 -->
<!ENTITY hellip   CDATA "&#8230;" -- horizontal ellipsis = three dot leader,
                                     U+2026 ISOpub  -->
<!ENTITY prime    CDATA "&#8242;" -- prime = minutes = feet, U+2032 ISOtech -->
<!ENTITY Prime    CDATA "&#8243;" -- double prime = seconds = inches,
                                     U+2033 ISOtech -->
<!ENTITY oline    CDATA "&#8254;" -- overline = spacing overscore,
                                     U+203E NEW -->
<!ENTITY frasl    CDATA "&#8260;" -- fraction slash, U+2044 NEW -->

<!-- Letterlike Symbols -->
<!ENTITY weierp   CDATA "&#8472;" -- script capital P = power set
                                     = Weierstrass p, U+2118 ISOamso -->
<!ENTITY image    CDATA "&#8465;" -- blackletter capital I = imaginary part,
                                     U+2111 ISOamso -->
<!ENTITY real     CDATA "&#8476;" -- blackletter capital R = real part symbol,
                                     U+211C ISOamso -->
<!ENTITY trade    CDATA "&#8482;" -- trade mark sign, U+2122 ISOnum -->
<!ENTITY alefsym  CDATA "&#8501;" -- alef symbol = first transfinite cardinal,
                                     U+2135 NEW -->
<!-- alef symbol is NOT the same as hebrew letter alef,
     U+05D0 although the same glyph could be used to depict both characters -->

<!-- Arrows -->
<!ENTITY larr     CDATA "&#8592;" -- leftwards arrow, U+2190 ISOnum -->
<!ENTITY uarr     CDATA "&#8593;" -- upwards arrow, U+2191 ISOnum -->
<!ENTITY rarr     CDATA "&#8594;" -- rightwards arrow, U+2192 ISOnum -->
<!ENTITY darr     CDATA "&#8595;" -- downwards arrow, U+2193 ISOnum -->
<!ENTITY harr     CDATA "&#8596;" -- left right arrow, U+2194 ISOamsa -->
```

```
<!ENTITY crarr    CDATA "&#8629;" -- downwards arrow with corner leftwards
                                  = carriage return, U+21B5 NEW -->
<!ENTITY lArr     CDATA "&#8656;" -- leftwards double arrow, U+21D0 ISOtech -->
<!-- Unicode does not say that lArr is the same as the 'is implied by' arrow
     but also does not have any other character for that function. So ? lArr can
     be used for 'is implied by' as ISOtech suggests -->
<!ENTITY uArr     CDATA "&#8657;" -- upwards double arrow, U+21D1 ISOamsa -->
<!ENTITY rArr     CDATA "&#8658;" -- rightwards double arrow,
                                  U+21D2 ISOtech -->
<!-- Unicode does not say this is the 'implies' character but does not have
     another character with this function so ?
     rArr can be used for 'implies' as ISOtech suggests -->
<!ENTITY dArr     CDATA "&#8659;" -- downwards double arrow, U+21D3 ISOamsa -->
<!ENTITY hArr     CDATA "&#8660;" -- left right double arrow,
                                  U+21D4 ISOamsa -->

<!-- Mathematical Operators -->
<!ENTITY forall   CDATA "&#8704;" -- for all, U+2200 ISOtech -->
<!ENTITY part     CDATA "&#8706;" -- partial differential, U+2202 ISOtech -->
<!ENTITY exist    CDATA "&#8707;" -- there exists, U+2203 ISOtech -->
<!ENTITY empty    CDATA "&#8709;" -- empty set = null set = diameter,
                                  U+2205 ISOamso -->
<!ENTITY nabla    CDATA "&#8711;" -- nabla = backward difference,
                                  U+2207 ISOtech -->
<!ENTITY isin     CDATA "&#8712;" -- element of, U+2208 ISOtech -->
<!ENTITY notin    CDATA "&#8713;" -- not an element of, U+2209 ISOtech -->
<!ENTITY ni       CDATA "&#8715;" -- contains as member, U+220B ISOtech -->
<!-- should there be a more memorable name than 'ni'? -->
<!ENTITY prod     CDATA "&#8719;" -- n-ary product = product sign,
                                  U+220F ISOamsb -->
<!-- prod is NOT the same character as U+03A0 'greek capital letter pi' though
     the same glyph might be used for both -->
<!ENTITY sum      CDATA "&#8721;" -- n-ary sumation, U+2211 ISOamsb -->
<!-- sum is NOT the same character as U+03A3 'greek capital letter sigma'
     though the same glyph might be used for both -->
<!ENTITY minus    CDATA "&#8722;" -- minus sign, U+2212 ISOtech -->
<!ENTITY lowast   CDATA "&#8727;" -- asterisk operator, U+2217 ISOtech -->
```

```
<!ENTITY radic    CDATA "&#8730;" - square root = radical sign,
                                    U+221A ISOtech -->
<!ENTITY prop     CDATA "&#8733;" - proportional to, U+221D ISOtech -->
<!ENTITY infin    CDATA "&#8734;" - infinity, U+221E ISOtech -->
<!ENTITY ang      CDATA "&#8736;" - angle, U+2220 ISOamso -->
<!ENTITY and      CDATA "&#8743;" - logical and = wedge, U+2227 ISOtech -->
<!ENTITY or       CDATA "&#8744;" - logical or = vee, U+2228 ISOtech -->
<!ENTITY cap      CDATA "&#8745;" - intersection = cap, U+2229 ISOtech -->
<!ENTITY cup      CDATA "&#8746;" - union = cup, U+222A ISOtech -->
<!ENTITY int      CDATA "&#8747;" - integral, U+222B ISOtech -->
<!ENTITY there4   CDATA "&#8756;" - therefore, U+2234 ISOtech -->
<!ENTITY sim      CDATA "&#8764;" - tilde operator = varies with = similar to,
                                    U+223C ISOtech -->
<!-- tilde operator is NOT the same character as the tilde, U+007E,
     although the same glyph might be used to represent both -->
<!ENTITY cong     CDATA "&#8773;"-approximately equal to, U+2245 ISOtech -->
<!ENTITY asymp    CDATA "&#8776;"-almost equal to = asymptotic to,
                                    U+2248 ISOamsr -->
<!ENTITY ne       CDATA "&#8800;" - not equal to, U+2260 ISOtech -->
<!ENTITY equiv    CDATA "&#8801;" - identical to, U+2261 ISOtech -->
<!ENTITY le       CDATA "&#8804;" - less-than or equal to, U+2264 ISOtech -->
<!ENTITY ge       CDATA "&#8805;" - greater-than or equal to,
                                    U+2265 ISOtech -->
<!ENTITY sub      CDATA "&#8834;" - subset of, U+2282 ISOtech -->
<!ENTITY sup      CDATA "&#8835;" - superset of, U+2283 ISOtech -->
<!-- note that nsup, 'not a superset of, U+2283' is not covered by the Symbol
     font encoding and is not included. Should it be, for symmetry?
     It is in ISOamsn  -->
<!ENTITY nsub     CDATA "&#8836;" - not a subset of, U+2284 ISOamsn -->
<!ENTITY sube     CDATA "&#8838;" - subset of or equal to, U+2286 ISOtech -->
<!ENTITY supe     CDATA "&#8839;" - superset of or equal to,
                                    U+2287 ISOtech -->
<!ENTITY oplus    CDATA "&#8853;" - circled plus = direct sum,
                                    U+2295 ISOamsb -->
<!ENTITY otimes   CDATA "&#8855;" - circled times = vector product,
                                    U+2297 ISOamsb -->
```

```
<!ENTITY perp     CDATA "&#8869;" -- up tack = orthogonal to = perpendicular,
                                    U+22A5 ISOtech -->
<!ENTITY sdot     CDATA "&#8901;" -- dot operator, U+22C5 ISOamsb -->
<!-- dot operator is NOT the same character as U+00B7 middle dot -->

<!-- Miscellaneous Technical -->
<!ENTITY lceil    CDATA "&#8968;" -- left ceiling = apl upstile,
                                    U+2308 ISOamsc  -->
<!ENTITY rceil    CDATA "&#8969;" -- right ceiling, U+2309 ISOamsc  -->
<!ENTITY lfloor   CDATA "&#8970;" -- left floor = apl downstile,
                                    U+230A ISOamsc  -->
<!ENTITY rfloor   CDATA "&#8971;" -- right floor, U+230B ISOamsc  -->
<!ENTITY lang     CDATA "&#9001;" -- left-pointing angle bracket = bra,
                                    U+2329 ISOtech  -->
<!-- lang is NOT the same character as U+003C 'less than'
     or U+2039 'single left-pointing angle quotation mark' -->
<!ENTITY rang     CDATA "&#9002;" -- right-pointing angle bracket = ket,
                                    U+232A ISOtech  -->
<!-- rang is NOT the same character as U+003E 'greater than'
     or U+203A 'single right-pointing angle quotation mark' -->

<!-- Geometric Shapes -->
<!ENTITY loz      CDATA "&#9674;" -- lozenge, U+25CA ISOpub -->

<!-- Miscellaneous Symbols -->
<!ENTITY spades   CDATA "&#9824;" -- black spade suit, U+2660 ISOpub -->
<!-- black here seems to mean filled as opposed to hollow -->
<!ENTITY clubs    CDATA "&#9827;" -- black club suit = shamrock,
                                    U+2663 ISOpub -->
<!ENTITY hearts   CDATA "&#9829;" -- black heart suit = valentine,
                                    U+2665 ISOpub -->
<!ENTITY diams    CDATA "&#9830;" -- black diamond suit, U+2666 ISOpub -->
```

24.4 Character entity references for markup-significant and internationalization characters

The character entity references in this section are for escaping markup-significant characters (these are the same as those in HTML 2.0 and 3.2), for denoting spaces and dashes. Other characters in this section apply to internationalization issues such as the disambiguation of bidirectional text (see the section on bidirectional text for details).

Entities have also been added for the remaining characters occurring in CP-1252 which do not occur in the HTMLlat1 or HTMLsymbol entity sets. These all occur in the 128 to 159 range within the cp-1252 charset. These entities permit the characters to be denoted in a platform-independent manner.

To support these entities, user agents may support full [ISO10646] or use other means. Display of glyphs for these characters may be obtained by being able to display the relevant [ISO10646] characters or by other means, such as internally mapping the listed entities, numeric character references, and characters to the appropriate position in some font that contains the requisite glyphs.

24.4.1 The list of characters

```
<!- Special characters for HTML ->

<!- Character entity set. Typical invocation:
     <!ENTITY % HTMLspecial PUBLIC
       "-//W3C//ENTITIES Special//EN//HTML">
     %HTMLspecial; ->

<!- Portions © International Organization for Standardization 1986:
     Permission to copy in any form is granted for use with
     conforming SGML systems and applications as defined in
     ISO 8879, provided this notice is included in all copies.
->

<!- Relevant ISO entity set is given unless names are newly introduced.
     New names (i.e., not in ISO 8879 list) do not clash with any
     existing ISO 8879 entity names. ISO 10646 character numbers
     are given for each character, in hex. CDATA values are decimal
     conversions of the ISO 10646 values and refer to the document
     character set. Names are Unicode 2.0 names.
->
```

```
<!-- C0 Controls and Basic Latin -->
<!ENTITY quot     CDATA "&#34;"   -- quotation mark = APL quote,
                                     U+0022 ISOnum -->
<!ENTITY amp      CDATA "&#38;"   -- ampersand, U+0026 ISOnum -->
<!ENTITY lt       CDATA "&#60;"   -- less-than sign, U+003C ISOnum -->
<!ENTITY gt       CDATA "&#62;"   -- greater-than sign, U+003E ISOnum -->

<!-- Latin Extended-A -->
<!ENTITY OElig    CDATA "&#338;"  -- latin capital ligature OE,
                                     U+0152 ISOlat2 -->
<!ENTITY oelig    CDATA "&#339;"  -- latin small ligature oe, U+0153 ISOlat2 -->
<!-- ligature is a misnomer, this is a separate character in some languages -->
<!ENTITY Scaron   CDATA "&#352;"  -- latin capital letter S with caron,
                                     U+0160 ISOlat2 -->
<!ENTITY scaron   CDATA "&#353;"  -- latin small letter s with caron,
                                     U+0161 ISOlat2 -->
<!ENTITY Yuml     CDATA "&#376;"  -- latin capital letter Y with diaeresis,
                                     U+0178 ISOlat2 -->

<!-- Spacing Modifier Letters -->
<!ENTITY circ     CDATA "&#710;"  -- modifier letter circumflex accent,
                                     U+02C6 ISOpub -->
<!ENTITY tilde    CDATA "&#732;"  -- small tilde, U+02DC ISOdia -->

<!-- General Punctuation -->
<!ENTITY ensp     CDATA " " -- en space, U+2002 ISOpub -->
<!ENTITY emsp     CDATA " " -- em space, U+2003 ISOpub -->
<!ENTITY thinsp   CDATA " " -- thin space, U+2009 ISOpub -->
<!ENTITY zwnj     CDATA "&#8204;" -- zero width non-joiner,
                                     U+200C NEW RFC 2070 -->
<!ENTITY zwj      CDATA "&#8205;" -- zero width joiner, U+200D NEW RFC 2070 -->
<!ENTITY lrm      CDATA "&#8206;" -- left-to-right mark, U+200E NEW RFC 2070 -->
<!ENTITY rlm      CDATA "&#8207;" -- right-to-left mark, U+200F NEW RFC 2070 -->
<!ENTITY ndash    CDATA "&#8211;" -- en dash, U+2013 ISOpub -->
<!ENTITY mdash    CDATA "&#8212;" -- em dash, U+2014 ISOpub -->
<!ENTITY lsquo    CDATA "&#8216;" -- left single quotation mark,
                                     U+2018 ISOnum -->
<!ENTITY rsquo    CDATA "&#8217;" -- right single quotation mark,
                                     U+2019 ISOnum -->
```

```
<!ENTITY sbquo    CDATA "&#8218;" -- single low-9 quotation mark, U+201A NEW -->
<!ENTITY ldquo    CDATA "&#8220;" -- left double quotation mark,
                                    U+201C ISOnum -->
<!ENTITY rdquo    CDATA "&#8221;" -- right double quotation mark,
                                    U+201D ISOnum -->
<!ENTITY bdquo    CDATA "&#8222;" -- double low-9 quotation mark, U+201E NEW -->
<!ENTITY dagger   CDATA "&#8224;" -- dagger, U+2020 ISOpub -->
<!ENTITY Dagger   CDATA "&#8225;" -- double dagger, U+2021 ISOpub -->
<!ENTITY permil   CDATA "&#8240;" -- per mille sign, U+2030 ISOtech -->
<!ENTITY lsaquo   CDATA "&#8249;" -- single left-pointing angle quotation mark,
                                    U+2039 ISO proposed -->
<!-- lsaquo is proposed but not yet ISO standardized -->
<!ENTITY rsaquo   CDATA "&#8250;" -- single right-pointing angle quotation mark,
                                    U+203A ISO proposed -->
<!-- rsaquo is proposed but not yet ISO standardized -->
<!ENTITY euro     CDATA "&#8364;" -- euro sign, U+20AC NEW -->
```

Appendix A

Changes

Contents

1. Changes between HTML 3.2 and HTML 4.0
    1. Changes to elements
        - New elements
        - Deprecated elements
        - Obsolete elements
    2. Changes to attributes
    3. Changes for accessibility
    4. Changes for meta data
    5. Changes for text
    6. Changes for links
    7. Changes for tables
    8. Changes for images, objects, and image maps
    9. Changes for forms
    10. Changes for style sheets
    11. Changes for frames
    12. Changes for scripting
    13. Changes for internationalization
2. Changes from the 18 December 1997 specification
    1. Errors that were corrected
    2. Minor typographical errors that were corrected

A.1 Changes between HTML 3.2 and HTML 4.0

A.1.1 Changes to elements

New elements

The new elements in HTML 4.0 are: ABBR, ACRONYM, BDO, BUTTON, COL, COLGROUP, DEL, FIELDSET, FRAME, FRAMESET, IFRAME, INS, LABEL, LEGEND, NOFRAMES, NOSCRIPT, OBJECT, OPTGROUP, PARAM, S (deprecated), SPAN, TBODY, TFOOT, THEAD, and Q.

Deprecated elements

The following elements are deprecated: APPLET, BASEFONT, CENTER, DIR, FONT, ISINDEX, MENU, STRIKE, and U.

Obsolete elements

The following elements are obsolete: LISTING, PLAINTEXT, and XMP. For all of them, authors should use the PRE element instead.

A.1.2 Changes to attributes

- Almost all attributes that specify the presentation of an HTML document (e.g., colors, alignment, fonts, graphics, etc.) have been deprecated in favor of style sheets. The list of attributes in the appendix indicates which attributes have been deprecated.

- The id and class attribute allow authors to assign name and class information to elements for style sheets, as anchors, for scripting, for object declarations, general purpose document processing, etc.

A.1.3 Changes for accessibility

HTML 4.0 features many changes to promote accessibility, including:

- The title attribute may now be set on virtually every element.

- Authors may provide long descriptions of tables (see the summary attribute), images and frames (see the longdesc attribute).

A.1.4 Changes for meta data

Authors may now specify profiles that provide explanations about meta data specified with the META or LINK elements.

A.1.5 Changes for text

- New features for internationalization allow authors to specify text direction and language.
- The INS and DEL elements allow authors to mark up changes in their documents.
- The ABBR and ACRONYM elements allow authors to mark up abbreviations and acronyms in their documents.

A.1.6 Changes for links

- The id attribute makes any element the destination anchor of a link.

A.1.7 Changes for tables

The HTML 4.0 table model has grown out of early work on HTML+ and the initial draft of HTML3.0. The earlier model has been extended in response to requests from information providers as follows:

- Authors may specify tables that may be incrementally displayed as the user agent receives data.
- Authors may specify tables that are more accessible to users with non-visual user agents.
- Authors may specify tables with fixed headers and footers. User agents may take advantage of these when scrolling large tables or rendering tables to paged media.

The HTML 4.0 table model also satisfies requests for optional column-based defaults for alignment properties, more flexibility in specifying table frames and rules, and the ability to align on designated characters. It is expected, however, that style sheets will take over the task of rendering tables in the near future.

In addition, a major goal has been to provide backwards compatibility with the widely deployed Netscape implementation of tables. Another goal has been to simplify importing tables conforming to the SGML CALS model. The latest draft makes the align attribute compatible with the latest versions of the most popular browsers. Some clarifications have been made to the role of the dir attribute and recommended behavior when absolute and relative column widths are mixed.

A new element, `COLGROUP`, has been introduced to allow sets of columns to be grouped with different width and alignment properties specified by one or more `COL` elements. The semantics of `COLGROUP` have been clarified over previous drafts, and `rules="basic"` replaced by `rules="groups"`.

The style attribute is included as a means for extending the properties associated with edges and interiors of groups of cells. For instance, the line style: dotted, double, thin/thick etc; the color/pattern fill for the interior; cell margins and font information. This will be the subject for a companion specification on style sheets.

The frame and rules attributes have been modified to avoid SGML name clashes with each other, and to avoid clashes with the align and valign attributes. These changes were additionally motivated by the desire to avoid future problems if this specification is extended to allow frame and rules attributes with other table elements.

A.1.8 Changes for images, objects, and image maps

- The `OBJECT` element allows generic inclusion of objects.
- The `IFRAME` and `OBJECT` elements allow authors to create embedded documents.
- The alt attribute is required on the `IMG` and `AREA` elements.
- The mechanism for creating image maps now allows authors to create more accessible image maps. The content model of the `MAP` element has changed for this reason.

A.1.9 Changes for forms

This specification introduces several new attributes and elements that affect forms:

- The accesskey attribute allows authors to specify direct keyboard access to form controls.
- The disabled attribute allows authors to make a form control initially insensitive.
- The readonly attribute, allows authors to prohibit changes to a form control.
- The `LABEL` element associates a label with a particular form control.

- The FIELDSET element groups related fields together and, in association with the LEGEND element, can be used to name the group. Both of these new elements allow better rendering and better interactivity. Speech-based browsers can better describe the form and graphic browsers can make labels sensitive.

- A new set of attributes, in combination with scripts, allow form providers to verify user-entered data.

- The BUTTON element and INPUT with type set to "button" can be used in combination with scripts to create richer forms.

- The OPTGROUP element allows authors to group menu options together in a SELECT, which is particularly important for form accessibility.

- Additional changes for internationalization.

A.1.10 Changes for style sheets

HTML 4.0 supports a larger set of media descriptors so that authors may write device-sensitive style sheets.

A.1.11 Changes for frames

HTML 4.0 supports frame documents and inline frames.

A.1.12 Changes for scripting

Many elements now feature event attributes that may be coupled with scripts; the script is executed when the event occurs (e.g., when a document is loaded, when the mouse is clicked, etc.).

A.1.13 Changes for internationalization

HTML 4.0 integrates the recommendations of [RFC2070] for the internationalization of HTML.

However, this specification and [RFC2070] differ as follows:

- The accept-charset attribute has been specified for the FORM element rather than the TEXTAREA and INPUT elements.

- The HTML 4.0 specification makes additional clarifications with respect to the bidirectional algorithm.
- The use of CDATA to define the SCRIPT and STYLE elements does not preserve the ability to transcode documents, as described in section 2.1 of [RFC2070].

A.2 Changes from the 18 December 1997 specification

This section describes how this version of the HTML 4.0 specification differs from the previous version released on 18 December 1997.

A.2.1 Errors that were corrected

Section 2.1.1

"http://www.w3.org/TR/PR-html4/cover.html" was said to designate the current HTML specification. The current HTML specification is actually at http://www.w3.org/TR/REC-html40.

Section 7.5.2

The hypertext link on name was incorrect. It now links to types.html#type-name.

Section 7.5.4

href was listed as an attribute of the DIV and SPAN elements. It is not.

Section 7.5.6

A P element was used in the example. It is invalid in ADDRESS.

Section 8.1

In the first example, which reads "Her super-powers were the result...", there was an extra double quote mark before the word "Her".

Section 9.3.4

The attribute width was not noted as **deprecated**.

Section 11.2.4, "Calculating the width of columns"

The sentence "We have set the value of the align attribute in the third column group to 'center'" read "second" instead of "third".

Section 11.2.6, "Cells that span several rows or columns"

The second paragraph read "In this table definition, we specify that the cell in row four, column two should span a total of three columns, including the current row." It now ends "...including the current column."

Section 13.2

The sentence beginning "User agents must render alternate text when they cannot support ..." read "next", instead of "text".

Section 13.6.2

The last sentence of the second paragraph applied to both the IMG and INPUT elements. However, the ismap attribute is not defined for INPUT. The sentence now only applies to IMG.

Section 14.2.3

The title attribute for the STYLE element was not listed as an attribute defined elsewhere.

Section 14.3.2

The second example set `title="Compact"`. It now sets `title="compact"`.

Section 15.1.2

The sentence ending "the align attribute." read "the align element."

Section 15.1.3.2

The CSS style rule "BR.mybr { clear: left }" was incorrect, since it refers to the class "mybr" and not the id value. The correct syntax is: "BR#mybr { clear: left }".

Section 16

All the examples containing a Document Type Declaration used something like "THE_LATEST_VERSION_/frameset.dtd" or "THE_LATEST_VERSION_" as the system identifier for the Frameset DTD. They now use "http://www.w3.org/TR/REC-html40/frameset.dtd" instead.

Section 16.3 and Section 16.3.1

The second example of 16.3 and the example of 16.3.1 used the wrong DTD; they now use the Transitional DTD.

Section 17.5

In "attributes defined elsewhere" for the BUTTON element, id, class, lang, dir, title, style, and tabindex were missing. Also, usemap has been removed.

Section 17.6/17.6.1

The "attributes defined elsewhere" for OPTION and OPTGROUP mistakenly listed onfocus, onblur, and onchange. The "attributes defined elsewhere" section was missing for the SELECT element (please see the DTD for the full list of attributes).

Section 17.9.1

The tabindex attribute was said to be defined for the LABEL element. It is not.

Section 17.12.2

The sentence "The following elements support the readonly attribute: INPUT and TEXTAREA." read "The following elements support the readonly attribute: INPUT, TEXT, PASSWORD, and TEXTAREA."

Section 18.2.2, "Local declaration of a scripting language"

The first paragraph read: "It is also possible to specify the scripting language in each SCRIPT element via the type attribute. In the absence of a default scripting language specification, this attribute must be set on each SCRIPT element." Since the type attribute is required for the SCRIPT element, this paragraph now reads: "The type attribute must be specified for each SCRIPT element instance in a document. The value of the type attribute for a SCRIPT element overrides the default scripting language for that element."

Section 24.2.1 and file HTMLlat1.ent

The comment for the character reference "not" read "= discretionary hyphen". This has been removed. The FPI in comment read "-//W3C//ENTITIES Full Latin 1//EN//HTML", instead this is now "-//W3C//ENTITIES Latin1//EN//HTML".

Section 24.3.1 and file HTMLsymbol.ent

The FPI in comment read "-//W3C//ENTITIES Symbolic//EN//HTML", instead this is now "-//W3C//ENTITIES Symbols//EN//HTML".

Section A.1.1, "New elements" (previously A.1.1) and Section A.1.1, "Deprecated elements" (previously A.1.2)

The S element which is **deprecated** was listed as part of the changes between HTML 3.2 and HTML 4.0. This element was not actually defined in HTML 3.2. It is now in the new elements list.

Section A.1.3 (previously A.3)

The longdesc attribute was said to be specified for tables. It is not. Instead, the summary attribute allows authors to give longer descriptions of tables.

Section B.4

The sentence "You may help search engines by using the LINK element with **rel="start"** along with the title attribute, ..." read "You may help search engines by using the LINK element with **rel="begin"** along with a TITLE, ..." The same stands for the companion example.

Section B.5.1

The sentence "This can be altered by setting the width attribute of the TABLE element." read "This can be altered by setting the width-TABLE attribute of the TABLE element."

Section B.5.2

The sentence "Rules for handling objects too large for a column apply when the explicit or implied alignment results in a situation where the data exceeds the assigned width of the column." read "too large for column". The meaning of the sentence was unclear since it referred to "rules" governing an error condition; user agent behavior in error conditions lies outside the scope of the specification.

Index of attributes

The href attribute for the BASE element was marked as **deprecated**. It is not. However, it is not defined in the Strict DTD either.

The language attribute for the SCRIPT element was not marked as **deprecated**. It is now, and it is no longer defined in the Strict DTD.

A.2.2 Minor typographical errors that were corrected

Section 2.1.3

"Relative URIs are resolved..." was "Relative URIsare resolved...".

Section 2.2.1

The second word "of" was missing in "Despite never receiving consensus in standards discussions, these drafts led to the adoption of a range of new features."

Section 3.3.3

The sentence "Element types that are designed to have no content are called empty elements." contained one too many "elements". The word "a" was missing in the sentence "A few HTML element types use an additional SGML feature to exclude elements from a content model".

Also, in list item two, a period was missing between "optional" and "Two".

Section 3.3.4

In the section on "Boolean attributes", the sentence that begins "In HTML, boolean attributes may appear in minimized..." included a bogus word "be".

Section 6.3

The sentence beginning "For introductory information about attributes, ..." read "For introductory about attributes, ...".

Section 6.6

In the first sentence of the section on Pixels, "is an integer" read "is integer".

Section 7.4.1

The first word "The" was missing at the beginning of the section title.

Section 7.4.4

The last word "a" was missing in the sentence "The meaning of a property and the set of legal values for that property should be defined in a reference lexicon called profile."

Section 7.5.2

"Variable déclarée deux fois" read "Variable déclaré deux fois".

Section 9.2.2

The language of the quotations was "en" instead of "en-us", while in British English, the single quotation marks would delimit the outer quotation.

Section 9.3.2

In the first line, the sixth character of "&#x000A" was the letter 'O' instead of a zero.

Section 10.3.1

"(they are case-sensitive)" read "(the are case-sensitive)".

Section 12.1.1

In the sentence beginning "Note that the href attribute in each source ..." the space was missing between "href" and "attribute".

Section 12.1.2

The sentence "Links that express other types of relationships have one or more link types specified in their source anchors." read "Links that express other types of relationships have one or more link type specified in their source anchor."

Section 12.1.5

The second paragraph reads "the hreflang attribute provides user agents about the language of a ..." It should read "the hreflang attribute provides user agents with information about the language of a ..."

Section 13.3.2

In the sentence beginning "Any number of `PARAM` elements may appear in the content of an `OBJECT` or `APPLET` element, ..." a space was missing between "`APPLET`" and "element".

Section 14.2.2

There was a bogus word "style" at the beginning of the sentence "The style attribute specifies ..."

Section 17.2

In "Those controls for which name/value pairs are submitted are called successful controls" the word "for" was missing.

Section 17.10

There was a bogus word "/samp" just before section 17.11.

Section 17.11

The first sentence read, "In an HTML document, an element must receive focus from the user in order to become active and perform their tasks" (instead of "its" tasks).

Section 18.2.2

Just before section 18.2.3, the sentence that includes "a name attribute takes precedence over an id if both are set." read "over a id if both are set.".

Section 19.1

The section title read "document Document Validation". It now is "Document Validation".

Section 21

The FPI for the Transitional HTML 4.0 DTD was missing a closing double quote.

Section B.5.1/B.5.2

This sections referred to a non-existent `cols` attribute. This attribute is not part of HTML 4.0. Calculating the number of columns in a table is described in section Section 11.2.4.3, in the chapter on tables. In sections B.5.1 and B.5.2, occurrences of `cols` have been replaced by "the number of columns specified by the COL and COLGROUP elements".

Section B.5.2

In the sentence "The values for the frame attribute have been chosen to avoid clashes with the rules, align and valign attributes." a space was missing between "the" and "frame" and the last attribute was "valign-COLGROUP".

Section B.10.1

The last sentence read "Once a file is uploaded, the processing agent should process and store the it appropriately." "the it" was changed to "it".

Index of Elements

"strike-through" in the description of the S element read "sstrike-through".

Appendix B

Performance, Implementation, and Design Notes

Contents

1. Notes on invalid documents
2. Special characters in URI attribute values
   1. Non-ASCII characters in URI attribute values
   2. Ampersands in URI attribute values
3. SGML implementation notes
   1. Line breaks
   2. Specifying non-HTML data
      - Element content
      - Attribute values
   3. SGML features with limited support
   4. Boolean attributes
   5. Marked Sections
   6. Processing Instructions
   7. Shorthand markup
4. Notes on helping search engines index your Web site
   1. Search robots
      - The robots.txt file
      - Robots and the META element
5. Notes on tables
   1. Design rationale
      - Dynamic reformatting
      - Incremental display
      - Structure and presentation
      - Row and column groups
      - Accessibility

2. Recommended Layout Algorithms
   - Fixed Layout Algorithm
   - Autolayout Algorithm
6. Notes on forms
   1. Incremental display
   2. Future projects
7. Notes on scripting
   1. Reserved syntax for future script macros
      - Current Practice for Script Macros
8. Notes on frames
9. Notes on accessibility
10. Notes on security
    1. Security issues for forms

The following notes are informative, not normative. Despite the appearance of words such as "must" and "should", all requirements in this section appear elsewhere in the specification.

B.1 Notes on invalid documents

This specification does not define how conforming user agents handle general error conditions, including how user agents behave when they encounter elements, attributes, attribute values, or entities not specified in this document.

However, to facilitate experimentation and interoperability between implementations of various versions of HTML, we recommend the following behavior:

- If a user agent encounters an element it does not recognize, it should try to render the element's content.

- If a user agent encounters an attribute it does not recognize, it should ignore the entire attribute specification (i.e., the attribute and its value).

- If a user agent encounters an attribute value it doesn't recognize, it should use the default attribute value.

- If it encounters an undeclared entity, the entity should be treated as character data.

We also recommend that user agents provide support for notifying the user of such errors.

Since user agents may vary in how they handle error conditions, authors and users must not rely on specific error recovery behavior.

The HTML 2.0 specification ([RFC1866]) observes that many HTML 2.0 user agents assume that a document that does not begin with a document type declaration refers to the HTML 2.0 specification. As experience shows that this is a poor assumption, the current specification does not recommend this behavior.

For reasons of interoperability, authors must not "extend" HTML through the available SGML mechanisms (e.g., extending the DTD, adding a new set of entity definitions, etc.).

B.2 Special characters in URI attribute values

B.2.1 Non-ASCII characters in URI attribute values

Although URIs do not contain non-ASCII values (see [URI], section 2.1) authors sometimes specify them in attribute values expecting URIs (i.e., defined with %URI; in the DTD). For instance, the following href value is **illegal**:

    <A href="http://foo.org/Håkon">...</A>

We recommend that user agents adopt the following convention for handling non-ASCII characters in such cases:

1. Represent each character in UTF-8 (see [RFC2044]) as one or more bytes.

2. Escape these bytes with the URI escaping mechanism (i.e., by converting each byte to %HH, where HH is the hexadecimal notation of the byte value).

This procedure results in a syntactically legal URI (as defined in [RFC1738], section 2.2 or [RFC2141], section 2) that is independent of the character encoding to which the HTML document carrying the URI may have been transcoded.

Note. Some older user agents trivially process URIs in HTML using the bytes of the character encoding in which the document was received. Some older HTML documents rely on this practice and break when transcoded. User agents that want to handle these older documents should, on receiving a URI containing characters outside the legal set, first use the conversion based on UTF-8. Only if the resulting URI does not resolve should they try constructing a URI based on the bytes of the character encoding in which the document was received.

Note. The same conversion based on UTF-8 should be applied to values of the name attribute for the A element.

B.2.2 Ampersands in URI attribute values

The URI that is constructed when a form is submitted may be used as an anchor-style link (e.g., the href attribute for the A element). Unfortunately, the use of the "&" character to separate form fields interacts with its use in SGML attribute values to delimit character entity references. For example, to use the URI "http://host/?x=1&y=2" as a linking URI, it must be written <A href="http://host/?x=1&y=2"> or <A href="http://host/?x=1&y=2">.

We recommend that HTTP server implementors, and in particular, CGI implementors support the use of ";" in place of "&" to save authors the trouble of escaping "&" characters in this manner.

B.3 SGML implementation notes

B.3.1 Line breaks

SGML (see [ISO8879], section 7.6.1) specifies that a line break immediately following a start tag must be ignored, as must a line break immediately before an end tag. This applies to all HTML elements without exception.

The following two HTML examples must be rendered identically:

```
<P>Thomas is watching TV.</P>

<P>
Thomas is watching TV.
</P>
```

So must the following two examples:

```
<A>My favorite Website</A>

<A>
My favorite Website
</A>
```

B.3.2 Specifying non-HTML data

Script and style data may appear as element content or attribute values. The following sections describe the boundary between HTML markup and foreign data.

Note. *The DTD defines script and style data to be CDATA for both element content and attribute values. SGML rules do not allow character references in CDATA element content but do allow them in CDATA attribute values. Authors should pay particular attention when cutting and pasting script and style data between element content and attribute values.*

This asymmetry also means that when transcoding from a richer to a poorer character encoding, the transcoder cannot simply replace unconvertible characters in script or style data with the corresponding numeric character references; it must parse the HTML document and know about each script and style language's syntax in order to process the data correctly.

Element content

When script or style data is the content of an element (SCRIPT and STYLE), the data begins immediately after the element start tag and ends at the first ETAGO ("</") delimiter followed by a name character ([a-zA-Z]); note that this may not be the element's end tag. Authors should therefore escape "</" within the content. Escape mechanisms are specific to each scripting or style sheet language.

ILLEGAL EXAMPLE:
The following script data incorrectly contains a "</" sequence (as part of "</EM>") before the SCRIPT end tag:

```
<SCRIPT type="text/javascript">
   document.write ("<EM>This won't work</EM>")
</SCRIPT>
```

In JavaScript, this code can be expressed legally by hiding the ETAGO delimiter before an SGML name start character:

```
<SCRIPT type="text/javascript">
   document.write ("<EM>This will work<\/EM>")
</SCRIPT>
```

In Tcl, one may accomplish this as follows:

```
<SCRIPT type="text/tcl">
   document write "<EM>This will work<\/EM>"
</SCRIPT>
```

In VBScript, the problem may be avoided with the Chr() function:

```
"<EM>This will work<" & Chr(47) & "EM>"
```

Attribute values

When script or style data is the value of an attribute (either style or the intrinsic event attributes), authors should escape occurrences of the delimiting single or double quotation mark within the value according to the script or style language convention. Authors should also escape occurrences of "&" if the "&" is not meant to be the beginning of a character reference.

- '"' should be written as """ or """
- '&' should be written as "&" or "&"

Thus, for example, one could write:

```
<INPUT name="num" value="0"
onchange="if (compare(this.value, &quot;help&quot;)) {gethelp()}">
```

B.3.3 SGML features with limited support

SGML systems conforming to [ISO8879] are expected to recognize a number of features that aren't widely supported by HTML user agents. We recommend that authors avoid using all of these features.

B.3.4 Boolean attributes

Authors should be aware than many user agents only recognize the minimized form of boolean attributes and not the full form.

For instance, authors may want to specify:

```
<OPTION selected>
```

instead of

```
<OPTION selected="selected">
```

B.3.5 Marked Sections

Marked sections play a role similar to the #ifdef construct recognized by C preprocessors.

```
<![INCLUDE[
 <!- this will be included ->
]]>
```

```
<![IGNORE[
 <!- this will be ignored ->
]]>
```

SGML also defines the use of marked sections for CDATA content, within which "<" is not treated as the start of a tag, e.g.,

```
<![CDATA[
 <an> example of <sgml> markup that is
 not <painful> to write with < and such.
]]>
```

The telltale sign that a user agent doesn't recognize a marked section is the appearance of "]]>", which is seen when the user agent mistakenly uses the first ">" character as the end of the tag starting with "<![".

B.3.6 Processing Instructions

Processing instructions are a mechanism to capture platform-specific idioms. A processing instruction begins with <? and ends with >

```
<?instruction >
```

For example:

```
<?>
<?style tt = font courier>
<?page break>
<?experiment> ... <?/experiment>
```

Authors should be aware that many user agents render processing instructions as part of the document's text.

B.3.7 Shorthand markup

Some SGML SHORTTAG constructs save typing but add no expressive capability to the SGML application. Although these constructs technically introduce no ambiguity, they reduce the robustness of documents, especially when the language is enhanced to include new elements. Thus, while SHORTTAG constructs of SGML related to attributes are widely used and implemented, those related to elements are not. Documents that use them are conforming SGML documents, but are unlikely to work with many existing HTML tools.

The SHORTTAG constructs in question are the following:

- NET tags:

`<name/.../`

- closed Start Tag:

`<name1<name2>`

- Empty Start Tag:

`<>`

- Empty End Tag:

`</>`

B.4 Notes on helping search engines index your Web site

This section provides some simple suggestions that will make your documents more accessible to search engines.

Define the document language

In the global context of the Web it is important to know which human language a page was written in. This is discussed in the section on language information.

Specify language variants of this document

If you have prepared translations of this document into other languages, you should use the LINK element to reference these. This allows an indexing engine to offer users search results in the user's preferred language, regardless of how the query was written. For instance, the following links offer French and German alternatives to a search engine:

```
<LINK rel="alternate"
      type="text/html"
      href="mydoc-fr.html" hreflang="fr"
      lang="fr" title="La vie souterraine">
```

```
<LINK rel="alternate"
      type="text/html"
      href="mydoc-de.html" hreflang="de"
      lang="de" title="Das Leben im Untergrund">
```

Provide keywords and descriptions

Some indexing engines look for META elements that define a comma-separated list of keywords/phrases, or that give a short description. Search engines may present these keywords as the result of a search. The value of the name attribute sought by a search attribute is not defined by this specification. Consider these examples,

```
<META name="keywords" content="vacation,Greece,sunshine">
<META name="description" content="Idyllic European vacations">
```

Indicate the beginning of a collection

Collections of word processing documents or presentations are frequently translated into collections of HTML documents. It is helpful for search results to reference the beginning of the collection in addition to the page hit by the search. You may help search engines by using the LINK element with **rel="start"** along with the title attribute, as in:

```
<LINK rel="begin"
      type="text/html"
      href="page1.html"
      title="General Theory of Relativity">
```

Provide robots with indexing instructions

People may be surprised to find that their site has been indexed by an indexing robot and that the robot should not have been permitted to visit a sensitive part of the site. Many Web robots offer facilities for Web site administrators and content providers to limit what the robot does. This is achieved through two mechanisms: a "robots.txt" file and the META element in HTML documents, described below.

B.4.1 Search robots

The robots.txt file

When a Robot visits a Web site, say http://www.foobar.com/, it firsts checks for http://www.foobar.com/robots.txt. If it can find this document, it will analyze its contents to see if it is allowed to retrieve the document. You can customize the robots.txt file to apply only to specific robots, and to disallow access to specific directories or files.

Here is a sample robots.txt file that prevents all robots from visiting the entire site

```
User-agent: *      # applies to all robots
Disallow: /        # disallow indexing of all pages
```

The Robot will simply look for a "/robots.txt" URI on your site, where a site is defined as a HTTP server running on a particular host and port number. Here are some sample locations for `robots.txt`:

Site URI	URI for `robots.txt`
http://www.w3.org/	http://www.w3.org/robots.txt
http://www.w3.org:80/	http://www.w3.org:80/robots.txt
http://www.w3.org:1234/	http://www.w3.org:1234/robots.txt
http://w3.org/	http://w3.org/robots.txt

There can only be a single "/robots.txt" on a site. Specifically, you should not put "robots.txt" files in user directories, because a robot will never look at them. If you want your users to be able to create their own "robots.txt", you will need to merge them all into a single "/robots.txt". If you don't want to do this your users might want to use the Robots META Tag instead.

Some tips: URI's are case-sensitive, and "/robots.txt" string must be all lower-case. Blank lines are not permitted.

There must be exactly one "User-agent" field per record. The robot should be liberal in interpreting this field. A case-insensitive substring match of the name without version information is recommended.

If the value is "*", the record describes the default access policy for any robot that has not matched any of the other records. It is not allowed to have multiple such records in the "/robots.txt" file.

The "Disallow" field specifies a partial URI that is not to be visited. This can be a full path, or a partial path; any URI that starts with this value will not be retrieved. For example,

```
Disallow: /help disallows both /help.html and /help/index.html, whereas
Disallow: /help/ would disallow /help/index.html but allow /help.html.
```

An empty value for "Disallow", indicates that all URIs can be retrieved. At least one "Disallow" field must be present in the robots.txt file.

Robots and the `META` element

The META element allows HTML authors to tell visiting robots whether a document may be indexed, or used to harvest more links. No server administrator action is required.

In the following example a robot should neither index this document, nor analyze it for links.

    <META name="ROBOTS" content="NOINDEX, NOFOLLOW">

The list of terms in the content is `ALL`, `INDEX`, `NOFOLLOW`, `NOINDEX`. The name and the content attribute values are case-insensitive.

Note. In early 1997 only a few robots implement this, but this is expected to change as more public attention is given to controlling indexing robots.

B.5 Notes on tables

B.5.1 Design rationale

The HTML table model has evolved from studies of existing SGML tables models, the treatment of tables in common word processing packages, and a wide range of tabular layout techniques in magazines, books and other paper-based documents. The model was chosen to allow simple tables to be expressed simply with extra complexity available when needed. This makes it practical to create the markup for HTML tables with everyday text editors and reduces the learning curve for getting started. This feature has been very important to the success of HTML to date.

Increasingly, people are creating tables by converting from other document formats or by creating them directly with WYSIWYG editors. It is important that the HTML table model fit well with these authoring tools. This affects how the cells that span multiple rows or columns are represented, and how alignment and other presentation properties are associated with groups of cells.

Dynamic reformatting

A major consideration for the HTML table model is that the author does not control how a user will size a table, what fonts he or she will use, etc. This makes it risky to rely on column widths specified in terms of absolute pixel units. Instead, tables must be able to change sizes dynamically to match the current window size and fonts. Authors can provide guidance as to the relative widths of columns, but user agents should ensure that columns are wide enough to render the width of the largest element of the cell's content. If the author's specification must be overridden, relative widths of individual columns should not be changed drastically.

Incremental display

For large tables or slow network connections, incremental table display is important to user satisfaction. User agents should be able to begin displaying a table before all of the data has been received. The default window width for most user agents shows about 80 characters, and the graphics for many HTML pages are designed with these defaults in mind. By specifying the number of columns, and including provision for control of table width and the widths of different columns, authors can give hints to user agents that allow the incremental display of table contents.

For incremental display, the browser needs the number of columns and their widths. The default width of the table is the current window size (`width="100%"`). This can be altered by setting the width attribute of the `TABLE` element. By default, all columns have the same width, but you can specify column widths with one or more `COL` elements before the table data starts.

The remaining issue is the number of columns. Some people have suggested waiting until the first row of the table has been received, but this could take a long time if the cells have a lot of content. On the whole it makes more sense, when incremental display is desired, to get authors to explicitly specify the number of columns in the `TABLE` element.

Authors still need a way of telling user agents whether to use incremental display or to size the table automatically to fit the cell contents. In the two pass auto-sizing mode, the number of columns is determined by the first pass. In the incremental mode, the number of columns must be stated up front (with `COL` or `COLGROUP` elements.

Structure and presentation

HTML distinguishes structural markup such as paragraphs and quotations from rendering idioms such as margins, fonts, colors, etc. How does this distinction affect tables? From the purist's point of view, the alignment of text within table cells and the borders between cells is a rendering issue, not one of structure. In practice, though, it is useful to group these with the structural information, as these features are highly portable from one application to the next. The HTML table model leaves most rendering information to associated style sheets. The model presented in this specification is designed to take advantage of such style sheets but not to require them.

Current desktop publishing packages provide very rich control over the rendering of tables, and it would be impractical to reproduce this in HTML, without making HTML into a bulky rich text format like RTF or MIF. This specification does, however, offer authors the ability to choose from a set of commonly used classes of border styles. The frame attribute controls the appearance of the border frame around the table while the rules attribute determines the choice of rulings within the table. A finer level of control will be supported via rendering annotations. The style attribute can be used for specifying rendering information for individual elements. Further rendering information can be given with the STYLE element in the document head or via linked style sheets.

During the development of this specification, a number of avenues were investigated for specifying the ruling patterns for tables. One issue concerns the kinds of statements that can be made. Including support for edge subtraction as well as edge addition leads to relatively complex algorithms. For instance, work on allowing the full set of table elements to include the frame and rules attributes led to an algorithm involving some 24 steps to determine whether a particular edge of a cell should be ruled or not. Even this additional complexity doesn't provide enough rendering control to meet the full range of needs for tables. The current specification deliberately sticks to a simple intuitive model, sufficient for most purposes. Further experimental work is needed before a more complex approach is standardized.

Row and column groups

This specification provides a superset of the simpler model presented in earlier work on HTML+. Tables are considered as being formed from an optional caption together with a sequence of rows, which in turn consist of a sequence of table cells. The model further differentiates header and data cells, and allows cells to span multiple rows and columns.

Following the CALS table model (see [CALS]), this specification allows table rows to be grouped into head and body and foot sections. This simplifies the representation of rendering information and can be used to repeat table head and foot rows when breaking tables across page boundaries, or to provide fixed headers above a scrollable body panel. In the markup, the foot section is placed before the body sections. This is an optimization shared with CALS for dealing with very long tables. It allows the foot to be rendered without having to wait for the entire table to be processed.

Accessibility

For the visually impaired, HTML offers the hope of setting to rights the damage caused by the adoption of windows based graphical user interfaces. The HTML table model includes attributes for labeling each cell, to support high quality text to speech conversion. The same attributes can also be used to support automated import and export of table data to databases or spreadsheets.

B.5.2 Recommended Layout Algorithms

If `COL` or `COLGROUP` elements are present, they specify the number of columns and the table may be rendered using a fixed layout. Otherwise the autolayout algorithm described below should be used.

If the `width` attribute is not specified, visual user agents should assume a default value of `100%` for formatting.

It is recommended that user agents increase table widths beyond the value specified by `width` in cases when cell contents would otherwise overflow. User agents that override the specified width should do so within reason. User agents may elect to split words across lines to avoid the need for excessive horizontal scrolling or when such scrolling is impractical or undesired.

For the purposes of layout, user agents should consider that table captions (specified by the `CAPTION` element) behave like cells. Each caption is a cell that spans all of the table's columns if at the top or bottom of the table, and rows if at the left or right side of the table.

Fixed Layout Algorithm

For this algorithm, it is assumed that the number of columns is known. The column widths by default should be set to the same size. Authors may override this by specifying relative or absolute column widths, using the `COLGROUP` or `COL` elements. The default table width is the space between the current left and right margins, but may be overridden by the width attribute on the `TABLE` element, or determined from absolute column widths. To deal with mixtures of absolute and relative column widths, the first step is to allocate space from the table width to columns with absolute widths. After this, the space remaining is divided up between the columns with relative widths.

The table syntax alone is insufficient to guarantee the consistency of attribute values. For instance, the number of `COL` and `COLGROUP` elements may be inconsistent with the number of columns implied by the table cells. A further problem occurs when the columns are too narrow to avoid overflow of cell contents. The width of the table as specified by the `TABLE` element or `COL` elements may result in overflow of cell contents. It is recommended that user agents attempt to recover gracefully from these situations, e.g., by hyphenating words and resorting to splitting words if hyphenation points are unknown.

In the event that an indivisible element causes cell overflow, the user agent may consider adjusting column widths and re-rendering the table. In the worst case, clipping may be considered if column width adjustments and/or scrollable cell content are not feasible. In any case, if cell content is split or clipped this should be indicated to the user in an appropriate manner.

Autolayout Algorithm

If the number of columns is not specified with COL and COLGROUP elements, then the user agent should use the following autolayout algorithm. It uses two passes through the table data and scales linearly with the size of the table.

In the first pass, line wrapping is disabled, and the user agent keeps track of the minimum and maximum width of each cell. The maximum width is given by the widest line. Since line wrap has been disabled, paragraphs are treated as long lines unless broken by BR elements. The minimum width is given by the widest text element (word, image, etc.) taking into account leading indents and list bullets, etc. In other words, it is necessary to determine the minimum width a cell would require in a window of its own before the cell begins to overflow. Allowing user agents to split words will minimize the need for horizontal scrolling or in the worst case, clipping the cell contents.

This process also applies to any nested tables occurring in cell content. The minimum and maximum widths for cells in nested tables are used to determine the minimum and maximum widths for these tables and hence for the parent table cell itself. The algorithm is linear with aggregate cell content, and broadly speaking, independent of the depth of nesting.

To cope with character alignment of cell contents, the algorithm keeps three running min/max totals for each column: Left of align char, right of align char and unaligned. The minimum width for a column is then: `max(min_left + min_right, min_non-aligned)`.

The minimum and maximum cell widths are then used to determine the corresponding minimum and maximum widths for the columns. These in turn, are used to find the minimum and maximum width for the table. Note that cells can contain nested tables, but this doesn't complicate the code significantly. The next step is to assign column widths according to the available space (i.e., the space between the current left and right margins).

For cells that span multiple columns, a simple approach consists of apportioning the min/max widths evenly to each of the constituent columns. A slightly more complex approach is to use the min/max widths of unspanned cells to weight how spanned widths are apportioned. Experiments suggest that a blend of the two approaches gives good results for a wide range of tables.

The table borders and intercell margins need to be included in assigning column widths. There are three cases:

1. **The minimum table width is equal to or wider than the available space.** In this case, assign the minimum widths and allow the user to scroll horizontally. For conversion to braille,

it will be necessary to replace the cells by references to notes containing their full content. By convention these appear before the table.

2. **The maximum table width fits within the available space.** In this case, set the columns to their maximum widths.

3. **The maximum width of the table is greater than the available space, but the minimum table width is smaller.** In this case, find the difference between the available space and the minimum table width, lets call it **W**. Lets also call **D** the difference between maximum and minimum width of the table.

   For each column, let d be the difference between maximum and minimum width of that column. Now set the column's width to the minimum width plus **d** times **W** over **D**. This makes columns with large differences between minimum and maximum widths wider than columns with smaller differences.

This assignment step is then repeated for nested tables using the minimum and maximum widths derived for all such tables in the first pass. In this case, the width of the parent table cell plays the role of the current window size in the above description. This process is repeated recursively for all nested tables. The topmost table is then rendered using the assigned widths. Nested tables are subsequently rendered as part of the parent table's cell contents.

If the table width is specified with the width attribute, the user agent attempts to set column widths to match. The width attribute is not binding if this results in columns having less than their minimum (i.e., indivisible) widths.

If relative widths are specified with the COL element, the algorithm is modified to increase column widths over the minimum width to meet the relative width constraints. The COL elements should be taken as hints only, so columns shouldn't be set to less than their minimum width. Similarly, columns shouldn't be made so wide that the table stretches well beyond the extent of the window. If a COL element specifies a relative width of zero, the column should always be set to its minimum width.

When using the two pass layout algorithm, the default alignment position in the absence of an explicit or inherited charoff attribute can be determined by choosing the position that would center lines for which the widths before and after the alignment character are at the maximum values for any of the lines in the column for which align="char". For incremental table layout the suggested default is charoff="50%". If several cells in different rows for the same column use character alignment, then by default, all such cells should line up, regardless of which character is used for alignment. Rules for handling objects too large for a column apply when the explicit or implied alignment results in a situation where the data exceeds the assigned width of the column.

Choice of attribute names. *It would have been preferable to choose values for the* frame *attribute consistent with the* rules *attribute and the values used for alignment. For instance:* `none, top, bottom, topbot, left, right, leftright, all`. *Unfortunately, SGML requires enumerated attribute values to be unique for each element, independent of the attribute name. This causes immediate problems for "none", "left", "right" and "all". The values for the frame attribute have been chosen to avoid clashes with the* rules, align, *and* valign *attributes. This provides a measure of future proofing, as it is anticipated that the* frame *and* rules *attributes will be added to other table elements in future revisions to this specification. An alternative would be to make* frame *a CDATA attribute. The consensus of the W3C HTML Working Group was that the benefits of being able to use SGML validation tools to check attributes based on enumerated values outweighs the need for consistent names.*

B.6 Notes on forms

B.6.1 Incremental display

The incremental display of documents being received from the network gives rise to certain problems with respect to forms. User agents should prevent forms from being submitted until all of the form's elements have been received.

The incremental display of documents raises some issues with respect to tabbing navigation. The heuristic of giving focus to the lowest valued tabindex in the document seems reasonable enough at first glance. However this implies having to wait until all of the document's text is received, since until then, the lowest valued tabindex may still change. If the user hits the tab key before then, it is reasonable for user agents to move the focus to the lowest currently available tabindex.

If forms are associated with client-side scripts, there is further potential for problems. For instance, a script handler for a given field may refer to a field that doesn't yet exist.

B.6.2 Future projects

This specification defines a set of elements and attributes powerful enough to fulfill the general need for producing forms. However there is still room for many possible improvements. For instance the following problems could be addressed in the future:

- The range of form field types is too limited in comparison with modern user interfaces. For instance there is no provision for tabular data entry, sliders or multiple page layouts.

- Servers cannot update the fields in a submitted form and instead have to send a complete HTML document causing screen flicker.

- These also cause problems for speech based browsers, making it difficult for the visually impaired to interact with HTML forms.

Another possible extension would be to add the usemap attribute to `INPUT` for use as client-side image map when "type=image". The `AREA` element corresponding to the location clicked would contribute the value to be passed to the server. To avoid the need to modify server scripts, it may be appropriate to extend `AREA` to provide x and y values for use with the `INPUT` element.

B.7 Notes on scripting

B.7.1 Reserved syntax for future script macros

This specification reserves syntax for the future support of script macros in HTML CDATA attributes. The intention is to allow attributes to be set depending on the properties of objects that appear earlier on the page. The syntax is:

```
attribute = "... &{ macro body }; ... "
```

Current Practice for Script Macros

The macro body is made up of one or more statements in the default scripting language (as per intrinsic event attributes). The semicolon following the right brace is always needed, as otherwise the right brace character "}" is treated as being part of the macro body. Its also worth noting that quote marks are always needed for attributes containing script macros.

The processing of CDATA attributes proceeds as follows:

1. The SGML parser evaluates any SGML entities (e.g., ">").

2. Next the script macros are evaluated by the script engine.

3. Finally the resultant character string is passed to the application for subsequent processing.

Macro processing takes place when the document is loaded (or reloaded) but does not take place again when the document is resized, repainted, etc.

DEPRECATED EXAMPLE:
Here are some examples using JavaScript. The first one randomizes the document background color:

```
<BODY bgcolor='&{randomrbg};'>
```

Perhaps you want to dim the background for evening viewing:

```
<BODY bgcolor='&{if(Date.getHours > 18)...};'>
```

The next example uses JavaScript to set the coordinates for a client-side image map:

```
<MAP NAME=foo>
   <AREA shape="rect" coords="&{myrect(imageuri)};" href="&{myuri};" alt="">
</MAP>
```

This example sets the size of an image based upon document properties:

```
<IMG src="bar.gif" width='&{document.banner.width/2};' height='50%' alt="banner">
```

You can set the URI for a link or image by script:

```
 <SCRIPT type="text/javascript">
   function manufacturer(widget) {
       ...
   }
   function location(manufacturer) {
       ...
   }
   function logo(manufacturer) {
       ...
   }
 </SCRIPT>
  <A href='&{location(manufacturer("widget"))};'>widget</A>
  <IMG src='&{logo(manufacturer("widget"))};' alt="logo">
```

This last example shows how SGML CDATA attributes can be quoted using single or double quote marks. If you use single quotes around the attribute string then you can include double quote marks as part of the attribute string. Another approach is use " for double quote marks:

```
<IMG src="&{logo(manufacturer(&quot;widget&quot;))};" alt="logo">
```

B.8 Notes on frames

Since there is no guarantee that a frame target name is unique, it is appropriate to describe the current practice in finding a frame given a target name:

1. If the target name is a reserved word as described in the normative text, apply it as described.

2. Otherwise, perform a depth-first search of the frame hierarchy in the window that contained the link. Use the first frame whose name is an exact match.

3. If no such frame was found in (2), apply step 2 to each window, in a front-to-back ordering. Stop as soon as you encounter a frame with exactly the same name.

4. If no such frame was found in (3), create a new window and assign it the target name.

B.9 Notes on accessibility

Note. *The following algorithm for generating alternate text may be superseded by recommendations by the W3C Web Accessibility Initiative Group. Please consult* [WAIGUIDE] *for more information.*

When an author does not set the alt attribute for the `IMG` or `APPLET` elements, user agents should supply the alternate text, calculated in the following order:

1. If the title has been specified, its value should be used as alternate text.

2. Otherwise, if HTTP headers provide title information when the included object is retrieved, this information should be used as alternate text.

3. Otherwise, if the included object contains text fields (e.g., GIF images contain some text fields), information extracted from the text fields should be used as alternate text. Since user agents may have to retrieve an entire object first in order to extract textual information, user agents may adopt more economical approaches (e.g., content negotiation).

4. Otherwise, in the absence of other information, user agents should use the file name (minus the extension) as alternate text.

When an author does not set the alt attribute for the `INPUT` element, user agents should supply the alternate text, calculated in the following order:

1. If the title has been specified, its value should be used as alternate text.

2. Otherwise, if the name has been specified, its value should be used as alternate text.

3. Otherwise (submit and reset buttons), the value of the type attribute should be used as alternate text.

B.10 Notes on security

Anchors, embedded images, and all other elements that contain URIs as parameters may cause the URI to be dereferenced in response to user input. In this case, the security issues of [RFC1738], section 6, should be considered. The widely deployed methods for submitting form requests—HTTP and SMTP—provide little assurance of confidentiality. Information providers who request sensitive information via forms—especially with the INPUT element, type="password"—should be aware and make their users aware of the lack of confidentiality.

B.10.1 Security issues for forms

A user agent should not send any file that the user has not explicitly asked to be sent. Thus, HTML user agents are expected to confirm any default file names that might be suggested by the value attribute of the INPUT element. Hidden controls must not specify files.

This specification does not contain a mechanism for encryption of the data; this should be handled by whatever other mechanisms are in place for secure transmission of data.

Once a file is uploaded, the processing agent should process and store it appropriately.

Reference

Index of Elements

*Legend: **O**ptional, **F**orbidden, **E**mpty, **D**eprecated, **L**oose DTD, **F**rameset DTD*

Name	Start Tag	End Tag	Empty	Depr.	DTD	Description
A						anchor
ABBR						abbreviated form (e.g., WWW, HTTP, etc.)
ACRONYM						
ADDRESS						information on author
APPLET				D	L	Java applet
AREA		F	E			client-side image map area
B						bold text style
BASE		F	E			document base URI
BASEFONT		F	E	D	L	base font size
BDO						I18N BiDi over-ride
BIG						large text style
BLOCKQUOTE						long quotation
BODY	O	O				document body
BR		F	E			forced line break
BUTTON						push button
CAPTION						table caption
CENTER				D	L	shorthand for DIV align=center
CITE						citation

(Continued–1)

CODE						computer code fragment
COL		F	E			table column
COLGROUP		O				table column group
DD		O				definition description
DEL						deleted text
DFN						instance definition
DIR				D	L	directory list
DIV						generic language/style container
DL						definition list
DT		O				definition term
EM						emphasis
FIELDSET						form control group
FONT				D	L	local change to font
FORM						interactive form
FRAME		F	E		F	subwindow
FRAMESET					F	window subdivision
H1						heading
H2						heading
H3						heading
H4						heading
H5						heading
H6						heading
HEAD	O	O				document head
HR		F	E			horizontal rule
HTML	O	O				document root element

(Continued–2)

I						italic text style
IFRAME					L	inline subwindow
IMG		F	E			Embedded image
INPUT		F	E			form control
INS						inserted text
ISINDEX		F	E	D	L	single line prompt
KBD						text to be entered by the user
LABEL						form field label text
LEGEND						fieldset legend
LI		O				list item
LINK		F	E			a media-independent link
MAP						client-side image map
MENU				D	L	menu list
META		F	E			generic metainformation
NOFRAMES					F	alternate content container for non frame-based rendering
NOSCRIPT						alternate content container for non script-based rendering
OBJECT						generic embedded object
OL						ordered list
OPTGROUP						option group
OPTION		O				selectable choice
P		O				paragraph
PARAM		F	E			named property value
PRE						preformatted text
Q						short inline quotation

(Continued–3)

S				D	L	strike-through text style
SAMP						sample program output, scripts, etc.
SCRIPT						script statements
SELECT						option selector
SMALL						small text style
SPAN						generic language/style container
STRIKE				D	L	strike-through text
STRONG						strong emphasis
STYLE						style info
SUB						subscript
SUP						superscript
TABLE						
TBODY	O	O				table body
TD		O				table data cell
TEXTAREA						multi-line text field
TFOOT		O				table footer
TH		O				table header cell
THEAD		O				table header
TITLE						document title
TR		O				table row
TT						teletype or monospaced text style
U				D	L	underlined text style
UL						unordered list
VAR						instance of a variable or program argument

Index of Attributes

Legend: **D**eprecated, **L**oose DTD, **F**rameset DTD

Name	Related Elements	Type	Default	Depr.	DTD	Comment
abbr	TD, TH	%Text;	#IMPLIED			abbreviation for header cell
accept-charset	FORM	%Charsets;	#IMPLIED			list of supported charsets
accept	INPUT	%ContentTypes;	#IMPLIED			list of MIME types for file upload
accesskey	A, AREA, BUTTON, INPUT, LABEL, LEGEND, TEXTAREA	%Character;	#IMPLIED			accessibility key character
action	FORM	%URI;	#REQUIRED			server-side form handler
align	CAPTION	%CAlign;	#IMPLIED	D	L	relative to table
align	APPLET, IFRAME, IMG, INPUT, OBJECT	%IAlign;	#IMPLIED	D	L	vertical or horizontal alignment
align	LEGEND	%LAlign;	#IMPLIED	D	L	relative to fieldset
align	TABLE	%TAlign;	#IMPLIED	D	L	table position relative to window
align	HR	(left | center | right)	#IMPLIED	D	L	
align	DIV, H1, H2, H3, H4, H5, H6, P	(left | center | right | justify)	#IMPLIED	D	L	align, text alignment
align	COL, COLGROUP, TBODY, TD, TFOOT, TH, THEAD, TR	(left | center | right | justify | char)	#IMPLIED			
alink	BODY	%Color;	#IMPLIED	D	L	color of selected links
alt	APPLET	%Text;	#IMPLIED	D	L	short description
alt	AREA, IMG	%Text;	#REQUIRED			short description
alt	INPUT	CDATA	#IMPLIED			short description
archive	OBJECT	%URI;	#IMPLIED			space separated archive list
archive	APPLET	CDATA	#IMPLIED	D	L	comma separated archive list

(Continued–1)

axis	TD, TH	CDATA	#IMPLIED			names groups of related headers
background	BODY	%URI;	#IMPLIED	D	L	texture tile for document background
bgcolor	TABLE	%Color;	#IMPLIED	D	L	background color for cells
bgcolor	TR	%Color;	#IMPLIED	D	L	background color for row
bgcolor	TD, TH	%Color;	#IMPLIED	D	L	cell background color
bgcolor	BODY	%Color;	#IMPLIED	D	L	document background color
border	IMG, OBJECT	%Length;	#IMPLIED	D	L	link border width
border	TABLE	%Pixels;	#IMPLIED			controls frame width around table
cellpadding	TABLE	%Length;	#IMPLIED			spacing within cells
cellspacing	TABLE	%Length;	#IMPLIED			spacing between cells
char	COL, COLGROUP, TBODY, TD, TFOOT, TH, THEAD, TR	%Character;	#IMPLIED			alignment char, e.g. char=':'
charoff	COL, COLGROUP, TBODY, TD, TFOOT, TH, THEAD, TR	%Length;	#IMPLIED			offset for alignment char
charset	A, LINK, SCRIPT	%Charset;	#IMPLIED			char encoding of linked resource
checked	INPUT	(checked)	#IMPLIED			for radio buttons and check boxes
cite	BLOCKQUOTE, Q	%URI;	#IMPLIED			URI for source document or msg

(Continued–2)

cite	DEL, INS	%URI;	#IMPLIED			info on reason for change
class	All elements but BASE, BASEFONT, HEAD, HTML, META, PARAM, ain SCRIPT, STYLE, TITLE	CDATA	#IMPLIED			space separated list of classes
classid	OBJECT	%URI;	#IMPLIED			identifies an implementation
clear	BR	(left | all | right | none)	none	D	L	control of text flow
code	APPLET	CDATA	#IMPLIED	D	L	applet class file
codebase	OBJECT	%URI;	#IMPLIED			base URI for classid, data, archive
codebase	APPLET	%URI;	#IMPLIED	D	L	optional base URI for applet
codetype	OBJECT	%ContentType;	#IMPLIED			content type for code
color	BASEFONT, FONT	%Color;	#IMPLIED	D	L	text color
cols	FRAMESET	%MultiLengths;	#IMPLIED		F	list of lengths, default: 100% (1 col)
cols	TEXTAREA	NUMBER	#REQUIRED			
colspan	TD, TH	NUMBER	1			number of cols spanned by cell
compact	DIR, MENU	(compact)	#IMPLIED	D	L	
compact	DL, OL, UL	(compact)	#IMPLIED	D	L	reduced interitem spacing
content	META	CDATA	#REQUIRED			associated information
coords	AREA	%Coords;	#IMPLIED			comma separated list of lengths

(Continued–3)

coords	A	%Coords;	#IMPLIED			for use with client-side image maps
data	OBJECT	%URI;	#IMPLIED			reference to object's data
datetime	DEL, INS	%Datetime;	#IMPLIED			date and time of change
declare	OBJECT	(declare)	#IMPLIED			declare but don't instantiate flag
defer	SCRIPT	(defer)	#IMPLIED			UA may defer execution of script
dir	All elements but APPLET, BASE, BASEFONT, BDO, BR, FRAME, plain FRAMESET, HR, IFRAME, PARAM, SCRIPT	(ltr | rtl)	#IMPLIED			direction for weak/neutral text
dir	BDO	(ltr | rtl)	#REQUIRED			directionality
disabled	BUTTON, INPUT, OPTGROUP, OPTION, SELECT, TEXTAREA	(disabled)	#IMPLIED			unavailable in this context
enctype	FORM	%ContentType;	"application/x-www-form-urlencoded"			
face	BASEFONT, FONT	CDATA	#IMPLIED	D	L	comma separated list of font names
for	LABEL	IDREF	#IMPLIED			matches field ID value
frame	TABLE	%TFrame;	#IMPLIED			which parts of frame to render
frameborder	FRAME, IFRAME	(1 | 0)	1		F	request frame borders?

(Continued—4)

headers	TD, TH	IDREFS	#IMPLIED			list of id's for header cells
height	IFRAME	%Length;	#IMPLIED		L	frame height
height	IMG, OBJECT	%Length;	#IMPLIED			override height
height	APPLET	%Length;	#REQUIRED	D	L	initial height
height	TD, TH	%Pixels;	#IMPLIED	D	L	height for cell
href	A, AREA, LINK	%URI;	#IMPLIED			URI for linked resource
href	BASE	%URI;	#IMPLIED			URI that acts as base URI
hreflang	A, LINK	%LanguageCode;	#IMPLIED			language code
hspace	APPLET, IMG, OBJECT	%Pixels;	#IMPLIED	D	L	horizontal gutter
http-equiv	META	NAME	#IMPLIED			HTTP response header name
id	All elements but BASE, HEAD, HTML, META, SCRIPT, STYLE, TITLE	ID	#IMPLIED			document-wide unique id
ismap	IMG	(ismap)	#IMPLIED			use server-side image map
label	OPTION	%Text;	#IMPLIED			for use in hierarchical menus
label	OPTGROUP	%Text;	#REQUIRED			for use in hierarchical menus
lang	All elements but APPLET, BASE, BASEFONT, BR, FRAME, FRAMESET, HR, IFRAME, PARAM, SCRIPT	%LanguageCode;	#IMPLIED			language code
language	SCRIPT	CDATA	#IMPLIED	D	L	predefined script language name
link	BODY	%Color;	#IMPLIED	D	L	color of links
longdesc	IMG	%URI;	#IMPLIED			link to long description (complements alt)
longdesc	FRAME, IFRAME	%URI;	#IMPLIED		F	link to long description (complements title)

(Continued–5)

marginheight	FRAME, IFRAME	%Pixels;	#IMPLIED		F	margin height in pixels
marginwidth	FRAME, IFRAME	%Pixels;	#IMPLIED		F	margin widths in pixels
maxlength	INPUT	NUMBER	#IMPLIED			max chars for text fields
media	STYLE	%MediaDesc;	#IMPLIED			designed for use with these media
media	LINK	%MediaDesc;	#IMPLIED			for rendering on these media
method	FORM	(GET | POST)	GET			HTTP method used to submit the form
multiple	SELECT	(multiple)	#IMPLIED			default is single selection
name	BUTTON, TEXTAREA	CDATA	#IMPLIED			
name	APPLET	CDATA	#IMPLIED	D	L	allows applets to find each other
name	SELECT	CDATA	#IMPLIED			field name
name	FRAME, IFRAME	CDATA	#IMPLIED		F	name of frame for targetting
name	A	CDATA	#IMPLIED			named link end
name	INPUT, OBJECT	CDATA	#IMPLIED			submit as part of form
name	MAP	CDATA	#REQUIRED			for reference by usemap
name	PARAM	CDATA	#REQUIRED			property name
name	META	NAME	#IMPLIED			metainformation name
nohref	AREA	(nohref)	#IMPLIED			this region has no action
noresize	FRAME	(noresize)	#IMPLIED		F	allow users to resize frames?
noshade	HR	(noshade)	#IMPLIED	D	L	
nowrap	TD, TH	(nowrap)	#IMPLIED	D	L	suppress word wrap
object	APPLET	CDATA	#IMPLIED	D	L	serialized applet file
onblur	A, AREA, BUTTON, INPUT, LABEL, SELECT, TEXTAREA	%Script;	#IMPLIED			the element lost the focus

(Continued-6)

onchange	INPUT, SELECT, TEXTAREA	%Script;	#IMPLIED			the element value was changed
onclick	All elements but APPLET, BASE, BASEFONT, BDO, BR, FONT, FRAME, FRAMESET, HEAD, HTML, IFRAME, ISINDEX, META, PARAMlain, SCRIPT, STYLE, TITLE	%Script;	#IMPLIED			a pointer button was clicked
ondblclick	All elements but APPLET, BASE, BASEFONT, BDO, BR, FONT, FRAME, FRAMESET, HEAD, HTML, IFRAME, ISINDEX, META, PARAM, SCRIPT, STYLE, TITLE	%Script;	#IMPLIED			a pointer button was double clicked
onfocus	A, AREA, BUTTON, INPUT, LABEL, SELECT, TEXTAREA	%Script;	#IMPLIED			the element got the focus
onkeydown	All elements but APPLET, BASE, BASEFONT, BDO, BR, FONT, FRAME, FRAMESET, HEAD, HTML, IFRAME, ISINDEX, META, PARAM, SCRIPT, STYLE, TITLE	%Script;	#IMPLIED			a key was pressed down
onkeypress	All elements but APPLET, BASE, BASEFONT, BDO, BR, FONT, FRAME, FRAMESET, HEAD, HTML, IFRAME, ISINDEX, META, PARAM, SCRIPT, STYLE, TITLE	%Script;	#IMPLIED			a key was pressed and released

(Continued–7)

onkeyup	All elements but APPLET, BASE, BASEFONT, BDO, BR, FONT, FRAME, FRAMESET, HEAD, HTML, IFRAME, ISINDEX, META, PARAM, SCRIPT, STYLE, TITLE	%Script;	#IMPLIED		a key was released
onload	FRAMESET	%Script;	#IMPLIED	F	all the frames have been loaded
onload	BODY	%Script;	#IMPLIED		the document has been loaded
onmousedown	All elements but APPLET, BASE, BASEFONT, BDO, BR, FONT, FRAME, FRAMESET, HEAD, HTML, IFRAME, ISINDEX, META, PARAM, SCRIPT, STYLE, TITLE	%Script;	#IMPLIED		a pointer button was pressed down
onmousemove	All elements but APPLET, BASE, BASEFONT, BDO, BR, FONT, FRAME, FRAMESET, HEAD, HTML, IFRAME, ISINDEX, META, PARAM, SCRIPT, STYLE, TITLE	%Script;	#IMPLIED		a pointer was moved within
onmouseout	All elements but APPLET, BASE, BASEFONT, BDO, BR, FONT, FRAME, FRAMESET, HEAD, HTML, IFRAME, ISINDEX, META, PARAM, SCRIPT, STYLE, TITLE	%Script;	#IMPLIED		a pointer was moved away

(Continued–8)

onmouseover	All elements but APPLET, BASE, BASEFONT, BDO, BR, FONT, FRAME, FRAMESET, HEAD, HTML, IFRAME, ISINDEX, META, PARAM, SCRIPT, STYLE, TITLE	%Script;	#IMPLIED			a pointer was moved onto
onmouseup	All elements but APPLET, BASE, BASEFONT, BDO, BR, FONT, FRAME, FRAMESET, HEAD, HTML, IFRAME, ISINDEX, META, PARAM, SCRIPT, STYLE, TITLE	%Script;	#IMPLIED			a pointer button was released
onreset	FORM	%Script;	#IMPLIED			the form was reset
onselect	INPUT, TEXTAREA	%Script;	#IMPLIED			some text was selected
onsubmit	FORM	%Script;	#IMPLIED			the form was submitted
onunload	FRAMESET	%Script;	#IMPLIED		F	all the frames have been removed
onunload	BODY	%Script;	#IMPLIED			the document has been removed
profile	HEAD	%URI;	#IMPLIED			named dictionary of meta info
prompt	ISINDEX	%Text;	#IMPLIED	D	L	prompt message
readonly	TEXTAREA	(readonly)	#IMPLIED			
readonly	INPUT	(readonly)	#IMPLIED			for text and passwd
rel	A, LINK	%LinkTypes;	#IMPLIED			forward link types
rev	A, LINK	%LinkTypes;	#IMPLIED			reverse link types
rows	FRAMESET	%MultiLengths;	#IMPLIED		F	list of lengths, default: 100% (1 row)
rows	TEXTAREA	NUMBER	#REQUIRED			
rowspan	TD, TH	NUMBER	1			number of rows spanned by cell

(Continued–9)

rules	TABLE	%TRules;	#IMPLIED			rulings between rows and cols
scheme	META	CDATA	#IMPLIED			select form of content
scope	TD, TH	%Scope;	#IMPLIED			scope covered by header cells
scrolling	FRAME, IFRAME	(yes | no | auto)	auto		F	scrollbar or none
selected	OPTION	(selected)	#IMPLIED			
shape	AREA	%Shape;	rect			controls interpretation of coords
shape	A	%Shape;	rect			for use with client-side image maps
size	HR	%Pixels;	#IMPLIED	D	L	
size	FONT	CDATA	#IMPLIED	D	L	[+|-]nn e.g. size="+1", size="4"
size	INPUT	CDATA	#IMPLIED			specific to each type of field
size	BASEFONT	CDATA	#REQUIRED	D	L	base font size for FONT elements
size	SELECT	NUMBER	#IMPLIED			rows visible
span	COL	NUMBER	1			COL attributes affect N columns
span	COLGROUP	NUMBER	1			default number of columns in group
src	SCRIPT	%URI;	#IMPLIED			URI for an external script
src	INPUT	%URI;	#IMPLIED			for fields with images
src	FRAME, IFRAME	%URI;	#IMPLIED		F	source of frame content
src	IMG	%URI;	#REQUIRED			URI of image to embed
standby	OBJECT	%Text;	#IMPLIED			message to show while loading
start	OL	NUMBER	#IMPLIED	D	L	starting sequence number
style	All elements but BASE, BASEFONT, HEAD, HTML, META, PARAM, SCRIPT, STYLEsed, TITLE	%StyleSheet;	#IMPLIED			associated style info

(Continued–10)

summary	TABLE	%Text;	#IMPLIED			purpose/structure for speech output
tabindex	A, AREA, BUTTON, INPUT, OBJECT, SELECT, TEXTAREA	NUMBER	#IMPLIED			position in tabbing order
target	A, AREA, BASE, FORM, LINK	%FrameTarget;	#IMPLIED		L	render in this frame
text	BODY	%Color;	#IMPLIED	D	L	document text color
title	STYLE	%Text;	#IMPLIED			advisory title
title	All elements but BASE, BASEFONT, HEAD, HTML, META, PARAM, SCRIPT, STYLEsed, TITLE	%Text;	#IMPLIED			advisory title/amplification
type	A, LINK	%ContentType;	#IMPLIED			advisory content type
type	OBJECT	%ContentType;	#IMPLIED			content type for data
type	PARAM	%ContentType;	#IMPLIED			content type for value when valuetype=ref
type	SCRIPT	%ContentType;	#REQUIRED			content type of script language
type	STYLE	%ContentType;	#REQUIRED			content type of style language
type	INPUT	%InputType;	TEXT			what kind of widget is needed
type	LI	%LIStyle;	#IMPLIED	D	L	list item style
type	OL	%OLStyle;	#IMPLIED	D	L	numbering style
type	UL	%ULStyle;	#IMPLIED	D	L	bullet style
type	BUTTON	(button | submit | reset)	submit			for use as form button
usemap	IMG, INPUT, OBJECT	%URI;	#IMPLIED			use client-side image map
valign	COL, COLGROUP, TBODY, TD, TFOOT, TH, THEAD, TR	(top | middle | bottom | baseline)	#IMPLIED			vertical alignment in cells
value	OPTION	CDATA	#IMPLIED			defaults to element content

(Continued–11)

value	PARAM	CDATA	#IMPLIED			property value
value	INPUT	CDATA	#IMPLIED			required for radio and checkboxes
value	BUTTON	CDATA	#IMPLIED			sent to server when submitted
value	LI	NUMBER	#IMPLIED	D	L	reset sequence number
valuetype	PARAM	(DATA | REF | OBJECT)	DATA			How to interpret value
version	HTML	CDATA	%HTML.Version;	D	L	Constant
vlink	BODY	%Color;	#IMPLIED	D	L	color of visited links
vspace	APPLET, IMG, OBJECT	%Pixels;	#IMPLIED	D	L	vertical gutter
width	HR	%Length;	#IMPLIED	D	L	
width	IFRAME	%Length;	#IMPLIED		L	frame width
width	IMG, OBJECT	%Length;	#IMPLIED			override width
width	TABLE	%Length;	#IMPLIED			table width
width	APPLET	%Length;	#REQUIRED	D	L	initial width
width	COL	%MultiLength;	#IMPLIED			column width specification
width	COLGROUP	%MultiLength;	#IMPLIED			default width for enclosed COLs
width	TD, TH	%Pixels;	#IMPLIED	D	L	width for cell
width	PRE	NUMBER	#IMPLIED	D	L	

About toExcel's Open Documents Standards Library

Welcome to the world of Open Publishing™ with toExcel.

The book you hold in your hand is just one part of toExcel's revolutionary publishing initiative, bringing important online and other documents to the public in printed form…quickly and efficiently.

toExcel is actively working with Web sites and other information providers to distribute information to the widest possible audience via our unique on-demand publishing technology. We are committed to bringing into print the titles the public needs and wants…from the works of the World Wide Web Consortium to the latest information from the open source movement. We get new and updated titles into your hands fast. What's more, all toExcel books in the Open Document Standards Library are always available to be read online, free at our site, in keeping with the core philosophy of the open documents movement.

Each title in the toExcel Open Documents series is a printed version of the latest industry-accepted specifications and contains the complete, unedited text of the original document. toExcel provides this book as a service to the developers' community for use as a handy desktop companion, saving you the time and expense of printing the documentation.

You can learn more about toExcel and how you can be a part of the on-demand publishing revolution by visiting our Web site at www.toExcel.com. You can also give us your feedback and let us know what online materials you'd like us to publish by e-mailing feedback@toExcel.com. We value your opinion.

Kenzi Sugihara
Publisher

About the W3C

The W3C was founded in October 1994 to develop common standards and protocols for the World Wide Web. The W3C is an international industry consortium, jointly hosted by the Massachusetts Institute of Technology Laboratory for Computer Science [MIT/LCS] in the United States; the Institut National de Recherché en Informatique et en Automatique [INRIA] in Europe; and the Keio University Shonan Fujisawa Campus in Japan. Services provided by the Consortium include: a repository of information about the World Wide Web for developers and users; reference code implementations to embody and promote standards; and various prototype and sample applications to demonstrate use of new technology.

For more information about the W3C see http://www.w3c.org/

More Titles in the toExcel Open Docs Series

Cascading Style Sheets Specification, Level 1

available 6/99

ISBN 1-158348-252-0

Ideal for program designers, HTML Web page authors, and others who need to keep abreast of current publishing standards for the World Wide Web, this book describes how to attach a style sheet to an HTML document so that its appearance (fonts, colors, spacing) can be accurately defined and explains the "cascading" nature of style sheets.

Cascading Style Sheets Specification, Level 2

available 6/99

ISBN 1-53848-253-9

A companion to CSS Level 1, this second book contains the complete and most up-to-date version currently available of the CSS2 specification, an enhancement of the earlier CSS1 specifications, that provide greater control and flexibility in rendering a page on screen or paper.

HTML 3.2 Reference Specification

available 6/99

ISBN 1-58348-258-X

This book is the complete text of the latest available version of the HTML 3.2 specifications and reference manual (also includes the HTML 2.0 specifications). It is a must-have resource for HTML Web page authors, Internet program developers, information technology managers, and anyone else who publishes documents on the World Wide Web.

toExcel Orders
Phone: 877-823-9235 (877-82EXCEL)
Fax: 408-260-3067
http://www.toExcel.com

Document Object Model Specification, Level 1

available 6/99

ISBN 1-58348-254-7

A handy resource for HTML Web page authors, Web and Internet program developers, Java and JavaScript programmers, and anyone else who publishes documents on the World Wide Web, this book describes what the Document Object Model is, and how it's used and includes full descriptions of all definitions used in the DOM Level 1 specification.

Document Object Model Specification, Level 2

available 6/99

ISBN 1-58348-255-5

The goal of the DOM specification is to define a programmatic interface for XML and HTML. Document Object Model Level 2 builds on DOM Level 1 by adding interfaces for a Cascading Style Sheets object model, an event model, and a query interface, among others. Specification 2 is designed to be a handy desktop companion, saving you the time and expense of printing the documentation yourself and for use when you can't be online.

Extensible Markup Language (XML) 1.0 Specifications

available 6/99

ISBN 1-58348-256-3

Representing the future of the World Wide Web, the Exensible Markup Language (XML) provides for an almost limitless variety of text and formatting for Web pages and other electronic documentation. The XML 1.0 specifications are the industry standard recommendation for this important new technology.

toExcel Orders
Phone: 877-823-9235 (877-82EXCEL)
Fax: 408-260-3067
http://www.toExcel.com

Extensible Stylesheet Language (XSL)

available 6/99
ISBN 1-58348-257-1

A complete and up-to-date version of the working draft specifications of Extensible Stylesheet Language (XSL), this book describes how XSL can be used to define the appearance of printed and displayed documents. It's the perfect companion for program developers, Web page authors, technology managers, and others.

toExcel Orders
Phone: 877-823-9235 (877-82EXCEL)
Fax: 408-260-3067
http://www.toExcel.com

Communicate with toExcel Online

There's lots to do at www.toExcel.com including:

Read Entire Books Online...Free

At toExcel, you have the opportunity to read this entire book and hundreds more online. You get to try it before you buy it. Our readers get more than just a description, table of contents and reviews. They can make their decision to buy based on viewing the whole book online at toExcel's ReaderCentral.

Get Hard-To-Find Titles

toExcel is amassing a huge collection of out-of-print titles and republishing them. If you're an Apple fan, you can get *Danny Goodman's AppleScript™ Handbook*, in a brand new printing, from toExcel.

Have Your Say

We value your opinion. At toExcel you can comment on each and every book and participate in discussions with other readers and authors. You can also e-mail confidential feedback to us at feedback@toExcel.com.

Decide What We Should Publish

toExcel is publishing hundreds of books per year. Help us decide what titles to publish by submitting your suggestions to suggest@toExcel.com.

toExcel
165 West 95th Street, Suite B-N
New York, NY 10025
www.toExcel.com
Phone: 212-663-6856
Fax: 212-866-4629
info@toExcel.com